Reading the Peak District Landscape

Reading the
Peak District Landscape

Snapshots in Time

John Barnatt

Published by Historic England, The Engine House, Fire Fly Avenue, Swindon SN2 2EH
www.HistoricEngland.org.uk
Historic England is a Government service championing England's heritage and giving expert, constructive advice.

The views expressed in this book are those of the author and not necessarily those of Historic England.

First published 2019

ISBN 978-1-84802-379-6

British Library Cataloguing in Publication data
A CIP catalogue record for this book is available from the British Library.

The right of John Barnatt to be identified as author of this work has been asserted by him in accordance with the Copyright, Designs and Patents Act 1988.

All mapping produced for this publication used Ordnance Survey data under Peak District National Park Authority License No LA 100005735 2009.

Application for the reproduction of images should be made to Historic England. Every effort has been made to trace the copyright holders and we apologise in advance for any unintentional omissions, which we would be pleased to correct in any subsequent edition of this book.

For more information about images from Historic England Archive, contact Archives Services Team, Historic England, The Engine House, Fire Fly Avenue, Swindon SN2 2EH; telephone (01793) 414600.

Brought to publication by Jess Ward, Publishing, Historic England.
Typeset in Georgia Pro 9.5/11.75pt
Edited by Stephanie Rebello
Proof read by Kim Bishop
Indexed by Caroline Jones
Page layout by Ledgard Jepson
Printed in Czech Republic by Akcent Media Ltd.

Front cover: Fossilised medieval open-field strips just outside Longnor (left), with the Upper Dove Valley close to Chrome Hill behind. [© John Barnatt]
Frontispiece: Ridge and furrow between Winster and Elton. [© Historic England Archive, 17428_52]

Contents

Acknowledgements   *vii*
Preface   *viii*

1   Introducing the Peak District – People, places and landscapes   1

2   Peak landscapes   13

3   Places to live   36

4   Land to farm   57

5   Using fields   79

6   Minerals from the ground   91

7   Quarrying stone   118

8   Travelling between places   130

9   Using water   149

10   Past landscapes   157

11   Roman occupation and medieval elites   177

12   Polite landscapes   185

13   Conflict landscapes   196

14   Inhabited places   202

15   Postscript – People, place and archaeology today   221

Appendix 1: The locations of Peak District places referred to throughout the book   *222*
Appendix 2: Historic landscape character assessment in the Peak District   *244*
Notes   *252*
Bibliography   *257*
Index   *264*

*This book is dedicated to Bren, my companion
through life, whose never-ending support over the years
has made my journeys into the past that much easier.
She has enriched my being in so many ways and I will
be eternally grateful to her for this.*

Acknowledgements

Many thanks to all those who helped with the preparation of this volume and undertook the archaeological projects which are referred to. The historic landscape character analysis for the Peak District was supervised by the author but the mapping was undertaken by Gill Stroud within the National Park, whilst Miles Johnson and Rowan May did this for those areas outside the Park; funding for this was provided by English Heritage (now Historic England), with special mention of Graham Fairclough for commissioning the work (Figs A2.1–A2.8).

Stewart Ainsworth and other staff of the Royal Commission on the Historical Monuments for England, with John Barnatt for the Peak District National Park Authority (PDNPA), carried out collaborative detailed metrical survey projects in the 1990s on Big Moor (Fig 10.4) and Gardom's Edge, whilst Nigel Sharpe provided GPS survey expertise above Burbage in 2015 (Fig 13.2). The majority of field assessments described or noted below were undertaken by the author for the PDNPA (Figs 3.12, 4.10–12, 5.6, 6.11, 6.13, 6.21, 6.26, 7.8, 8.6, 8.8, 8.10, 8.16, 10.4, 10.5, 11.2, 11.4, 12.7, 13.2, 13.4, 14.20), with surveys at some industrial sites undertaken in his own time (Figs 6.9, 6.12, 6.17–18, 6.20, 6.24, 6.26, 7.2, 7.5, 8.17), where help and advice were given by Richard Carr, Chris Heathcote, David Kitching, Phil Pritchard, Phil Shaw and Dave Williams. David Kitching also advised on field kilns. Bill Bevan also did rapid fieldwork surveys for PDNPA (Fig 6.29) and historical data on charcoal burning was compiled by Gill Stroud. Alice Ullathorne did the rapid fieldwork survey at Thorpe Pasture (Fig 11.3). The Reeve Edge Quarry survey was undertaken by Eric Wood and Margaret Black (Fig 7.9) and the survey of remains at One Ash was assisted by a fieldwork team provided by the Manpower Services Commission (Fig 3.17).

Surveys of underground mine workings were done in collaboration with Terry Worthington (Fig 6.18), and at Ecton also with the late Paul Deakin (Figs 6.11, 6.21) and with Garth Thomas (Fig 6.11). The survey of Speedwell Cavern is adapted from one by Richard Shaw (Fig 6.20). Jim Rieuwerts worked with the author on the Masson Cavern survey data (Fig 6.17) and a plan of Hillcarr Sough is based on one of Jim's drawings (Fig 6.8). Advice on the interpretation of underground features was given by Richard Shaw and Terry Worthington in particular.

Survey work at Chatsworth (Figs 4.10, 4.12, 7.8, 8.8. 8.10, 10.5, 12.4, 12.7), and the mapping of survival and loss of lead-mining remains (Fig 6.4), was partially funded by English Heritage, whilst survey and assessment at Bakewell (Fig 5.6) was funded by the Local Heritage Initiative. The excavations at mine engine houses were directed by the author, with a team of excavators provided by the Peak District Mines Historical Society (Figs 6.9, 6.12). The survey of the Grin Hill limekilns (Fig 7.2) was done with a grant from Derbyshire County Council.

Surface photographs were taken by the author, with the exception of the fine images taken by Anthony Hammerton who kindly granted permission for their use (Figs 6.28, 7.6–7, 8.3, 9.1, 9.6), and two photographs taken as part of the Gardom's Edge Project undertaken jointly by John Barnatt and Bill Bevan for the PDNPA and Mark Edmonds of Sheffield University (Figs 2.17, 10.3). Underground photographs were taken by the late Paul Deakin (Figs 6.5–7, 6.22), the late Jon Humble (Fig 6.19), and Mat and Niki Adlam Stiles (Fig 7.4). Aerial photographs were provided by the Historic England Archive at Swindon (Frontispiece and Figs 3.4, 3.16, 5.7, 7.3, A1.5), and by the late Derrick Riley (Figs 5.5, 6.16, 10.1, 11.1, 14.10). Angie Johnson helped with the preparation of the drawn illustrations and historic landscape character mapping for publication.

The PDNPA contributed the author's time to write the volume, whilst Historic England kindly funded its publication, with special thanks to Ken Smith (PDNPA) and John Hudson (HE) for their support. Ken Smith proofread an early draft of the text and made many valuable suggestions. The two anonymous referees who commented on a draft text also made invaluable suggestions for improving the book. Also from Historic England, I would like to thank Stephanie Rebello for copy editing the text and Jess Ward and Victoria Trainor for project managing the book through to publication.

Preface

The Peak District is a vital place for many in its surrounding cities, somewhere to spend leisure time, to escape to another world that contrasts with the places they live and work. It has landscapes of great beauty with wild moorland and walled fields around picturesque villages, all of which are imbued with great time depth. Even the open moorlands are not 'natural places' but have been shaped by people over millennia. There are few places in the world where such a rich history is still visible in one relatively small but varied landscape. It is a very special place.

This book goes beyond the Peak District places that usually feature in accounts of the region's archaeology and history, such as Arbor Low and Chatsworth House. It introduces a wealth of little-explored sites and landscapes, all imbued with people from the past who shaped these special upland places. Whilst the Peak as experienced by humans is underpinned by the geology and topography, there is not a single square metre that has not been shaped by people; there is no such thing as a natural landscape in the Peak, rather it is land made and remade by people over many generations. Whilst it has many vibrant and in some cases rare ecological habitats, containing a rich variety of plants and wildlife, these communities would not appear as they do if it were not for the activities of people over the last 10,000 years.

What is written here builds upon much research into the Peak's past undertaken over decades, but here things are presented differently, with its character described thematically rather than the story of change given chronologically.

The starting point and anchor throughout is cultural mapping of the landscape through time. However, on the way it explores patterns of settlement, contrasting zones where villages dominate or where scattered farmsteads are the norm. These settlements are found in radically different farming landscapes, some with medieval origins, others coming later when extensive upland commons were enclosed. Today's fields have many fascinating archaeological details such as limekilns, dew ponds and wall furniture. Medieval landscapes were dominated by structures built in wood and earth, contrasting with later ones where building in stone became the way forward.

Industrial sites and landscapes are examined, including those where quarrying for stone and mining for lead and coal have taken place. Minerals were smelted or used as fuel, whilst stone was used for building, production of lime and specialist products such as millstones, grindstones and crushing stones. People have always travelled through the Peak, with many routeways now abandoned but still visible. The use of water in the Peak, for milling and provision of drinking water for cities, is described.

There are many archaeological sites that tell of ancient landscapes, now overwritten by later changes, where people organised themselves differently. The landscape has many surviving prehistoric sites. There are also Roman and medieval remains built by church and state. Similarly, there are polite landscapes created by the wealthy for their delectation contrasting with conflict landscapes where men trained for war, whilst others defended their homeland.

The work concludes with a description of the ways individual communities have long cross-cut local differences in landscape character, each using a wide variety of different resources.

Introducing the Peak District – People, places and landscapes

The Peak District is a very special place with a host of vibrant visual contrasts, from its vast swaths of drystone-walled fields, open moorlands, villages with stone-built houses in a distinctive vernacular style, ancient archaeological sites, industrial remains as at abandoned lead mines and quarries, to stately homes in picturesque parkland. But it is more than this, for every nook and cranny has a past and the varied Peak District landscapes are imbued with great time depth, with the whole being greater than the sum of its parts. Within the region there are contrasting landscapes sitting cheek by jowl with each other, including the busy 'White Peak' farming landscape, the 'Dark Peak' with brooding heather moorlands, and the deep valleys between the two that have long been focal points for settlement. Being an upland region, much has survived for centuries rather than being swept away to cater for the needs of intensive agriculture and by urban development. Its exceptionally rich past is still here for all to see.

The Peak District landscapes, havens of tranquil beauty with spectacular views, are the life's breath for many who live and work in the surrounding cities such as Manchester, Sheffield and Derby, all only a short drive away. It includes parts of seven different counties, with the surrounding urban sprawl contrasting with the Peak's rural landscapes (Fig 1.1). There are many scheduled monuments and listed buildings, and the Derwent Valley World Heritage Site starts in the Peak and runs southwards to Derby. Whilst these are jewels in the crown, the landscape in its entirety has great cultural value. It is not a coincidence that the Peak District was chosen as the first national park in Britain; it is one the most heavily visited national parks in the world.

The Peak has many archaeological sites, all to be cherished, but the landscape as a whole, or rather several very different and contrasting landscape areas, is equally exciting. Often many details, such as its drystone walls, old limekilns and moorland guide stones, which taken individually are interesting but commonplace, when placed in the landscape context become very special.

The author has been lucky to work here as a landscape archaeologist for four decades and a synthesis of some of what he has learnt is presented here. This new book, which covers the whole of the Peak District region rather than just the national park at its heart, builds upon a previous volume published in 2004.[1] However, it takes a different approach, looking at aspects such as landscape, settlement, agriculture and industry separately, rather than the story of the Peak and its archaeology being told chronologically. At its core is a vision of the meaning of Peak landscapes as a whole, where all the places here have a rich past still visible today, which once looked at with new eyes adds greatly to our understanding of those who live and visit here. The book is designed to impart a deeper appreciation of how this cultural landscape came into being and what makes it special today.

Snapshots in time

The Peak District, for expediency from now on will usually be referred to as the Peak, is an upland region at the southern end of the Pennines. It has a rich variety of standing buildings, field boundaries and roads that are still in use today even though some are many hundreds of years old. Well-preserved prehistoric and later earthworks, as well as ruined buildings and old industrial sites such as mines and quarries, have not been subject to the ravages of arable farming that are the norm in lowland England. Together, the used and redundant relics of past times, some thousands of years old, come together in a vibrant historic landscape with many local variations that add to its diversity; its time depth

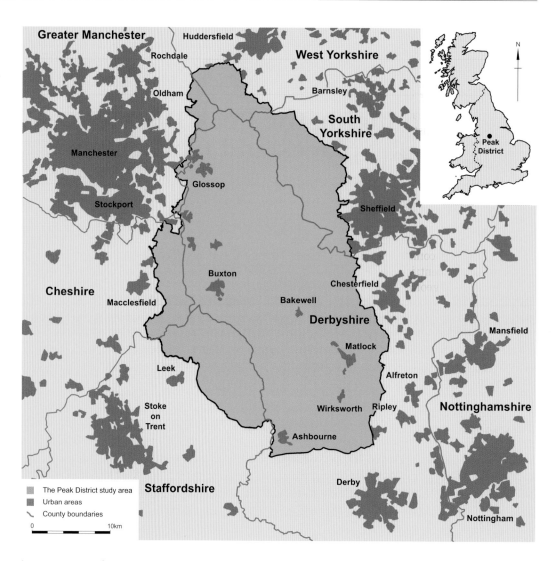

is not surpassed anywhere in the country. Each feature or group of features present today represents a snapshot in time that we can use to explore the landscape's past.

This book aims to describe and interpret the Peak landscape, exploring what we have inherited from past generations and how this differs from place to place. Amongst the underlying themes are regional and local patterns and the reasons for these in terms of geology and how many generations of people and communities have shaped this land: the influence people have had on the ecology of the region; the rich time depth in its settlement, farmland and industrial sites; and the rich diversity of local archaeological detail which adds much to the character of the landscape. It is a work not so much about the archaeology of people but the time depth of today's landscape, which celebrates the rich diversity that has built up over the last 10,000 years.

A historic landscape character assessment that underpins the book builds upon much research into the archaeology and history of the Peak undertaken over the last century.[2] Throughout, the book draws on the extensive fieldwork and analyses undertaken by the author for the Peak District National Park Authority and as part of his own research over five decades, as well as presenting new studies undertaken especially for this work. It does not aim to be comprehensive, but picks out key themes, highlighting those that seem the most interesting in terms of the development of the landscape and what from the past has heavily influenced the look of today's landscape. It inevitably reflects the author's interests, hence will have idiosyncratic biases. Some important details are ignored, such as the meaning of place-names and what we can learn from the Domesday survey of 1086, as they have been presented elsewhere.[3] In other cases, such as medieval churches and castles, only summaries are given. Similarly, this book concentrates on the core parts of the Peak, not those areas around the fringes of the national park that in effect are parts of 'other places'. Also, no attempt has been made to place the Peak archaeology and historic landscape in its national and international context; a book that covered everything with equal weight would be prohibitively long.

People and place

In the Peak, as with elsewhere, there has long been an intimate connection between people and their environment; in some ways the natural topography and geology, and the potential for habitation and use, have shaped the way people have lived in particular places. However, culturally determined values and the way people interact socially, and their different emphases on technology, have had a greater impact at any moment in time.

The geology and topography of the Peak have had an impact on people and what they have chosen to do here. Being dissected upland, some places are more favourable than others for settlement and farming; places with shelter were important, whilst altitude also governed rainfall levels and thus soil fertility. As for example the character of ancient woodland ranged from dense forest in valley bottoms to more open habitats on higher land. Different geologies also influence soils, with good if usually thin acidic soils on the limestone plateau, heavy clay lands and glacial terraces in some valleys, and once-fertile but stony sandy soils on the gritstone scarp and shelf tops. These soils were fragile once the natural woodland cover was removed, leading long-term to much now being peaty and waterlogged. Topographically the Peak landscape has a variety of valley bottoms, shelves and plateau tops where people have concentrated activities, interspersed with steep and often boulder-strewn slopes, steep-sided dry valleys and limestone gorges (Fig 1.2), some of which

Fig 1.2
A drystone valley on the limestone plateau, at Cressbrook Dale near Wardlow Mires, with Peter's Stone to the right.
[John Barnatt]

Fig 1.3
A limestone plateau landscape, with 19th-century mine buildings at Watergrove Mine with Tideslow on the skyline.
[John Barnatt]

Fig 1.4
High on the eastern gritstone upland, with Parsons House built close to the 1812 turnpike road from the Derwent Valley to Sheffield. Behind, Over Owler Tor (left) and Stanage (centre) are so high that nobody has ever lived here, although the cliffs were sources of good stone.
[John Barnatt]

have impacted on travel between zones and created gaps between communities. The geology has also provided specific opportunities for mineral extraction. Limestone areas traditionally have been quarried for lime production and have rich mineral resources (Fig 1.3). Notable were lead ores and associated fluorspar, barytes and calcite, whilst copper ores have been locally important; these are all now largely worked out. In contrast, the gritstone uplands, including much bleak moorland, have provided good building stone, high-grade sandstone for specialist products and coal (Fig 1.4).

Climate has also been critical and fluctuations have led to periodic use of land which at other times has been above the altitude threshold for sustainable farming; where global warming will take us in the future remains to be seen but potential increased emphasis on arable production could lead to radical impacts on the fabric of the historic landscape.

All this said, people faced with the same natural constraints and opportunities have responded very differently through time; hence for example we had people living in small scattered communities on the eastern gritstone moors in prehistory with significant contraction later, partly at least due to settlement foci growing in the nearby valleys. Romano-British farms on the limestone plateau were widely spread, whilst people were brought together into villages set at a distance from each other in the medieval period. Large settlements on the fringes of the Peak only became possible with the coming of local industry, and today's global communication and long-distance transport links have led to many local people not having the same intimate links with, and understandings of, the local landscape.

The Peak landscape has been increasingly shaped by people over the 10,000 years since the end of the last glaciation; for generation upon generation alterations to the natural environment have modified viable choices for the future. Sometimes options have been closed down, for instance once wild food sources are reduced, hunting becomes an unviable option for communities as a whole. Similarly, over-farming has led to soil deterioration and the change from relatively intense farming to using whole swaths of land for only moorland grazing. In contrast, new choices have opened up. Forest clearance has allowed for greater emphasis on arable and pastoral farming, and the discovery of mineral resources has led to the potential for creating wealth.

Maps through time

Much of the assessment of historic landscape character of the Peak given in subsequent chapters is underpinned by detailed digital mapping and analyses undertaken in the 1990s. This included mapping the predominant character of land on a field-by-field basis, identifying such things as fields with ancient origins, new post-medieval enclosure, unenclosed land, industrial land, parkland and woodland (Fig 1.5). Time-slice maps showing the situation at 50-year intervals from 1600 to the present day were produced, based on what is shown on available historic maps, including those made for enclosure awards and tithes, others drawn for large estates for their own management

Fig 1.5
An example of mapping derived from historic landscape character analysis, centred on Taddington, Flagg and Monyash, showing fields with medieval origins around villages, contrasted with extensive surrounding areas that were open commons until post-medieval times (for the original mapping for 1650 and present day see Figs A2.7 and A2.8).

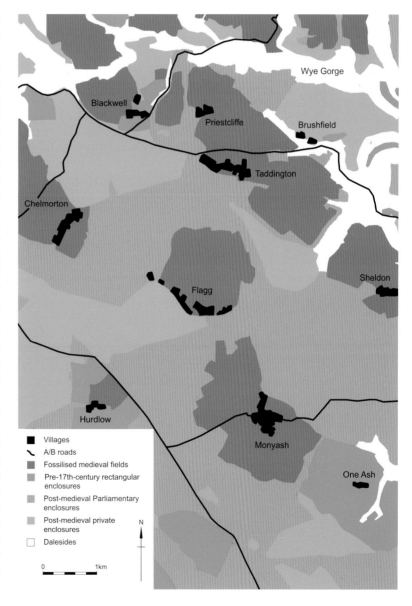

purposes, and those surveyed by the Ordnance Survey from the 1830s onwards. Details of the methodology are given in the Appendix at the end of the book.

Of course, what are shown on these time-slice plots are only data that can be derived from maps; radical changes within the skeleton formed by field boundaries have taken place and continue to do so; for instance, hay meadows have been replaced by silage fields, whilst walls and hedges have sometimes been replaced by barbed wire. The countryside lost many agricultural workers as mechanisation increased in the 20th century and today villages and scattered dwellings are occupied by communities within which some families have lived for generations and others are incomers who often work elsewhere or who have retired to their countryside idyll.

The Peak mapping shows the predominantly agricultural 'dominant character' and this is reviewed at a landscape scale in Chapter 2. Other aspects of historic landscape character, such as settlement, industry and past landscapes are just as important and these are best reviewed separately when considering detail, as attempts to combine all leads to such a wealth of information that a coherent overview of the main aspects and trends through time easily becomes obscured; different themes pertinent to the Peak landscape are discussed separately in Chapters 3 to 13. Things are drawn back together again in Chapter 14, with the emphasis on how communities have used different resources available to them.

The area studied

As this book is underpinned by historic landscape character mapping, the data collected for this determined the boundary of the area considered in the book. The same mapping methodology was employed in both the national park and Derbyshire beyond the park, but this has not been done for other adjacent areas in Staffordshire, Cheshire, Greater Manchester, West Yorkshire and South Yorkshire, thus the area to be studied stops at the park boundary in these counties.

Local boundaries

A word needs to be said about the terms 'parish', 'manor' and 'township'. Whilst the main administrative unit today is the 'civil parish', these are in effect what used to be known as townships, although sometimes the boundaries have been rationalised. The traditional use of the word 'parish' was normally for 'ecclesiastical parishes' and sometimes these included several townships. Similarly, a comparable civil division sometimes with several townships, was the 'manor', usually held by the lord of the manor. To confuse matters, the parish and manorial boundaries do not always match each other. Similarly, on the wastes and commons, particularly where these were extensive, exact boundaries were sometimes not formalised until post-medieval times. Whilst beating the bounds was often undertaken to formalise what a settlement controlled, and 18th- and 19th-century records of these activities survive, we know that in the medieval period there were sometimes complex arrangements for sharing upland grazing between several communities, a practice known as inter-commoning, which is now not well understood in the Peak.

Regional character

The Peak can be divided into five basic topographic character zones, each of which is heavily influenced by the geology, which contrast with their neighbours (Fig 1.6).[4] The traditional way of dividing the region into just Dark Peak and White Peak is far too simplistic. Whilst all the five zones are significantly different from each other and in some cases have clear-cut boundaries, in other places a precisely drawn boundary line on a map represents what in reality is a somewhat fuzzy interface.[5] Places mentioned in this chapter are given on Figure A1.1 (see p 223).

White Peak

This block of Carboniferous limestone at the heart of the region, together with shale valleys around the edges, have always been the region's core settlement areas and the limestone area was particularly important for its rich lead mines (Figs 1.7 and 1.8). Much of the land is a high plateau.[6] This is often steep-sided at its edges and is cut by limestone gorges and steep-sided dry valleys with narrow bottoms. It can be subdivided into different parts: the high, rolling, spinal ridges to the west and south-east; more fertile upland shelves at the eastern edge and at the centre above the gorges of the rivers Wye and Lathkill; and a similar area to the south-west above the rivers Dove and Manifold, which pass through the plateau in gorges. Much of the zone is enclosed agricultural land and there is also extensive evidence for quarrying and old lead mining.

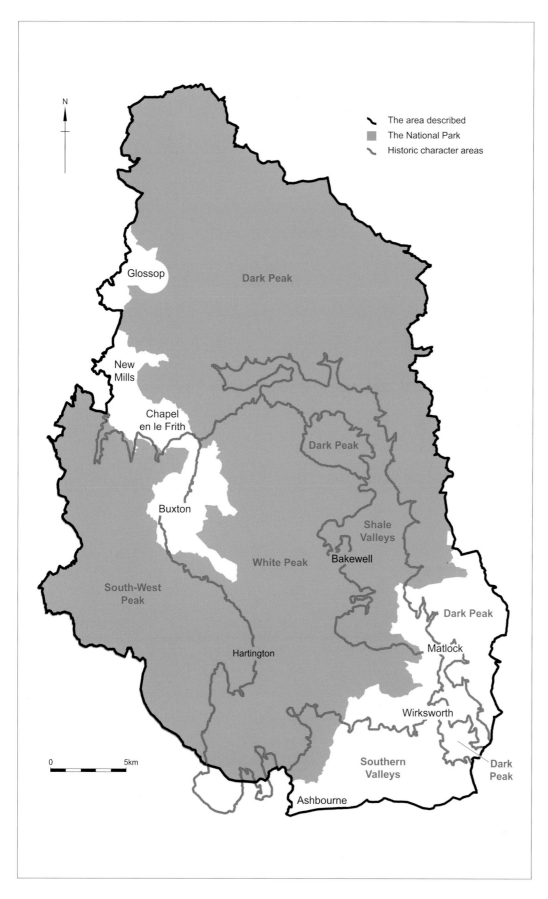

Fig 1.6
The Peak District – historic character areas, major places, the area described and the national park.

Fig 1.7
Fields on the limestone
plateau close to Foolow, with
Wardlow Hay Cop on the
horizon, taken from close
to the top of the gritstone
scarp of Hucklow Edge.
[John Barnatt]

Fig 1.8
Tideslow Rake, one of the
main lead-mine workings
on the limestone plateau.
[John Barnatt]

Shale valleys

Between the White and Dark Peak areas there is a series of deep valleys, containing the River Derwent and part of the River Wye, all eroded into thick beds of Carboniferous shales and thin beds of sandstones. The zone includes land between these two valleys, comprising low shelves and small islands of gritstone upland at Calton Pasture, Harthill Moor and Stanton Moor. It can be divided into two parts. The first comprises the broad upper valleys to the north, including the Hope Valley and Edale.[7] Further south the Derwent and Wye valleys, with associated shelves between, are again often wide.[8] Both have long been focal areas for settlement.

Dark Peak

High uplands of Carboniferous Millstone Grit and the Lower Coal Measures sandstones surround the central limestone plateau on all sides but the south. Those to the north and east are included here, whilst those to the west are described under the South-West Peak. The Dark Peak can be divided into a large area to the north that is predominantly high moorland, and the eastern moors, which are lower.[9] The former includes the highest windswept parts of the Peak at Kinder Scout and Bleaklow; this area is predominantly moorland and only fringes to the east and west are enclosed and have ever attracted settlement. This high area is dissected by the narrow river valleys of the upper Derwent, Alport and Ashop. To the north-west there is also the upper valley of the River Etherow known as Longdendale. The eastern moors, with a prominent western shelf, are different in that they are in part enclosed today, whilst on the moorlands there is extensive evidence of prehistoric settlement and small monuments (Figs 1.9 and 1.10). The zone includes an island of upland west of the Derwent centred on Abney, Offerton and Eyam Moors.

Fig 1.9
The main western shelf of eastern moorlands below the southern end of Stanage Edge, high above the Hope Valley visible in the distance on the left. The small Overstones Farm is a particularly exposed farmstead.
[John Barnatt]

Fig 1.10
The prehistoric Barbrook 1 stone circle, with upright stones peeping above the coarse grassland, in the heart of the eastern moors. [John Barnatt]

South-West Peak

These Millstone Grit uplands are similar to those to the north and east but they are more dissected, whilst land has been enclosed to a higher average altitude when compared with the eastern moors. The zone can be divided, firstly into valleys not as favourable for settlement as the shale valleys east of the limestone. Notable are the upper reaches of the Rivers Dove, Manifold and Hamps draining south, and those of the Goyt and Dane to the west. This part of the zone also includes low and often enclosed ridges between the valleys and has scattered farmsteads throughout. The second part comprises the higher ridges, with the highest parts still moorland.[10]

Southern valleys

A small area just beyond the southern edge of the limestone plateau, between Ashbourne and Wirksworth, cannot be excluded as a fringe area because of the importance of the villages here, which are an integral part of what culturally has traditionally been the Peak. Here broad shale valleys separated by low sandstone ridges have long been settled.

Fringes

Other areas, around the edges of the Peak and termed here 'fringes', are not fully described as these are interface areas at the edges of landscape zones beyond the region. For the most part they comprise valleys, shelves and foothills between the high gritstone areas and the lowlands that flank the region to the east and west.[11]

Perspectives

The Peak landscape can be viewed at a variety of scales, ranging from the region as a whole, down to the five main character areas, and focusing further to the local when individual parishes or farms can be examined. Each approach gives different perspectives that provide different insights into the region, its historic complexity and how what remains today contributes to the richness of the landscape.

This much-loved landscape can be seen from an archaeological stance, where the development through time of its buildings, field boundaries and earthworks can be studied. This in turn allows consideration of the interaction between people and place, and the influence of different types of society and peoples' changing lifeways through history. All these have affected choices made and the look of the land. Or, the landscape can be viewed from broader perspectives, as a significant part of cultural, aesthetic, ecological, topographical and geological overviews. All these contribute to today's landscape character, influencing how people choose to appreciate, visit or inhabit the Peak.

Taking the Peak as a whole, this has an identity as a well-inhabited upland at the southern end of the Pennines, where the high moorlands on three sides may well have helped forge the cultural identity of the core part of the Peak District from early times. However, as we have seen above, the region has several component parts. The gritstone Dark Peak and limestone White Peak have been identified for several decades by people promoting the region, both with easily recognised distinct character with different things to offer. A more nuanced approach, as adopted here, is to hive off the eastern shale valleys of the Derwent and Wye, the southern valley below the southern edge of the limestone plateau, and the varied landscape of the South-West Peak. These are treated here as different from the White and Dark Peak. Each of these five landscapes is different geologically and topographically, and each has a different historic landscape character from its neighbours. Looking locally, as with the various case studies given below, there is a great deal that demonstrates similarities and differences between neighbouring communities and their parish landscapes; thus we can identify both what is special about each place and underlying commonalities.

Whilst much of the Peak lies within Derbyshire, there are smaller parts to the west in Staffordshire and Cheshire, and land on the fringes is in different counties again. These administrative divisions cross-cut real landscape distinctions. If you live in the Upper Dove Valley, for example, you will probably see yourself as much the same as people who live on the other side of the river in a different county, whilst from a broader perspective, the Peak is very different from the rest of the counties that have land here, which have contrasting histories. For example, the industrial areas around Chesterfield, Alfreton and Ripley in North-East Derbyshire and those to the north-west on the fringe of Stockport and Manchester have little in common with the Peak, and it seems remote from Derby and other communities in the Trent Valley lowlands.

Another way of viewing the Peak landscape is to think about it as a place where many people have spent much of their time and to consider the distances over which they have interacted with others. These range through local contact with neighbours, through to longer-distance contact for trading commodities and ideas; and these have changed through time. Until relatively recently, many people have stayed within their local community, rarely travelling beyond their market town. Each local community drew on a range of topographies with complementary resources that they had access to, so that with basics at least they were relatively self-sufficient; other items were brought into the region by tradesmen and carriers. Local accents were more pronounced than now; often people from only 50 miles away, and sometimes far less, could barely be understood. The local gentry and aristocracy had wider contacts and this helped them maintain their differences from the common people. New ways were often introduced from outside, sometimes at times when crises meant a breakdown of traditional ways, rather than because adoption of the new was led by notions of progress and modernity.

A minority of people, particularly from the 19th century onwards, moved away following new jobs that sprang up in developing industrial areas and associated cities. This trend started earlier for people with specific occupations; for example, drovers, packhorse drivers and miners. Similarly, there have always been people with wanderlust, often young people who take off to see the world, and others who move to be with marriage partners. This has always happened and people have sometimes returned with ideas from other counties, countries and continents.

Looking at the complexity of today's landscape and understanding something of the rich and varied past that influences today's character, allows decisions for the future to be made on a more informed basis. No doubt there are going to be changes imposed by global warming and developments in farming practice, together with choices made that further accommodate the desires of the many visitors to the Peak. Ethical choices revolving around the desirability or otherwise of livestock farming may also come into stronger play. Animal welfare and present farming are seen by some as in conflict with each other; we need to consider animal rights against the look of the landscape we cherish; removal of grazing animals, unless much land goes to arable, will inevitably lead to widespread scrub growth and later to tree regeneration. In the last two decades reduction of stocking levels and ceasing of heather burning on parts of the eastern moors has been carried out following ecological imperatives; a side effect have been that many of the important prehistoric features that tell of ancient settlement and farming are now no longer visible; whilst still there for future generations, now it is that much harder to foster public interest as there is little to see and grab the imagination. Some ecologists go further and advocate that the landscape should be allowed to return to nature but the implications of this approach, if taken to the extreme, are that most if not all parts of the Peak would return to thick woodland, with a resulting reduction of habitat variation. I, for one, would be horrified if we lost the landscape views that the Peak is famous for as the trees encroached (Fig 1.11). Rather, should we not celebrate the rich and varied landscape we have now, accommodating this for the future wherever possible, and husband the great wealth of interest created by people in the past?

Fig 1.11
If trees were allowed to regenerate across the Peak, with these 'going on forever' as they last did about 6000 years ago, then most of our cherished landscape views would be lost from sight; as here from within planted woodland on Longstone Edge.
[John Barnatt]

2

Peak landscapes

As introduced in Chapter 1, the Peak District is a place of different landscape characters, with contrasts between the limestone plateau, the shale valleys, the high gritstone uplands, the south-western landscape and the southern valleys. This chapter considers each of these areas in general terms at a landscape scale, as well as introducing the component aspects of their character that are considered in subsequent chapters. Each area is now discussed in turn, presented together with vignettes to illustrate common themes and contrasts in more detail. Places mentioned in Chapter 2 are given on Figure A1.2 (*see* p 225).

White Peak

At the heart of the Peak lies the large limestone plateau, where the historic landscape character has great time depth, focused on villages and monastic farms known as granges with easily recognised medieval pasts (*see* p 18 and Chapter 3). Today's field layouts reflect medieval open fields but with their cultivation strips enclosed long ago. Extensive commons were also enclosed, mostly in the 18th and 19th centuries, and there are thousands of miles of ruler-straight drystone walls defining rectangular fields. New farmsteads were also built when some farmers moved out from the traditional village centres to live at the heart of their newly allocated land.

The plateau has a high rolling top, and often drops off steeply at its edge, where rivers have eroded deep valleys through the shale rocks that millions of years ago once overlay the Carboniferous limestone (Fig 2.1). Rivers such as the Wye, Lathkill, Dove and Manifold have cut deep gorges through the limestone. Once these main valleys, often with cliffs at their sides, had impenetrable woods and formed barriers to easy transport from one side to the other. Similarly, many side valleys run down to the gorges that have only ever been suitable for

wood pasture and open grazing. Above the gorges there are shallow but broad upland basins formed many millennia ago before the deep cliff-lined gorges were cut. These basins have rich if shallow soils that have attracted farmers from prehistory onwards. The small Staffordshire part of the limestone plateau has its own distinctive character, criss-crossed by gorges, with small but fertile shelves above, and a line of high hills at its northern edge.

When setting settlement character against landscape potential, available water supply and altitude have always been critical factors, particularly when people were living here in a sustained way rather than passing quickly through. There are only a few watercourses that run year-long, except for those in the deep gorges of the rivers Wye, Dove and Manifold, as much water flows through caves rather than at surface. Above were a few natural meres and latterly many dew ponds were placed in walled fields to provide water for stock.

In the heart of the plateau there are villages and hamlets in the upper basins and similar situations, created where permanent habitation was made possible by reliable springs, often following the line of outcropping impervious volcanic beds in the limestone. Notable are concentrations of villages in the Wye and Lathkill basins, those on the shelves above the Via Gellia, and others to the south-west on the shelves above the Dove and Manifold.[1]

Many of the communities that farmed on the plateau lived in villages within the shale valleys at the edge, taking advantage of sheltered environments, whilst exploiting the rich resources on the limestone above. Those to the east and south in the main shale valleys are discussed below in 'Shale valleys' and 'Southern valleys'.[2] An atypical situation at the plateau-edge occurs to the north-east between Bradwell and Stoney Middleton, where there is an adjacent high gritstone upland rather than shale valley; here

Fig 2.1
A limestone plateau landscape photographed from above Taddington, with Fin Cop with a hillfort on its crest seen on the skyline high above the River Wye, and the side valley of Taddington Dale in the middle distance to the left, with the Millstone Grit scarp behind. The Wye and Derwent valleys lie behind Fin Cop but are shrouded in mist.
[John Barnatt]

settlements concentrate at streams before they flow underground as the limestone is reached.[3] To the west, away from the most-favourable valleys, there are settlements close to the upper River Wye before it passes eastwards through a gorge dissecting the limestone plateau. These centre on Burbage, Buxton and Fairfield, with small settlements nearby on shelves on the plateau itself.[4] Further south the topographically isolated upper valley of the Dove has the market village of Hartington nestled below the edge of the plateau; again there are smaller places on the limestone above.[5] To the south-west, the plateau again rises to gritstone uplands, where there are settlements at plateau level that focus on the geological interface (*see* pp 30–33).[6]

The historic character of the present agricultural landscape has many clear-cut patterns. Most obvious are the large fossilised open fields, often showing much of the medieval layout. These sit as islands in a sea of later rectangular fields superimposed on former commons, some after Parliamentary Enclosure Awards, others done privately without recourse to formal arbitration. Less common are rectangular fields that early estate maps show, which were laid out before the 17th century, often around what had been monastic granges. Elsewhere the date of fields is unclear, as at the former foresters' centre of Peak Forest at the heart of the royal hunting preserve of the Royal Forest of the Peak.

Chelmorton, Taddington and Flagg

This area is one of the classic limestone landscapes and is illustrated in Chapter 1 (*see* Fig 1.5). It is characterised by clearly visible, large but now fossilised medieval open fields around villages, with many narrow sinuous walled enclosures. These are contrasted with rectangular fields on former commons, large parts of which were enclosed following Parliamentary Enclosure Awards in the late 18th and early 19th centuries;[7] other areas were enclosed privately somewhere between the late 17th century and when the Enclosure Awards were drawn up.[8]

The three townships centre on the high Taddington Moor rising to well over 400m OD, which provided a strong boundary between them. Each of the three settlements, all part of the large Crown estates in the Peak for centuries, are at focal points within good agricultural land on broad shelves (Fig 2.2). The medieval fields of Chelmorton and Taddington were largely bounded by steep slopes to moors above and dry valleys and the Wye gorge below.

However, Flagg, which is sited in the broad but high upper Lathkill basin, had no such constraints and was laid out following a coherent simple plan, with all its strips running gently downslope in a large 'potato-shaped' field surrounded on all sides by common. Here we see the medieval design reflecting the ideal concept of what should exist, unfettered by topographical constraint.

All three villages have planned medieval village layouts, with Taddington having back lanes as well as a main street. Priestcliffe lies within the township of Taddington and has an irregular layout; first recorded in Domesday Book, it was probably a subsidiary place established before the Norman Conquest, perhaps created in response to people not wanting to walk excessive distances to the north-western parts of the open fields. Alternatively, it was an earlier independent hamlet, where the size of open fields in the township militated against full nucleation at the planned village of Taddington. In contrast, the carefully planned village of Chelmorton, at a high location but sheltered from the north, does not appear in documents until 1101; when it was established is unclear.[9]

Fig 2.2
The medieval open fields crossing the rolling shelf north of the large village of Taddington later had parcels of strips walled out to create a distinctive enclosed field landscape.
[John Barnatt]

Hartington

The exceptionally large parish of Hartington, divided into four 'quarters' with their boundaries rationalised after the enclosure of the commons in the 19th century, provides another fine example of a complex landscape, here focused around the old market centre of Hartington itself (*see also* pp 216–7) (Fig 2.3).[10] At Domesday in 1086 all in and around Hartington was 'waste' but soon the area was developed by the Earls of Derby followed later by the Duchy of Lancaster. A market charter was granted in 1203. The land was divorced from the Duchy in 1603 and the lordship was purchased by the 3rd Earl of Devonshire in 1663. Understanding the landscape history of Hartington is helped by a wonderful multicoloured map now at Chatsworth House

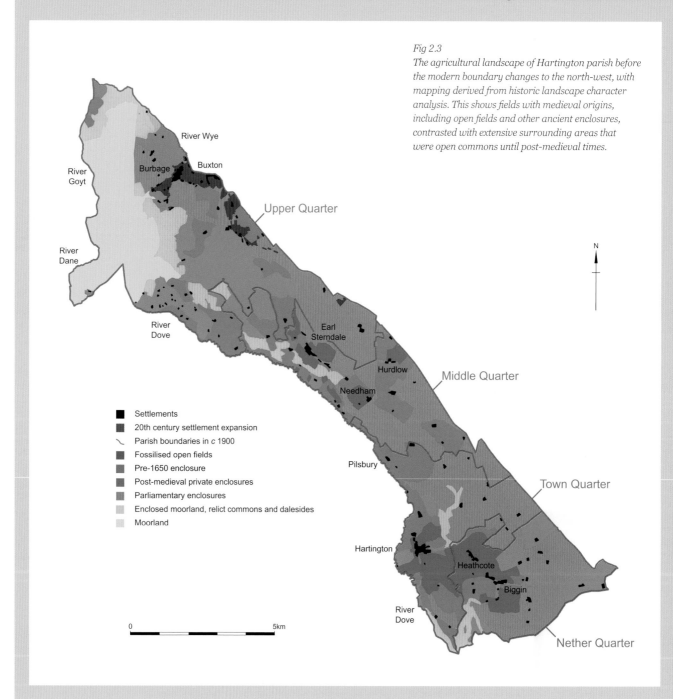

Fig 2.3
The agricultural landscape of Hartington parish before the modern boundary changes to the north-west, with mapping derived from historic landscape character analysis. This shows fields with medieval origins, including open fields and other ancient enclosures, contrasted with extensive surrounding areas that were open commons until post-medieval times.

Settlements
20th century settlement expansion
Parish boundaries in *c* 1900
Fossilised open fields
Pre-1650 enclosure
Post-medieval private enclosures
Parliamentary enclosures
Enclosed moorland, relict commons and dalesides
Moorland

River Wye
River Goyt
River Dane
Burbage
Buxton
Upper Quarter
River Dove
Earl Sterndale
Hurdlow
Middle Quarter
Needham
Pilsbury
Town Quarter
Hartington
Heathcote
Biggin
River Dove
Nether Quarter

N

0   5km

and drawn in 1614. It is over 5.5m long and now in two pieces, but it still can only be viewed where there is a large space available to unroll it.[11] The history of Hartington parish from medieval times onwards is well documented and there is much value in combining historic documents with study of the historic landscape.[12]

The Hartington open fields extended onto heavy soils of the flood plain of the River Dove where there is still ridge and furrow, with one part later enclosed in a way that disregarded the former layout. However, for the most part the medieval open fields were on limestone plateau shelves above, which had thin but rich soils. Within the highest extremities to the east are the small subsidiary planned linear villages of Biggin and Heathcote, both sited within fields that were a long walk from Hartington in the valley below.

On higher land beyond the open fields there are large expanses of ancient rectangular fields to the north and south of Hartington together with new farmsteads in fields with ruler-straight boundaries post-dating the Hartington Enclosure Award of 1807 and others that were privately enclosed (Fig 2.4). The earlier intakes, sub-divided by less-regular fields, were mostly once surrounded by common. Some focused on monastic granges.[13] Others include the hamlets of Pilsbury, Hurdlow, Needham, Earl Sterndale and Burbage, the last now subsumed within the urban sprawl of Buxton. The farmsteads in the Goyt Valley were removed when reservoirs were created in the 20th century (*see* p 156). In the far north-west there are still large expanses of open moorland on the highest land.

Fig 2.4
Typical high limestone scenery above Hartington that until the post-medieval period was part of the commons. The field barn belongs to the long-established Bank Top Farm in the valley bottom below, while the high hill of Carder Low to the left has late rectangular fields. [John Barnatt]

Hurdlow and the granges

Fig 2.5 (below, right) The three remaining farmsteads at Hurdlow Town all have sturdy houses, including this one at Hurdlow Hall with a 1689 date stone, added when the building was remodelled. [John Barnatt]

Fig 2.6 (below) Hurdlow Town and monastic granges north-west of Hartington, showing farmsteads and enclosure in the early 17th century.

Located high on the limestone plateau, in Hartington Middle Quarter, is Hurdlow Town. This isolated hamlet now comprises three farmsteads on a single planned street (Fig 2.5); when first mapped in 1614, there were five properties and a funnelled way led westwards onto the commons (Fig 2.6). There is a block of readily recognised open-field arable strips, now fossilised by walls, between the hamlet and the straight parish boundary that follows the plateau spine. This reflects the line of a Roman road from Buxton leading south-eastwards towards the now lost Lutudarum (*see* p 177). To the west and north of Hurdlow more pre-1614 fields may have always been rectangular in shape and there was a small isolated farmstead called Street against the Roman road.

Hurdlow land abutted that of Cronkston Grange, which once belonged to the Cistercian

abbey of Merevale in Warwickshire. The whole was surrounded by wastes and commons until the enclosure of the commons. This is one of four isolated monastic granges within the commons here. Needham and Pilsbury granges also belonged to Merevale Abbey, whilst Cotesfield Grange belonged to the Cistercians of Combermere Abbey in Cheshire.

All but Cotesfield have surviving bank and ditch earthworks at the edge of the commons. In the case of Cronkston, it appears a sub-oval enclosure was enlarged to take in more of the common, and there was a similarly shaped one at Pilsbury, whilst those at Needham and Cotesfield are distinctly more rectangular; here the enclosure follows lead mines that must have been in work when it was laid out. Needham has a parcel of fossilised open-field strips and it seems there was once another hamlet here similar to that at Hurdlow. In the case of Pilsbury it is unclear whether the grange buildings were down in the valley at the hamlet, with motte-and-bailey castle not far away, or high on the plateau above as with the others.

Farmsteads at Wheeldon Trees and Custard Field were here by 1614, as were enclosed parcels of land at Clemonseats and Parsley Hay (see Fig 2.6). The name of the last suggests the Hay was a medieval enclosure, perhaps created to contain deer.[14]

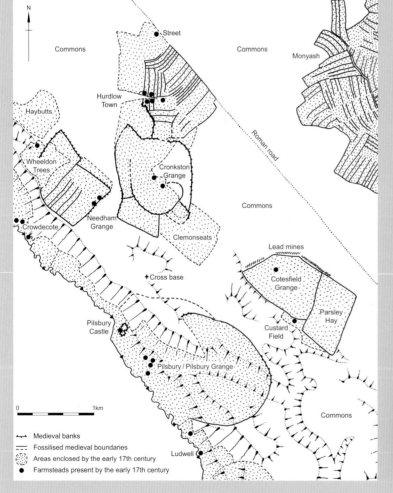

N

Commons

Street

Commons

Monyash

Roman road

Hurdlow Town

Haybutts

Wheeldon Trees

Cronkston Grange

Commons

Crowdecote

Needham Grange

Clemonseats

Lead mines

Cross base

Cotesfield Grange

Parsley Hay

Pilsbury Castle

Custard Field

Pilsbury / Pilsbury Grange

Commons

0   1km

Ludwell

⌐ Medieval banks
══ Fossilised medieval boundaries
▒ Areas enclosed by the early 17th century
● Farmsteads present by the early 17th century

Alstonefield

This large village in the heart of the Staffordshire part of the limestone plateau has long been an important place within what was once a very large manor.[15] There was an Anglo-Saxon church, now rebuilt from the 12th century onwards but still with fragments of several Anglo-Saxon crosses. The complex irregular village plan has evolved at a criss-crossing of routeways heading in all directions, with small greens at their intersections. Most of today's roads have medieval origins, except around the church to the south-east where there was re-organisation in the 18th century. There are interesting details, such as 16th- to 19th-century inscriptions on buildings, a 19th-century workhouse, an old reading room and a walled village well.[16]

The modern civil parish of Alstonefield, traditionally just one township within the ecclesiastical parish and manor, has distinct parts (Fig 2.7). Around the village itself, the

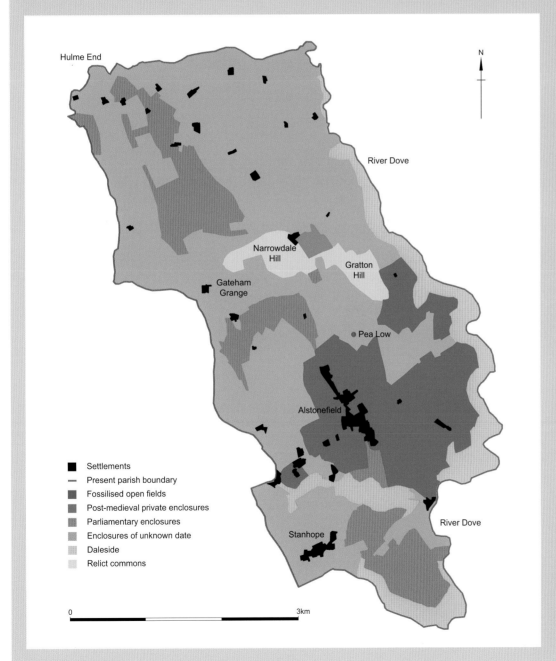

Hulme End

N

River Dove

Narrowdale Hill

Gratton Hill

Gateham Grange

Pea Low

Alstonefield

River Dove

Stanhope

■ Settlements
— Present parish boundary
■ Fossilised open fields
■ Post-medieval private enclosures
■ Parliamentary enclosures
■ Enclosures of unknown date
■ Daleside
■ Relict commons

0   3km

Fig 2.7
The agricultural landscape of the present-day Alstonefield parish, with mapping derived from historic landscape character analysis.

Fig 2.8
Alstonefield village, partially masked by trees, has surrounding walled enclosures that include narrow fields with curved boundaries that tell of previous medieval cultivation strips. Pea Low on the ridge above, crossed by a wall catching the light, is thought to be the best-preserved Neolithic chambered tomb in the Peak, with its chambers still awaiting discovery. [John Barnatt]

layout of large medieval fields can still be traced in the pattern of fossilised field strips with their distinctive sinuous walled boundaries (Fig 2.8). This area is overlooked by the massive prehistoric round barrow of Pea Low on a ridgetop north of the village (*see* p 165). Beyond to the north, centred on the high Narrowdale Hill and Gratton Hill, were once limestone commons. Nearby at Gateham Grange there is a farmstead which has origins as a monastic farm owned by Combermere Abbey in Cheshire.

To the south is the hamlet of Stanshope, first recorded in Domesday Book of 1086, which occupies a limestone shelf separated from Alstonefield by a steep-sided valley running up from Dove Dale. Common to the east of the settlement was not enclosed until the 19th century.

To the north the landscape running to Hulme End is very different in character, once comprising low moorland with waterlogged ground that had heavy clay soils over shale bedrock. Today there are scattered farmsteads and houses, some with medieval origins, but most of those on less advantageous ground are of 18th- and early 19th-century date, with the last fields added as a mopping-up operation after a Parliamentary agreement of 1839.

In the medieval period, the Manor of Alstonefield extended about 17km north-westwards, reaching as far as Three Shires Head near the head of the River Dane, at what was the boundary between Staffordshire, Cheshire and Derbyshire. Much of the more remote parts to the north-west were set aside as a hunting forest known as Alstonefield Frith or Malbanc Frith (*see* Chapter 12).

Shale valleys

The main sheltered valley running through the heart of the Peak, cut into the shale beds above the Carboniferous limestone and running to the east of the limestone plateau, is that of the River Derwent. Linked with this to the north are the River Noe and Peakshole Water in Edale and the Hope Valley respectively. Further south there are also the lower reaches of the River Wye around Ashford and Bakewell after it emerges from the gorge that crosses the limestone plateau west to east. In this general area there are also sandstone ridges in a dissected area between the two river valleys. These ridges continue south of the Wye near the lower stretch of the River Lathkill coming eastwards from Youlgreave. Going south again, the Derwent itself runs through a limestone gorge between Matlock and Cromford. Valleys to the south side of the limestone plateau are discussed separately below.

Spaced throughout these shale valleys are many of the larger villages of the Peak, together with the market centre of Bakewell. This has long been an important place, with surviving Anglo-Saxon cross fragments indicating a probable original association with a minster church and monastery here. Another market centre was Castleton to the north, a planned medieval 'town' with stone castle, within the Crown's hunting preserve of the Royal Forest of the Peak. Important medieval royal manorial centres lie along the main valleys at Hope, Ashford, Bakewell, Darley Churchtown and Matlock Churchtown. Other centres in private

hands since before the Norman Conquest included Hathersage and Edensor (Fig 2.9).

Many of the villages lie at the interface with the limestone plateau, allowing their occupants access to the complementary resources within their manors that the plateau and valley bottom provided.[17] Others similarly had access to valley and gritstone upland and ridgetop resources.[18]

The historic landscape character of the main shale valleys is, for the most part, one of diverse fragmented patterns, often with parcels of unknown date interspersed with woodland and partially surviving fossilised medieval strip fields. This fragmentation reflects long continuous use and modification, rather than radical points of change, and in contrast to the patterns seen on the limestone plateau that are more clear-cut. A major exception to fragmentation lies to the north where the western half of the Hope Valley has extensive fossilisation of open fields around Castleton, Bradwell and Hope. This contrasts with Edale, a more remote valley, where there was never nucleated settlement; here a series of medieval hamlets and later farmsteads have small irregular fields, many of which may well be ancient, but a lack of early maps prevents confirmation of details. One exceptional landscape that breaks all the above generalities is the large landscape park around Chatsworth, with work beginning in the mid-18th century and the park enlarged in the 19th century (*see* Chapter 4). This is one of the key landscapes of the Peak, imposed on the agricultural landscape as a radical transformation made for the Dukes of Devonshire.

Fig 2.9
The estate village of Edensor, near Chatsworth House, lies in the heart of the Derwent Valley and has long been a focal point for settlement.
[John Barnatt]

Hope Valley and Edale

The deep and wide valley centred on Hope, sandwiched between the high limestone plateau to the south-west and high gritstone moorlands elsewhere, has long been a focal point for settlement (Fig 2.10). Here lies the large Iron Age hillfort on Mam Tor high above, overlooking the Roman fort at Brough and medieval castles at Castleton, Hope and Hathersage (*see* Chapters 10 and 11).

In the western half of the valley, fossilised open fields exist at Castleton, Hope, Aston, Thornhill and Bradwell (*see* Fig A2.5; *see also* the case study on pp 206–7) (Fig 2.11). All but the last took advantage of the south-facing valley side and valley bottom, whilst at Bradwell the open fields extended up the side of the limestone plateau as the slope here, whilst relatively steep, is not as precipitous as at Castleton. Immediately above the open fields of Castleton some of the land had already been enclosed into rectangular and irregular fields by the time a map of 1639 was drawn; elsewhere in the valley there are no early maps to determine when similar-looking fields were created. Whilst much of the surrounding high land was enclosed in post-medieval times, previously all was open commons. The modern Hope Valley cement works has quarried away a significant area between Bradwell and Castleton.

Fig 2.10
The Hope Valley from the edge of the limestone plateau, looking down Winnats Pass at its western end, with Castleton below within a hedged and walled landscape.
[John Barnatt]

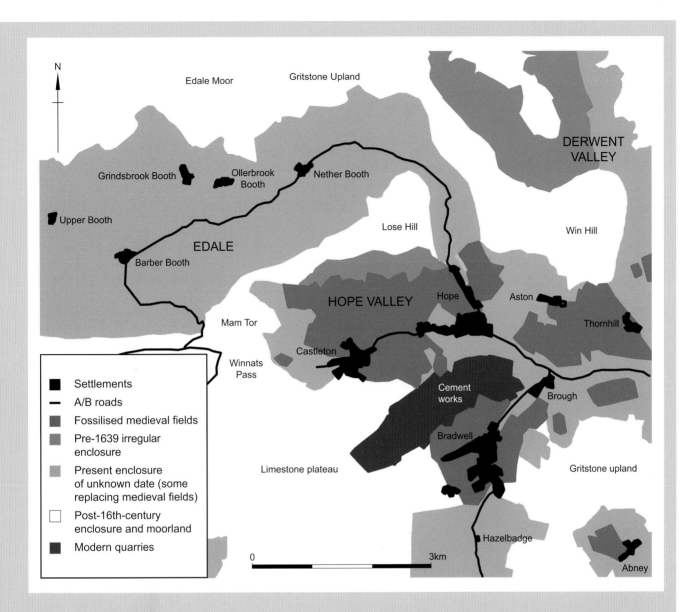

N

Edale Moor

Gritstone Upland

DERWENT
VALLEY

Grindsbrook Booth

Ollerbrook
Booth

Nether Booth

Upper Booth

Lose Hill

Win Hill

EDALE

Barber Booth

HOPE VALLEY

Hope

Aston

Mam Tor

Thornhill

Winnats
Pass

Castleton

Cement
works

Brough

Settlements

A/B roads

Fossilised medieval fields

Pre-1639 irregular
enclosure

Present enclosure
of unknown date (some
replacing medieval fields)

Post-16th-century
enclosure and moorland

Modern quarries

Bradwell

Limestone plateau

Gritstone upland

Hazelbadge

Abney

0   3km

At the eastern end of the Hope Valley the present field layout incorporates less complete evidence for former medieval open-field strips at Bamford, Hathersage and Offerton, the last on the south side of the valley with a shrunken settlement where the main survival is the mid-17th-century hall. Much of the valley land has enclosures of unknown date, presumably telling of gradual modification of the farming landscape over the centuries.

Edale is a second deep valley north-west of Hope, but one where the settlement pattern stands in contrast. It is more remote and surrounded by high land with only one lowland way in, following the River Noe upstream from Hope (*see* Fig A2.5; *see also* the case study in

Chapter 14). Here there were five medieval farmsteads or hamlets known as 'Booths', with a scattering of other isolated farmsteads being established later. The Booths all lie on the south-facing slope, avoiding the north-facing land opposite that is often in shadow. The whole agricultural landscape of the valley comprises small irregular and rectangular fields, traditionally bounded by hedges, but on the valley-side slopes replaced by walls by 1839 at latest (*see* Chapter 4). Unfortunately there is no detailed map of Edale from before this date that would allow the development of this interesting atypical historic landscape to be easily unravelled.

Fig 2.11
The western half of the Hope Valley and much of Edale, with mapping derived from historic landscape character analysis, showing fields with medieval origins around villages, contrasted with extensive surrounding areas that were open commons until post-medieval times.

Baslow, Bubnell, Hassop and Pilsley

Baslow lies where the Derwent Valley opens out from a narrow upriver section. The landscape running west from the River Derwent to the River Wye at Bakewell, centred on Hassop and Pilsley, is atypical in that it is dominated by a series of dissected gritstone hills and shelves that do not reach the same altitude as the gritstone uplands elsewhere. Here there are small medieval villages and hamlets in a palimpsest of historic landscapes of different date and character, most changed through time under heavy influence from three large estates that farmed here (*see* the case study on pp 208–9) (Fig 2.12).[19]

The village of Baslow has long been relatively important, with a planned medieval layout now altered in parts. The southern parts of its fields were swept away in the 1820s and 1830s when incorporated into Chatsworth Park, whilst an estate farm to the west of here lies on the floodplain and may never have had open fields (*see* Fig 8.10).

On the other side of the river, the smaller medieval linear village of Bubnell has a much-altered estate landscape, once part of the Duke of Rutland's holding but again transferred to the Duke of Devonshire in the earlier 19th century. The hamlet of Bramley nearby once also had an open field but now the landscape is dominated by a pre-19th-century ruler-straight, estate-planned, set of rectangular fields.

In a set of strong contrasts, coming away from the Derwent, Pilsley has extensive fossilised medieval fields, whilst the settlement of Birchills is now much shrunken. In the early 17th century parts of its open fields remained, used as a sheepwalk, whilst later estate rationalisation led to large fields being created, now largely swept away again as Chatsworth Estate has developed the area into a 'prairie farm'. At Hassop there is another estate landscape, with fields of post-medieval or undated type, with a park around Hassop Hall developed from the later 18th century, the home of the Earls of Newburgh in the earlier 19th century (*see* Chapter 12).

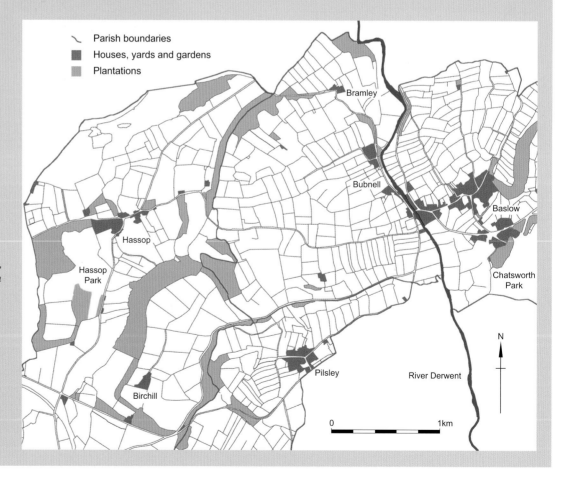

Fig 2.12
The parishes of Hassop, Pilsley and Baslow with Bubnell as they were in 1897, with data from Ordnance Survey mapping revised in that year. The different field layouts include fossilised medieval strips and later more rectangular fields, with plantations often on steeper slopes or flanking parkland.

Haddon Hall

This well-known stately residence, just over the hill from Chatsworth House, has a landscape history that is very different to that at Chatsworth. The present small park, east of the A6 road and divided from this by tree screens, is a late 19th-century creation, made when there was a revival of interest in what had been a neglected house.[20] It is this neglect that led to the survival of one of the finest medieval halls in England; unlike many such houses it was never replaced by something more fashionable. Haddon Hall had been an important residence for several centuries, standing in an extensive deer park that appears to have been, in part, carved out of the parishes of Bakewell and Rowsley, which have long been part of the same estate (Fig 2.13). Today's hall dates from the 12th century onwards, with substantial additions made through to the 14th century. Across the river to the west was the medieval village of Nether Haddon, then surrounded by extensive open fields, with much of its ridge and furrow remaining visible today.

The village of Nether Haddon was much reduced in size by the time it was mapped in about 1717; the former western part of the village was used as a rabbit warren known as the Little Park.[21] At this date Haddon's medieval open field had become a massive sheepwalk, with another known as the Ox Close nearby.[22] By 1793 an estate map shows only a central area of Haddon Field remained unenclosed but this had gone when mapped again in 1799. Ancient fields were confined to the valley-bottom land and an area near the hamlet of Alport.[23]

Haddon Park was still in use in the 17th century and additions were made, with surviving archaeological remains included three bowling greens, one in the garden and two in the old deer park, one of which was previously an 'archery ground'. An 'avenue' with multiple lines of very mature lime and oak trees survives running between the hall and one of the bowling greens.

In the 18th century the Manners family, previously Earls of Rutland, and then Dukes from 1703, for the most part lived at their main residence at Belvoir Castle in Leicestershire. Haddon was old-fashioned and largely ignored; the old deer park was eventually enclosed as farmland, probably in the 1770s. Similarly, the sheepwalks were probably divided in the same period.

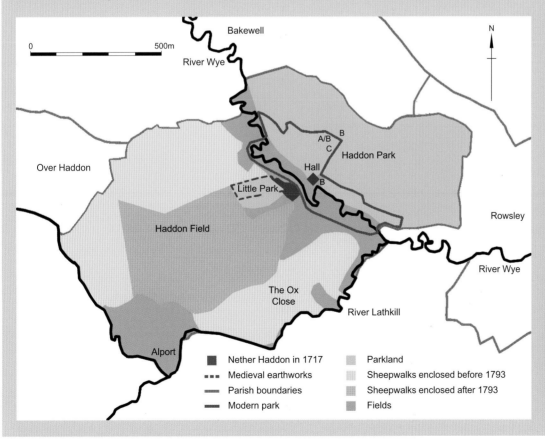

Fig 2.13
Nether Haddon in the 18th century. The medieval deer park was abandoned and enclosed later in the 18th century. Today there is evidence for an archery ground (A), three bowling greens (B) and an avenue of veteran trees in multiple rows (C). The parish boundaries shown for Nether Haddon and adjacent parishes held by the Duke of Rutland are those of the 1790s; that for Nether Haddon was later modified.

Fig 2.14
*The high shelves below
Stanage Edge were farmed
in prehistory and again
in the 19th century after
enclosure walls were built.
However, the scarp slope
below the edge defied
improvement and a
plantation, only part of
which remains, did not
thrive. The edge itself has
always been a remote place
overlooking everything else.
[John Barnatt]*

Dark Peak

The Dark Peak is dominated by open moorland, often not inhabited at any period except by sheep and cattle owned by farmers living around the fringes, or in the case of the eastern moors, farmed in a more intensive way in prehistory, but again open grazing for the last 2000 years. This stands in strong contrast to the main shale valleys of the region and the limestone plateau beyond.

This gritstone upland zone can be divided into various parts. To the north the high swaths of moorland run for kilometre after kilometre, and include Kinder Scout and Bleaklow. There were scattered farmsteads in the narrow upper reaches of the River Derwent Valley, and those of tributaries dissecting this upland, running southwards to the main shale valleys. Similarly, Longdendale, west of Glossop, and shorter valleys elsewhere run down to the west, north and east to pass through peripheral hills.

To the east side of the Peak, in contrast, there is a broad area of gritstone upland which on average is lower in altitude than the moors to the north. These eastern moors in their northern parts again are dominated by heather and coarse grasses but in favourable areas, particularly on

shelves, there have long been scattered farmsteads with fields; elsewhere small areas have been taken into cultivation later, some after Parliamentary Enclosure Awards. At the northern end of the eastern moors, whilst the shelves at Bamford Moor have prehistoric settlement, the land above Stanage Edge is too high and this in effect is a southward-running spur of ground of the northern zone (Fig 2.14). To the south an area of topographically comparable upland, running southwards from above Darley, was fully enclosed by 18th- and 19th-century Parliamentary Enclosure Awards. Now there are extensive areas of forestry interspersed by farmland with ruler-straight field walls.

As well as the main block of upland east of the River Derwent, there are two islands of similar land west of the river. That at Abney, Offerton and Eyam Moors remains partially unenclosed, with two other parts divided into fields after Parliamentary Enclosure Awards. To the south, the fully enclosed land around Alderwasley is at a comparable altitude to the old moors east of here. To the west side of the Peak, the moorland landscape is more broken and described below under South-West Peak.

There are scattered farmsteads in upland locations around the fringes of the Dark Peak moorland; these were always relatively remote places to live, placed high above villages at township centres in the valleys below. In some cases, notably in the Upper Derwent Valley, early estate maps and documentary evidence show that farmsteads have medieval and early post-medieval origins. For the most part, the peripheral areas have undated or post-medieval fields. Where undated some farmsteads may have relatively early origins, as illustrated for example by historical research north of Bradfield, where several farmsteads have been shown to have existed before the Black Death in the 14th century.[24]

In the valleys that flank the Dark Peak upland there are larger settlements that have medieval origins, such as the village of Bradfield with its church and two motte-and-bailey castles. To the west, around Glossop, Whaley Bridge and Chapel en le Frith, landscape evidence for medieval origins is heavily masked by the development of these valleys as industrial settlements that grew around textile mills.

Upper Derwent

In the 19th century the valley of the River Derwent in its upper reaches, along with those of its tributaries the rivers Ashop and Alport to the west, was a classic example of a landscape with a dispersed settlement pattern. These deep valleys, which have narrow bottoms and steep sides with bleak moorlands above, did not have enough good land for large villages, but rather had many scattered farmsteads, with just one small hamlet, Derwent, located just east of the River Derwent. However, from early in the 20th century onwards much of this pattern was disrupted, first by the building of the Derwent and Howden reservoirs in 1901–16 and then in 1935–44 with the downriver addition of Ladybower Reservoir (see Chapter 9). The best farmland was flooded and a number of dwellings were demolished. Other buildings under Ladybower Reservoir were left; they are now ruinous and can be seen when water levels are very low.

Reconstruction through time of Hope Woodlands parish, which includes all land west of the River Derwent, is made possible by a study of medieval documentation and mapping in 1627 by William Senior for the Cavendish Family at Chatsworth.[25] This shows 22 tenanted farmsteads here, all within a complex agricultural landscape in the valley bottoms, with small irregular fields interspersed with managed woodlands (Fig 2.15). Above were large areas of moorland, each allocated to individual farmsteads as private upland grazing areas, edged by lines of boundary cairns and/or banks.

Nine of the farmsteads can be traced in documents back to the 14th century. At that date two were monastic granges owned by the Premonstratensian monks of Welbeck Abbey in Nottinghamshire. Their grant of land at Crookhill to the south was confirmed by King John in 1215, with 'One Mans Field' grange at Abbey further north added in the 1250s (see Chapter 3). The extent to which the monks took over an existing farmed landscape is not clear. Whilst the land lay within the Norman Royal Forest of the Peak, we know that this did not exclusively comprise unsettled land, but also had pre-Norman habitations and fields around its fringes. This said, at Hope Woodlands much of what was there in 1627 no doubt comprised intakes made within the forest from the 13th century onwards at a time when the forest was little used (*see* Chapter 12).

The situation in 1627 can be compared with the late 19th-century Ordnance Survey mapping done before the reservoirs were created.

The number of farmsteads and other dwellings had grown, mostly with infilling between the earliest farmsteads, whilst two of the 1627 farmsteads in the upper reaches of the Derwent Valley had gone. Similarly, the enclosed fields had been modified and somewhat expanded.

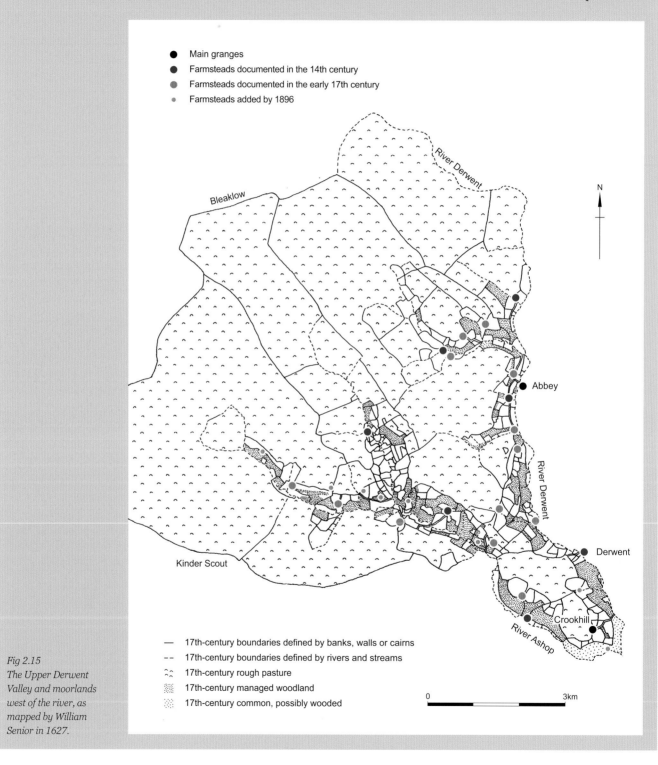

- ● Main granges
- ● Farmsteads documented in the 14th century
- ● Farmsteads documented in the early 17th century
- · Farmsteads added by 1896

— 17th-century boundaries defined by banks, walls or cairns
-- 17th-century boundaries defined by rivers and streams
᷍ 17th-century rough pasture
17th-century managed woodland
17th-century common, possibly wooded

0   3km

Fig 2.15
The Upper Derwent Valley and moorlands west of the river, as mapped by William Senior in 1627.

Gardom's Edge through time

The Gardom's Edge shelf on the gritstone upland east of Baslow is typical of the most favourable areas above the main scarp flanking the Derwent Valley. It is a landscape of great complexity and time depth (Fig 2.16). Investigation has included extensive archaeological survey and excavation.[26] An aid to interpreting late features is provided by historic maps dating from 1799 onwards.

The 1799 map shows a 1759 turnpike road, with one part already diverted east of Robin Hood. There was also a later diversion and new turnpike roads were built. Settlement comprises the hamlet of Robin Hood, with it roadside inn, and the Moorside farmstead further north. Prehistoric fields with field clearance and houses are found amongst the more recent fields and also more extensively on the moorland northern half of Gardom's Edge and to the east above Birchen Edge.

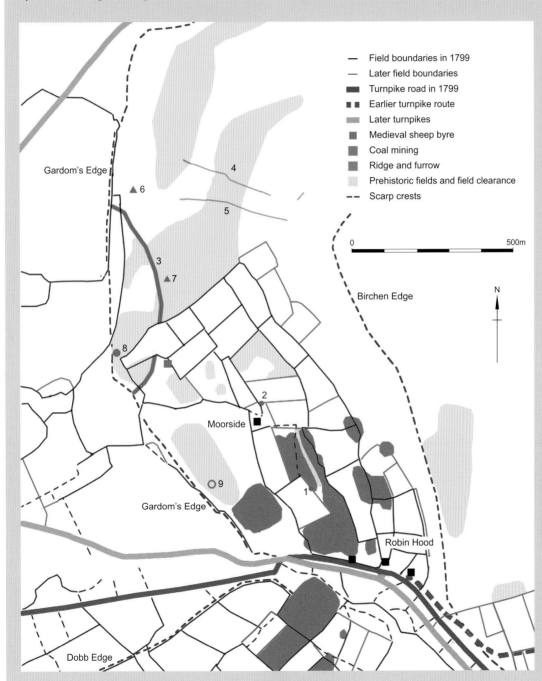

Field boundaries in 1799
Later field boundaries
Turnpike road in 1799
Earlier turnpike route
Later turnpikes
Medieval sheep byre
Coal mining
Ridge and furrow
Prehistoric fields and field clearance
Scarp crests

0   500m

N

Gardom's Edge

Birchen Edge

Moorside

Gardom's Edge

Robin Hood

Dobb Edge

Fig 2.16
The Gardom's Edge palimpsest. A snapshot for 1799 is provided by an estate map which shows field boundaries (those now removed shown dashed). Further field walls have been added subsequently; two have date stones (1: 1853; 2: 1861). Prehistoric features include a large prehistoric enclosure (3), a cross ridge bank (4), a pit alignment (5), a tall standing stone (6), rock art (7), a round barrow (8) and a ring cairn (9).

The main contrast today is between the northern and southern halves of the shelf. At the former there are extensive prehistoric remains (Fig 2.17). For the most part these comprise low stony mounds buried in the heather and bracken, which mark the sites of prehistoric settlement and fields, where people once lived in scattered round houses and cleared stone to use the land. There are also monuments and cross-ridge earthworks (*see* Chapter 10). All was abandoned sometime in the 500 years before the Romans arrived, with wetter climatic conditions in the first millennium BC having led eventually to the abandoning of these houses and fields. Since then, for over 2,000 years, the land has been open grazing, with the livestock keeping tree growth at bay.

Looking at the Gardom's Edge shelf as a whole, farming probably contracted rather than all that had been there in prehistory being abandoned.

Fig 2.17
An excavated prehistoric cairn on Gardom's Edge, comprising field clearance stone placed on an earthfast boulder, with further stones placed around the edge.
[Gardom's Edge Project]

The southern half is somewhat more advantaged, as the slope is south-facing, and there may well have been sustained farming in fields here for something like 4,000 years. Moorside Farm was already here when an estate map of 1799 was drawn.[27] This sits amongst improved fields interspersed with an area of stony ground near the Edge, and another area where there are extensive coal-mining remains, some probably going back to medieval times, that had inhibited farming (*see* Chapter 6). In both areas prehistoric features remain, whereas in the improved areas all such have presumably been swept away. After the coal mining had ceased, further field walls were built here as new farming ground was taken in and the layout modified; unusually two of these walls have mid-19th-century date stones.

Scattered across this southern area are archaeological features that suggest the farming shown on the 1799 map was not a recent development but previously had been sustained over a long period; these features include stony banks defining what may well be a medieval sheep byre at the edge of rough ground.[28] The footings of a stone-built rectangular house lie nearby, perhaps of 17th-century date and presumably lived in before a move to the present farmhouse site. There is also ridge and furrow of medieval or post-medieval date near the scarp edge in an area never enclosed by field walls.

South-West Peak

This part of the Peak is distinct. It comprises upland valleys and high moors on a gritstone and shale substrate. For the most part the moorlands are more broken up by valleys than those of the Dark Peak. A dispersed settlement pattern reflects the relatively restricted potential of the land compared with the adjacent limestone plateau and the main eastern and southern valleys.

The highest parts of the South-West Peak comprise gritstone and sandstone that have resisted erosion, whilst the valleys are dominated by shales. High and relatively continuous stretches of moors, comparable to those of the Dark Peak, are confined to Combs Moss to the north and a larger area west of Buxton centred on Goyt's Moss (Fig 2.18). Elsewhere there are unenclosed ridges, as at Shutlingsloe, The Roaches, Middle Hills and Revidge, whilst

Fig 2.18 (opposite)
The high and inhospitable gritstone moorlands found in the Dark Peak to the north extend to the South-West Peak, as here at Black Edge on Combs Moss.
[John Barnatt]

a long high ridge to the south, the Morridge, was fully enclosed in post-medieval times.

The most important valleys comprise those at the upper reaches of the rivers Dove, Manifold and Hamps, all with broad waterlogged bottomlands, that downstream lead to gorges running through the limestone plateau. To the north and west, the rivers Goyt and Dane respectively flow down to the Peak foothills around New Mills and Macclesfield.

The Staffordshire villages of Warslow, Butterton, Grindon, Waterfall, Waterhouses and Cauldon lie close to the edge of the limestone plateau, which here extends a short distance west of the gorges of the rivers Manifold and Hamps; the change from shale to limestone here has no strong topographic contrast. The limestone plateau in Staffordshire, whilst complementing the shale and gritstone landscape described here, has been covered above.

The majority of the South-West Peak landscape is populated by many dispersed farmsteads and cottages, together with small hamlets, scattered widely across the land except at the highest areas. Some of these are recorded in the medieval period and could have even earlier origins, whilst others were built in post-medieval times as farmers expanded into more marginal areas. The notable exception are the limestone-edge villages noted above and that of Longnor further north. This market village was super-imposed on the hamlet zone, probably in the medieval period, with its market charter granted in 1293 (*see* the case study on pp 214–5).

Longnor also stands out as having well-preserved fossilised field strips for open fields on the ridgetop near the village and in the Upper Dove Valley below (Fig 2.19). No other settlements in this part of the South-West Peak have such remains, indicating medieval Longnor was atypical, presumably because of its market. Other large open-field layouts are confined to the villages at the edge of the limestone plateau to the south-east, although one at Upper Elkstone indicates such fields also existed at hamlets.

Like the southern valleys described below, much of the land in the South-West Peak has irregular and roughly rectangular fields that cannot be easily dated from their form and there are usually no early maps to indicate their age. In the valleys some of these fields may well have been here in the medieval period and like their farmsteads may have earlier origins. Others at the moorland fringes are recognisable from the layout of the fields as intakes into former commons, although in some cases this may have happened long ago.

There are exceptions; estate maps show that some fields around Grindon and Wincle have medieval or early post-medieval origins, whilst in contrast there are areas enclosed from moorland as the result of Parliamentary Enclosure Awards, notably around Roche Grange, Longnor and Butterton. Elsewhere, in some instances mapping and field shape show fields that are relatively late in date. There are also two areas of parkland, at Swythamley and at the northern fringe around the grand house at Lyme. Open expanses of moorland to the north include Goyt's Moss and Combs Moss, whilst on lower ridges further south remaining moorland tends to be divided into large grazing parcels.

Fig 2.19
Fossilised medieval open-field strips on the high ridge just outside Longnor (left), with the Upper Dove Valley close to the prominent Chrome Hill behind.
[John Barnatt]

Warslow and Elkstone

The village of Warslow lies close to the interface between shale beds and the gritstone moors above with the limestone land below. Close by is the gorge of the River Manifold cut deep into the limestone. The village itself has an unusual plan, radically changed from an irregular layout of spaced properties after two turnpike roads were added, following Acts of Parliament in 1770 and 1833, with new houses springing up against them (*see* 'Living differently' on p 47).

The Warslow and Elkstone landscape has the main village at the most advantageous point, with fossilised open-field strips adjacent and below the houses leading down to the top of the Manifold gorge (Fig 2.20). The fields here have good limestone soils, whereas above and to the west is heavy-clay land on shale. Here there are scattered farmsteads away from the village amongst extensive tracts of small rectangular and irregular fields which, in the absence of pre-19th-century maps, are hard to date. Some may be ancient, whereas higher up the slopes they may have been added later. Two exceptions are relics of small areas of fossilised open-field strips associated with the two hamlets at Elkstone. As a last stage of landscape development, some parcels were taken in from moorland following a Parliamentary Enclosure Award of 1839, with a smaller area taken in as private enclosure at a somewhat earlier date. Above there is still unimproved moorland, divided into large parcels by criss-crossing walls and boundaries. In contrast the adjacent village of Butterton to the south had already had all its moorland common enclosed after an Award of 1776.

For several centuries much of the land was owned by the Harper Crewe family, who owned Warslow Hall but had their main residence at Calke Abbey near Ticknall south of the Trent. However, in the 1980s the moorland and some of the farmland were accepted by HM Treasury in lieu of death duties and given to the National Park Authority to manage.

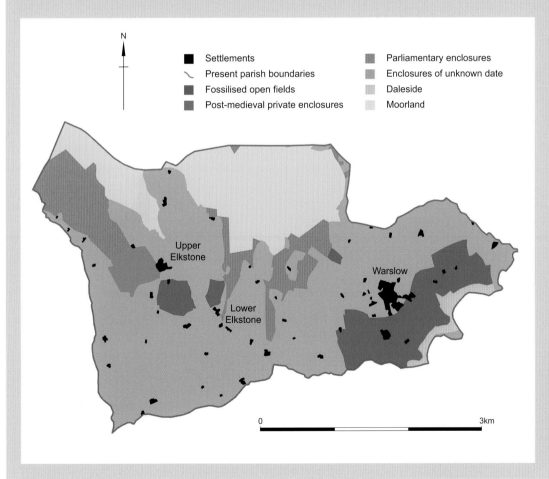

N

■ Settlements	Parliamentary enclosures
＼ Present parish boundaries	Enclosures of unknown date
Fossilised open fields	Daleside
Post-medieval private enclosures	Moorland

Upper Elkstone

Warslow

Lower Elkstone

0   3km

Fig 2.20
The agricultural landscapes of Warslow and Elkstone parish, with mapping derived from historic landscape character analysis.

Southern valleys

Immediately south of the limestone plateau, beyond where it drops off steeply close to the villages of Ilam (Fig 2.21), Blore, Thorpe, Tissington, Parwich, Ballidon, Brassington, Carsington and Hopton, and also the town of Wirksworth, there is a series of sheltered valleys running southwards between low rolling ridges. However, these valleys shortly run through the low, flat-topped, sandstone and mudstone hills of Permian and Triassic age. These are relatively infertile and in the medieval period including the large hunting forest of Duffield Frith to the east; much of this land lies outside the scope of this volume. The valleys, from west to east, include those of Bletch Brook, Bradbourne Brook, Haven Hill Brook, Scow Brook and the River Ecclesbourne.

This low-lying area immediately south of the plateau is a landscape where settlement is dominated by villages. Some, as named above, take advantage of the shelter and springs at the edge of the plateau. Others, further south, include Ashbourne, Mappleton, Fenny Bentley, Bradbourne, Kniveton, Hognaston and Kirk Ireton. Amongst them were important medieval manorial centres at Ashbourne, Parwich and Wirksworth. The last was particularly important because of rich lead mines nearby and, as well as an agricultural market centre, it has long been the administrative centre for the lead trade in the southern half of the orefield. Brassington is also large because of the extensive lead mines on the plateau nearby.

The settlements lie within a relatively rich and advantaged agricultural landscape of enclosed fields. The villages normally had medieval open fields around them, sometimes with extensive tracts still identifiable in fossilised form as at Ashbourne, Parwich and Brassington in particular. There are also areas that we know were enclosed after 18th- and 19th-century Parliamentary Enclosure Awards, as for example at Hognaston, Callow and Wirksworth. Also present are small areas where privately enclosed fields are distinctively late in form with straight edges and rectangular shape. Several local halls lie within small areas of parkland, as at Ilam Hall, Hopton Hall and Alton Manor. The first, to the far west next to the River Manifold where it emerges from a gorge through the limestone plateau, is owned by the National Trust and has public access.

Although the distinctive forms noted above exist, the most common element of today's agricultural landscape character comprises irregular and roughly rectangular fields that, with the absence of early estate maps, cannot be easily dated. These are likely to vary widely in inception; some are probably medieval or earlier in date, whilst many may be later with the majority created between the 16th and 18th centuries.

Fig 2.21
Ilam church lies within the parkland of Ilam Hall, the owners of which transformed the local fertile landscape here. Thorp Cloud at the edge of the limestone plateau is visible in the distance. [John Barnatt]

Parwich and Newton Grange

In medieval times this large village was a royal manorial centre which had three small outlying subsidiary settlements, called 'berewicks', on less favourable ground to the west.[29] The village itself nestles under the steep edge of the limestone plateau, with broad valleys and a low ridge running away southwards. Of its medieval subsidiary settlements, Alsop le Dale lies nestled near the head of the narrower valley of Bletch Brook, whilst Hanson, which became a monastic grange of Burton Abbey in Staffordshire, and Cold Eaton, both lie on the limestone plateau further west. Newton, again on the plateau, was a separate holding at Domesday and later became a grange of the Cistercian Combermere Abbey in Cheshire.

The parishes of Parwich and Newton Grange have no early maps and this case study provides an example of what can be determined from field shapes alone (Fig 2.22). South and west of Parwich village the soils are mostly clays and there is an extensive area of fossilised open fields, with much ridge and furrow, found both in the valley bottom and on a low, steep-sided ridge between Bradbourne Brook and Bletch Brook (Fig 2.23). To the north-west of the village there was another open field. Whilst the fossilisation pattern here is far from complete, ridge and furrow and lynchets in other fields confirm a large medieval cultivation area here. This field extended a short way up onto the limestone plateau, where the slope is less steep when compared with Parwich Hill just north of the village. This hill and much of the rest of the

plateau land was open common until enclosed into rectangular fields in post-medieval times. In contrast, the land on the limestone plateau to the west around the outlying settlements has fields that are mostly of undiagnostic type and uncertain date.

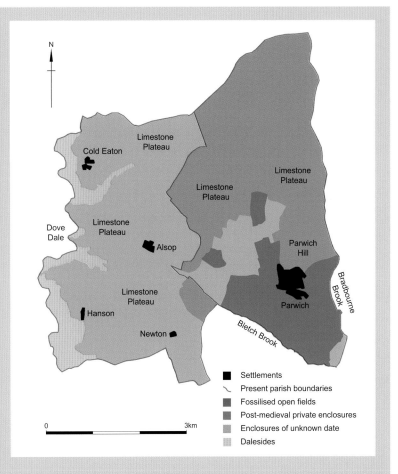

Settlements
Present parish boundaries
Fossilised open fields
Post-medieval private enclosures
Enclosures of unknown date
Dalesides

0   3km

Fig 2.22
The agricultural landscapes of Parwich and Newton Grange parishes, with mapping derived from historic landscape character analysis.

Fig 2.23
Parwich village nestles amongst trees in the Bradbourne Brook valley below the edge of the limestone plateau. The photograph looks north-west from Bradbourne; to the right Parwich Hill rises steeply above the village, while to the centre and left there are low 'shale' ridges where open-field ridge and furrow can still be seen. [John Barnatt]

3

Places to live

Settlements are a vital part of the landscape character. Most of the towns and villages in the Peak, and a proportion of scattered farms and hamlets, have medieval origins and indications of this can often be seen in the buildings and in historical documentation. Places named in Chapter 3 are located on Figure A1.2 (*see* p 225).

Many of the villages of the Peak have medieval churches, although in a significant number of cases these were restored or rebuilt in the 19th century. There are only few medieval castles in the Peak, mostly comprising motte-and-bailey earthworks, with only one stone-built example at Peveril Castle at Castleton. Both churches and castles are returned to in Chapter 11.

With the exception of medieval churches, few standing buildings date to before the mid-16th century; the main exceptions are Peveril Castle at Castleton and halls at Haddon, Upper Padley, Fenny Bentley and Throwley. From the mid-16th century onwards many medieval manor houses of the minor gentry and the homes of wealthy yeomen farmers were rebuilt or newly erected in stone. There is a significant number of small but sturdy halls surviving, scattered through the Peak, with distinctive mullioned windows and stone-slate roofs, many thought to have been afforded on the back of wealth acquired through involvement in the lead trade (*see* Chapter 12) (Fig 3.1).[1] In the 18th and 19th centuries the rebuilding of houses and outbuildings in stone migrated down the social hierarchy. This is part of a wider trend, with many thousands of miles of field boundaries

Fig 3.1
A classic small hall at Highlow in the gritstone upland south of Hathersage built by the Eyre family and of probable late 16th-century date. The photograph is taken from a long but now-abandoned formal terrace.
[John Barnatt]

built or remodelled in the later 18th and earlier 19th centuries (*see* Chapter 4). By the mid-19th century even humble outbuildings such as pigsties and cart sheds were built in stone as a matter of course. Although there were once many medieval and early post-medieval farmhouses, cottages and outbuildings built with timber frames, wattle-and-daub walls, and thatch roofs, today virtually all these buildings have been swept away as and when the time came for rebuilding or abandonment. The exceptions are a number of in-situ later medieval cruck frames, now not usually recognised from the outside because they have been encased by stone walls. These are particularly common on the eastern gritstone moorland fringes but are also found elsewhere across the region. More common are displaced crucks reused in later buildings, which often form the only visible indicator of an earlier build.

Vernacular buildings

Most vernacular buildings in the Peak, which have a distinctive local style and are a strongly defining feature of this upland region, are built in limestone or gritstone with this reflecting the locally available stone. Where constructed in limestone, if it could be afforded, gritstone was used for details such as lintels and quoins because it was more readily shaped. Bricks were not normally used before the 20th century, for these were expensive to make/import. The exceptions are a few high-status buildings, such as 18th-century examples at Longstone Hall in Great Longstone and the Duke of Devonshire's coaching inn at Edensor. Whilst many buildings were once thatched, such roofs are now very rare, with but two surviving examples near Baslow in the Derwent Valley. An 1850 survey of the buildings in Beeley, made for the Duke of Devonshire, showed that a significant proportion of his properties were thatched.[2] The other common traditional roofing material, with many examples surviving, was stone slate, quarried locally at specific thin beds of coarse sandstone. These demanded a lower pitch to the roof, and often when thatched buildings were to be re-roofed with stone slate, or from the later 19th century with Welsh slate brought in by railway, the upper walls of the building were heightened to make the re-roofing possible.

In villages a whole range of traditional buildings often exists. As well as church, vicarage, manor house or hall, others were erected as farmsteads, houses, cottages, shops, workshops and outbuildings. At farmsteads, whether in villages or scattered across the countryside, there is often a house, cow houses, loose boxes, stables, haylofts, cart sheds, pigsties, storage sheds, livestock yards and stack yards. Sometimes there are threshing barns and large open-sided hay-storage barns; field barns are returned to in Chapter 5. Traditional buildings can have external stone staircases and dog kennels. At cow houses and loose boxes, pitch-holes or picking holes are common, which are small shuttered square doors for importing hay for first-floor storage. Old cheese presses are sometimes retained as ornamental features. Until a few decades ago, cottages and small-holdings often also had small cow houses and/or stables, as well as pigsties and cart sheds. All these features tell of local farming practices over the last few hundred years, providing evidence for the use of animals on farms, and the mixed farming practice of this upland region.

Traditionally, the farms of the Peak needed to supply a large population, some of which earned their living from industry rather than agriculture, especially lead mining and textile production. New impetus to farmers was provided with the growth of surrounding cities in the 19th century, with livestock and dairy products sent here; how the farm buildings and their uses changed through time, which can be set against historical records and contemporary descriptions, is a subject where much research is still needed.[3]

Nucleated and dispersed ways

In the medieval period a central part of the Peak was, and still is, dominated by villages. Whilst known early isolated farmsteads are likely to be under-represented as they commonly went undocumented in medieval sources, it is clear that in the village-dominated area the majority of the scattered farmsteads that exist today beyond the villages were created in the 18th and 19th centuries on sites where nothing stood before, built when the wastes and commons were enclosed. In contrast, it is in the 'mixed' and 'dispersed' settlement areas, to the west, north and east, where there is often uncertainty over the age of particular farmsteads. Before the mid-18th century when enclosure and industrialisation started, the contrast between the nucleated and dispersed settlement areas was even stronger than it is today (Fig 3.2).

Fig 3.2
Medieval settlement patterns in the Peak, showing zones of 'nucleated', 'mixed' and 'dispersed' habitation. In the 'dispersed' and 'mixed' zones many places are shown as only possible examples because of ambiguous historic reference in published sources; conversely there may well have been other scattered farmsteads, not shown here as they have gone undocumented. The two nucleated settlements in the 'dispersed' zone are the superimposed market centres of Chapel en le Frith and Longnor.

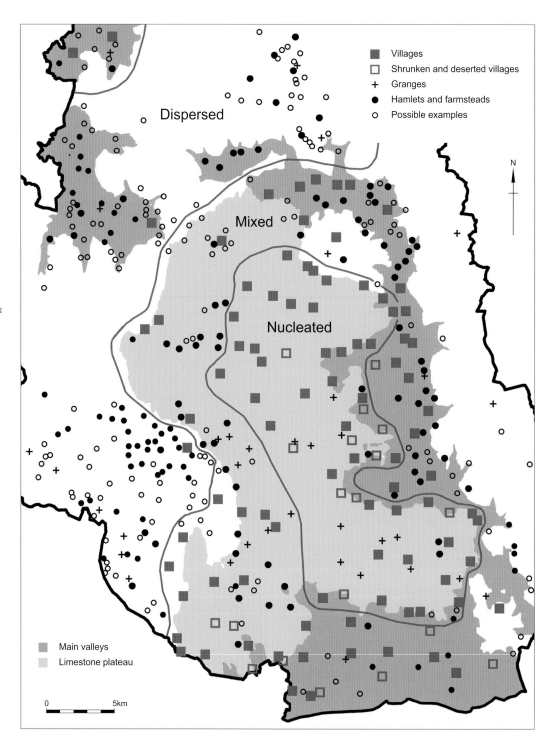

On the limestone plateau, at its heart and eastern edge, the medieval landscape was dominated by nucleated villages, whilst the number of dispersed farmsteads was small and largely confined to a scattering of monastic granges in less advantaged areas. For the most part the insignificant numbers of other minor medieval settlements here today are now deserted or shrunken settlements and their original size is unknown. Today's large numbers of farmsteads away from the villages are of later 18th and earlier 19th centuries; some farmers chose to move out of the villages and built houses and farm outbuildings amongst their new fields once the limestone heaths were divided.

In a halo around the limestone nucleated settlement core there is a zone where settlement is mixed, with villages, hamlets and scattered farmsteads all common. This area includes the higher spinal ridges of the limestone plateau to the west where monastic granges are common; high swaths of the limestone plateau to the north; and the Derwent Valley to the east. There is also a small area of mixed settlement to the far north-west around the lower end of Longdendale at the fringe of the Royal Forest of the Peak (*see* pp 186-7).

A third settlement zone, which lies to the north and west, is one of predominantly dispersed settlement. This includes the Staffordshire moorlands to the west and the upper parts of the Derwent Valley and its tributaries to the north (Fig 3.3). To the north-west the valleys of the rivers Goyt and Etherow, which run down from the Peak into the plain beyond, once also had predominantly dispersed settlement, now masked by the proliferation of housing built in post-medieval times associated with textile mills and other industry. The main medieval settlement of any size was at Chapel en le Frith; this exceptional site was the market centre at the heart of the royal hunting forest.

In the mixed and dispersed zones the settlement comprises both single scattered farms and clusters of dwellings forming hamlets, some in tight groups, but more often in loose clusters (Fig 3.4). Many non-nucleated settlements existed in the western and northern parts of the Peak, or at less favourable spots within the mixed zone, which never have been township foci.

The plotting of small settlements on Figure 3.2 is only a first attempt at this, based on easily available sources.[4] Many farmsteads and hamlets are plotted as only possible examples, where detailed future research may confirm their age.[5] Plotting of dispersed settlement still needs much research, but where this has happened, as with scattered farms north of Bradfield in South Yorkshire, medieval dates for some have been confirmed.[6]

Fig 3.3
Dispersed farmsteads are common on the Staffordshire moorlands, as here at Lower Green Farm in the uppermost reaches of the Hamps Valley. [John Barnatt]

Fig 3.4
Little Hucklow on the
limestone plateau is a small
linear village surrounded
by fossilised medieval fields
crossed by small lead-mine
workings, while the hamlet
of Coplow Dale in the
foreground straddles a
parish boundary and is
post-medieval in date.
[© Crown copyright.
Historic England Archive,
17196_01]

Little of the medieval layout of small settlements can now be reconstructed where they are still occupied. Earthworks at deserted medieval farmsteads are rare in the Peak, but one at Lawrence Field on the eastern gritstone upland above Padley has a single longhouse, with outbuilding, associated with an oval intake surrounded by moorland common.[7] On the opposite side of the steep Burbage Brook valley, about 0.5km away, there is an irregular cluster of five or six longhouses at Sheffield Plantation.[8] Another longhouse has been excavated at Staden near Buxton.[9]

Further spatial patterning can be seen when the distribution of planned and non-planned villages is examined. Almost all of the villages in the heart of the limestone plateau are planned. Of the exceptions, Monyash was a market centre and includes the addition of a planned row, whilst Alstonefield had origins as an early major manorial focal point and Peak Forest was an atypical settlement that grew around the foresters' chamber at the heart of the Royal Forest. The only smaller villages/hamlets that stand out as unplanned are Aldwark and Stanshope. In contrast to the limestone heart, the villages along the plateau edge and the shale valleys are more mixed in type, some with overt planned layouts, others not. The layouts of manorial centres and other villages are returned to below.

The dichotomy between the limestone plateau and elsewhere suggests that at some point there was a radical change made to how these limestone areas were farmed, with feudal lords imposing planned villages. When this took place in the Peak is unclear. Whilst most of the settlements are recorded in Domesday, this gives no guarantee they nucleated by 1086, indeed many were recorded as berewicks. Did the nucleation take place with the later fragment-ation of the large royal estates centred at Hope, Ashford, Bakewell, Darley Churchtown, Matlock Churchtown, Wirksworth, Parwich and Ash-bourne, or did it already exist?

Taking a more local perspective, a few villages are clearly secondary sites, some at least probably developing because of the distance of medieval open fields from the main village. The classic cases are at Tideswell which has the smaller village of Wheston to the west, and Eyam with Foolow again to the west. In both examples the civil parish boundaries at the end of the 19th century stood out from elsewhere because of their complex series of irregular partitions and detached parcels of one parish's land within the other. Wheston is first documented in 1225 and Foolow in 1269, whereas the primary villages are listed at Domesday.[10] In the case of Priestcliffe, which lies a short distance from Taddington, in post-medieval times both places were administered together rather than having separate townships but both appear in Domesday. In the case of Bonsall, which again is recorded in 1086, the nearby Upper Town to the west was first recorded in 1297, whilst for Slaley, a short distance to the south-west, it is 1326; all are in the same 'parish' but it is not known whether the primary reason for the creation of these smaller settlements was agricultural or because there were extensive lead mines nearby.

Whilst all village nucleation across the Peak is likely to have taken place by the mid-13th century at latest, and in some cases perhaps long before, we do not know whether there was a discrete short period of change, or whether the planned sites were slowly imposed from the 10th or 11th century onwards.

Manorial centres and markets

Most of the main manorial centres lie along the plateau edge and the shale valleys, including those at the centre of large late-Saxon royal estates (Fig 3.5).[11] These valley areas were clearly settlement heartlands, undoubtedly already of long standing by the time of the Norman Conquest.[12]

Of these manorial centres, Ashford, Bakewell, Matlock Churchtown, Wirksworth and Parwich have irregular settlement plans or have only specific parts that are planned. The village of Hope is largely planned, but the focal point around the church and nearby motte-and-bailey castle may be earlier than the rest and form an irregular focal point. Similarly, whilst Ashbourne

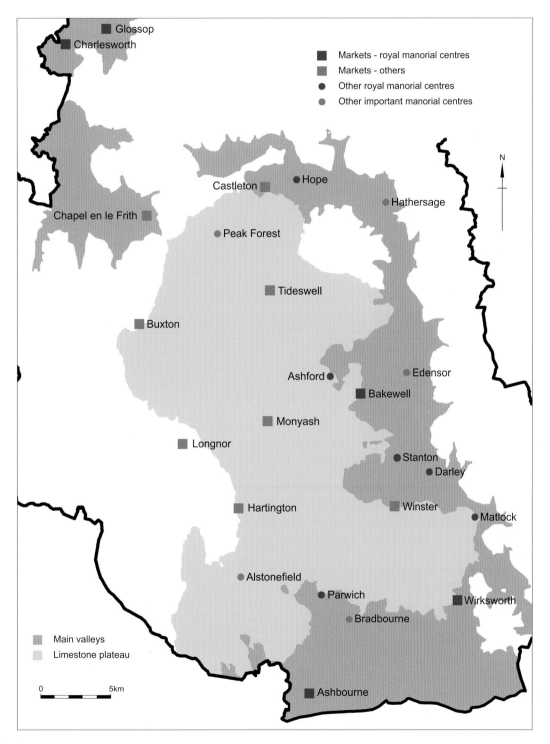

■ Markets - royal manorial centres
■ Markets - others
● Other royal manorial centres
● Other important manorial centres

■ Main valleys
□ Limestone plateau

0   5km

Fig 3.5
The distribution of medieval markets and manorial centres in the Peak.

41

has a planned main street, the market place at one end could be an initial irregular focal point. Darley Churchtown is now shrunken and its medieval layout is unclear.

Four places that may have been important manorial centres, but which were in private hands by the immediate pre-Norman period, are similar. As noted above, Alstonefield is irregular in plan and Edensor and Hathersage are again irregular but have appended linear streets, whilst the layout-type of Stanton in Peak is ambiguous.

In summary, it appears that there is a small number of important places that evolved as irregularly planned settlements at an early date, probably before the advent of planned villages made when a pattern of hamlets and dispersed farms was largely swept away on the limestone plateau and in parts of the Derwent Valley. A notable exception is the planned town at Castleton surrounded by a rectangular bank and ditch, which was probably created in the late 12th century, built below the Royal Forest stronghold of Peveril Castle, superseding Hope as the main centre in the western part of the Hope Valley.

Many of these focal places are where markets and fairs were held in the medieval period and another important aspect of their distribution is their relationship to topographical zones.[13] The majority, at Castleton, Bakewell, Winster, Wirksworth, Buxton, Longnor and Hartington, were at or close to the interface between the limestone plateau and the shale valleys with gritstone uplands beyond, ideally placed for exchange of complementary produce from these contrasting areas. Similarly, those at Wirksworth, Ashbourne, Charlesworth and Glossop are placed between the Peak upland and the lowlands. This leaves three others at places a long way from the markets noted above. That at Chapel en le Frith is in the heart of the western valleys of the Royal Forest, whilst Tideswell and Monyash are placed in the heart of the limestone plateau at its central shelves that were an important settlement focal area.

Planned villages

The plans of Peak villages, as today and shown on 16th- to 19th-century historic maps, are very variable and often still reflect something of their medieval character in the layout of streets, lanes and holding boundaries. Whilst buildings moved within plots as rebuilding took place, the plots themselves remained relatively constant. There are villages that were obviously planned, whilst at the other extreme some appear to be very irregular in form and presumably reflect a more gradual aggregation of dwellings rather than the superimposition of a manorial lord's ideas as to how a feudal community should be organised. The types of village forms and their degree of variation are typical of what is found throughout much of northern England and beyond.[14] The descriptions that follow are intended to give a flavour of the range of variation at Peak villages.

The classic form taken by planned villages in the Peak is a single straight street with the houses and yards, usually referred to as the 'crofts and tofts', in rows that run back from the street, usually with a common orientation to the cultivation strips in the open-field furlongs immediately beyond. Wardlow and Chelmorton are classic examples with houses in two rows, one on each side of the street, with now fossilised open fields beyond (Figs 3.6 and 3.7). Chelmorton also has a substantial bank and ditch separating the open fields from the commons beyond.[15] As is often the case, both had funnel-shaped entries to the village at the edge of the fields, so that stock could be more easily brought to the village or open fields. Unlike the two villages noted above, at Wormhill the linear village has farmhouses built at right angles to the street, some set back as if there was once a green that has now been largely enclosed (Fig 3.8).

In contrast, Little Longstone and Fairfield were probably planned to have crofts in a single row along only one side of the street. Some villages are now somewhat shrunken, as at Blackwell where there are earthworks within now unoccupied 'tofts' spaced down the street and beyond its present eastern end. In contrast, Youlgreave is exceptionally large and for centuries has been a rich farming and mining settlement; there has been expansion away from the main street, especially down the slope into Bradford Dale. Expansion up from the medieval core towards mines is a strong characteristic of the medieval settlements of Bradwell and Winster.

The small linear village of Abney is exceptional in that it lies in an isolated site on a high gritstone shelf; much of its fossilised open-field layout remains. In contrast, with the exception of the village of Birchover, elsewhere on the high gritstone shelves there were only small 'open fields' where the associated settlements appear to have been minor hamlets lying within the townships of larger villages on lower, better ground. There are also a number of one-street hamlets that are planned, such as Hurdlow, planted high on the limestone plateau with its surrounding small fossilised open field; similar examples exist to the north-western fringe of the Peak at Chunal and Padfield.

A number of planned villages have more complex layouts than just the single street. The large village of Taddington has two back lanes flanking the main street, with a series of narrow ginnels running between 'tofts' and linking all three; the village water supply was at a spring line partway up the steep slope to Taddington Moor from where paths lead down to the village nestled below. The smaller village of Elton is similar in that part has a single back lane, whilst Well Street leads off the main street at right angles, going a short distance to the water supply. The small village of Calton also has one back lane.

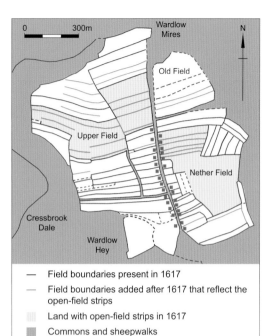

— Field boundaries present in 1617
— Field boundaries added after 1617 that reflect the open-field strips
Land with open-field strips in 1617
Commons and sheepwalks
Planned streets ▪ Buildings in 1617

Fig 3.6
Wardlow in 1617, based on a map by William Senior for the Cavendish family. Field boundaries shown in 1617 and still present today are shown as solid lines, while those no longer extant are dashed.

Fig 3.7
Chelmorton, high on the limestone plateau, is a classic medieval linear village with fossilised medieval field strips running away from the long-established house plots. The contrasting landscape beyond to the south was once part of the commons. [John Barnatt]

Fig 3.8
Wormhill village as it was in 1897, as depicted on Ordnance Survey mapping revised in that year. Buildings include church, vicarage, hall with outbuildings, school and other dwellings. The layout of some medieval crofts and open-field strips are easily identified. Most buildings are set back from the street, suggesting a former green; to the north those at Wormhill Hill appear to be planned separately.

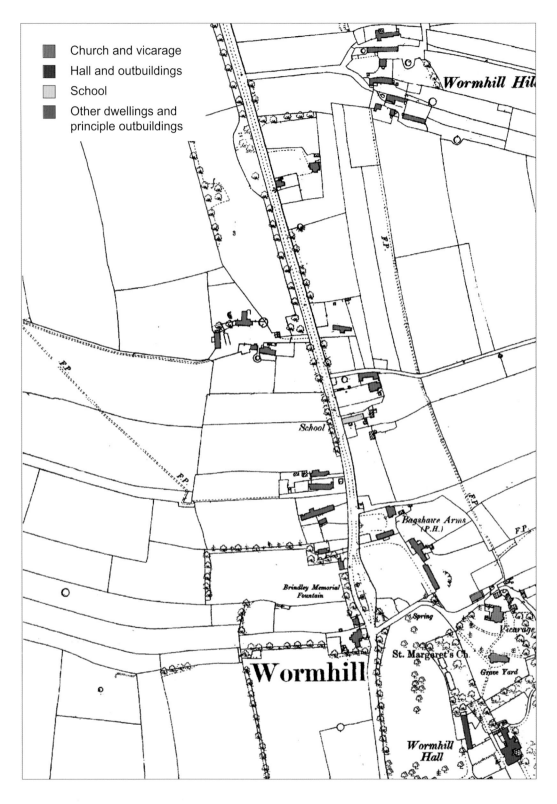

Church and vicarage
Hall and outbuildings
School
Other dwellings and principle outbuildings

Wormhill Hill

School

Bagshawe Arms (P.H.)

F.P.

Brindley Memorial Fountain

Spring

Vicarage

Wormhill

St. Margaret's Ch.

Grave Yard

Wormhill Hall

Wetton is atypical in that it has a grid-like arrangement of streets that is probably imposed on an older through route and settlement core (the case study below). Thorpe appears to be similar in that the plan is also grid-like.

There is a series of other villages similar to all those described above, but which are less obviously carefully planned, as the main streets are sinuous rather than straight. However, in most cases planning is likely, but with topography influencing the layout. A classic case is the large market village of Tideswell, which winds with the valley it follows. Along the valley bottom there is a long but narrow market place, with a second smaller example further up the village. There are also back lanes on the valley sides with linking ginnels running through the toft rows. Hope, which was a royal manorial centre before being superseded by Castleton, has a long street with its church and nearby motte at one end. In its northern part the street curves to follow the River Noe, with a toft row on the opposite side of the street to the river; this may have been added to a non-planned core at the south end. The important village of Eyam has the most sinuous main street of all, but even here it appears the curves are designed primarily to follow the topography, weaving between the heads of dry valleys and intervening ridges to follow a relatively level course; whether this constitutes purposeful planning of the village as an entity is unclear. Flagg is somewhat different from the other villages in the group in that the village street follows the curved edge of the large open field, with crofts on the field side but not that of the common.[16] The overall open-field plan here is still visible in the landscape, fossilised by field walls, and comprises a large 'potato-shaped' area, just under 2km across, occupying gently sloping ground and totally surrounded by common. The field and village at the bottom end were undoubtedly planned together as an ambitious venture to exploit relatively high limestone plateau land at an altitude that even

then was probably only just viable for arable farming.

The village of Castleton is exceptional in that it is a small planned town, which replaced a less grand settlement, presumably close to the entrance to Peak Cavern. The planned town, with a grid of streets around a church at the centre, lies within defensive earthworks at the base of the slope up to Peveril Castle, the only stone-built castle in the Peak.[17]

Even some of the large focal villages with more irregular and part-agglomerated plans have elements that were planned. Monyash, in the heart of the limestone plateau but with a small area of impermeable ground with ponds, was an obvious place to become a market place for livestock. The focal point was the central space, with dwellings at the sides of four roads leading to it (see Fig 3.14). However, one part of the village, on the north side of the road entering from the east, has a planned row of 'crofts and tofts' with a back lane behind. At Hartington the market place is again at a focal point of roads, whilst many of the main farmsteads were built to one side, alongside a road running northwards at the base of the plateau slope, and again this is perhaps a planned element. Chapel en le Frith is similar in that its market place and church were at the top end of a linear street. Ashbourne is also comparable but appears more planned, with a large triangular market place with 'crofts and tofts' on all three sides, which is perhaps an early irregular focus, but with the settlement dominated by a long linear street and back lane leading to the church at the other end.

Wetton

This village, 2km west of Alstonefield, is a medieval planned settlement.[18] Wetton was first recorded in the late 12th century and was one of the townships of Alstonefield.[19] The Cavendish family, later Dukes of Devonshire, became lords of the manor in the late 16th century and today they still own properties in the village.

The street pattern comprises a rectangular grid with parallel streets, seemingly an ambitious scheme by a medieval lord of the manor which never reached its full potential as some streets remained largely undeveloped (Figs 3.9 and 3.10). This grid overlies an older routeway running diagonal to the planned village, with the church aligned on this. This

long-distance route probably came from Cheshire to the north-west, going to Ashbourne and beyond to the south-east. Surviving estate maps of 1587 and 1617 show that the size and layout of the village has changed little since then. However, in 1587 the village was largely surrounded by open fields except to the north where Wetton Hill was a high windswept common, and at crofts around the houses and a few enclosures nearby.[20] By 1617 the process of enclosure had progressed, with more former open strips being taken into permanently bounded fields. Wetton Hill is still largely unenclosed today, but its relatively flat top has walled fields that were built by 1809, the date of the next available map after that of 1617.

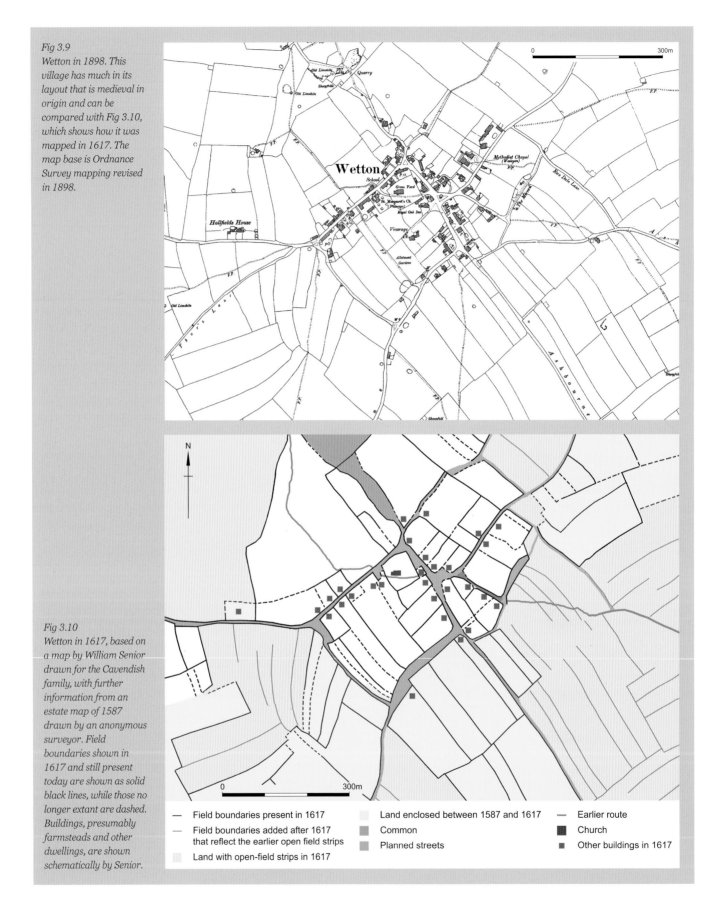

Fig 3.9
Wetton in 1898. This village has much in its layout that is medieval in origin and can be compared with Fig 3.10, which shows how it was mapped in 1617. The map base is Ordnance Survey mapping revised in 1898.

Fig 3.10
Wetton in 1617, based on a map by William Senior drawn for the Cavendish family, with further information from an estate map of 1587 drawn by an anonymous surveyor. Field boundaries shown in 1617 and still present today are shown as solid black lines, while those no longer extant are dashed. Buildings, presumably farmsteads and other dwellings, are shown schematically by Senior.

— Field boundaries present in 1617

— Field boundaries added after 1617 that reflect the earlier open field strips

Land with open-field strips in 1617

Land enclosed between 1587 and 1617

Common

Planned streets

— Earlier route

Church

Other buildings in 1617

Living differently

Other important medieval places have irregular plans, as at Alstonefield, which has a complex criss-crossing of streets with several small triangular greens at intersections. This village has long been at the centre of a huge parish, with a 'minster' church founded in 892 where fragments of several Anglo-Saxon crosses have been found in its post-Norman fabric. The important market centre of Bakewell also has a 'minster' church, with many surviving Anglo-Saxon cross fragments; a 'burh' was built in 920 somewhere in the vicinity but perhaps on the other side of the river. The street layout has hints of a grid layout, perhaps similar in character to that at Castleton, but alternatively much can be seen as less regular and organically formed through time; post-medieval prosperity has led to the masking of any immediately clear medieval plan. At Wirksworth (Fig 3.11), the market place is at a focal point with roads approaching it from all directions, whilst what was probably an early 'minster' is off to one side. Other places with irregular, sinuous but grid-like street layouts are Ashford and Parwich. Both were important royal manors that, as nucleated settlements, also probably pre-date the Norman Conquest. Hathersage was another large manor and on a high point there is a ringwork and church, whilst in the valley below there is a second settlement focus comprising a long but somewhat sinuous single main street.

Smaller agglomerated layouts include Foolow that focuses on an irregularly shaped small green, Beeley that has intersecting streets and Curbar that has a complex plan of mostly sinuous intersecting lanes, with dwellings in and around the small islands of land thus created. Warslow was once similar, as shown by surviving earthworks, but was radically altered when turnpikes were built through the village (Fig 3.12). Grindon nearby appears to have a similar layout. At Nether Haddon the village is abandoned but a winding street flanked by 'crofts and tofts' can still be seen in earthwork form.[21] Whether or not these smaller places have long histories that pre-date the planned villages nearby is currently not known.

Fig 3.11
Part of an Anglo-Saxon grave slab in Wirksworth Church that may well have been in the early minster here. [John Barnatt]

Fig 3.12
Turnpike roads were imposed in Warslow in 1770 and 1833 on a less regular pattern of lanes and paths. Associated with the traditional islands of ground between the old routes were houses, yards and gardens. Beyond the village there are field boundaries reflecting former open-field strips, while to the north was an open common with a major braided hollow-way passing the edge of the village. After the turnpikes were created, settlement nucleated against these two roads in the eastern half of the village.

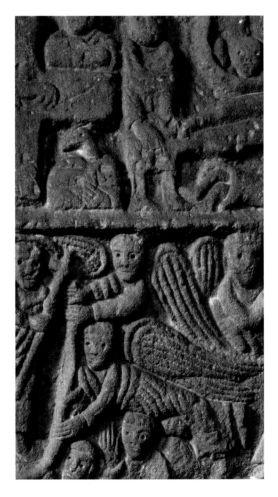

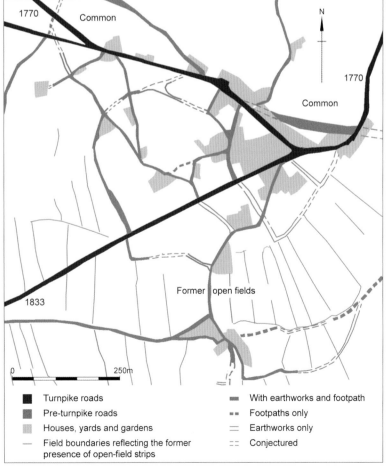

Turnpike roads
Pre-turnpike roads
Houses, yards and gardens
Field boundaries reflecting the former presence of open-field strips

With earthworks and footpath
Footpaths only
Earthworks only
Conjectured

Peak Forest

This village is an exceptional place, in the heart of the medieval Royal Forest of the Peak where the main foresters' chamber stood, located on a low knoll at a site that commands wide views (*see* Chapter 12). There is a degree of nucleation along the 18th-century turnpike road, which probably follows an earlier route, but elsewhere there is a loose agglomeration of farmsteads across the broad valley bottom running from north-west to south, often with wide spaces from one to the next (Fig 3.13). At the centre of the basin, at Old Dam, there is a pond suitable for watering stock. There is also a small unusual block of narrow but straight-edged enclosures of presumed later 17th-century or 18th-century date, created after the forest had fallen out of use. Similarly, there are irregular co-axial fields with aligned farmsteads scattered amongst them, which appear to be of similar date.

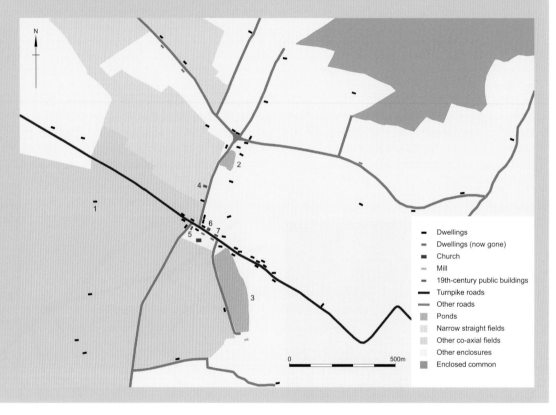

Fig 3.13
Peak Forest in 1807, including the site of the foresters' chamber (1), the Old Dam (2) and a mill pond (3). Later buildings comprise the Methodist chapel of 1851 (4), the reading room of 1880 (5), the school of 1868 (6) and the Devonshire Arms (7).

Legend:
- Dwellings
- Dwellings (now gone)
- Church
- Mill
- 19th-century public buildings
- Turnpike roads
- Other roads
- Ponds
- Narrow straight fields
- Other co-axial fields
- Other enclosures
- Enclosed common

0   500m

Village greens

These communal open spaces at settlements are not common at Peak villages but a few still exist (Fig 3.14). The best known is at Monyash, with its medieval cross and public house that was used for lead miners' Barmote courts. This green started life as a market place and was once larger, with associated ponds for watering livestock.

Very few of the single-street villages had linear greens but instead seem to have always had narrow main streets, but one small example does survive at Little Hucklow. At Wormhill there is a much larger but now partially infilled green.[22] Litton is in one sense also a single-street village, of a type again normally categorised as a double row village where the 'crofts and tofts' flank a long linear green. But, in this case, the green is somewhat triangular, with a medieval cross at the widest end and a short third row of 'tofts' at the end. A possible infilled green has been illustrated above (*see* Fig 3.8).

At Biggin, a village that was within one of the Quarters of the massive manor of Hartington, there are earthworks defining what was named a 'green' in 1614. This former large open space lay to one side of, and at right angles to, the single main street with a narrow linear green, with the larger green paralleled by one at Pilsley in the sense that the green is not the main settlement focal point. King Sterndale, although a very small settlement, has farmsteads that flank a fine surviving green (Fig 3.15).

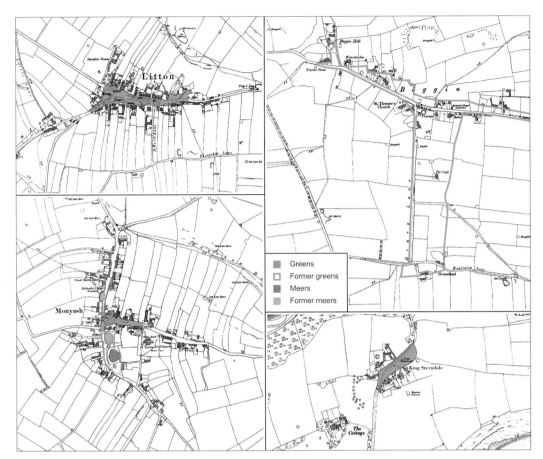

Fig 3.14
Examples of village greens
and former greens at Litton,
Biggin, Monyash and
King Sterndale, all with
Ordnance Survey backdrops
dating from revisions made
in 1897–8. Watering ponds
at Monyash, often referred
to as 'meres', include one
still extant today and four
former examples.

Greens
Former greens
Meers
Former meers

Fig 3.15
The green at the small
village of King Sterndale,
with its medieval cross shaft
and base restored in 1937.
[John Barnatt]

At the majority of villages it seems people were content to do without a green, perhaps because of the extensive wastes and commons within easy reach.

Deserted villages and farms

There are settlements that have long lain within their own townships but that are now only small hamlets or single farmsteads; a few have been abandoned altogether. Where there is an absence of medieval settlement earthworks their original plans and size are unknown. Some, as at Shatton and Offerton, have evidence for relatively large open fields and thus may well have once been villages. Others, as at Hazlebadge, have no such evidence and have perhaps always been non-nucleated hamlets or isolated farmsteads.

On the opposite side of the road to the drive to Haddon Hall, there is the site of Nether Haddon village, with only one house at the southern end still inhabited. There are extensive earthworks defining the sites of at least ten houses with associated yards and garden plots.[23] Later, these earthworks were overlain by artificial mounds known as pillow mounds where rabbits were reared and trapped for the table at the hall. By the 18th century this area was surrounded by a large open sheepwalk (see Chapter 4).

Darley Churchtown has what may have started as a minster-type church and was a royal manorial centre in the Norman period, but by the 19th century was reduced to a very small linear settlement with less than a handful of traditional properties still occupied; platforms at the sites of further houses have not been identified.

Unlike Darley Churchtown, the village of Smerrill was always small and unimportant. It has long been deserted but survives in earthwork form, with only nine 'tofts' in two rows flanking a single street (Fig 3.16).[24] Earthworks of other small places are found at Burton just south of Bakewell and at Ballidon,

whilst at Conksbury, located on a shelf above the River Lathkill, earthworks are thought to be extensive but no published plan exists.[25]

Some settlements declined at an early date and were superseded in the medieval period, as at the monastic granges of One Ash, Newton, Hanson and Musden. At One Ash, there are the footings of what seems to be a stone-built hall and fragments of Anglo-Saxon cross have been found nearby (Fig 3.17).[26] Whether the grange was on the same site is unknown, but by the early 17th century the One Ash Grange farmstead was on more sheltered ground just over 0.5km away to the north-east.

Like Nether Haddon, other villages declined until all that remained was a hall, as at Offerton, Holme, Throwley and Castern, whilst at Chatsworth, Harthill and Blore these were also associated with deer parks (see Chapter 12). Several other places contracted markedly but still have farmsteads, as at Brushfield, and there is a variety of others where earthwork evidence or documentation suggests contraction or abandonment has taken place.[27]

Fig 3.16
At Smerrill near Middleton by Youlgreave, low earthworks at crofts and tofts with medieval origins are clearly visible on this aerial photograph along one side of the village street. [© Crown copyright. Historic England Archive. 17036_67]

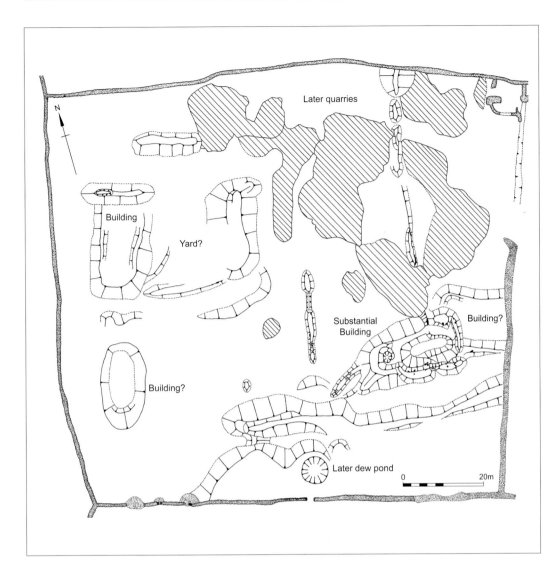

Later quarries

Building

Yard?

Building?

Substantial
Building

Building?

Later dew pond

0   20m

Fig 3.17
Earthworks at One Ash,
surveyed shortly after
discovery in 1984. These
include footings of a
substantial building that
was probably a stone-built
hall, perhaps for the
grange, while other
platforms on a different
orientation may have had
earlier timber buildings.
Surrounding fields have
been improved and it is
unclear how large the
original settlement was.

Medieval granges

One of the characteristics of the Peak settlement
landscape is the number of farms that in the
medieval period belonged to monasteries and
were normally known as 'granges'.[28] These were
outlying properties granted to abbeys and
priories by landowners to help provide income
for the monks, often in return for intercessions
for the donors' souls. When these granges were
first founded, often in the 12th and 13th
centuries, they were farmed directly by the
monasteries, sometimes with lay-brethren doing
the work. However, after the Black Death in the
mid-14th century, usually the farms were let to
lay-tenants.

A variety of monastic orders held granges in
the Peak, but all mother houses were in more
favourable lowland areas rather than in the Peak
(Fig 3.18).[29] The nearest were the small but
wealthy Beauchief Abbey for Premonstratensian
monks in the foothills to the east, south-west of
Sheffield, and the Cistercian Dieulacres Abbey
just outside Leek.[30] The conventional wisdom is
that the upland granges concentrated on sheep
farming, an idea based on known practices of
Cistercian Monks in the Yorkshire Dales and
elsewhere; this was the case at Dieulacres, which
grew wealthy through engaging in the wool
trade, but taking the Peak granges as a whole,
whilst in part true, this interpretation is over-
simplistic (*see* Chapter 4).

Sometimes what were probably always small
and sometimes perhaps failing settlements were
granted to abbeys and priories, as at Musden,
Newton, Hanson and Ivonbrook on the
limestone plateau, and at Harewood on the
eastern moors. At some places it appears that a
village and nearby grange happily coexisted and
both are still occupied today, as at Abney in an

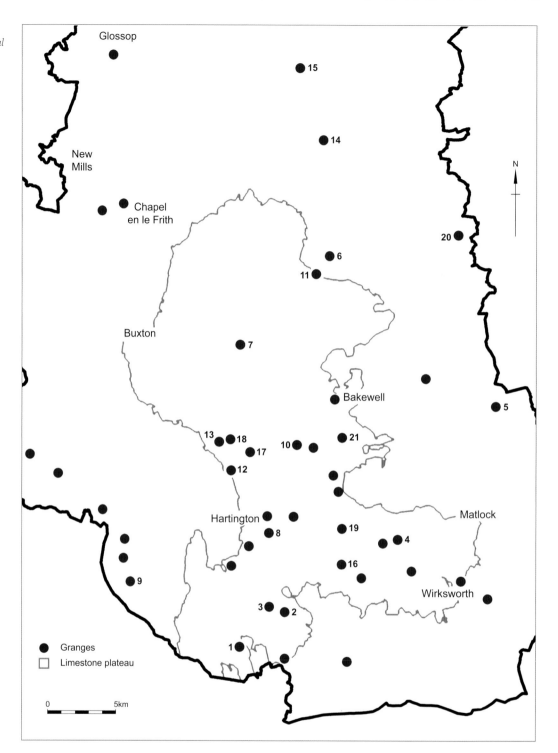

Fig 3.18
The distribution of medieval
monastic granges in the
Peak, with the highest
density on the limestone
plateau. Those mentioned
in the text are:
1: Musden
2: Newton
3: Hanson
4: Ivonbrook
5: Harewood
6: Abney
7: Blackwell
8: Biggin
9: Onecote
10: One Ash
11: Grindlow
12: Pilsbury
13: Needham
14: Crookhill
15: Abbey
16: Roystone
17: Cotesfield
18: Cronkston
19: Mouldridge
20: Strawberry Lee
21: Meadow Place

isolated gritstone valley, Blackwell and Biggin on the limestone, and at Onecote high on the Staffordshire gritstone uplands. At One Ash near Monyash there are earthworks at a different site to what became called One Ash Grange by early post-medieval times (*see* Fig 3.17). Either the grange farmstead itself moved or the documented pre-existing village was at a

different site and may have continued in existence for some time alongside the grange. A small village exists today at Grindlow near Great Hucklow whilst there is now no trace of the grange; similarly at Pilsbury it is not known whether the grange was alongside the hamlet in the Dove Valley or on the high limestone land above. In contrast, at Needham Grange nearby

on the high western part of the limestone plateau, a farmstead of this name survives and an adjacent medieval hamlet may also have existed, for there are arable strips in a small open field that were retained in multiple ownership for long enough to eventually be fossilised into walled parcels (*see* Fig 2.6). In the Upper Derwent Valley a large area with scattered medieval farmsteads included two granges belonging to Welbeck Abbey, at Crookhill and Abbey (*see* Fig 2.15).

Other granges may well have been founded at 'new' sites upon the grant of land to a monastery, as at Roystone Grange in a remote limestone dry valley, where there do not appear to have been houses since this small valley was occupied in Roman times.[31] Other 'new' monastic farmsteads

may include those at relatively inhospitable limestone sites at Cotesfield, Cronkston and Mouldridge granges (*see* Fig 2.6).[32]

High on the eastern gritstone moors there was a series of medieval crosses, some of which survive, as near Shilito Wood, which are thought to mark monastic property boundaries associated with the Strawberry Lee Grange and Harewood Grange, both of which belonged to Beauchief Abbey (Fig 3.19).[33]

Today the surviving grange farmsteads are indistinguishable from others around them, for they were rebuilt in stone in the 17th to 19th centuries, long after they were first in secular hands. Some were well-to-do properties, as at Cronkston and Meadow Place held by the Chatsworth Estate.

Fig 3.19
The medieval cross on Hewitt Bank near Shilito Wood at the eastern edge of Ramsley Moor was erected on land farmed by Beauchief Abbey.
[John Barnatt]

Fig 3.20
A small but carefully considered and architect-designed 19th-century farmstead at Cronkston Lodge high on the limestone plateau in Hartington Middle Quarter, with trees planted for shelter. [John Barnatt]

New farmsteads on old commons

When the extensive wastes and commons of the limestone plateau were enclosed in the later 18th and earlier 19th centuries, a significant number of new farmsteads were built; this is particularly noticeable in the nucleated settlement zone where farmsteads away from the villages were a rarity before this date (*see* Fig 3.2). The new buildings were placed within blocks of land allocated to specific farmers at the time of allotment. Whilst some people chose to continue to farm from their village farmstead, others must have thought it more convenient to live amongst their new fields. Much research is needed on underlying factors here: was the choice to move made by those who had inadequate facilities on restricted sites within villages; or those who were given a single coherent block of land; and/or those who created one 'ring-fenced' holding by exchanging parcels of land with other farmers in the community? Similarly, the role of larger estates and the desire to rationalise needs to be studied.

New farmsteads were built all across the newly enclosed higher parts of the limestone plateau. A smaller number of such farms is also found in parts of the gritstone uplands.

Occasionally the enclosure-period farms have distinctive non-medieval names, as at Organ Ground and South Carolina Farm. For the most part these workaday places are architecturally indistinguishable from other farmsteads across the region, primarily because the latter were also being rebuilt in stone in the same period. However, there are exceptions, such as Cronkston Lodge a short distance south of the medieval monastic grange farmsteads at Needham and Cronkston; here a small farmstead is laid out as a miniature version of a planned courtyard farmstead as found in fashionable contemporary manuals on how to farm (Fig 3.20). Another oddity is Fivewells Farms, high on Taddington Moor, built from the outset as a pair of small semi-detached farmsteads under one roof.

Towards urbanisation

There are a number of market towns in the Peak with medieval origins, notably Bakewell, Hartington, Wirksworth, Ashbourne and Chapel en le Frith. Other towns grew as a response to their popularity as spas at Buxton, Matlock Bank and Matlock Bath, whilst industry elsewhere provided the impetus for growth, particularly on the north-western fringe of the region.

The long-used market centres are often located at interfaces between different topographic zones where contrasting products could be exchanged and goods brought from outside the region could be acquired. They tend to be widely spaced apart, each with its own catchment from which people in the surrounding countryside came; market days were something exciting that people looked forward to.

Buxton and Matlock Bath grew into small towns when it became fashionable for the well-to-do to take the waters at the thermal springs here, with visitor numbers growing exponentially from the 18th century onwards. They have magnificent and distinctive buildings such as the Crescent at Buxton and its plethora of grand hotels. Matlock Bank grew when a hydro was built in the 19th century high in the valley side, now used as the County Council offices.

Bakewell: Anatomy of a market town

Historic maps provide snapshots of the development of Bakewell from the late 18th century onwards (Fig 3.21).[34] Maps of this date show the town had developed from medieval origins, with a somewhat irregular grid of streets at its core and housing also following roads radiating outwards, particularly to the north-east to where a medieval bridge crosses the Wye and to the north-west to the corn mill on the road to Buxton. The western half of the town, including the minster church with pre-conquest

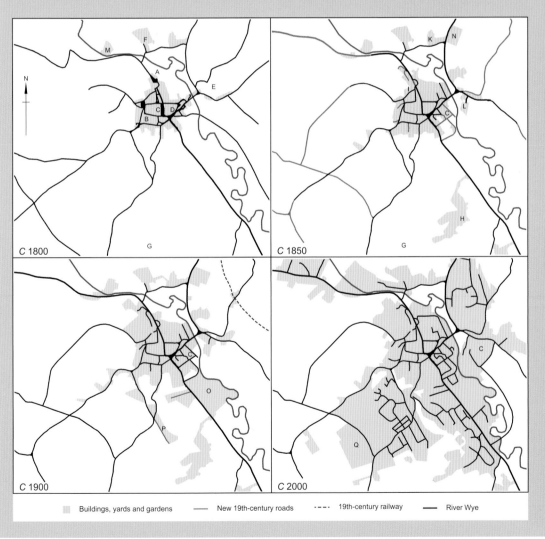

C 1800

C 1850

C 1900

C 2000

▨ Buildings, yards and gardens ⎯ New 19th-century roads ╌╌ 19th-century railway ⎯ River Wye

Fig 3.21
The development of Bakewell through time at 50-year intervals, with the historic mapping based on maps of 1796, 1799, 1852 and 1898. Places include the corn mill (A), the church (B), the cattle market (C), the main market (D), the motte-and-bailey castle (E), Holme Hall (F), the site of Burton village (G), Burton Closes (H), Endcliffe House (I), Castle Hill (J), Burre House (K), the marble mill (L), Lumford textile mill (M), the workhouse (N), the recreation ground and adjacent allotments (O), the cemetery (P) and Lady Manners School (Q).

origins, which still has a fine Norman west end, occupies a relatively steep slope rising towards the best agricultural land on the limestone shelf above. There were two market places; the cattle market ran along the base of the slope, whilst the general market, with market hall, was on the road crossing the floodplain to the bridge; by

Fig 3.22
Burton Closes on the outskirts of Bakewell, built in the mid-19th century in Tudor Gothic style for John Allcard, a Quaker stockbroker, designed by Joseph Paxton and his assistant John Robertson, both of whom were based at Chatsworth, with interiors by the well-known architect and designer Augustus Pugin; it is now an old people's home.
[John Barnatt]

1796, the date of the earliest detailed map, this market place had probably been partially infilled. The presence of housing here suggests the river was not prone to regular flooding. Across the river was the site of a hilltop medieval motte-and-bailey castle. Further upriver was the deserted medieval settlement of Holme, now occupied by a fine 1626 hall and its gardens.

The Parliamentary Enclosure Award of 1810 led to the rearrangement of roads in the old open fields and commons. In about 1845 the grand house at Burton Closes was built close to the deserted medieval settlement of Burton, whilst other houses for the wealthy were built at Endcliffe House, Castle Hill and Burre House (Fig 3.22). The cattle market was moved to a site by the river. Industrial premises also lay out in the fields, including a 'marble' works and the large textile mill at Lumford, whilst the large purpose-built workhouse, later a hospital, was finished in 1841. In the later 19th century ribbon development gradually extended along the Monyash and Matlock roads, and a cemetery and recreational ground were added.

In the 20th century the town became much larger, with housing estates added on surrounding fields. Lady Manners School, the grammar school, was moved to new premises at the town outskirts in 1938.

Industrial sprawl

For the most part the Peak is unaffected by urban sprawl; the national park with its enhanced planning powers was created just in time to stop much development from surrounding cities; in places such as Grindleford and parts of the Hope Valley this was a close-run thing and desirable residences had been built for wealthy commuters before the park was created. We perhaps get a flavour of what would have happened if the national park had not been created if you follow the A6 from Northwood through Darley Dale to Matlock, with its almost continuous spread of houses of all types and sizes, where the character is suburban, with countryside for the most part only glimpsed as a backdrop.

Whilst towns such as Buxton, Matlock and Wirksworth have some modern housing development around their edges, the one significant area of the Peak where the traditional settlement pattern has changed beyond recognition is to the north-west around Glossop,

Marple, New Mills, Whaley Bridge and Chapel en le Frith. Here there have been radical industrial transformations over the last 200 years associated with the building of mills for cotton and silk production, and factories associated with allied trades such as bleaching and cloth printing. Nearby coal mines provided fuel for steam engines at mills and elsewhere. All these industrial developments went hand in hand with new housing to accommodate radical increases in population. The first large industrial-scale mills were created in the later 18th century in nearby Macclesfield and an exponential transformation of the Peak fringe area as a whole took place in the 19th century. The focal areas, along the river valleys between high hills or flanking their western edges, have an urban character typical of mill towns of the Southern Pennines. Although the mills have mostly closed and the iconic chimneys felled, some mills survive, either derelict or dilapidated, or converted to flats, whilst much of the terraced housing remains.

4

Land to farm

The Peak landscape we have inherited is one where past and present agricultural features often come together to make the dominant character of the land. It has a rich palimpsest of field boundaries and other features, mostly created and added to over the last 650 years.[1] Some parts, with small narrow fields, have origins in the medieval period, whilst others come with the frequent building of many rectangular fields with ruler-straight walls 250 to 150 years ago, dating to when many of the region's commons were enclosed (Fig 4.1). Elsewhere there are irregular fields around isolated medieval and later farmsteads, many with complex but little-understood developments and expansions that took place slowly over hundreds of years, whilst on the gritstone uplands there are still large areas of unenclosed grazing. Those places mentioned in Chapter 4 are shown on Figure A1.3 (*see* p 227)

The medieval villages of the Peak were once surrounded by large 'open fields', often two to four in number, but with hamlets with only one and the town of Bakewell having an exceptional six.[2] Each field was divided into a multitude of narrow strips, in blocks known as furlongs, with each strip redistributed annually so that everyone, in theory, got a fair share of good, middling and poor land. The lord of the manor also had blocks of open-field land known as the 'demesne', which were farmed for him by the village tenants. The ideal was that field use was rotated so that each field was used for cereal cultivation, growing root crops, and then left fallow with grazing and thus manuring. In practice, the situation was clearly more complex, with much variation in practice to suit local needs, with strips redesigned periodically as each generation adapted to new circumstances.

Fig 4.1
The land around the village of Litton has well-preserved fossilised open fields defined by drystone walls, as seen here from Litton Edge. In the middle distance is land that was once open common until enclosed in 1764.
[John Barnatt]

After the Black Death of 1348, with a significant loss of population, the feudal farming regime started to break down and the farming emphasis went from extensive arable towards pasture. Livestock needed fewer people to tend them and there was greater scope for cash profit rather than working in customary ways designed for feeding the local population and supporting the manorial lord. In many places cultivation strips stopped being redistributed annually and this allowed individual farmers to fence out small parcels of these into permanent fields. This was a slow process; in the late 16th and early 17th centuries, when the earliest surviving detailed maps were drawn, parts of open fields had often gone, whilst some extensive areas of strips, sometimes now as bounded parcels, were still used in traditional ways (Fig 4.2).[3] Sometimes the demesne was enclosed early because the lord had free rein here. The process of enclosure of former open fields accelerated through the 17th and 18th centuries. However, exceptionally, at Bakewell large parts of the open fields survived until 1810; a large number of people in the township had traditional rights here and it took a Parliamentary Enclosure Award to resolve permanent redistribution.[4]

Radical change to the landscape came with the enclosure of many of the traditional commons surrounding the old open fields and their villages, dividing these areas into a multitude of rectangular fields with ruler-straight boundaries (Fig 4.3). This allowed village farmers and manorial farms to have greater control over grazing and thus improve bloodstock, manure land in controlled ways, and have more choice over how specific fields were used from year to year. The limestone plateau's open grazing was virtually all lost, whilst significant contraction occurred on the gritstone uplands (see Fig 4.19). Here, much of the moorland was enclosed to the west, whereas less occurred to the east because some of the moors here were set aside for grouse shooting by ducal owners.

Where decisions to enclose were contentious, commonly when there were large numbers of people with traditional grazing rights, enclosure of open fields and commons was achieved through a Parliamentary Enclosure Award, following the passing of an Act of Parliament for each manor, where independent commissioners determined allotment. Acts were passed in the second half of the 18th century and the first half of the 19th century. Starting in the 17th century if not before, other enclosure was agreed privately, often where the lord of the manor had exclusive ownership or where amicable agreements between a few people could be reached.

One interesting aspect of Parliamentary Enclosure is the affect the process had on field size. Where there were several blocks of common within a township, each with the same number of people with grazing rights, small blocks had smaller fields and vice-versa. This is well illustrated by the fields around Tideswell and Wheston (Fig 4.4). Also, there was an underlying general trend for enclosures to be larger with increased altitude, as on the high western and northern limestone areas, where there were fewer people with common grazing rights.

Fig 4.2
Part of what was once a large oval open field surrounded by common at Flagg on the gentle slopes of the upper basin above Lathkill Dale in the heart of the limestone plateau. Long thin parcels of strips have been enclosed in post-medieval times by walls. The sinuous road bisects the field following the contour through the middle of the field, while the medieval village lies at the bottom of the slope out of sight to the left.
[John Barnatt]

Fig 4.3
Ruler-straight walls at rectangular post-medieval fields north of Wheston, laid out on the former common after the Tideswell Parliamentary Enclosure Award of 1821.
[John Barnatt]

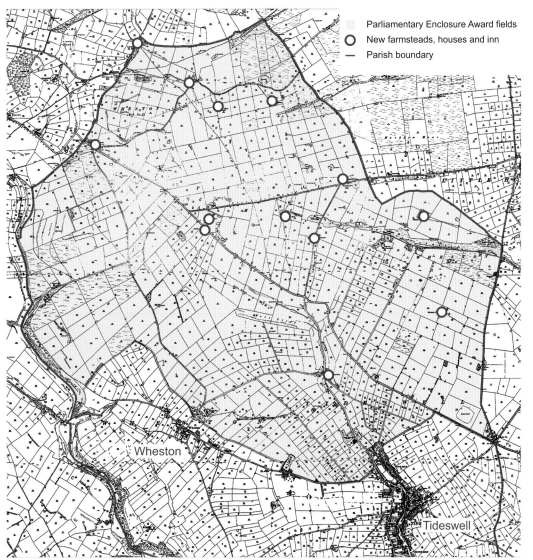

Parliamentary Enclosure Award fields
O New farmsteads, houses and inn
— Parish boundary

Fig 4.4
Parliamentary Enclosure Award fields in the northern part of the parishes of Tideswell and Wheston, created after an Award of 1821, with farmsteads, houses and an inn built amongst the fields. Blocks of fields of different sizes can be identified. The map base is Ordnance Survey mapping revised in 1897.

Fig 4.5
The limestone plateau between Foolow and Eyam, photographed from the gritstone scarp of Hucklow Edge. The fields include rectangular layouts on former commons and fossilised strips on lower ground to the right. The mounds are at the sites of air shafts on an 18th-century mine drainage level at Old Grove Mine.
[John Barnatt]

From a historic landscape perspective, these 18th- and 19th-century landscapes are just as important as the more ancient ones with their narrow fields. The rectangular fields on the old commons tell much of the rational reorganisation of the landscape and social change that went hand in hand with the age of enlightenment, the maximisation of profit, and the move to farming following the then latest ideas on good practice (Fig 4.5).

In the western parts of the Peak, and to the north flanking the high moorlands, the grain of the agricultural landscape is different. Here the non-nucleated farmsteads, some with medieval or earlier origins, are each surrounded by enclosed fields. At the oldest settlements the parcels are often small and irregular in shape, whilst moving upslope they shade into more typical post-medieval rectangular fields with straight boundaries (Fig 4.6). Normally the fields of individual farms are conjoined with those of their neighbours, whereas at the edge of the commons, the curved top edges of individual intakes that have encroached onto the open moorland can sometimes be seen (Fig 4.7).

Fig 4.6
*To the western parts of the
Peak, valleys often have
irregular ancient fields
around farmsteads, as
here around Haylee Farm
south-west of Combs.*
[John Barnatt]

Fig 4.7
Agricultural enclosure
on the uplands west of
Longnor and Warslow is
predominantly piecemeal
in character and of
uncertain date. There are
enclosed commons on
higher ground above, in
places 'chewed' into by
obvious intakes. Exceptions
include small areas at
Upper and Lower Elkstone
that can be seen from their
form to be ancient and
others that were enclosed
after a Parliamentary
Enclosure Award of 1839.
The map base is Ordnance
Survey mapping revised
in 1897.

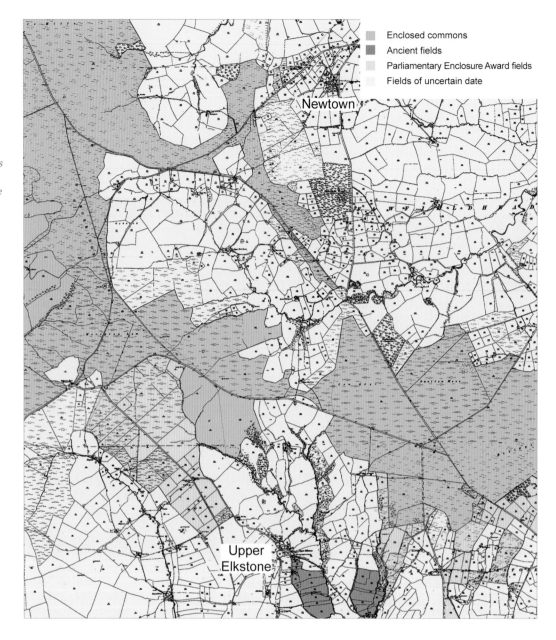

Enclosed commons
Ancient fields
Parliamentary Enclosure Award fields
Fields of uncertain date

Open moorlands are as much farmland as the enclosed landscapes; grazing is vital for the maintenance of the moors and without it all but the highest parts would revert to woodland. The biggest change here over recent centuries is the loss of common rights, often with privatisation coming in the later 18th and earlier 19th centuries.

A glance at White Peak and Dark Peak Ordnance Survey 1:25,000 maps reveals strongly distinctive field patterns. Where these are clear-cut, the field boundaries take on added value as exemplars of the landscape character types introduced above (*see also* Appendix 2). Many fine examples of fossilised open-field systems with Parliamentary Enclosure Award fields beyond are found around villages on the limestone plateau, as at Wheston, Tideswell and Litton north of the Wye, and south of the river at Chelmorton, Taddington, Flagg and Monyash. Other good Parliamentary Enclosure Award fields to the south-east lie above Elton, Winster and Bonsall, complemented by medieval 'fossilisation' at Bonsall and nearby Ible. To the northern end of the plateau another enclosed medieval field extends upslope from Bradwell and other more fragmented examples occupy the base of the Hope Valley around Castleton, Hope and Thornhill. Private enclosure award fields above Castleton are important because of their proven 1691 date, whilst at Peak Forest there is an unusual block of many small but ruler-straight walled fields which pre-date the 19th century and may be significantly earlier. A classic example of rigid grid-patterning, laid out by the Chatsworth Estate, can be seen high on the gritstone upland at Rodknoll near Wadshelf. In the non-nucleated zone, good examples of small ancient fields leading uphill to later straight-walled enclosures on former commons can be seen to the south-west around Fawfieldhead, Elkstone and Onecote, at Edale to the north and Bradfield to the north-east. Elsewhere, sometimes all the different pattern types have become blurred through time as change occurred, as for example where narrow strip fields have been combined by removal of walls and new straight-line walls added at right angles to divide the new parcel into sub-rectangular units, or where rectangular grids have been modified by modern boundary loss.

There are a number of rarer types of agricultural landscape across the Peak. A series of farms, often in relatively remote places, has origins as medieval monastic granges. High on the limestone plateau, by the early 17th century at the latest and with presumed medieval origins, these embanked or walled areas lie surrounded by extensive open commons, each divided into large rectangular fields. Some open grazing areas by the 17th century were not common land but managed as private 'sheepwalks', often referred to as 'joists', where farmers rented the right to graze sheep, cattle and horses, or where the manorial lords kept their own stock. Examples survive at Thorpe Pasture and Carsington Pasture, whilst well-documented examples formerly existed around Chatsworth.[5] Here the medieval deer park east of the house, Calton Pasture and the nearby warren,[6] and Cracknowl Pasture north of Bakewell, all feature in 18th-century estate accounts.

Not only deer but also rabbits were once regarded as high-status food. There were medieval deer parks at Haddon, Chatsworth, Harthill and Blore. Warrens also existed, where the rabbits were carefully bred in artificial mounds for the table and sale, with their fur also prized. A classic example was the massive open 'cunigre' at Edensor, with a warrener's lodge at the centre, shown on Senior's 1617 map,[7] whilst at Nether Haddon pillow mounds were placed on the site of the deserted medieval village.

Landscape parks were created as backdrops to stately homes in the 18th and 19th centuries; now open to the public are those at Chatsworth and Lyme, with smaller private examples at Hassop and Swythamley.

Historic landscapes through time

The Peak has contained radically different agricultural landscapes over the last few hundred years; there is no such thing as a timeless historic landscape. In the 11th to 14th centuries there was a largely unencumbered open landscape over much of the limestone plateau and parts of the Derwent Valley, with open fields divided into unfenced strips, sometimes separated from extensive commons by banks.

In contrast, from the later 14th to earlier 18th centuries there was an increased trend for enclosure around villages, where the open fields slowly became fragmented, with narrow fields created. However, walls may have been rare, even in the west and north where the norm was dispersed farmsteads with no local village, with each farmstead having enclosed fields below the upland commons; hedges or fences may have been the norm.

In some cases farmsteads in sheltered locales are surrounded by small irregular closes and it may be that these are medieval or earlier in date. However, as for example to the west around monastic granges, and to the east in places where villages have shrunk or been abandoned, large sub-rectangular fields were also common at an early date. These are clearly seen in the two early 17th-century books of surveys produced by William Senior that map the Cavendish family holdings scattered through the Peak and elsewhere.[8] The presence of these large fields is now masked by almost universal subdivision in the 17th and 18th centuries and thus they are not readily recognised as a distinctive element in today's landscape.

The most radical change, described above, was the landscape transformation with the enclosure of the limestone commons, and reductions in open land elsewhere, in the later 18th and earlier 19th centuries. This new landscape was one where stone dominated, in buildings in villages and countryside, and with the creation of a multitude of field walls. From the mid-19th century through to today, change to boundary patterns has been slow and relatively minor; despite boundary loss, the overall landscape character developed before 1850 has been retained.

Bakewell before and after enclosure

Fig 4.8
The parish of Bakewell was radically transformed in 1810 when surviving open fields and commons were enclosed. This map, which shows the situation from the 1790s to 1890s, is based on historic maps of 1796, 1810 and 1897. The six open fields of Bakewell are Far Field (A), Middle Field (B), Stonedge Field (C), Moor Hall Field (D), Nether Cowden Field (E) and Swindale Field (F). Other features noted in the text are the site of Moor Hall (G), Cowden sheepwalk (H), the site of Burton (I) and Holme Hall (J).

The farming landscape around the market town of Bakewell is unusual in that its extensive open fields survived exceptionally late, with large areas not swept away until after the Parliamentary Enclosure Award of 1810 (Fig 4.8).[9] In 1782 a German traveller, Carl Philipp Moritz, passed through Bakewell and noted its open fields: 'This field, as if it had been in Germany, was not enclosed with hedges but every spot in it was uninterruptedly diversified with all kinds of crops and growths of different greens and yellowish colours which gave a most pleasing effect.'[10]

The parts of the six medieval open fields of Bakewell that survived until 1810 were those that were traditionally used by the residents of Bakewell (Fig 4.9). Enclosure at an earlier date seems to have been impeded by there being an exceptional number of people, including inn keepers and tradesmen, with traditional rights to

use the land; the subdivided landscape in 1810 reflects this, particularly on the limestone shelf above the town where there are an exceptional number of smallholders' field barns. That part of the open field held for the lord of the manor, south-west of Moor Hall Field around the site of Moor Hall near where Lady Manners School now stands, had been enclosed into rectangular fields at an earlier date. Between the open fields and common to the west there was a sheepwalk that was originally taken in from the common for the use of the medieval Cowden Grange.

At the fringes of the parish, there are areas that once lay within different townships. To the west there is land that went with the now-deserted settlement of Burton, originally with two open fields and a moor but by the late 18th century having two large sheepwalks, an open riverside meadow, a small park and enclosures. At Holme Hall across the river, the fine early 17th-century hall lies at the site of another former medieval settlement. The surrounding land had been enclosed by the 1790s.

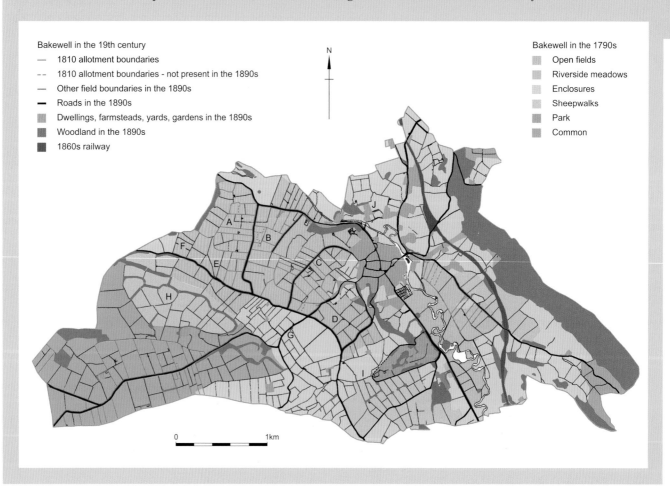

Bakewell in the 19th century
— 1810 allotment boundaries
-- 1810 allotment boundaries - not present in the 1890s
— Other field boundaries in the 1890s
— Roads in the 1890s
▨ Dwellings, farmsteads, yards, gardens in the 1890s
▨ Woodland in the 1890s
▨ 1860s railway

N

Bakewell in the 1790s
▨ Open fields
▨ Riverside meadows
▨ Enclosures
▨ Sheepwalks
▨ Park
▨ Common

0   1km

Fig 4.9
Broad but low ridge and furrow in Middle Field at Bakewell, running down a slope near Crowhill Lane on the main limestone shelf above the town, in a fertile landscape that remained largely unenclosed and still farmed in traditional ways until the early 19th century.
[John Barnatt]

Walls and hedges

The Peak is well known for its many drystone walls defining large swaths of agricultural landscape, particularly on the limestone plateau and the areas that fringe the gritstone moorlands; the patterning has just been discussed and boundaries are described in more detail below and in Chapter 5.

Field walls are not found everywhere. For instance, hedges are the norm in the bottom of Edale, the Hope Valley and parts of the Derwent Valley further south. A mixture of hedges and walls are commonly found in the valleys that fringe the southern edge of the limestone plateau. In the South-West Peak, a wall/hedge mixture is again intermittently common, especially in the valleys of the Dove, Manifold and Hamps, with hedges dominating in parts, but with the mixed-boundary regime extending onto higher ground. Here mixing of boundary types is even true within single boundaries, where sometimes there are short stretches of wall, hedge, and ditch with adjacent bank. The variation appears to relate directly to topography, with walls found where the ground is dry with good building stone beneath, whereas hedges occur where

there is shale beneath, whilst at boggy ground only banks and ditches are found.

A classic example that illustrates a former hedged landscape is provided by Chatsworth Park; here there are a multitude of low hedge banks that defined a series of former small fields that were swept away when 'Capability' Brown's landscape park was created from 1759 into the 1760s (Fig 4.10).[11]

A different situation is illustrated by a detailed archaeological assessment of much of the Edale Valley (Fig 4.11).[12] The valley bottom is dominated by hedges, many now in poor condition, but with walls common on the higher slopes. There is an interface zone where hedge banks tended to be abandoned as boundary layout was modified, with these replaced by walls on new alignments. Much of the present field layout was already established by 1839, the date of the first detailed maps of Edale township, but it is suspected that these hedges were probably replaced in the hundred years or so before this map was drawn.

Several decades ago it was suggested that hedges across England could be dated relatively precisely from the number of shrub species they contained, with diversity increasing with time.[13]

It is now known that applying this counting method can be fraught with problems and in the Peak for instance it cannot be used; any patterns are subsumed by changes in altitude as valley sides are ascended that adversely affects species-richness. Similarly, changes in how well hedges have been maintained have had an effect; today often hedges are no longer stock-proof, with barbed wire now fulfilling this function; sometimes only the occasional shrub remains. This said, where hedges are dominated by hawthorn they are likely to be relatively recent

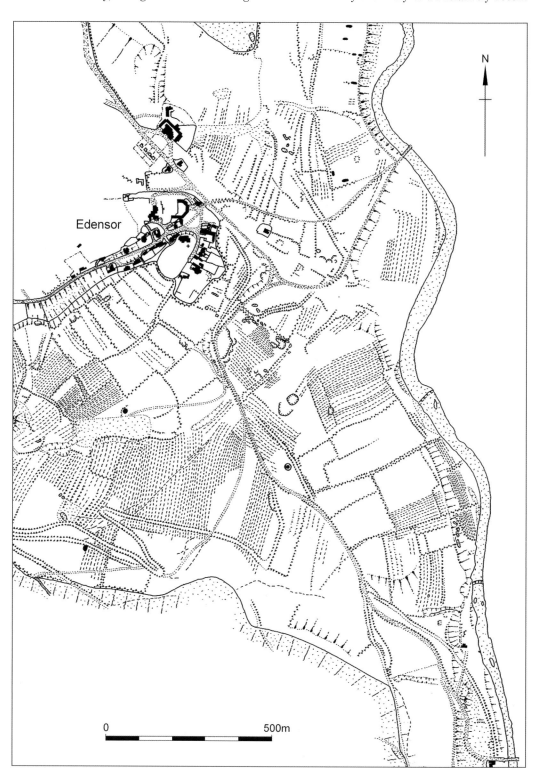

Fig 4.10
Parts of Chatsworth Park, west of the River Derwent, provide a classic example where low banks show that the landscape was covered in hedged fields, some containing ridge and furrow, in a fossilised landscape mostly dating to immediately before 'Capability' Brown had them swept away. Some of the unbounded ridge and furrow on higher land to the south-west is earlier. Other field boundaries immediately south of Edensor were removed in the 1820s when the park was enlarged.

Walls
Hedges
Extant boundaries 1993
Relict boundaries 1993
Moorland and semi-improved enclosure
Settlement
River Noe and streams
Assessment boundary
Parish boundary

Not assessed

0   1km

in date, most probably planted from the later 18th century onwards. In contrast, some hedges in the gritstone fringes contain significant amounts of holly and these may be earlier; traditionally this species has been used as winter fodder for cattle.

It is suspected that hedges were once more common than now in many areas of the Peak with fields that pre-date the later 18th century, even on the limestone plateau where only walls are found today. Comparison between what exists today and boundaries shown on detailed estate maps produced for the Cavendish Family in the 1610s to 1630s covering extensive estates

across the Peak, may be telling. In those few instances where boundaries have been moved, in places such as the limestone plateau, the 17th-century features are consistently relict hedge banks rather than ruined walls, whilst nearby boundaries still in use have been rebuilt in stone. This raises the possibility that replacement of hedges with walls was a common phenomenon in the 17th and 18th centuries, although there is need for systematic study to confirm this hypothesis, particularly as it suggests a radical change to our understanding. How many Peak drystone walls pre-date the 18th century is far from clear, but it is suspected

Fig 4.11
Edale in the late 19th century, showing walls and hedges. Boundary data is derived from an Environmentally Sensitive Area archaeological assessment undertaken by the author in 1993. Some boundaries shown on 19th-century mapping had been removed by 1993 and these are omitted when their construction type is unknown.

67

this is significantly fewer than has been previously assumed. Even in areas where walls are the norm, as on land that was being enclosed from wastes and commons, in some instances the making of banks or planting of hedges may have been done as a temporary measure to comply with the rules imposed by Parliamentary Enclosure Awards that insisted the boundaries of allocated land parcels were physically defined within a set period.

Whatever the scale of replacement of hedges with walls, in the 18th and 19th centuries there was a veritable mania for building in stone, creating new farmhouses, outbuildings and many thousands of miles of drystone field walls. This transformed huge swaths of land that had been wastes and commons and, similarly, there was radical impact on the areas that had once been open fields around villages, with many walls suspected to largely date to the 17th and 18th centuries, with only a minority of earlier date.

There are pros and cons with building hedges or walls. Hedges had the advantage of being relatively quick to plant, especially after hawthorn saplings became available in large numbers from commercial or estate nurseries during the Enclosure Award period. Against them is the need for ongoing maintenance to keep them stock-proof, with periodic 'laying' required to keep the growth close to the ground. In the Peak an added problem was that often hedges were close to the altitude limit for growth to thrive and with climatic fluctuations they sometimes struggled. Walls were more time-consuming to build but once erected were relatively maintenance-free, although over decades parts collapse and gaps need rebuilding, whilst every generation or

so more continuous rebuilding is desirable. Typically, what stands today is no more than about 50 years old, although specific features such as the footings or placed uprights can be significantly older.

Today, both field walls and hedges are expensive and time-consuming to maintain. Whilst there has not been the wholesale removal of boundaries in recent decades that has been seen in many lowland parts of England, there have been subtler losses in the Peak.

Walls have traditionally been repaired on an ad-hoc basis, with gaps rebuilt, but when this is no longer enough, then sometimes they are rebuilt. Some farmers have made sterling efforts to maintain all their walls. However, often only particular walls are kept in good repair, especially those at property boundaries, against roads and at internal divisions of the farm creating large grazing units; these walls are often top-wired, with barbed wire strands making doubly sure the boundary is stock-proof. Elsewhere, walls often remain dilapidated or ruined, with barbed wire and sheep netting used where a stock barrier is needed, or they are swept away with the stone sometimes robbed to maintain or rebuild other walls on the farm. Over several decades grants have been given by Government agencies and the National Park Authority to part-fund wall rebuilding in an attempt to maintain landscape character and aid upland farmers.

Maintenance issues also exist with hedges, which can naturally grow out if not carefully managed and replenished; the trend has been to keep them stock-proof with the aid of barbed wire. In some instances little remains except the wire, whilst elsewhere new boundaries have been made with post and wire only.

Chatsworth and Edensor before the landscape park

Chatsworth Park is an exceptional landscape, comprising extensive parkland of great if artificial beauty to either side of the River Derwent, with the mansion and gardens to the eastern side (Fig 4.12). This park was designed by 'Capability' Brown, with work starting in 1759. Later, in the 1820s, it was significantly enlarged around Edensor and to the north-east on the other side of the river.[14]

Looking closely at the swaths of grass, especially when close-cropped in winter, large numbers of low earthworks can be seen. Plotting these shows that the majority related to an agricultural landscape of medieval and post-medieval date, which was fossilised when the parkland was created. There is extensive ridge and furrow of a variety of dates, together with hedge banks defining the sites of field boundaries.

To the east of the river, much of the land belonged to the now-deserted and lost small medieval settlements of Chatsworth, Langley and Besley, all within the township of Chatsworth. Whilst there are medieval cultivation strip earthworks today, by 1617 when first mapped, the valley land was divided into a few large irregularly shaped fields, which had been farmed from Chatsworth Hall from the late medieval period.[15] Brown also swept away 16th-century formal gardens sited north of the house. Further north, the land belonged to Baslow until the 1820s, with a large number of fields and a farmstead at their heart; all were removed when the park was enlarged northwards.

To the west of the river the land was in the township of the large village of Edensor.[16] There are extensive medieval ridge and furrow earthworks, with cultivation abandoned prior to 1617 when the landscape was dominated by a large sheepwalk and a warren. In the 17th and earlier 18th centuries, all was divided into hedged fields, only to be swept away again a few decades later.

To the north of Edensor there were probably once further agricultural earthworks in the park, but this area was ploughed and cultivated in the 1939–45 war. To the south-west, on Calton Pasture, designed by Brown as an outer park, there are further earthworks related to pre-1759 fields; these have also been extensively damaged by ploughing in modern times.

Fig 4.12
Within the present Chatsworth Park, and Calton Pasture to the south-west, extensive earthworks show the layout of hedged fields swept away from 1759 into the 1820s. In 1617 when the land was mapped by William Senior the landscape was very different and, as well as larger fields by the river, there were gardens, a deer park, a warren and a sheep walk.

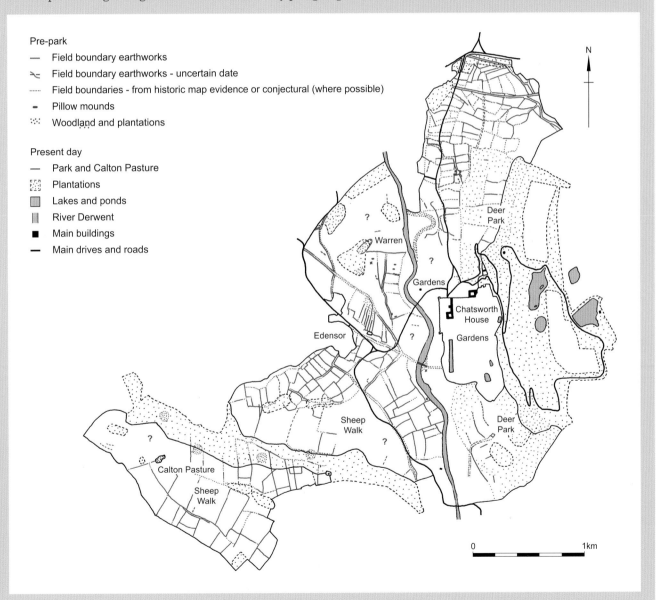

Pre-park

— Field boundary earthworks

⊰ Field boundary earthworks - uncertain date

⋯ Field boundaries - from historic map evidence or conjectural (where possible)

• Pillow mounds

⋮⋮ Woodland and plantations

Present day

— Park and Calton Pasture

⬚ Plantations

▢ Lakes and ponds

▍ River Derwent

■ Main buildings

— Main drives and roads

69

Medieval islands – Granges on the commons

Scattered throughout the Peak were nearly 50 granges, farms owned and sometimes run by abbeys and priories, with the mother houses spread through the surrounding lowlands and up to about 170km away.[17] The granges themselves were often situated in remote places. On the higher parts of the limestone plateau, where there were extensive tracts of wastes and commons, they formed a very distinctive element to the settlement pattern. The vast majority of people lived in villages surrounded by open fields, whilst, in contrast, many of the granges were within islands of enclosed land surrounded by a sea of heathland. Notable clusters exist north of Hartington,[18] south-east of Monyash,[19] east of Hartington[20] and east from here on the south-eastern plateau.[21] In the same high limestone zone, there was also a few small villages with open fields high on the commons.[22]

Some of these granges were primarily sheep farms, but at others, contrary to conventional wisdom, they practised mixed farming and sometimes this seems to have included using small open fields.[23] This may include the narrow co-axial fields running up the daleside within an oval boundary south-east of the buildings at Roystone Grange, which when first studied were interpreted as Romano-British in date but upon re-examination are argued to be more likely to be medieval.[24] Some granges in core settlement areas were at sites of small villages and hamlets that existed before the monastic farms were established, or the granges were established adjacent to them.[25]

Some of the boundaries to the grange lands, as with medieval open fields around villages, were defined by large banks, with notable surviving examples at Needham, Cronkston, Pilsbury and Mouldridge. At Cronkston, there are two such adjacent banks, suggesting the grange farmland was enlarged after it was first established. In other cases they built walls of vertically set stones rather than boundary banks, as at Roystone and Biggin.[26] The enclosed monastic farms, where surrounded by common, often have boundaries that tend to be roughly oval or 'potato-shaped', although more rectangular examples also occur, with little direct relationship to topographic changes that would have been obvious choices to follow; this is also the case with open fields around medieval villages. The reasons for the choices again need further study.

Parliamentary and private enclosure

Post-medieval fields that have been laid out as a result of an Enclosure Award are very distinctive in that normally they are part of planned blocks, with each of rectangular shape and having straight-sided boundaries. These characteristics result from large moorland parcels being subdivided on a map, using a ruler, and agreed before the boundaries were actually built (Fig 4.13).

These sets of fields are fundamentally different from those created or modified by individual farmers who made or moved boundaries to suit changing needs in organic fashion over decades as and when there was time and/or money to make this possible. Planned enclosure layouts were normally paid for by owners of large estates, or by individual farmers who grasped the opportunity for more land when commons were being enclosed. A great deal of initial effort was required to make this viable but often, if the family farm was to remain workable, this was necessary because the Parliamentary Enclosure Award, whilst awarding a share of the land, took away traditional grazing rights over the former commons. In contrast, intakes made by individual farmers on commons without an Award, from the medieval period into the 19th century, tend to be small irregular or 'potato-shaped' areas, found either at common edges or sometimes as islands of enclosed land within the common. These are often impossible to date unless documentary evidence for the farmsteads exists; on the limestone plateau and to the east they are rare, but on the western and northern moorland fringes whole swaths of landscape fall into this category.

In the core of the Peak, amongst the first Parliamentary Enclosure Awards were those for Litton and Winster in 1764, whilst the last was for Bamford Common in 1857. Something like half of the limestone plateau's commons were enclosed by Parliamentary Awards, whilst on the less-favourable gritstone uplands enclosure was significantly more restricted, with the former commons becoming privately owned grouse-shooting and/or stock-grazing moors. Awards tended to be sought from Parliament when there was a large population in the township with land rights, where agreement over how the commons were to be divided would have been difficult to reach without independent commissioners whose job it was to make the allocation; often it was powerful landowners who were treated the most favourably. Sometimes those cottagers who only had limited rights, often comprising grazing for just a few sheep or cows, appear to have been treated badly; for example, in the Baslow Award of 1826 they were allocated small parcels of high moorland at a distance from the village, perhaps for peat cutting; these were never enclosed but eventually became part of the Duke of Devonshire's grouse moor, presumably after being purchased from the villagers.

Parliamentary Enclosure Plans and Awards for the most part survive and form a valuable resource for understanding 18th- and 19th-century landscape development. However, they can trap the unwary, for the mapping shows the boundaries of land parcels allotted to individuals, but not how these people subdivided large blocks into fields that suited their agricultural practice.

Planned private enclosure was equally common but is often harder to date as documentation has not survived; the earliest example where a detailed map does exist is for 1691, covering part of the Castleton Commons to be divided between the village freeholders and copyholders. Earlier outline information also exists for enclosure on Crown land, done by Charles I in the north-western part of the Royal Forest of the Peak in the 1630s to raise funds.[27] These areas have long, ruler-straight boundaries that still exist today, which if the map did not exist would be assumed to be 19th century in date. Large estates with wealthy owners tended to make changes on a grand scale, sometimes sweeping away what was there formerly and starting again, creating what were 'modern' farms following contemporary thought on how to farm effectively. For example, the township of Brushfield, which was owned by the Dukes of Devonshire, had only three tenanted farmsteads in the old village by the early 19th century and the former 'High Field' had previously been divided into a large number of small fields. Similarly, the old deer park at Chatsworth, on high land east of the house, was subdivided into fields by ornamental shelter belts of trees, whilst land just outside to the north in Baslow Parish was transformed from small irregular fields in the early 19th century. Once the Duke of Devonshire's estate acquired this land from the Duke of Rutland in the 1820s, new blocks of rectangular fields were created, still here today, that replaced the old fields and extended onto former moorland.[28]

Fig 4.13
Just west of Rushup Hall, on Rushup Edge near Sparrowpit, is this 19th-century enclosure, which was drawn on a map with straight edges before the wallers built what had been designed in a land surveyor's office.
[John Barnatt]

Castleton Commons

A large area of the former commons of Castleton, high on the limestone plateau behind Cave Dale and west of Pin Dale, is divided today by drystone walls of the local limestone into rectangular to irregularly shaped fields of a wide variety of sizes. The archaeologist who once described them as 19th-century walls is to be forgiven for this is exactly what they look like. Many of the boundaries are ruler-straight and clearly planned on a map before being built. This is confirmed by a surviving enclosure map for one part dating to the late 17th century (Fig 4.14).[29] This shows that part of the wastes and commons of Castleton was divided amongst the freeholders and copyholders of the 'Liberty of Castleton' as agreed by 'their Ma[jes]ties writ of partition' on 3 September 1691. This is the only known 17th-century map for the Peak showing details of partition, and its existence illustrates that the process of sub-division of commons started well before the well-known Parliamentary Enclosure Awards of the later 18th and earlier 19th centuries. What happened at Castleton was part of a broader trend, with the Stuart Kings rationalising unenclosed land within the Royal Forest, dividing it between the Crown and tenants in order to help realise assets, as is known for example to have happened around Taddington and Chelmorton, and further north around Chapel en le Frith and Glossop.[30] Other parts of the Castleton Commons on the limestone plateau to the north, including Winnats Pass and Treak Cliff, also belonged to the Duchy of Lancaster but were the share held by the Crown; there is no historic map showing when these were enclosed.

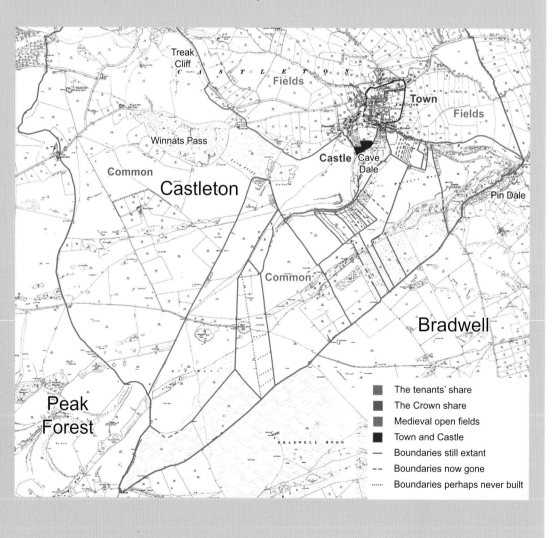

Fig 4.14
The southern part of Castleton Commons, showing the villagers' share of these as enclosed by agreement in 1691, the Crown's share of the common, now-fossilised medieval open fields, and the town and castle.

Many of the 1691 boundaries are still visible as walls. In three areas there is no evidence that the boundaries shown on the 1691 map were ever built; it may be that individuals rationalised their allotted holdings by exchange or sale of parcels. The map base is Ordnance Survey mapping revised in 1897.

The tenants' share
The Crown share
Medieval open fields
Town and Castle
— Boundaries still extant
-- Boundaries now gone
···· Boundaries perhaps never built

Traditional meadows and modern grazing

Whilst some grass pasture is used by farmers to graze livestock whenever needed, other fields are set aside in the spring and summer as meadows to provide feed for animals in winter. Traditionally hay was grown in these meadows, but today the grass is often cut and stored as silage, which in upland areas such as the Peak has the advantage that the grass does not have to come to full maturity; in some years the weather is such that periods of rain mean the hay crop is poor or fails altogether. Before modern times and the viable importation of winter fodder from other regions and/or the use of silage stored in plastic bags or silos, this limited the number of animals, and cattle in particular, that could be overwintered.

Whilst traditional hay meadows are often ecologically rich, with a wide variety of wild flowers and grasses, together with the numerous insect and mammal species they support, where silage is grown the fields have usually been ploughed and reseeded as 'monocultures' dominated by rye grass. The number of traditional meadows that survive today is a small fraction of what once existed and they have often been protected by conservation initiatives.[31]

One of the knock-on effects of periodic ploughing and reseeding in the last few decades has been damage or destruction of many slight archaeological earthworks that were the vestiges of medieval and earlier settlement, agriculture and other activity.

Arable in the 19th century

As one moves around the Peak today, in most parts, seeing a ploughed field is a rare event; sometimes the ploughing is done to plant arable crops, whilst elsewhere it is for periodic reseeding of pasture. In contrast, there was more arable in the mid-19th century, as shown by detailed records of what was being grown when parishes were assessed for tithe in the 1830s to 1840s. For example, the 1842 Taddington and Priestcliffe tithe assessment recorded 302 acres of arable, with 3,624 bushels of oats grown that year on 151 acres, with smaller amounts of turnips, potatoes, cabbages, seeds and dead fallow (Fig 4.15).[32] Taking four selected groups of parishes: the Edale, Hope and Derwent valleys had 16 per cent arable; parishes that straddled the limestone shale interface had 6 per cent; the limestone plateau had 10 per cent; and the southern valleys had 12 per cent.[33] The reasons for this greater emphasis on arable compared with today are complex. One factor is that arable production went up in response to the Napoleonic war and continued at a similar level due to the Corn Laws, which protected British farmers from foreign imports until repealed in 1846. In the 1870s there were several wet summers that damaged grain crops leading to an agricultural depression that lasted well into the 20th century; the small amount of arable continues to today because of difficulty in competing with intensive lowland production. Another important factor leading to the former high levels of arable was the cost of importing basic foodstuffs until the introduction of bulk transport on the railways reduced this. For most central parts of the Peak this came from the 1860s onwards. Before this, for many communities, if they wanted a varied diet, foodstuffs had to be grown locally. That said, the region was still deficient in wheat in the earlier 19th century, with local cereal growth being dominated by oats, whilst barley was grown for brewing. Although wheat was grown locally, a significant proportion of wheat flour was imported into the region from the lowlands of the Midlands for purchase by those wealthy enough to eat white bread.

Beyond the fields

Beyond the enclosed agricultural landscape of the Peak there are the large swaths of moorland on the gritstone uplands and also vestiges of former commons on the limestone plateau, the majority of which were swept away in the 17th to 19th centuries. These areas, traditionally often referred to as 'wastes and commons', were an important agricultural resource used for open grazing of stock.

Limestone commons

In the period before the enclosure awards of the later 18th and earlier 19th centuries the limestone plateau of the Peak was a very different place to that we see today. There were extensive open commons, vegetated by limestone heath, with heathers and coarse grasses dominating the landscape. Today only small vestiges remain, the only ones of any size on two of the highest parts of the plateau, at the western end of Longstone Edge and on Bradwell Moor (see Fig 4.19).[34]

Fig 4.15
The tithe schedule for
Taddington and Priestcliffe
of 1847, as mapped in
1848, is an agricultural
snapshot in time. The map
shows the widespread
distribution of arable
across both the old open-
field areas and 1790s'
Parliamentary Enclosure
Award fields beyond.
The arable is interspaced
with hay meadows and
pasture. Plantations and
'waste' are rare and there
were also three meres and
two small quarries.

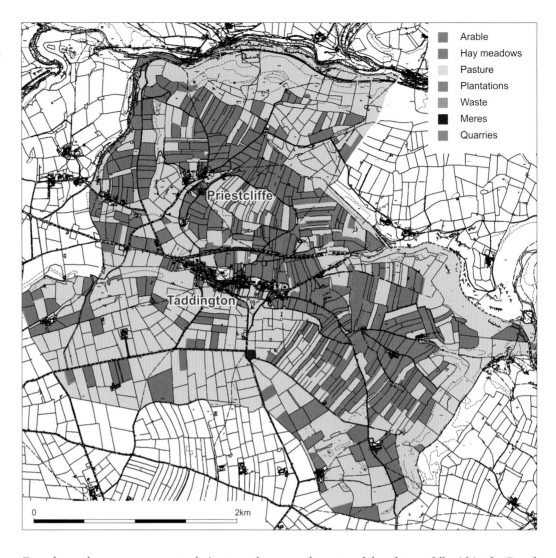

Even here, these areas are not obvious on the map, for they lie within large upland enclosures, surrounded by similarly shaped parcels where there has been 'improvement' of the pastures so that grass dominates.

In the mid-17th century the limestone commons were one of two dominant aspects to the landscape; there were swaths of limestone heath surrounding islands of fields around villages. Throughout the medieval period, to after 1650, it would probably have been possible, by sticking to the high ground, except where the gorges of the Lathkill and Wye needed to be crossed, to walk from Castleton to Wirksworth without crossing a single field boundary. These commons were a valuable resource, with complex traditional rights, where lords and commoners alike grazed livestock, collected firewood and cut peat for fuel.[35] Often areas of common well away from villages were shared with adjacent communities. To the

north, parts of the plateau fell within the Royal Forest of the Peak and came under forest law, but, as far as grazing by local villagers was concerned, the situation was effectively similar to elsewhere.

From the 17th century onwards there was gradual enclosure of the commons, for example, with the division into fields of part of Castleton Moor in 1691, but with large-scale removal from about 1750 onwards. Some of the first areas to go were those parts where communal rights had lapsed, in areas set aside for the Lords of the Manor or the Crown. Eventually the Parliamentary Enclosure Awards removed those areas of common where legal recourse was needed to remove traditional rights. Enclosure included some areas such as steep limestone dalesides unsuitable for arable, where common rights were removed and each dale divided into privately held grazing areas.

Carsington Pasture and Thorpe Pasture

At the southern edge of the limestone plateau there are rare survivals of ancient commons, now privately owned but looking much as they have done for several hundred years except perhaps for improvements in the quality of the grassland. Whilst they were once part of a more extensive unenclosed landscape, they now are walled at their edges and, as large 'sheepwalks', stand in contrast with the 'normal-sized' post-medieval fields that surround them.

Carsington Pasture, on high ground that drops off steeply to the southern edge, is located between Carsington and Brassington. Today it is divided into two parts by a modern fence and has only footpath access at its edges; masts of a windfarm dominate the scene (Fig 4.16). Its extensive old lead-mining remains are interspersed with low earthworks left by medieval cultivation and enclosure, telling of a time when more land was put over to arable before the population declines that came with the Black Death in the 14th century.[36]

Thorpe Pasture and the adjacent Thorpe Cloud now have 'Open Access' and occupy a dissected landscape to the east side of the mouth of Dove Dale (Fig 4.17). The Cloud is steep-sided and has never been cultivated, whilst to the east Thorpe Pasture has medieval cultivation strips at its southern and eastern fringes, again telling of contraction of cropping since the high medieval period. These earthworks are interspersed with Roman-period boundary banks with an abandoned farmstead in the dry valley at its heart that has associated fields and house platforms (*see* Chapter 11).

Fig 4.16
The open sheepwalk on the limestone plateau at Carsington Pasture has recently had a visual transformation; these symbols of our modern 'green' world are not to everyone's taste.
[John Barnatt]

Fig 4.17
Thorpe Cloud, always part of the commons, dominates its local landscape, whereas the large open grazing area of Thorpe Pasture has earthworks from past land-use. These include the low medieval ridge and furrow just visible in the foreground.
[John Barnatt]

Lathkill Dale

This impressive valley, long popular with walkers, forms a deep gash across the landscape, with precipitous dalesides and sometimes vertical cliffs (Fig 4.18). Whilst it is now easy to follow the path along the bottom of the dale, before it was cleared of natural woodland it would have been a difficult landscape to negotiate. People for the most part are likely to have crossed from side to side only when travelling beyond their home landscape. Change probably came in the early post-medieval period, brought about by over-use of the wood pasture here and the felling of trees for mining purposes. However, it was probably still a liminal place only occasionally visited, with the river forming a boundary between parishes.

In the last three centuries Lathkill Dale has been divided into large parcels by private owners. Today some areas are private sheep grazing, but the downriver parts are mostly steep slopes and are wooded. These plantations are a product of 19th-century replanting and woodland management by the Melbourne, Rutland and Devonshire estates. Some are in areas where there had long been ancient woodland, whilst others were planted after earlier woodland had been decimated by lead miners or where the daleside had become well-established open grazing.[37]

Lathkill Dale has long only been used by local people in a restricted number of specific ways.[38] Small caves have provided occasional refuge. Lead mining and to a lesser extent quarrying for limestone and tufa have been important; once there were impressive leats leading to two massive waterwheels and a Cornish steam engine used for driving pumps at the mines. For farmers the Lathkill has also been an important source of water at the heart of the dry plateau. At a time when there were commons to either side, stock would have been brought down to drink; but although lead-mining drainage soughs may well have had a detrimental effect on flow, it is suspected the river may well have always run dry from time to time in the summer. Later, a tradition of washing animals at specific places along the river continued and trout were bred and fished. Over Haddon Mill was long in use, whilst Carter's Mill further upstream existed by 1826 when it was known as 'New Mill'.

Fig 4.18
The precipitous upper part of Lathkill Dale below One Ash Grange, which is out of view to the left. From much of the surrounding landscape the gorge cannot be seen from a distance, and for a stranger it suddenly surprises as the dale top is reached.
[John Barnatt]

Grouse shooting or agricultural improvement

Most of today's gritstone moorlands in the Peak, with the exception of the higher northern and western parts, are at an altitude that would have made them suitable for enclosure and improvement in the 19th century (Fig 4.19).

This is particularly the case with the eastern moors, where there are large swaths of moorland at similar altitude to land on the western moors that have been enclosed; this is despite the western moors having a higher rainfall, making them less suitable for improvement. Large tracts of moorland to the east were owned by the Dukes of Devonshire and Rutland.

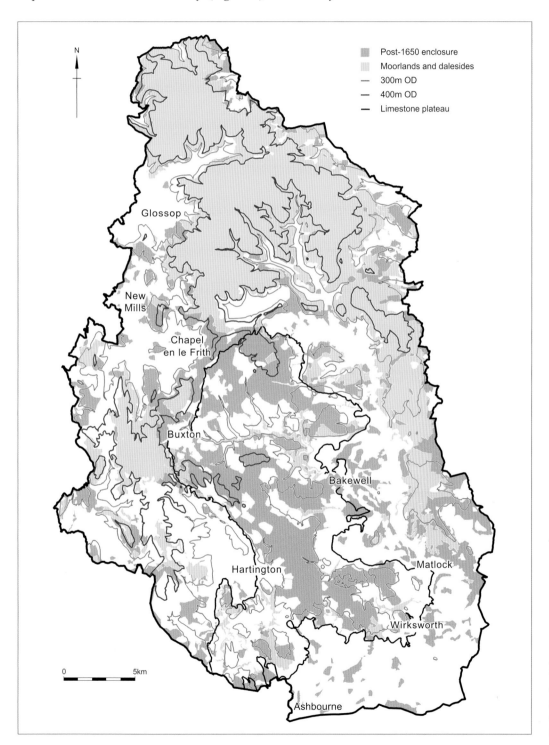

Key:
- Post-1650 enclosure
- Moorlands and dalesides
- 300m OD
- 400m OD
- Limestone plateau

Fig 4.19
The Peak showing the relationship between altitude, post-1650 enclosure and today's moorland and dalesides.

Fig 4.20
Traditional moorland management for grouse involves burning a mosaic of heather so that it is of different ages to maximise food and shelter for the birds, as here on Derwent Moors. Close inspection of burning nearby, several decades ago, revealed a prehistoric cairnfield, with small low mounds of stone, that otherwise would have remained invisible.
[John Barnatt]

Both families consciously developed these estates for grouse shooting at a time when this was becoming popular. This land-use led to the survival of some of the most important sets of prehistoric settlement and agricultural remains in Britain, which would have been easily swept away if the land had been cleared for arable or reseeded using palatable grass strains (Fig 4.20).[39]

The moors above Chatsworth were sufficiently close for shooting parties to foray out from the house. In contrast, the Dukes of Rutland, whose main family residence was Belvoir Castle in Leicestershire, developed a large lodge at Longshaw from the 1820s to the 1830s, at the centre of their shooting estate. Across the Longshaw Estate, there was a series of drives, some now abandoned and grassed over, that allowed visitors to be taken by carriage to all parts of the extensive moors. There were also imposing gamekeepers' lodges placed at prominent spots.

Shooting cabins were common on grouse moors, now often ruined, where refreshment could be taken and braces of birds stored. Lines of old shooting butts can still be seen, usually carefully placed out of sight so that birds could be driven over them without sufficient warning that they were there. These butts have a wide variety of designs, traditionally often built of turf with stone-lined interiors. Sometimes short but high walls were built midway between butts to prevent inexperienced members of the shooting parties from killing each other.

5

Using fields

The region's enclosed agricultural landscapes have a variety of details that add to their interest, as with field walls, wall furniture, field barns, ridge and furrow, strip lynchets, dew ponds and field kilns. Where they survive they are important in that they illustrate past agricultural practices and add to the rich diversity of archaeological features within the landscape. Places named in Chapter 5 are located on Figure A1.3 (*see* p 227).

Field walls

In 1991 it was proposed that Peak walls could be divided into five types, each of different design and date.[1] The earliest, Type 5, comprised horizontally laid stone slabs in a single line at a small enclosure, the remains being presumably only residual remnants of the original structure; these were argued to be prehistoric on the basis of early finds made in a small excavation. Type 4 walls are more common and have lines of vertically set slabs and blocks placed at the two edges, with a rubble core, and were thought to be Romano-British in date. Type 3 walls have a single line of large vertically set boulders and were argued to be medieval. Type 2 walls were of standard drystone type, built from rounded surface-gathered stones and thought to be of roughly early 17th-century date based on the known history of the property, whilst Type 1 walls were of about 1800 date, built as straight drystone walls of angular quarried stone that were more vertically sided.

This work, which was based on Roystone Grange, an isolated farm at the heart of the highest part of the limestone plateau, cannot be simplistically applied to other parts of the Peak. At Roystone itself the dating of some boundaries originally interpreted as Romano-British has more recently been argued to have been built in the medieval period.[2] What the Types 5 to 3 walls at Roystone have in common is that they incorporate large natural boulders; whilst initial clearance of land here was early, focused on both a Romano-British settlement and a medieval monastic grange, in other places in the Peak the first improvement for agriculture can be as late as the 19th century and large boulders are still used then where they occur naturally.[3] Similarly, Type 4 walls have been identified in prehistoric (probably Early Iron Age) rather than Roman-British contexts at excavations on Gardom's Edge.[4] This type of boundary appears not to be period-specific but rather is associated with boundaries that had an earthen core or upper part, much like a 'Cornish hedge', that would support a live hedge above and provide soil for its roots. In theory these can be anticipated to potentially be of prehistoric to medieval date in the Peak. The dating of typical Peak drystone walls on the basis of the types of stone used, which as we have argued above may be largely of 18th- and 19th-century date, is fraught with uncertainty; they are continuously falling down, with farmers repairing gaps or undertaking wholesale rebuilding, sometimes using stone imported from elsewhere or robbed from nearby ruined walls that are not to be retained. Occasionally walls in the Peak landscape stand out as built in a style that is 'foreign', which is particularly noticeable around reservoirs, where such things as crenellated coping stones were used; it seems some water companies employed their own wallers who learned their skills in other regions.

Often the best way of dating post-medieval walls is from existing historic estate, enclosure or tithe maps; this sometimes allows whole then-new field systems to be identified, whilst elsewhere study of the earliest available maps of a site can give clues as to relative age, by looking at the horizontal stratigraphy and thinking about, for instance, the sequence of boundary construction at T-junctions. Another technique that has been attempted is to study wall junctions to see what butts what; this is also fraught with problems as what relationships exist often relate to the latest rebuilds rather than the original sequence.

Wall furniture

Drystone walls, and sometimes hedges, contain a variety of traditional stone details that add greatly to their character, including gateposts, stiles, sheep-throughs also known as 'creeps', and smaller openings for rabbits or water called 'smoots'. For the most part they are 18th and 19th century in date.

Gateways into or between fields are often closed using five-bar gates between two posts of gritstone or limestone; commonly today they have metal gates hung on hinges set into the posts; sometimes modern posts are made of concrete. Such gates had become the norm by the end of the 19th century but a little under a hundred years earlier a different way of securing gateways was described; 'a hole through the stone near its top held a timber bar that had a wooden hoop that surrounded the top of the stone post, which in turn held the top of one end of a gate with its bottom set in a holed stone on the floor'.[5] Before that time it was also common for one, two or more frequently three horizontal wooded bars to be placed across a gateway, fitted into slots or holes in the gateposts; if the gap needed to be stock-proof, then a hurdle was attached to these (Fig 5.1).

Those gateposts made of limestone slabs are usually carefully selected pieces chosen for their shape, but with little in the way of dressing as this hard rock was difficult to shape. Sandstone examples are usually dressed to be neat rectangular posts. Here a variety of tool marks are common, with pick marks commonly seen; those stones of 18th-century date, especially where used on land held by wealthy estates, are finely dressed with semi-circular tops, smooth bands along the edges and/or fine parallel lines forming geometrically shaped panels.[6]

Traditional stone-built stiles also come in two forms; sometimes long slabs were placed horizontally through the wall to create steps, often with two to three forming a diagonal 'stair'; occasionally lintels and other pieces of dressed stonework from demolished buildings were reused. Elsewhere, two vertical posts were set close together to form squeezer-stiles, placed too close for stock to pass through; occasionally these were finely dressed to shape. When there were lambs in a field the stile was temporarily blocked using stones. Although stiles are commonly found along public footpaths, it should not be assumed that elsewhere they indicate the presence of a public route; sometimes they were built by farmers for their exclusive use.

Sheep-throughs usually comprise low openings through walls, usually around 0.6m and 0.8m high, with a simple slab of stone above forming a lintel. These were once common and allowed sheep to pass from field to field whilst cattle or horses were contained by closed gateways. When farmers did not want the sheep to move, the throughs were stopped up with crude drystone walling.

Smoots are small holes no more than 30cm high with vertical sides of two to three courses of stonework. They are not common and were often built to allow rabbits to pass; once they used these regularly, snares were set. Occasionally identical-looking holes are seen that may well have been made to allow water to flow that otherwise would pond up beside a wall or undermine foundations.

Fig 5.1
A gatepost at Ramshaw Rocks with slots for traditional closing bars; the opposite post has chiselled circular holes through which the other end of the bars were inserted before then slotting them into place.
[John Barnatt]

As dilapidated drystone walls are periodically brought into good order, much of the wall furniture is not retained upon rebuilding as these are anachronistic. In the case of stiles, with increased awareness of the requirements of those with special needs, timber wicket gates have been placed along the lines of paths, although in some instances, the traditional stiles have been retained with a modern foot gate placed adjacent. At gateways, it is common for one gatepost to have been removed or reset, for traditional gateways, which can occasionally still be seen at long-disused openings, are too narrow for modern farm machinery.

Field barns

There are many isolated farm buildings in the Peak, built away from the farmsteads, found in both nucleated and dispersed settlement areas; they were once vital to the farming economy.[7] These are all termed here 'field barns' for simplicity's sake; many are barns with upper floors or lofts where hay was stored for feeding to livestock in stalling on the ground floor; a minority are small single-storey sheds that were built for a variety of purposes, including storage and hencotes. A few are 'bank barns' built into a slope so that the top floor can be accessed upslope at ground level; more common, at sites on flatter land, there are external flights of stone steps to the top floor, whilst most two-storey barns have internal ladders. A small number of isolated barns have tall cart-sized doors showing these were used as threshing barns, but these are the exceptions to the rule; field barns usually contained livestock. A common feature at field barns are square window-like openings on the upper floor, originally with shutter-like doors, known locally as 'pitch-holes' or 'picking holes', designed primarily for throwing hay into the loft from a cart outside using a pitchfork, rather than to let in light (Fig 5.2). The ground floor of the building, known as the 'shippon' or 'cowhouse', was used for cattle and often divided into stalled areas locally often known as 'boskins' or 'booses'. Where there was a hay loft above, this helped keep the stock warm. Sometimes more than one outbuilding is found, together with walled yard, places for hay stacks, and dew pond, and these can be termed 'outfarms'.

Fig 5.2
A typical small field barn at Gateham, north of Alstonefield. The external stairs lead to the hay loft, while the shuttered picking hole allowed hay to be thrown with a pitchfork from a cart into the loft. The slots keep the barn well ventilated, reducing the risk of self-combustion of damp hay. The ground floor doors for stock are on the other side.
[John Barnatt]

Often field barns are imposing and sturdy structures in plain vernacular style, made to withstand Peak winters (Fig 5.3). Mostly the stone local to the site was used for building, but in limestone areas, sandstone was sometimes used for lintels and quoins, as this stone was more easily shaped than limestone. Traditional roofs were commonly of local sandstone slates or from the later 19th century onwards Welsh grey slate. In the South-Western Peak traditionally 'Staffordshire Blue' clay tiles were also used.

The majority of field barns were built in the 19th century, although others date to the early 20th century. Some have architectural details such as large irregular and often roughly triangular lintels suggesting they were built in the 17th or 18th century. One such example just outside Peak Forest has a 1781 date carved into a lintel. Many field barns are found in areas first enclosed from commons in the later 18th and earlier 19th centuries, but they were also frequently built in landscapes with a much longer period of farming within fields.

Field barns allowed cattle, and occasionally sheep or horses, to be kept away from the main farmsteads, often built in places at some distance away, or at the main farm building where smallholders had few or no outbuildings

adjacent to their dwelling. Not only did they provide shelter that allowed overwintering, but milking could also take place there; today both functions are provided at large sheds at the main farm complex.

Whilst field barns are found throughout the region, except on the moorlands, there are specific areas where they were particularly common.[8] Notable is the concentration around Winster and Bonsall in the south-east part of the limestone plateau; there was much lead mining here, and in post-medieval times, rather than there being a few large mines, the many small mines were worked by independent miner-farmers. These people not only mined but also had smallholdings so that when the mining was proving unproductive they still had food on the table. Another classic example of dual economy is provided by the large number of barns immediately outside Bakewell, particularly within the enclosed old medieval fields on the limestone shelf at the edge of town. Here townspeople had traditional land rights; but here it was not miners but tradespeople, such as inn- and shop-keepers and craftsmen, who had need for grazing for horses and livestock as well as having smallholdings to supplement their incomes.

Fig 5.3
This dilapidated but sturdy field barn south of Wetton is typical of many built in the Peak, with doors for stock, picking holes above and slots for ventilation. [John Barnatt]

Most areas have field barns of a variety of dates, built in response to the needs of individual farmers. In contrast, at Edensor a group of 13 barns, of which only nine now survive, are thought to have been erected by Chatsworth Estate. They lie in a discrete area of fields that were allocated to the smallholders of Edensor when the landscape park nearby was created in the 1760s. The buildings themselves mostly date between the 1830s and 1850s, erected after the park was enlarged in the 1820s and 1830s, associated with the remodelling of the village in the late 1830s and early 1840s.[9]

For the last few decades field barns have become increasingly anachronistic, and now for the most part have little or no agricultural usefulness. Most have become increasingly dilapidated and many have been demolished. Some are in good repair, either because farmers still value them, or because they now have other functions such as camping barns. Because they have often had little use for decades, some still contain fine examples of original wooden stalling and hay feeding racks, occasionally with vertical stone slabs dividing stalls. Around Bonsall a local initiative aimed at saving some of these interesting buildings led to basic repairs of over 20 examples. More fundamentally, whilst some people have wanted to convert these isolated farm buildings to dwellings, this has been resisted by the National Park Authority because to do so across the region would lead to radical and irrevocable changes to settlement patterns, landscape character and population density, which would place unsustainable stress on the existing local road network and public services.

Ridge and furrow/strip lynchets

The 'corrugated' ground often seen in fields, with low raised banks flanked by slight hollows, is known as 'ridge and furrow'. It has different forms and a variety of dates. In simplistic terms, broad ridges, often 5–10m across and up to 1m high, have origins in the medieval period, whereas 'narrow-rig' usually only 1–2m across, is often 19th and 20th century in date.[10]

Broad ridge and furrow is a product of the medieval feudal practice of dividing open fields into narrow strips and reallocating these each year to individual farmers. They were usually ploughed using oxen teams and the sinuous shape as seen on maps is thought to reflect the turn needed at the headlands. It is unclear whether or not the raised character of the ridges was purely a coincidental product of always ploughing in the same way with fixed mouldboard ploughs. Having furrows between each ridge helps with drainage. Also, the presence of a ridge slightly increases the surface area for growing and thus crop yield when compared with flat ground, but we do not know whether Peak farmers in the medieval period were aware of this.

A common variation in form resulting from medieval cultivation is the strip lynchet; these are formed on slopes where cultivation followed the contour or went up the slope at an angle, so that soil was cut away on the upslope side of the strip and accumulated on its downslope side. The result is a stepped landscape, with sharp breaks of slopes between each strip (Fig 5.4). What is often unclear is if the lynchets are solely the product of ploughing through time, or whether they were engineered at the outset by constructing terraces to make them flat enough to plough. Similarly, some broad ridge and furrow was hand dug; an example near Ashford on the steep side of the Wye Valley has ridges at right angles to a narrow natural terrace; these are so short that it would have been impossible to plough them.

Whilst broad ridge cultivation is often thought of as a medieval phenomenon, in the Peak the actual earthworks visible today can be as late as 18th or even early 19th century in date. The open fields were becoming increasingly fragmented by enclosure of specific parts into hedged or walled fields, a process that can be demonstrated to have started by the 17th century with potential origins from the 14th century onwards. However, relatively large parcels of land continued to be farmed in the traditional way and estate and township maps show them still subdivided into strips. In some instances, this may be a cartographic convention that was designed to illustrate how grazing rights were divided between several farmers using this land. In other cases, it is thought that the strips continued to be ploughed, with periodic changes made to strip layout to meet the needs of each generation of farmers.

In the Peak there are strong contrasts in the form ridge and furrow takes between the limestone plateau and the surrounding shale valleys. This results from differences in the character of the soils; those on the limestone plateau are often so thin that even with regular

Fig 5.4
Near Priestcliffe there is a
fine group of strip lynchets,
well known because they
are visible from the A6.
[John Barnatt]

Fig 5.5
Across the 'dry-valley' from
Wensley, at the crest of the
steep slopes at the edge of
the limestone plateau, there
are well-preserved
medieval strip lynchets
intermixed with ridge and
furrow; these have been cut
by lead mining following
small veins. Traces of
Romano-British banks can
be seen to the lower right.
In some fields post-
medieval ploughing has
removed earlier features.
[Derrick Riley]

ploughing only slight or no ridges were formed; frequently we only know of the former presence of strips because later piecemeal enclosure has drystone walls that follow the strip layout. Occasionally on the plateau, where strips were created on slopes, patterns of strip lynchets are visible, as for example near Priestcliffe, Youlgreave, and between Wensley and Snitterton (Fig 5.5). The last area is exceptional in extent and is a palimpsest landscape of Romano-British and medieval earthworks.

In contrast, on the deep clays in the shale valleys, and where shale occurs on shelves at the edge of the limestone plateau, cultivation ridge formation is good and these are often well defined. Good examples are found in Chatsworth Park and above Bakewell (Fig 5.6). The most extensive area with broad ridge and furrow is to the south at the plateau fringe, around Brassington, Carsington, Bradbourne, Ballidon, Parwich and Tissington (Fig 5.7); whilst some fields have been ploughed flat in modern times, survival is extensive and this ridge and furrow is an important example. A hundred years ago this was a small part of an extensive lowland tract of ridge and furrow landscape across

much of the English Midlands; however, with widespread destruction by modern ploughing in richer farming areas, the Peak fringe takes on added archaeological importance.

Narrow-rig is the product of ploughing with a small, horse-drawn plough that has a fixed mould-board so that the sods were always turned to the same side. If ploughing was up and down the field, returning in the opposite direction to the adjacent turned sods, then narrow ridges were formed. However, in contrast, if ploughing was in broad rectangular blocks, as much 20th-century ploughing has been, then most adjacent lines of sods went the same way leaving only spaced ridges and hollows at the edges of the blocks. In the Peak, which in the first half of the 20th century was predominantly turned over to livestock farming, much of the surviving narrow-rig dates to 1939–45, made when farmers were required by government to grow crops as part of the war effort; they pulled out grandfather's 19th-century plough from the back of the shed and used this. Surviving examples of narrow-rig are only found occasionally, usually on land which is marginal and has never been ploughed again in modern decades.

Fig 5.6
An extract from the survey drawings made for the Bakewell Parish survey undertaken in 2002, showing extensive areas of surviving medieval strip lynchets and ridge and furrow on the limestone shelf above the market town in the valley bottom to the east (areas not surveyed are stippled). Some earthworks are in good condition (A) and above there are interesting little-used strip boundaries created at the time of maximum extent of expansion onto the common, presumably in the 12th to 14th century (B). Other highlights include the site of a former main road (C), limestone and chert quarries (D) and what may be a 17th-century bowling green (E) overlooking the town.

Fig 5.7
Parts of the southern valleys flanking the limestone plateau often have extensive swaths of ridge and furrow, as here around the shrunken village of Ballidon. In the foreground on higher ground there are small lead mines where veins run across slighter cultivation earthworks on the limestone. [© Historic England Archive, 17433_51]

Dew ponds and meres

Scattered through the fields of the limestone plateau there are many small dew ponds made to water stock (Fig 5.8). Each comprises a circular hollow dug into the ground that originally was lined with lime to discourage worms, then covered with clay, mixed with straw as a binder, to stop leakage into the pervious limestone bedrock. Stones were added to create a durable surface that would prevent damage by hooves. On sloping ground the pond's top was carefully levelled, with the upcast material placed on the downslope side as a revetment bank. Occasionally pre-existing features were utilised, as with hollows within lead-mine hillocks; care must have been needed here not to allow water to drain from the surrounding mineral waste as this could result in poisoning. Commonly dew ponds were carefully sited so that they were crossed by field walls; hence two to four fields were served by the same pond.

Although the limestone plateau is the main place where these artificial ponds were created, made as a response to the lack of standing water over much of this landscape, they also occur occasionally in the gritstone upland landscapes, built where there was no good natural water source available.

Dew ponds probably mostly date from the 18th to earlier 20th century and many were made with the enclosure of the commons.[11] Prior to this, these extensive unenclosed areas were grazed by livestock that could walk to water sources when they were thirsty, either at the occasional natural mere on the plateau, or at springs and the year-round or seasonal rivers and streams found in the gorges and 'dry-valleys' that bisect the plateau. The livestock were attended by cow-herds and shepherds who ensured that the animals were moved through the day so that they could not only drink but move to where there was fresh grazing; they also ensured the animals did not stray into areas of limestone heath beyond the limits of their community's grazing rights, and protected them from wolves.

There were only ever a small number of meres on the limestone plateau, at places where drainage into the fissured limestone substrate was impeded.[12] A notable example is at Monyash, sited on a small inlier of shale bedrock, where five ponds became the focus for gathering stock at a medieval market. Elsewhere, some are now filled and forgotten, but examples remain at the restored High Mere on the moor-top south of Taddington and at another at Heathcote.

From the later 17th or earlier 18th centuries the traditional practices may have been under pressure, for some of the traditionally used springs were presumably drying up and the upper courses of rivers such as the Lathkill may have been flowing less frequently. This was due to the lowering of the water table by lead miners' drainage soughs that allowed mines to be worked at depth, taking water straight out to valley bottoms or beyond the plateau edge. With the coming of the wholesale enclosure of commons from the mid-18th century to earlier 19th century, a radically new way of managing stock was needed, as placing farm animals in walled fields took away their access to water over whole swaths of land; the answer was the dew pond. Despite their name, much of the water they contain is rainwater or surface run-off arriving after the rain has fallen. Cows need to drink daily, as do pregnant ewes.

Farey noted that the circular 'cattle ponds' were mostly built in response to the then-recent enclosure but that making them was an ancient practice.[13] 'Ancient' examples must have been rare, for dew ponds would not be generally needed until enclosure of the land.

Looking down from hilltops, working dew ponds often catch the light, reflecting the sky, and form an interesting and valuable detail that add to the character of the landscape. Nobody has counted the number of dew ponds there once were but it must be in the low thousands. Now some have been filled as it is illegal to water dairy cattle from these; tanks with piped water are used instead. Although significantly reduced in number they are still relatively common, although many are now dry or have been relined with concrete (Fig 5.9).

Fig 5.8
Dew ponds, which collect rainwater, are common on the limestone plateau. This one, close to a field barn south of Foolow, has had its traditional cobbled surface sealed under 20th-century concrete to stop it leaking.
[John Barnatt]

Fig 5.9
A dew pond, now relined with concrete, built on high limestone plateau ground above Pilsbury after the land was enclosed in the early 19th century.
[John Barnatt]

Field kilns

There are two basic types of limekiln in the Peak landscape, those at specific places where lime was produced in quantity for sale, and those out in the fields where farmers made their own lime. The commercial kilns are returned to in Chapter 7 (*see* pp 118–121). Field kilns were once common on the limestone plateau; today here and elsewhere in the region, all are dilapidated, ruined, buried or removed, as they have not been used for many decades. From an archaeological perspective commercial kilns, which tend to be larger or in early cases found in clusters, are usually distinguished from field kilns by the presence of associated waste heaps; the burnt lime was carefully picked from the coal ashes to provide a high-quality product, whereas at field kilns both lime and ashes were spread on the field. The product as it came out of the kiln was quicklime (CaO), whereas slaked lime (Ca(OH)2) was made with the addition of water and was commonly used for mortar as well as sometimes spread on fields; the former is caustic and has to be handled with great care if burns are to be avoided.

Most and perhaps all of the old field kilns seen today were built in the 18th and 19th centuries. There are two main ways lime was used agriculturally: spread thinly it is a de-acidifier;[14] most of the soils on the limestone plateau are acidic, resting on a clay subsoil, and lime increases grass yield by adding alkaline nutrients. In contrast, spread thickly, quicklime will burn off existing vegetation. This burning was particularly useful when fields were first created following Parliamentary Awards of the later 18th and earlier 19th centuries, or at post-medieval private enclosures, as it was the easiest way to remove the limestone heath vegetation prior to ploughing and seeding with a better-quality grass mix. It is suspected that this second use was the prime reason for the building of many of the kilns we see today, although detailed research is needed to confirm this. This hypothesis would explain the often very small size of associated quarries, which indicate that only a few firings were made, rather than lime being produced decade after decade.

Whilst much of the limestone plateau commonly has a scattering of kilns, sometimes with more than one per farm, when land was being farmed close to the main commercial lime production centres, for some farmers it may have been easier to go to those kilns for lime.

These commercial kilns sold impure lime waste and ashes from their waste heaps at a much reduced price. However, there is no clear-cut halo around commercial production centres such as Grin Hill at Buxton. Close to these commercial kilns there are several field kilns, although it is suspected these were built on farms tenanted from the Dukes of Devonshire, as several such have been noted in the estate accounts for the 1780s and 1790s, and the estate may well have encouraged 'state of the art' farming on their properties; Farey notes the improvements made in this area of the Hartington commons from 1783 by the Duke of Devonshire where huge swaths of 'heath' were replaced by grass.[15]

Away from the limestone plateau there are further field kilns in the South-West Peak, some of these located at very distinctive sites of thin beds of limestone amongst the predominant shales and sandstone, where linear quarries following outcrops can still be traced north of Mixon and on the high ridge west of Upper Elkstone. Elsewhere, kilns are sited on acidic ground over shale/sandstone bedrock.[16]

On the limestone plateau it made more sense to transport coal, the fuel used in the burning, to the limestone, where the lime was to be used. In the South-West Peak, it was viable to build kilns away from the limestone near local coal outcrops and bring the limestone to the coal-bearing area. On the eastern gritstone moors where there are further coal mines and lime would also have been used in the local enclosures, it seems that for the most part they imported lime from commercial kilns.

There is a variety of designs of field kilns in the Peak; these fit within a broad range of similar structures found through Britain.[17] However, there are regional variations in architecture and how they were used, and no overall typology has been agreed; whilst significant differences in how they worked are known, it is sometimes impossible when looking at field remains to apply terminology derived from historical or technological perspectives.[18] A fundamental difference in kiln-use is whether it was 'intermittent' or 'continuous-running'. With the former the kiln pot was loaded with layers of coal and limestone, burnt, then allowed to cool before emptying between each firing. With continuous-running kilns, which sometimes were significantly taller, the kiln was charged at the top whilst lime was being drawn from the bottom; these kilns could be used at one continuous firing until the required amount of lime had been made or the kiln pot needed relining.

The simplest field kilns in the Peak are what are termed here 'circular clamp kilns';[19] they have early origins but were commonly used in the 18th and 19th centuries.[20] These kilns comprise a central circular pot, up to about 3m high, into which the limestone to be burnt was tipped and they were of 'intermittent' type. It is documented that other small kilns were of 'continuous-running' type, and these were traditionally termed 'running kilns' or 'draw' kilns but these normally cannot easily be identified in the field.[21] Many 19th-century circular field kilns are larger than what has just been described, built up to about 7m high. Some of intermediate height were also faced externally on their downslope side to help ensure they did not collapse; it is often unclear whether they were 'running kilns' or 'intermittent kilns', especially where dilapidated. Tall kilns were certainly sometimes 'continuous-running' and these are typically but not always faced with high walls, often rectangular in external plan, with a stone-lined drawing tunnel on the downslope side. These are perhaps expediently termed 'faced field kilns'[22] rather than 'clamp kilns' or 'running kilns', but there is a significant grey area between the three types, especially where preservation is not good, where a distinction between 'intermittent' and 'continuous-running' cannot be drawn and thus the typology not easily applied (Fig 5.10).

Fig 5.10
This example of a 'faced field kiln', built in the 19th century high in the Goyt Valley, is unusual in that it was built close to the coal source and limestone was imported from over 3km away; it provided lime for the isolated farms in the valley bottom. The main opening let in draught and was also used for emptying the burnt lime. The small hole above was probably for a rod for poking the material as it burnt.
[John Barnatt]

The pots of the circular kilns were usually lined with local stone, and where visible today have near-vertical sides, tapering inwards towards the bottom. The whole was encased in a circular mound made of stone and/or earth. On the downslope side there is often a visible stone-lined 'drawing tunnel'. Looking at the field remains today, what is often unclear is whether these tunnels were primarily designed to draw air or also for removing the lime. With the former, the tunnel led to a small hole to the base of the pot which allowed a draught to be drawn up through the pot. However, when the kilns were for 'continuous-running', the inner end of the tunnel was also used to draw out the burnt lime. At many kilns a second small hole in the draw tunnel, placed above the first, was used for stoking with a bar that was poked into the pot to clear any blockages that formed during the firing when limestone blocks could become fused together or excessive clinker developed. In contrast to 'continuous-running' kilns, intermittent 'circular clamp kilns' were emptied from the top, with the downslope side of the kiln apparently lowered each time to allow lime to be more easily thrown out; these could also have drawing holes for air. With larger field kilns in particular, a cart to take the lime away for spreading was drawn up to the kiln in a flat-bottomed hollow with a cart-track leading away.

Another type of field kiln, but one of distinctive and readily recognised design, is what is termed here for convenience an 'oval clamp kiln' (Fig 5.11).[23] These kilns are oval in plan and rarely more than 1m to 2m high. When cut into a slope the material from the pit was placed as a bank on the downslope side to form the pot side. Here there were between one and three draughting flues or 'eyes' leading to the pot. This shallow pot, once charged with layers of coal and limestone, was clamped over with small stones surmounted by cut turves of grass, added so that the correct temperature could be achieved during firing. 'Oval clamp kilns' were fashionable in the early 19th century, with their virtues extolled by John Farey in his book on the minerals and agriculture of Derbyshire.[24] Eventually it was realised that they were no more efficient that the region's circular 'running kilns'.[25] About 30 oval kilns were known in 1995 when first studied, but now significantly more have been identified by fieldwork.

Fig 5.11
On the crest of Litton Edge there is a fine example of an 'oval clamp kiln' with triple draught-openings at the edge of a shallow limestone quarry (right), with a circular clamp kiln behind.
[John Barnatt]

6

Minerals from the ground

The Peak is rich in minerals of value to people in the past as well as the present. These range from metal ores, including those of lead, zinc and copper that are found in and around the central limestone plateau, to coal and associated fireclay and ganister that have been mined on the gritstone uplands to the east and west (Fig 6.1).

In addition to the mines there are important smelting sites and places where timber was grown and prepared for fuel. Industrial features again add vital elements to the character of the cultural landscape. Those places named in Chapter 6 are shown on Figure A1.4 (*see* p 229).

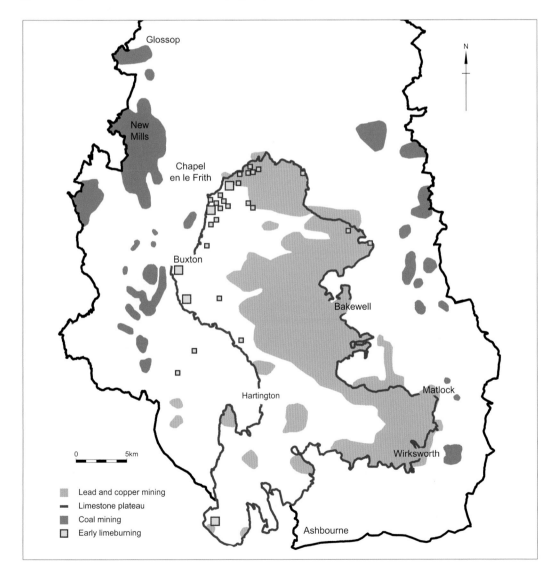

Fig 6.1
The distribution of the main lead and copper mining locations in relation to the limestone plateau, with coal mining beyond to the east and west. Early limeburning centres discussed in Chapter 7 are also shown, with a distinction drawn between major (large-square) and minor (small-square) examples.

Metal mining

The Derbyshire lead orefield has been one of the most important in Britain, with extraction starting in earnest in the Roman period, reaching a climax in the 16th and 17th centuries, and continuing into the 20th century.[1] The ores are found both in veins, the larger of these termed 'rakes', and in irregular deposits of various types traditionally known as 'pipes' and 'flats' (Fig 6.2). Mining took place across the orefield as a whole from early to modern times. Traditional Derbyshire mineral laws allowed lead miners to extract ores from land irrespective of who owned it.[2] Over the centuries a wealth of fascinating dialect mining terms evolved; without knowing these, the modern researcher would be forgiven for thinking the historic texts being studied were written in a foreign language.[3]

In the 16th to 17th century, lead mining was in crisis as the main veins had been taken out down to the water table and the bottoms of workings now flooded. Local miners introduced new infrastructure and technology to make ongoing extraction viable. Given the dissected topography of the region, often the easiest way to lower the water was to drive a level, known as a sough, from a nearby valley. Later, waterwheels were used for pumping but these were not as commonly used as elsewhere, for often there was no available water to drive the wheel unless the mine entrance was in one of the major valleys. Most miners had to wait until the 18th century and the invention of the steam engine to provide a realistic means of pumping below the horizon soughs could reach.

Another solution in the 16th and 17th centuries, used to access ores that previously were hard to exploit, was the reintroduction of an old mining technique known as 'firesetting', which was the application of intense heat to rock to fracture it. Limestone is a very hard rock to remove if all you have are hand picks and chisels, thus firesetting allowed thin ore deposits to be followed by removing adjacent stone deposits, which previously had been ignored whilst ever there had been richer pickings. However, in the 1660s the use of gunpowder for blasting rock was introduced into the region at Ecton and Cromford Sough. As this became more readily available it revolutionised mining across the

Fig 6.2
Typical well-preserved lead-mine waste hillocks on Wellfield Rake below Carder Low north of Hartington.
[John Barnatt]

orefield from the early 18th century onwards, for rock could be broken with relative ease and the extraction process became quicker. In the second half of the 19th century output increased exponentially with the introduction of compressed air for drilling shotholes. New techniques to smelt ores were also developed, allowing lower-grade ores to be processed. Bonfires on hilltops and other draughty places started to be replaced in the mid-16th century by smelting heaths with waterwheels producing the draught; in the 18th century a further change came when cupola furnaces were introduced.[4]

In the 19th century large mines, which often had steam-powered pumping and winding engines, reached depths where the cost of pumping and extraction infrastructure increasingly made them unprofitable (Fig 6.3). By the 1890s many mines closed as they could not compete with cheap lead that was coming in ever-greater quantities from other parts of the world. There was one notable exception, Millclose Mine near Darley Bridge, which has significant pipe deposits deep under the Derwent Valley that were worked to 1939.[5]

From the 17th century onwards larger mines required funding to cover the cost of expensive drainage and haulage, often provided by the local nobility, landed gentry, industrialists and tradespeople. In the 19th century there was a growing trend for shareholders inexperienced in mining to invest in mines they knew little about in the hope of 'getting rich quick'; for the most part investment in mines proved to be a liability rather than providing income.

Running parallel with 'professional' mining, there were many people working in mines part-time, taking full advantage of the traditional mine laws that allowed this irrespective of who owned the land. These 'miner-farmers' continued mining throughout the history of the orefield, working small mines to supplement incomes and in the expectation of rich returns. Even full-time miners needed a second source of income because if they failed to find the ore that a mine owner had agreed to pay for, then they would starve if they had no small holding or other way of making money.

The archaeological remains of the lead-mining industry, despite radical destruction through much of the 20th century, still retain great interest where remaining extant and are of vital importance in defining the character of the region, both at surface and in many places still explorable underground (Fig 6.4).[6]

Fig 6.3
A small 1870 engine house for a steam engine that both pumped water and wound ore, at Ashton's Mine, at Pin Dale near Castleton.
[John Barnatt]

Whilst the main product of the Derbyshire orefield has traditionally been lead, zinc from the same veins has been processed in smaller quantities, whilst fluorspar has been sold as a smelting flux since the 18th century. Blue John, a banded fluorspar from Blue John Mine, Treak Cliff Cavern and other mines near Castleton, has been used for ornaments and jewellery for over 200 years.[7]

Copper ores have been found in large quantities at Ecton and to a lesser extent in various other places in the Staffordshire uplands, where it is found together with lead and zinc ores in veins and pipe deposits.[8] Ecton has provided only the second example in England of copper mining in prehistory,[9] dating to about 2000 to 1600 BC, whilst between the 1740s and 1780s the Duke of Devonshire's Deep Ecton Mine was one of richest in the country and eventually reached a staggering 300m below river level, which is roughly 100m below sea level.[10] Those parts of the Ecton Mines with surface remains and accessible underground remains are of exceptional archaeological importance.

Fig 6.4
The Peak orefield,
traditionally primarily
mined for lead and centred
on the outcropping
limestone, has had many
of its surface waste heaps
removed with less than
25 per cent remaining in
relatively good condition.

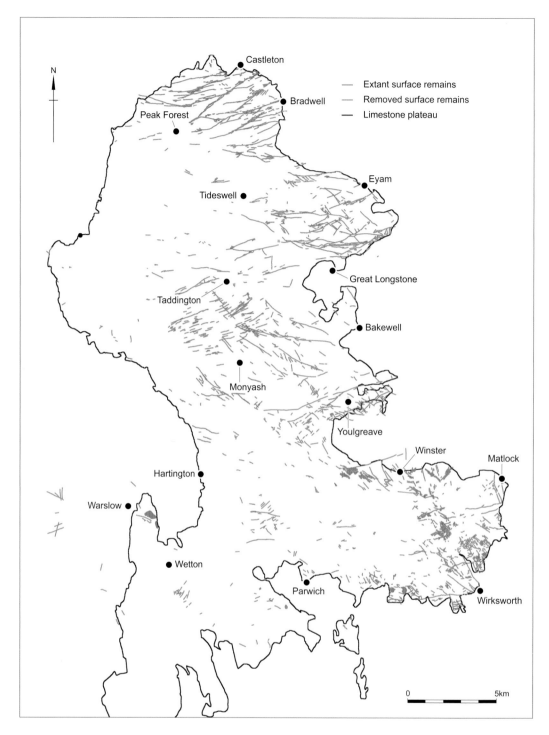

The coal mines of the Peak are little known to the general public but include nationally important archaeological remains.[11] The seams are relatively poor quality or thin compared with the best coal in adjacent major coalfields located to the east and west in adjacent foothills and lowlands.[12] Peak coal mining started in medieval times and reached its height in the 18th century as the demand for coal increased hand in hand with local industries such as limeburning, as well as a growing need for house coal. Increasingly through the 19th century, local workings were abandoned as transport networks improved and better coal could be imported from the nearby lowland mines. Whilst the Peak mines were relatively small, many archaeological features have survived where the surface remains are on moorland, whereas in the lowlands only rare isolated survivals exist. On the moors, the seams exploited were close below surface and many shafts were sunk as mining followed the seam; thus, at the larger sites used over long periods, whilst production and workforces were small, there can be in excess of a hundred hollows at run-in shafts, usually with associated mounds of shaft-sinking waste. Thus, the archaeological character is very different from that at deep mines in the main coalfields. Unlike the metal mines, old underground coal workings should never be explored because of the danger of poisonous and flammable gases.

At some coal mines the seat earth immediately beneath the seam, in the form of fireclay and ganister, was also mined.[13] Extraction of these was common from the later 18th century onwards, with ganister crushed and used for crucible making for the steel industry, and the fire clays used for firebrick production.

Wood had mining-related uses. Charcoal was produced for iron and lead smelting, with notable examples of platforms where the charcoal was made still to be found in woodlands at Gradbach behind The Roaches and in the Upper Derwent Valley.[14] Kiln-dried wood, traditionally known as 'white coal', was used for lead smelting and several kilns still exist in woodlands along the sides of the Derwent Valley.[15]

The archaeological survivals of lead mining in the Peak range from surface and underground remains at the mines themselves, to drainage levels and smelting sites. They include not only worked veins and waste hillocks but also a variety of mine buildings and the sites of horse-drawn engines, waterwheels and steam engines, and also ore dressing and smelting structures.

Rakes, scrins, pipes and flats

To use Derbyshire miners' terminology, a 'rake' is a large mineral vein in a fault, a 'scrin' is a small offshoot or minor mineralised fault fracture, whilst a 'pipe' is a cover-all term for irregular mineral deposits, and a 'flat' is a horizontal mineralised horizon. There are many important surviving archaeological sites, both at surface and underground.[16] Rakes have wide mineral deposits, often 1m to 5m across, which run deep into the ground; not all was lead ore, which was normally less than about 5 per cent of the whole, with the bulk comprising the non-metallic minerals, commonly fluorspar, barytes and calcite (Fig 6.5).[17] Occasionally the metal ores could belly-out and rich strikes were made.

Scrins are similar to rakes except that the veins were only a few centimetres thick and limestone to the side had to be removed to follow the mineralisation. As with rakes, pipes often contain minerals deposited about 300 million years ago by hot mineralised fluids, but formed in ancient pre-mineralisation caves (Fig 6.6). Other 'pipes' are later caves, part-filled with sediments derived from mineral veins, with galena found in nuggets in the cave clays, sands and gravels. Flats often follow the sedimentary bedding, with minerals deposited in open bedding planes, sometimes where caves have widened them.

Fig 6.5
Rake vein workings at the Coalpit Rake lead mine at Matlock Bath, now better known as Devonshire Cavern. [© Historic England Archive (Paul Deakin Photographic Archive of Mines and Caves, PDA01/03/056/10/11)]

At large rakes, there are sometimes large mined cavities still open, for example at Odin Mine near Castleton, where a surface opencut extends deep underground.[18] At Coalpit Rake at Matlock Bath there are several semi-parallel sets of stopes in an intricate maze. Similarly, pipe workings are sometimes extensive; one at Old Millclose Mine has 16km of passages deep underground, including caverns that were sediment-filled before the miners dug them out. Examples of ancient pipe workings can be visited at the showcaves at the Heights of Abraham above Matlock Bath, formerly known as the Nestus Pipes; similarly, the mined flats at Old Ash Mine near Snitterton are accessible to cavers. Long-term access to pipe and flat workings has been helped by them having rock roofs. In contrast, in vein workings, which at large mines can go down hundreds of metres, miners commonly stacked waste rock above their heads on timbers placed horizontally across the workings to save hauling them to surface; after being there for hundreds of years the timbers have rotted. The stone stacks, now partially or fully collapsed, can sometimes make such places extremely dangerous.[19]

Underground old lead mines have a wealth of archaeological interest, including stopes, stacked waste, levels and shafts. Sometimes there are engine chambers and drainage passages, as well as features to do with ore-winding, water-pumping and ore-processing. Details include for instance narrow-gauge tramways, ladders and inscriptions.

At surface, the mine sites are equally interesting, with a variety of mine entrances, hillocks and buildings, with occasional features such as the 'gin circles' where horses walked in a circle turning timber winding drums, and stone-lined troughs known as 'buddles' where ore was processed. The hillocks themselves are of great interest as they tell us much about what was being done. Some are made up of discarded waste minerals that had little ore in them. Often they comprise finely crushed mineral dumped after the ore had been extracted by sieving or buddling. Others are made up of only limestone when shafts or levels were being created in unproductive ground.

Battles with water and ore-winding from depth

In the struggle with water at depth, miners devised two important ways of combatting this, driving horizontal soughs to drain water into a nearby valley, and using engines to pump water up shafts to surface or to pumpways that led, like soughs, to nearby valleys.[20] A few large pumping engines were horse- or water-powered, but the majority were powered by steam.

The earliest lead-mine soughs in the Peak date to the first half of the 17th century (Fig 6.7). They continued to be driven until the late 19th century, as with the impressive Magpie Sough driven with high explosives. Some were only designed to reach specific mines. Others were more impressive schemes aimed at draining whole areas of the orefield, as at Stoke, Hillcarr and Meerbrook, which entered the Derwent respectively near Stoke Hall north of Calver, between Rowsley and Darley Bridge, and between Cromford and Whatstandwell (Fig 6.8). Often the sough drivers had agreements with mines that they would be paid 'compensation' according to how much the sough lowered the water table. Some soughs still function hundreds of years after they were driven; others have blockages and the water has backed up.

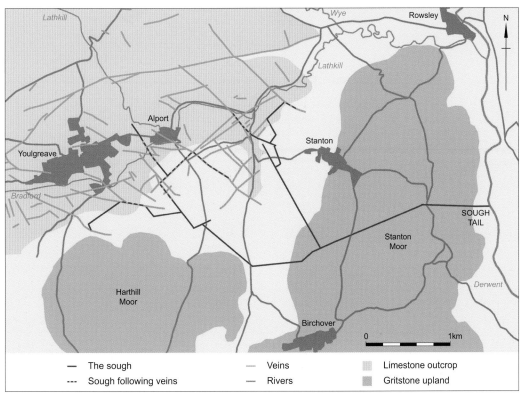

Fig 6.8
Hillcarr Sough was one of the most ambitious drainage levels in the lead orefield, driven from a tail next to the River Derwent and passing under Stanton Moor to the Alport mining field. The sough had various branches, some of which followed veins, reaching them at depth. These veins had been mined previously from surface where the limestone bedrock was exposed, with the miners using the sough branches to follow the mineralisation under the overlying shales.

97

The earliest steam pumping engines are of 18th-century date and were of a type first developed by the ironmonger and engineer Thomas Newcomen from Devon early in the century. Whilst there were 44 Newcomen engine installations at metal mines in the Peak, built between 1717 and 1825, none of their engine houses have survived in good condition. One of the few with any surface remains was archaeologically excavated in 2010–13 at Watergrove Mine near Foolow (Fig 6.9).[21] It is known from documentation that it was installed in 1794–5 and worked intermittently to 1819. It was anticipated before excavation that it would be an essentially single-phased structure but this proved not to be the case. Although everything had been reduced to footings, except the lower part of the end wall of the engine house adjacent to the shaft, which is still over 2m high, it was possible to identify five phases of build, alteration and demolition. These included the initial build, which comprised a tall engine house, with coal chute upslope to the east and opposite an

external circular boiler plinth on the downslope side. This plinth supported a type of boiler known as a 'haystack' and had an adjacent square chimney to the west side. The boiler was replaced, probably in 1803, by a rectangular 'waggon' boiler on the upslope side, with adjacent square chimney and shovelling floor, which in turn were replaced by a larger 'haystack' boiler, new chimney and coal hopper in 1819. A small lean-to building was added to the north side of the engine house after it ceased to be used for pumping. In the 1850s to 1870s everything was demolished.

An exceptional engine house still stands high on Ecton Hill (Fig 6.10). This was erected in 1788 and held one of the first ever mine winding engines, built by the firm of Boulton and Watt, the well-known engine designers based in Birmingham, to a design by James Watt.[22] It wound ore from deep in the mine, which was unloaded underground at river level, taken down the pumpway towards the surface and then brought up a short shaft to the dressing floors.

Fig 6.9
The excavated features at the Watergrove Mine, including the 1794–5 Newcomen engine house (A), its original 'haystack' boiler base, ash pit and chimney base (B), the original coal chute and a later coal hopper (C), the ash pit, shovelling floor and chimney bases for later 'waggon' and 'haystack' boilers (D), a 1794–5 paved path (E), a late stone-floored outbuilding abutted to the engine house (F) and the capped engine shaft (G).

*Fig 6.10 (opposite, top) This building high on Ecton Hill was erected in 1788 for a Boulton and Watt steam engine and is the oldest surviving well-preserved mine winding engine house in the world.
[John Barnatt]*

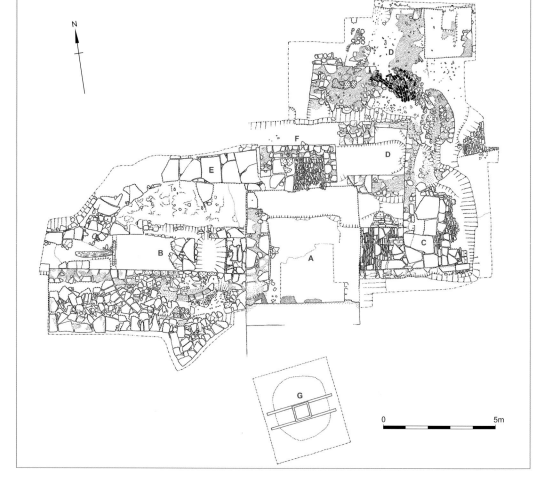

Although a second storey to one side was removed after the engine house was converted to a field barn, the rest of the building remains intact. One half contained the pumping engine with vertical cylinder, the other the boiler, whilst outside was a large horizontally placed winding drum. Archaeological excavations in 2012–14 revealed the footings of the basement plinth within the building that supported the engine, whilst outside investigations showed that the boilers had been replaced twice and new chimney and flue arrangements put in place.[23] Whilst the original engine was kept in repair and worked until the 1850s, the original copper 'haystack' boiler was replaced by a larger one in 1809, presumably of riveted iron, and then again by a rectangular one of 'waggon-type' in the early 1820s. The only other Boulton and Watt engine in the Peak was at Ashover, installed to pump water in 1779–81; this is long gone.

Deep under Ecton Hill, reached by a long pumpway at river level, there were unusual engines installed in the 1780s (Fig 6.11).

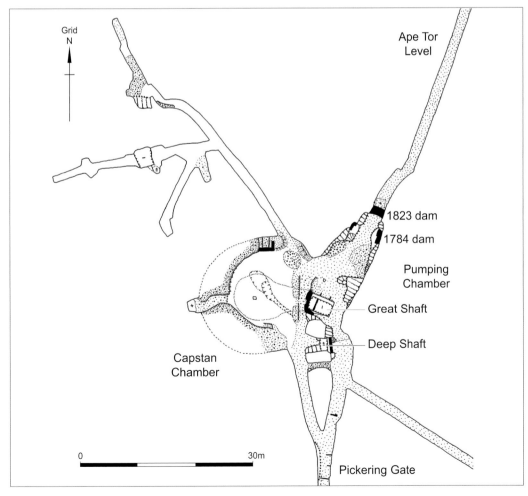

Fig 6.11
The underground chambers at river level in Deep Ecton Mine. Deep Shaft was finished in 1773 and used for winding ore up to this horizon. It was then taken towards surface along Pickering Gate. Adjacent to these, two large chambers were created from 1780 to 1784, primarily for pumping water up the then-new Great Shaft. Ape Tor Level was driven at this date to bring water from the River Manifold to operate a water-powered pumping engine in the eastern chamber; this was replaced by a massive waterwheel in 1823. The west chamber, later partially backfilled, had a machine, called 'the capstan' by the miners, which lowered equipment down the shaft.

One was worked by water brought from the river down a long tunnel, replaced in 1823 by a massive waterwheel. An adjacent engine was designed both for horse winding and as a capstan operated by miners. In contrast, at nearby Clayton Mine there was a series of steam engines installed deep underground from 1814 to the 1880s; such arrangements are rare because of the inherent problems of preventing fumes suffocating miners.

Several large 19th-century pumping engine houses remain in the Peak, including impressive examples at Magpie Mine near Sheldon, Mandale Mine in Lathkill Dale and Watt's Engine House at Old Millclose Mine near Darley Bridge. Another, at High Rake near Little Hucklow, had disappeared from view until excavated in 2000–08 (Fig 6.12).[24] It had an unusual and relatively early Peak example of a Cornish-type engine, installed in 1844 to a design by the engineer James Sims of Cornwall. This had a large low-pressure cylinder and a smaller high-pressure cylinder above. The lower cylinder was set in a deep basement and this had survived demolition of the engine house in the 1920s. Nearby there were the remains of the boiler house, chimney and balance bob, a cobbled coal yard, a platform for a capstan later used for a horse-drawn engine, and a horse-drawn ore crusher. To the north were the footings of an 1847 winding engine with boiler house and chimney, and various stone structures on a dressing floor of the same date. The mine failed to find rich ore deposits at depth, which were assumed to exist in limestone below a thick deposit of volcanic rock; it may be that they were in a volcanic vent that went to the core, and the mine was abandoned in 1852.

Fig 6.12

The excavated features in the southern part of High Rake Mine, centred at the 1844 Sims pumping engine house. The reconstruction drawing shows this, with its twin cylinders (A), cast iron beam (B), pump rods (C) and condenser pit (D).

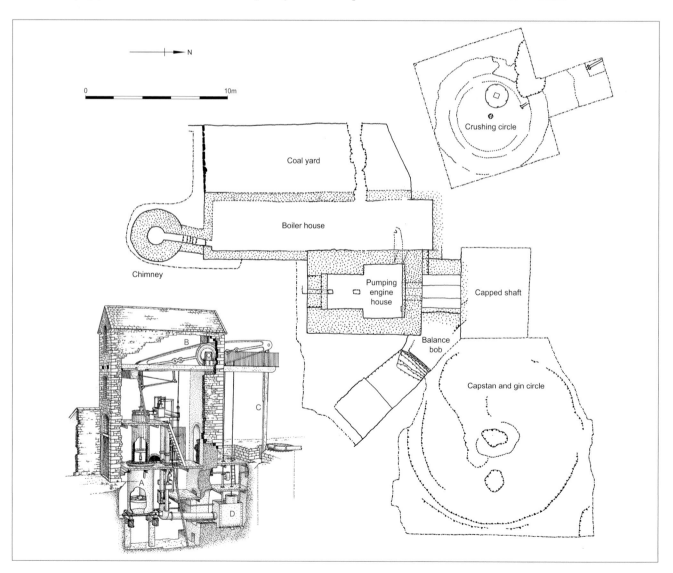

Magpie Mine

At the heart of this evocative site located south of Sheldon, the 1868 pumping engine house towers above a diverse range of other ruined buildings.[25] There has been mining here since the late 17th century and probably before; however, Magpie Mine came into its own in the 19th century. As is often the case it has a history of intermittent mining, with new generations of miners coming back to try their luck as technology improved or because it had been forgotten just how hopeless a working it was. Magpie was revived from 1800 with the mine agent from the 1820s being the local mining entrepreneur William Wyatt, who was involved in ventures across the orefield, including High Rake described above. In 1839 John Taylor, Britain's most respected mine

manager of the day, took charge and worked the mine to 1846. It opened again in 1868 when a Sheffield consortium led by the entrepreneur John Fairbairn invested heavily before all was sold in 1883. There followed several short-lived and unsuccessful operations, the last of which was in the 1950s.

What remains today is the most iconic mining site in the Peak (Figs 6.13 and 6.14). Originally some of the mines here, as at Maypits, Redsoil, Horsesteps and Dirty Redsoil, were independent ventures to Magpie Mine and only later was the title consolidated. One of the earliest recognisable features is the engine shaft with adjacent gin circle at Shuttlebark Shaft at the western end of the site, which dates to about 1760. The first Magpie Mine winding engine was installed in 1801, when the shaft was 360ft (110m) deep.

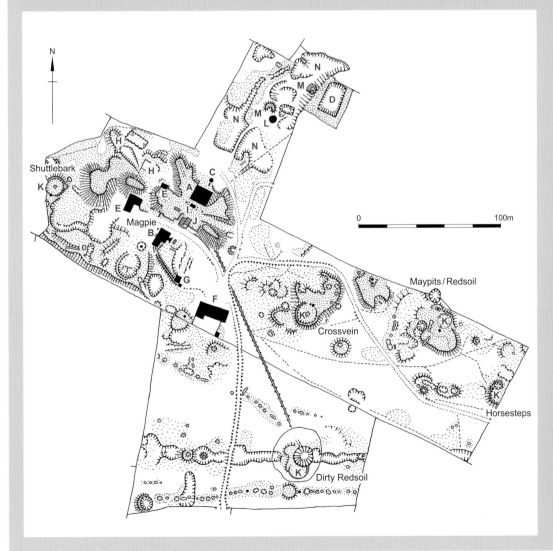

Fig 6.13
The surviving features centred on Magpie Mine. The features include the 1868 pumping engine house (A) and winding house (B), an 1840 chimney first built for an earlier engine (C), the engine house reservoir (D), the 1870 ore-crusher house and ore house (E), the 1840 office and smithy (F), a second 1840 chimney and one end of its boiler house (G), the dressing floor, settling ponds and waste heaps (H), the main shaft and 1950s' headframe (I), the 1950s' winding shed (J), five gin circles (K), the powder house (L), two limekilns (M) and quarries (N).

Fig 6.14
Magpie Mine is the most visually impressive set of lead-mine remains in the Peak, with extant built structures dating from the 1840s to the 1950s. The large pumping engine house was built in the late 1860s.
[John Barnatt]

Other good examples of hillock-top gin circles to the east include the 480ft (146m) deep Crossvein Shaft of 1833, whilst beyond is the 420ft (128m) deep Redsoil Engine Shaft of 1831. When this shaft was sunk Redsoil was an independent mine to Magpie and there were protracted disputes between the two, which culminated in 1833 when three of the Redsoil miners died, smoked out by the Magpie miners, several of whom were tried for murder. They were acquitted, it is believed, because Wyatt could afford better legal representation than the Redsoil men.

Three structures from Taylor's time remain, all dating to 1840. The mine office and smithy, which form a single building, have been re-roofed and are now a field study centre, whilst there is a round chimney for the pumping house and square chimney for the winding house, with these engine houses now both largely removed.[26] The 1840 pumping house was the second on site; the first was for a pumping engine of Newcomen type, built in 1825 two years after the engine shaft was started, and the last of this engine design erected in the orefield; it was idle by 1830.

Two of the three 1868–70 engine houses held steam pumping and winding engines, whilst the third was for a small engine that drove stone rollers for crushing ore. They reflect the high investment needed to mine at increasing depth; the shaft reached its full depth of 684ft (208m) in 1882. To alleviate the high cost of pumping water to surface, a sough from the side of the River Wye about 1.6km away to the north was started in 1873 and finished in 1881, reaching the engine shaft at 575ft (175m) down. Even with this taking away the water, the mine did not pay and it was closed soon afterwards.

The mine dressing floor was to the north-west of the main shaft, associated with two dressing ponds and a buddle dam, with nearby low mounds of mineral clay that comprise waste material from the last stages of dressing. To the north, on higher ground, is a now-dry reservoir for the steam engines, whilst at the irregular ground between it and the pumping engine house are the stone quarries for the 1820s' to 1860s' buildings, with two small associated limekilns for producing the lime mortar. There is also a circular powder house of Cornish design, set aside from the main buildings in case of explosion.

The headframe over the shaft, and the adjacent tin shed containing a winder comprising a fishing trawler engine and drum, date to the 1950s. The ground level at the shaft top was heightened in the 20th century; originally the 1868 engine house would have appeared more imposing.

In many ways Magpie Mine is atypical in that most lead mines in the Peak had only hillocks and small buildings at surface, as with the well-preserved hillocks seen on site and continuing to the south and west. In several important senses it is such hillocks rather than imposing buildings that are the important mining archaeology, telling much about lead mining in the Peak.

Hillock today, gone tomorrow

From analysis of aerial photographs it is estimated that only about a quarter of the metal-mine hillocks present in the Peak at the turn of the twentieth century still remained 100 years later (*see* Fig 6.4).[27] Losses have commonly resulted from both agricultural 'improvement' and removal by mineral operators wanting to reprocess them for fluorspar and barytes; this dual threat has put the mining remains amongst the archaeological features at greatest risk in the region. Over the last two decades there have been concerted efforts by conservation agencies to secure the future of key sites by designation, when of national importance, and also more generally through voluntary conservation agreements and the good will of landowners.[28] It has been recognised that the resource is so diverse, with multiple cultural and natural aspects to the conservation interest, ranging from landscape character through archaeology, social, economic and industrial history, to geology and ecology, that in many cases the removal of specific sites takes away the only places where particular facets of interest remain. Consequently, an inventory of 292 sites of significant national and regional conservation interest at surface has been drawn up,[29] with a further 42 where this is confined to underground interest.[30]

The northern part of the orefield has good examples illustrating survival and loss at large veins where miners dug deep workings, created extensive hillocks and built a variety of structures. Two of the best survivals are Tideslow Rake north of Tideswell and Oxlow Rake north-east of Peak Forest. The former has been worked from medieval times if not before until the 19th century, leaving opencuts along the vein and massive hillocks to the sides, with occasional other features such as old water-leat and pond earthworks. Careful study of the remains shows that what is visible today is primarily 19th century in date, resulting from reworking hillocks to recover residual amounts of ore left by previous generations, with all anticipated earlier features such as gin circles and dressing floors badly damaged or removed. The opencut sides are much earlier, but it is unclear whether these sides have always been visible or have been unburied during later activity. Further east, the same vein has been heavily reworked in the 20th century; the important archaeological survivals here, at High Rake noted above, were recently uncovered by the Peak District Mines Historical Society.[31]

Oxlow Rake is similar, but there is more of a palimpsest of remaining features of different dates and functions. Although there has been much later reworking, the larger mines along it can still be recognised from their hillock character. There are also leat and pond earthworks, small ruined sheds, an ore-washing hopper and ore-dressing hillocks known as buddle dams.

In contrast, at Dirtlow Rake nearby and at Moss Rake west of Bradwell very little of interest has survived 20th-century ravages (Fig 6.15). The exceptions are a small archaeologically excavated mine complex on Dirtlow Rake with shed, crushing circle and buddles at How Grove.[32] A gin circle remains at Hazard Mine at the top end of the rake. There are also opencuts, hillocks, ponds and a robbed crushing circle at the very west end of Moss Rake. Examination of detailed Ordnance Survey maps surveyed in the 1890s is useful in that it shows many more then-remaining features at the abandoned mines, spaced at intervals along both veins, including small buildings, gin circles, crushing circles and ponds.

A further contrast is provided by extensive hillocks surviving in the southern part of the orefield. At Bonsall Lees, centred on Slaley Corner, there are many smaller hillocks and capped shafts on a multitude of semi-parallel veins documented

Fig 6.15
Examples of large lead mines that have now been largely removed, as shown on Ordnance Survey maps revised in 1897. All has now gone to fluorspar extraction at the central section of Moss Rake on Bradwell Moor, while only opencuts and shafts have survived reworking at the north-eastern end of Dirtlow Rake. At the south-western end of Dirtlow Rake little remains today of the large Hazard and Hollandtwine mines, except the walled gin circle and shaft at the south side of the former.

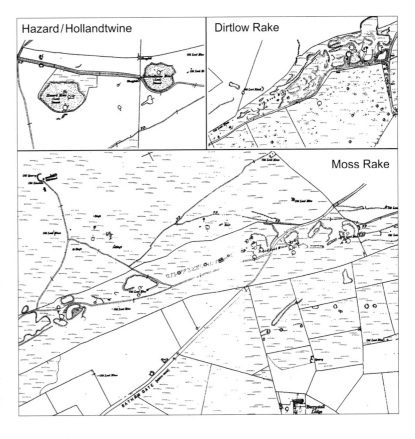

Fig 6.16
Extensive and for the most part well-preserved lead-mine remains at a complex swarm of veins around Slaley Corner on Bonsall Lees, mostly within post-medieval enclosures just beyond the medieval fields of Bonsall (bottom right). Some of the fields have been 'improved', but here slighted hillocks can sometimes still be made out. [© Derrick Riley]

as worked from medieval time onwards (Fig 6.16). Here there are ruined sheds, walled hillock-top dressing floors, and small stone ore-washing troughs known as 'buddles'. At the Dunnington Mines west of Elton there is an area with interlinked hillocks over a broad area, where miners worked an extensive 'pipe' close to surface. Similarly, extensive remains are found on Carsington Pasture and nearby west of Brassington, where there is more of a mixture of vein and pipe hillocks.

Exploring hidden worlds

Some underground mines created in the search for minerals over the last 2,000 years can still be explored. For most people this hidden world is only occasionally glimpsed. The earliest known metal mines in the Peak are at the Earlier Bronze Age copper workings at Ecton. There are also accessible ancient lead workings of Roman or medieval date around Matlock Bath. However, the majority of still-accessible mines were created in post-medieval times. Exploration presents an evocative if sometimes uncomfortable experience unlike anything at surface. This short section of text gives five examples to show something of the range of underground workings that can be explored, some easy to access as they are show mines/ caves open to the public, others only accessible with specialist equipment and accompanied by experienced explorers.

Nestus Pipes

These are an ancient set of lead mines, parts of which are open today at the Heights of Abraham at Matlock Bath as the Great Masson and Rutland Caverns (Fig 6.17).[33] The workings here are first documented in 1467 but by then were already extensive. Miners revisited it over the next 400 years, looking for lead that had been missed and extended the workings a long distance to the north-west beyond the area shown in the figure. The galleries were reworked again in the early to mid-20th century when fluorspar was extracted; parts were wholly removed by opencasting later in the century. Fluorspar as well as lead had long been taken from these mines, for it is documented as going to Ecton as a smelting flux in the late 18th century. The earliest workings have very distinctive pickwork, nicknamed 'woodpecker work', where a small pick with handle or a chisel was used to carefully remove the lead in lumps so that it could easily be smelted in early hearths known as 'boles'.

Fig 6.17
The south-eastern and central parts of the Nestus Pipes on Masson Hill, where evidence for medieval lead mining can be seen in the form of distinctive pickwork known as 'woodpecker work'. Parts of these extensive pipeworkings leading off Bacon Rake are open to the public.

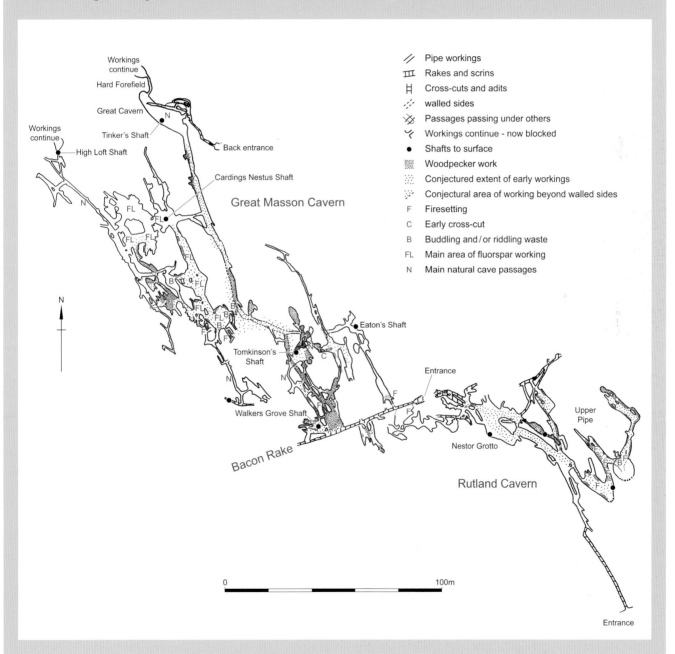

Old Ash Mine

This mineral working in Northern Dale near Snitterton is another ancient lead mine (Fig 6.18).[34] Here miners had followed cave passages developed along mineralised bedding, taking out lead ores from the passage sides using the ancient technique of firesetting to remove limestone, thus making the extensions high enough to enter. Radiocarbon dating of the twigs used to light the coal fires indicate the firesetting is likely to have taken place in the 16th to 17th centuries AD. This is not an easy mine to explore, involving low crawls, tight squeezes and good route-finding skills in order to avoid deep drops.

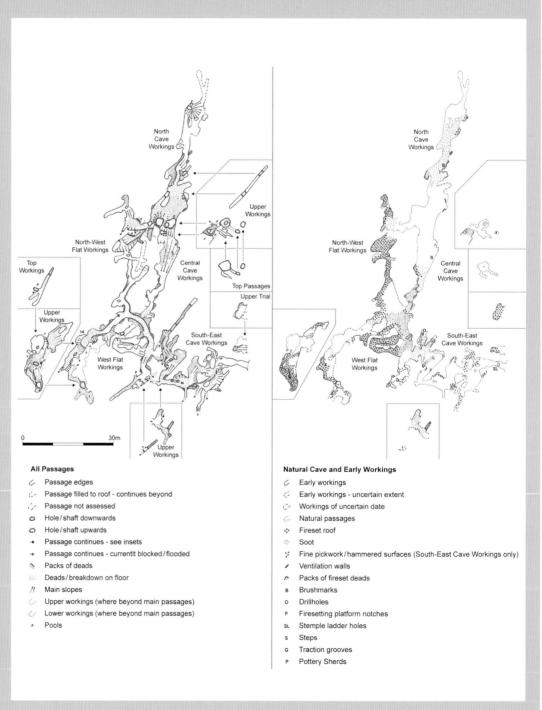

All Passages

- ⌐ Passage edges
- ⌐: Passage filled to roof - continues beyond
- ⌐: Passage not assessed
- ⌀ Hole / shaft downwards
- ⌀ Hole / shaft upwards
- → Passage continues - see insets
- → Passage continues - currentlt blocked / flooded
- ⌐ Packs of deads
- ⁘ Deads / breakdown on floor
- ⁄⁄ Main slopes
- ⌐ Upper workings (where beyond main passages)
- ⌐ Lower workings (where beyond main passages)
- ⌐ Pools

Natural Cave and Early Workings

- ⌐ Early workings
- ⌐: Early workings - uncertain extent
- ⌐· Workings of uncertain date
- ⌐ Natural passages
- ⁙ Fireset roof
- ⁘ Soot
- ⁛ Fine pickwork / hammered surfaces (South-East Cave Workings only)
- ⌐ Ventilation walls
- ⌐ Packs of fireset deads
- B Brushmarks
- D Drillholes
- F Firesetting platform notches
- SL Stemple ladder holes
- S Steps
- G Traction grooves
- P Pottery Sherds

Fig 6.18
Old Ash Mine, showing all passages, including natural cave, early workings and 18th- to 19th-century mining where gunpowder was utilised (left). The early workings, of 16th- and 17th-century AD date, using firesetting are extensive (right).

Speedwell Mine

This lead mine near Castleton at the northern edge of the limestone plateau has an ambitious underground canal driven in 1771 to 1782 as a then state-of-the-art way of taking out ore from deep underground (Fig 6.19 and 6.20).[35] It was accessed via a shaft and nearby incline. The canal led to a major cave system deep under the high limestone upland that rises steeply above the entrance, which had intersected several mineral veins that previously had been worked closer to surface. From the canal a series of raised plankways over underground streams allowed access through the cave passages. The mineral deposits proved disappointing here and by 1802 at latest the canal was opened to the paying public as a tourist attraction. A boat trip today still goes as far as the Bottomless Pit, a natural chamber intersected by the canal.

Fig 6.19
The ambitious underground canal at Speedwell Mine was driven in 1771–82. Here an original ore boat lies on the bottom with its back broken. [© Jon Humble]

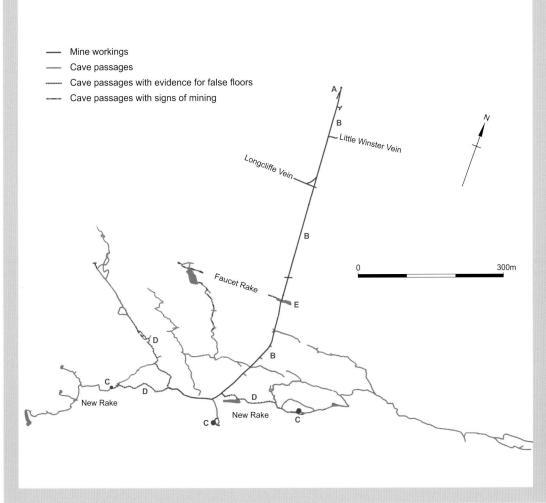

— Mine workings
— Cave passages
---- Cave passages with evidence for false floors
— Cave passages with signs of mining

Fig 6.20
Speedwell Mine, with the main natural cave passages and mined passages (with upper natural passages omitted for clarity). From the entrance incline and shaft (A) the canal extends for over 800m (B). Three main places have been identified where ore-rich sediments in cave passages and in-situ mineralisation were mined (C). False floors on timber beams were laid to help move ore to the canal (D). The present tourist trip stops at the Bottomless Pit (E).

Clayton Mine

A long, wet and cold trek down a level that drains water from this mine leads to a chamber of exceptional interest, one of several highlights at the internationally important and extensive accessible working at Ecton Hill (Figs 6.21 and 6.22).[36] Here there is a deep shaft forming the main way down into later 18th- and 19th-century workings that went down nearly 300m below river level. From 1814 onwards a series of steam engines were installed in the chamber to bring up ore and keep the mine clear of water. In the 1880s there were three engines here, a large one winding ore and pumping water, another producing compressed air for shothole drilling and ventilation, and a third for electric lighting. The challenge with having boilers underground was how to prevent the smoke suffocating the miners. A series of flues, chimneys and air doors were installed, which allowed the smoke to be let into older workings going near-vertically to surface high on the hill.

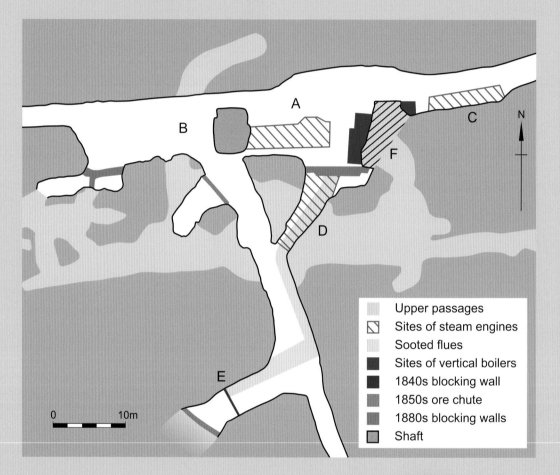

Upper passages
Sites of steam engines
Sooted flues
Sites of vertical boilers
1840s blocking wall
1850s ore chute
1880s blocking walls
Shaft

0   10m

Fig 6.21
The main chamber in Clayton Mine had a series of steam engines, the sites of which can be identified, with smoke vented into upper passages to surface. Successive engines did the winding and pumping: one dating to 1814, another to the 1840s and three to 1884. They were placed in the main chamber (A) at a point east of the engine shaft going to depth. The area west of the shaft (B) was used for unloading ore brought up the shaft to take it westwards along the main level. In the 1880s two other small engines were installed, one for producing compressed air (C), the other for a dynamo (D) used for electric lighting in the main chamber. This is the earliest known accessible underground archaeological evidence for the use of electricity in a mine anywhere in Britain. The side chamber used for the dynamo had probably been created for the 1814 boiler and later contained a flue from the 1840s' boiler in the main chamber. This flue can still be identified from sooting, running to a wooden blocking wall across a side passage going upwards (E). In contrast, the first engine had its boiler smoke taken away in cast-iron pipes. At the end of the chamber a massive chimney base was built in 1884 (F), which supported four vertical boilers with pipes leading through the wall to an old working rising behind. There are also ore chutes and stone-built blocking walls dating to the 1850s and 1880s.

Fig 6.22
*Around the corner
from the main engine
chamber at Clayton
Mine at Ecton, this late
18th-century passage
was adapted in the
1880s to contain a small
steam engine bolted to
the floor that produced
compressed air for rock
drilling and ventilation.
Steam was produced in
a vertical boiler set on
the wall beyond, which is
the back of the chimney
base that took the fumes
up into old workings
above. The walls were
whitewashed to make
it lighter and thus easier
to work the machinery.
[© Historic England
Archive (Paul Deakin
Photographic Archive
of Mines and Caves
PDA01/03/064/15/06)]*

Moorland coal

The gritstone moorlands to the east and west sides of the Peak have a variety of surface remains that tell of past mining for coal and associated products, including shafts with associated waste heaps, ruined engine houses, access causeways and tramways.

Western moors

Parts of the Peak's western moorlands have extensive coal-mining remains, often comprising hollows at the sites of shafts with surrounding mounds formed where miners dumped the shaft-sinking dirt. There are also, for instance, gin circles, ruined engine houses, sites of adits and sough entrances, causeways linking shafts across marshy ground and access roads.[37] Noteworthy concentrations occur at Ollersett Moor east of New Mills; Combs Moss high above Dove Holes; Goyt's Moss, Thatch Marsh and Orchard Common west of Buxton; Danebower close by in the Upper Dane Valley (Fig 6.23); and Goldsitch Moss north-east of The Roaches.[38] Many of the mines worked the Ringinglow Seam, which was relatively thick and of reasonable quality, whilst others exploited seams higher in the sequence, as at the Yard Seam, a sulphurous coal often used for industrial purposes. Three sites are described to illustrate the character of the moorland coalmines, all with some or all of their surface features on Open Access moorland.

Fig 6.23
At Danebower Colliery in the Upper Dane Valley south-west of Buxton, this chimney stands at the upper end of a flue that came from a steam engine down the hillside and out of sight, from where a cable ran down a shaft and hauled coal up an underground incline. Behind there are trackways that led to other parts of the colliery in the valley bottom.
[John Barnatt]

Thatch Marsh and Goyt's Moss collieries

To the west of Buxton there are mines of exceptional archaeological interest, for the most part worked for the Earls and then Dukes of Devonshire. They lie high on the moors at Thatch Marsh behind Axe Edge, extending southwards onto Orchard Common in Staffordshire where they were in different ownership (Fig 6.24). The coal is the Ringinglow Seam, worked from the late 16th century if not before. Extraction at the more remote Goyt's Moss Colliery at the head of the Goyt Valley, working the Yard Seam, had started by the late 17th century at the latest; a small part to the west was once in Cheshire and until 1778 was owned independently. Production from both seams was at its highest in the 18th and 19th centuries, and at Thatch Marsh continued until 1918.

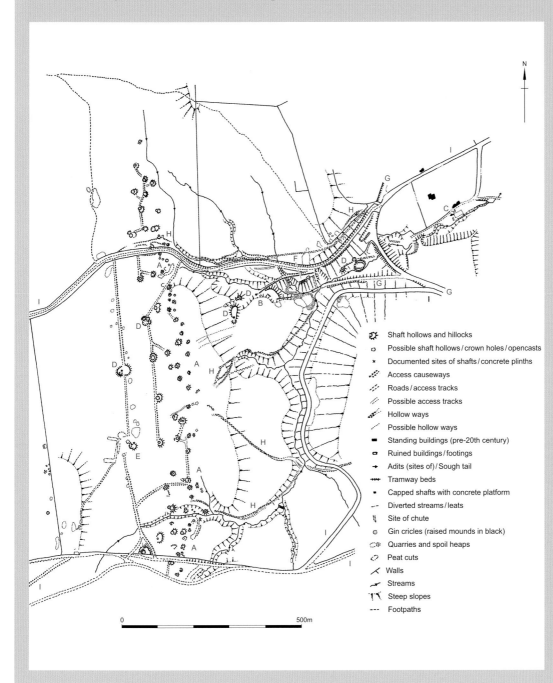

Shaft hollows and hillocks
Possible shaft hollows / crown holes / opencasts
Documented sites of shafts / concrete plinths
Access causeways
Roads / access tracks
Possible access tracks
Hollow ways
Possible hollow ways
Standing buildings (pre-20th century)
Ruined buildings / footings
Adits (sites of) / Sough tail
Tramway beds
Capped shafts with concrete platform
Diverted streams / leats
Site of chute
Gin cricles (raised mounds in black)
Quarries and spoil heaps
Peat cuts
Walls
Streams
Steep slopes
Footpaths

0   500m

Fig 6.24
The northern half of the Thatch Marsh Colliery, with early workings near outcrop (A), the mid-18th-century upper Burbage adit (B), the early 19th-century lower Burbage adit (C), ventilations shafts to the two levels (D), the site of a later 19th-century steam winding engine (E), coking ovens (F), the Cromford and High Peak Railway and a siding (G), various early hollowways (H) and later turnpike roads (I). For the southern half of the colliery, see Figure 8.17.

Coal went to the local domestic market and was burnt in great quantities at the important nearby industrial limeburning complex at Grin Hill (*see* Chapter 7).

Much of the archaeological surface evidence at the Buxton mines relates to close-spaced shaft mining, with 347 to 383 sites of shafts identified, usually with associated waste heaps of sinking dirt. Mining migrated from shaft to adjacent shaft as the seam was followed, with recently redundant ones allowing circulation of air. The earliest and shallowest shafts were hand wound and in places there are associated hollow-ways heading eastwards towards Buxton and Grin Hill. From the second half of the 18th century onwards shafts had horse gins and were linked by access causeways to turnpike roads. Close-spaced shaft mining continued until halfway through the 18th century at Thatch Marsh, until viable shallow coal reserves were exhausted and deeper mining methods were developed. However, at Goyt's Moss the use of close-spaced shafts continued into the mid-19th

century as the coal seam did not go to depth. Technological developments at the Buxton collieries came in the mid-18th century with the driving of soughs and the first long access adit from Burbage; in the later 18th century there was an underground canal here. In the 19th century a still longer adit was driven and coal was extracted via this on tramways. There were a small number of shafts used for ventilation, including two to the south with small fire houses built to improve their air-drawing capability. From the second half of the 19th century steam engines were used for winding, both at a small number of shafts and an inclined drift. At this date coal again was brought out of the upper Burbage adit, which was reused and extended, to bring it underground from Goyt's Moss. Some of this coal was converted to coke in a small bank of kilns. This coal and coke was shipped on the Cromford and High Peak Railway which passed close by (*see also* the case study 'Burbage Colliery' on p 148).

Ollersett Moor Mines

The coal mines here, which worked the Yard Seam, have a long history and there are extensive remains that include 125 to 138 shaft mounds, together with access tracks and gin circles, found in a band where the coal was followed westwards downdip from outcrop, with the workings drained by two or more soughs driven into the hillside from downslope. Mining probably started in the 17th century or earlier, and a rare survival of a detailed account book documents continuous mining from 1711 to 1757. Shallow shaft mining continued into the

early 19th century. At Burnt Edge to the north there are tramways, the sites of three steam engine houses and surviving reservoir ponds at deep shafts that date to the mid-19th century and were used into the 1880s and 1890s. Further south, in the 18th to early 20th centuries mining also extended downdip to the west, with the coal reached via deep shaft mines, including that at Dolly Pit where a steam engine house survives, now converted to a house.[39] A fine early 19th-century engine house for a vertical-cylindered steam engine, later converted to a ventilation fire house, stands on Bings Road at Whaley Bridge.

Combs Moss Colliery

At the centre of the high and bleak Combs Moss between Buxton and Chapel en le Frith there were two clusters of shafts, each with roughly 60 to 65 very close-spaced, systematically arranged shaft mounds. These lie at the north-west and south-east ends of an isolated oval outcrop of the Ringinglow Seam. Here there are also opencast pits, and each cluster has a possible collapsed

adit or sough entrance. Both areas were worked in at least two phases and the colliery is documented as active in the 18th century but may well have earlier origins. Whilst it is tempting to see this colliery providing the limekilns at Dove Holes below to the east, which are documented as active from the early 17th century into the 18th century, hollow-ways lead from the colliery going north-westwards to the farmsteads in the valleys.

Eastern moors

There are coal-mining remains scattered intermittently across the moorlands over much of the eastern gritstone upland, again concentrating on the Ringinglow coal seam, but also including several others in the Millstone Grit and Lower Coal Measure beds.[40] For the most part they comprise small clusters of close-spaced shaft hollows and adjacent upcast mounds, with the occasional linking causeway, sites of adit entrances and gin circles (Fig 6.25). Concentrations with a large number of shafts occur around Ringinglow, Owler Bar, Robin Hood and Beeley Moor.

Fig 6.25
One of several circular hollows at Oaking Clough behind Stanage Edge, located east of the two collieries here given as a case study below, which are at the tops of collapsed coal-mining shafts at a third small remote mine where coal was worked a short distance below surface.
[John Barnatt]

Baslow Colliery

At Robin Hood there are the remains of the largest of the eastern moors mines. To the north of the settlement there are 69 to 82 surviving shaft hollows and mounds, whilst to the south there are 91 to 114. It is likely that coal working here, at the Ringinglow Seam, started in medieval times and was certainly active by 1636. In this year there was an agreement made to drive a sough, probably under the northern workings, whilst another agreement for 1692 may well be for another sough running southwards with its tail still visible today against the Heathy Lea Brook. By 1764 this sough had been extended southwards as far as a point below the boundary of Chatsworth's old deer park and coal working was extended under here in subsequent decades but closed before 1811. Although worked by the same men, this was called 'Chatsworth Park Colliery' as it lay under land owned by the Duke of Devonshire, with royalties paid separately, for all to the north then was held by the Duke of Rutland. North of the deer park a lower level was driven southwards, with water brought up to the upper level using an underground waterwheel probably installed in the late 1780s. By the 1830s mining north of the deer park had ceased, shortly after the land was taken over by the Chatsworth Estate. Further trial workings at the colliery were undertaken by them in the 1870s and during the 1914–18 war.

Stanage Collieries

Above the crest of Stanage Edge, there are two typical small coal mines, but at particularly high and exposed locations, both working in the 18th and/or earlier 19th centuries. To the south at Stanage Pole Colliery, intersected by the late 18th-century Long Causeway, there are 14 to 18 shafts (Fig 6.26). These mostly have adjacent sinking mounds, some linked to the adjacent road by causeways across marshy ground. To the north, behind High Neb on Stanage Edge, there were a further 15 shafts at Stanage Colliery, including a later one to the east with a large hillock for a deep shaft.

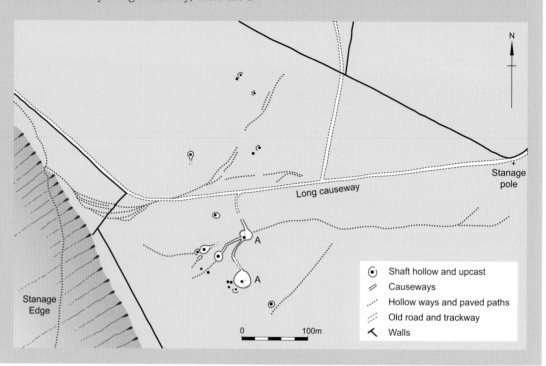

Fig 6.26
The small Stanage Pole Colliery, with hollows at backfilled shafts within sinking-dirt upcast heaps. Some are connected by causeways leading to the Long Causeway road where coal-laden carts turned towards Sheffield. Two of these hillocks (A), where the coal was accessed at its deepest point, are flat-topped and large enough to have had horse gins for winding the coal to surface. The others would have had hand-wound windlasses.

Legend:
- Shaft hollow and upcast
- Causeways
- Hollow ways and paved paths
- Old road and trackway
- Walls

0   100m

Smelting and associated industries

Most of the smelting of ores took place away from the mines themselves, located at places near necessary fuel sources, including coal and wood, or sited beside streams and rivers that powered bellows. Sites used for preparation of fuels include places where charcoal and kiln-dried wood, known as 'white coal', were made.

Processing metals

The way lead has been smelted changed radically through time.[41] Medieval sites known as 'bole hearths' were little more than open-air bonfires, comprising layers of timber and ore. These continued to be used to the late 16th century and these post-medieval boles were sometimes well-organised operations using large boles fired seasonally when weather conditions were right. Only lumps of dressed ore would smelt successfully, whilst that reduced to gravel and finer material would not, but instead dropped down through the fire. Windy sites were required to ensure that the fires became sufficiently hot to melt the ore, thus hilltops and scarp edges were commonly used, although other boles were placed in valleys that funnelled the wind, as shown by the excavated sites at Linch Clough in the Upper Derwent Valley.[42] Slags produced in the boles would be sorted and re-smelted nearby using charcoal to reach the necessary higher temperatures.

From the mid-16th century, a significant development in smelting technology was introduced, known as the 'ore hearth'. Here bellows were used to raise temperatures, often using waterwheels but at some small sites they were operated by hand. 'Ore hearths' were more efficient than boles and smaller-sized ore could be smelted; the normal fuel was 'white coal'.

Slags were again re-smelted, at first using charcoal or coal, with coal and coke becoming dominant from the late 17th century through to the late 18th century when the last 'ore hearths' fell out of use.

A second radical change came from the 1730s onwards with use of 'cupola furnaces'. Lead dust and lower grades of ore could be smelted; coal was used for both the smelting and slag re-smelting. The smelting process at some larger sites of 19th-century date was made more efficient by having long condensing flues where residual lead deposits were periodically scraped out at great risk to the health of the workers given the task.

Smelters were rarely sited at the mines.[43] Ore buyers would visit mines and purchase dressed ore and it would be shipped to smelters located close to where fuel was available and/or from where the smelted product, in ingots known as 'pigs', could easily be shipped to market. Whilst some lead was used locally, much went eastwards to Hull to be shipped elsewhere. The majority of smelting sites were placed near the northern or eastern edges of the orefield, or further east in the Derwent Valley, on the eastern gritstone upland or its eastern foothills. Exact siting preferences changed through time. 'Boles' were often on the eastern gritstone upland because of good opportunities for catching the wind. 'Ore hearths' needed the many streams running into the Derwent or further eastwards to the Don, Rother and Amber, to power their bellows. Often these had coppiced woodland nearby to produce their 'white coal'. 'Cupolas' did not need to be near water and their sites are near local coal sources and transport routes. It is salutary to note that in post-medieval times there was a significant number of smelters putting significant amounts of toxic fumes into the air that were sited upwind of nearby population centres such as Sheffield and Chesterfield.

'Bole hearths' have left few obvious above-ground remains, except for slag deposits, often robbed later for re-smelting, with scattered material sometimes only obvious because plants upon them that tolerate heavy metals grow well; in some places the ground is still bare because of the toxicity. Often others can be identified from 'bole' place names. In one rare instance, at Lodge Moor north of Stanage Edge, there is an intact slag heap. Slags can also be found at sites where they were washed prior to re-smelting. Most 16th- to 18th-century 'ore hearths' have disappeared from sight, presumably as the hearth was placed in timber rather than stone buildings. However, this was not always the case, as witnessed by

ruined stone structures hidden in woodland north of Froggatt that appear to date to the 17th century. Another rectangular ruined building in woodland close to Bar Brook, with leat and header pond, appears to be a slag smelter, but it is uncertain whether this was associated with the 17th- to 18th-century 'ore hearth' upstream, or an 18th-century 'cupola' across the valley. Evidence for 'cupolas' can still be seen, with a fine standing chimney at the 1770 to 1860 Stone Edge smelter on high ground between Rowsley and Chesterfield, and long but ruined flues at Alport, Brough and Crich (Fig 6.27).[44]

From 1764 onwards 'cupolas' and 'calciners' were built at the Ecton copper mines, each with a specific task, processing the copper, lead and lead slags. However, in the 1770s the copper smelting was transferred to Whiston a short way outside the Peak to the south-west. This was close to where the coal needed for fuel was mined in the Duke of Devonshire's own mines and conveniently sited for shipping the processed copper from the Caldon Canal wharf at Froghall in the Churnet Valley near Cheadle. Little remains at Ecton or Whiston except disturbed piles of slag and slag blocks. These rectangular blocks were cast in moulds and were used, for example, at the coal yard floor at the 1788 Boulton and Watt engine house at Ecton.[45] At Whiston there are buildings still standing in the village built from these near-black and sometimes iridescent blocks.

Fig 6.27
In the Hope Valley the flues from the Brough Cupola, opened in 1860, went to a chimney on the hillside above. These have now largely gone, but these earth-covered tunnels remain, where part way up, the flue was taken horizontally and then returned on an adjacent line, to lengthen the flue to improve condensation of lead from the fumes. In the section illustrated the outgoing flue (left) is ruined, but the return (right) is still relatively intact. [John Barnatt]

White coal

Between the mid-16th and 18th century coppiced wood was grown to produce 'white coal'.[46] This kiln-dried wood, made from about 0.05 to 0.10m diameter poles chopped into short lengths, was produced specifically for smelting lead ores, often in 'ore hearths' with bellows powered by waterwheels; the heat was not as intense as that produced by charcoal and thus the lead did not evaporate.

Commonly, both in the Peak and in the woods in the foothills around Sheffield and north-east Derbyshire, the archaeological remains of white coal kilns comprise simple shallow pits with a gully running out to one side where the draughting flue was; these have been nicknamed 'Q-pits'. Often when found singly or in small numbers their interpretation in the absence of archaeological excavation is ambiguous. Other white coal kilns are easier to recognise (Fig 6.28). A classic example has been found in woodland near North Lees above Hathersage, where there was a later 17th- to earlier 18th-century 'ore-hearth' smelter sited by Hood Brook. A well-preserved circular kiln of about 4m diameter has its side defined by a drystone wall, whilst a short, walled, draughting flue passes through the retaining bank on the downslope side. A similar but larger example is to be found in overgrown woodland just north of Froggatt, covered in ivy, ferns and bracken, sited close to a ruined 'ore-hearth' smelter downslope. This is the only known example where there were stone beams set horizontally, two of which

are in situ, placed above a draughting 'chamber' to support the base of a stack of the 'white coal' that was to be dried.

At white coal kilns it may be that the drying fire was normally lit outside the kiln, in or close to its draughting flue, thus preventing the chopped 'white coal' from accidentally setting alight. Not all kilns were circular, for rectangular examples have been identified in woodlands flanking the Derwent between Cromford and Whatstandwell, and also probably further north below Gardom's Edge and in Padley Wood.

At North Lees the smelter was surrounded by three small plantations, sited on wooded land unsuitable for agriculture, each with its own white coal kiln. Here there are narrow woodland management tracks and a platform, presumably for preparing the wood, on the slopes above the kilns. In the 1760s the smelt mill was converted for paper making and most of the ruined structures remaining today belong to this phase, although one half of the dam above may be earlier and lead slag can still be found nearby.

In some Peak coppices used for 'white coal' production, archaeological evidence seems to show that charcoal was also made in the wood, as for example at Shacklow Wood west of Ashford. This lies close to the site of an ore hearth built sometime between 1574 and 1581 and used until 1781; this smelter provided the lead used during the rebuilding of Chatsworth House in 1690 to 1697. Whether dual fuel production in Peak woodland was contemporary or use of the coppices changed through time needs further research.

Fig 6.28
The white coal kiln at North Lees (top left), with draughting flue to the left. Overgrown remains in Froggatt Wood, with the white coal kiln (bottom left) and a stone-lined water channel leading to the ore hearth.
[© Anthony Hammerton; John Barnatt]

Charcoal making

Burning coppiced wood to make charcoal is a traditional industry which was widely practised. The evidence can be elusive, but in particular Peak woods there are oval and circular platforms cut into steep wooded hillsides that can be readily recognised, especially when fragments of charcoal are eroding from them or have been thrown up by rabbits.

Close to Caster's Bridge near Gradbach and behind The Roaches, both steep sides of a side valley have a number of charcoal-burning platforms, some retained downslope by drystone walls, some linked by trackways. In the valley bottom there are three large mounds of slag from iron bloomery smelting. There is no convincing evidence for an iron source in the immediate vicinity and it may be that the ore was brought from a distance for local use and to take advantage of the woodland fuel source here. Archaeological evidence for bloomery smelting is rare in the Peak, with only two other sites known, both on the eastern gritstone upland. One comprises three large mounds of slag in two clusters high in the Burbage Valley.[47] Another single mound has recently been identified at Moscar further north, which together with the Gradbach site was noted by Farey in 1811 as sites of 'old bloomeries'. The Moscar site has recently been radiocarbon-dated from charcoal amongst the slags to the late 12th or 13th centuries.

The largest known concentration of charcoal-burning platforms occurs in the Upper Derwent Valley on steep valley sides flanking both the River Derwent and River Alport (Fig 6.29).[48] Over 250 oval platforms are recorded. Production may have started in medieval times, but charcoal making was at its height in the 18th century when large amounts were produced for local industrialists. In the mid-decades of this century the Duke of Devonshire sold rights to the woods to Wortley Top Forge near Stocksbridge, Mousehole Forge at Malin Bridge and Attercliffe Forge in Sheffield. These are linked with the upper Derwent area by packhorse routes coming eastwards across the moors. Traditional wisdom is that charcoal did not travel well and iron producers used woods local to their forges; the upper Derwent evidence illustrates that this was not always the case.

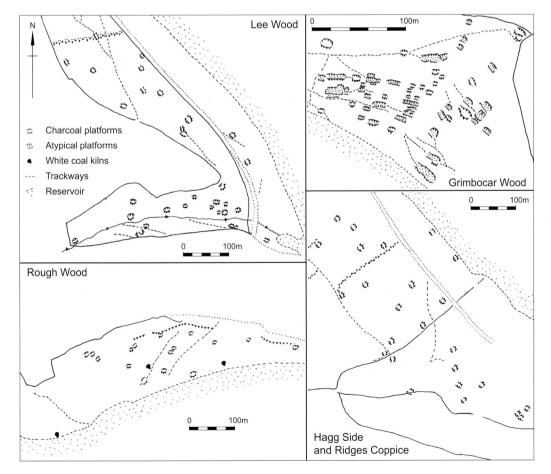

Fig 6.29 Charcoal-burning platforms in the Upper Derwent Valley on the steep slopes above Ladybower Reservoir. A few are linked by trackways. Some within Grimbocar Wood are unusual, in that they are atypically closely spaced and include platforms of uncertain function. These have straight-sided retaining walls and may be later in date than the more typical oval to sub-rectangular examples nearby. In Rough Wood there are three structures interpreted as 'white coal' kilns.

117

7

Quarrying stone

The region has a variety of types of useful stone that have been quarried over the centuries. Local limestone and sandstone have been important for building, whilst many tonnes of the former have also been converted to lime.[1] Specialist products have included Ashford Black Marble and Bakewell Chert. Limestone extraction is still an important industry in the Peak. Sandstones have been important for building stone and millstone production in the past but only a few small quarries which specialise in high-grade stone for such things as fireplaces are currently in business. Very little on the history and archaeology of Peak quarrying has been published. Places named in Chapter 7 are located on Figure A1.4 (p 229).

Limestone

Today, limestone quarrying is one of the main industries in the Peak, with limestone for aggregate and concrete being quarried around Buxton and Peak Dale to the west, at Hope to the north, and Caldon Low to the south-west.

Local limeburning is first documented in the early 17th century and was a major industry from the late 18th century onwards as demand from agriculture and the chemical industry increased with the Industrial Revolution, hand in hand with large quantities of lime needed for building with the growth of associated towns and cities. Large numbers of early kilns exist around Grin Hill at Buxton, Dove Holes, Peak Forest and Caldon Low, whilst banks of tall 19th-century kilns lie next to canals, as at Bugsworth and Marple.

Traditionally burnt limestone, generally referred to as lime, has been used as a de-vegetater and de-acidifier spread onto fields to aid fertility, for mortar when building, and in the chemical industry. As seen in Chapter 5, field kilns were commonly built on farms to produce their own lime. Much lime was also produced commercially in the Peak, with operations at a larger scale than that on farms, often at what were called 'sale kilns'. These produced a purer product, with the lime separated from the slags and other waste such as half-burnt coal.

Early clusters of kilns are found at a number of sites across the Peak.[2] These are characterised by circular mounds with a central pot of 'intermittent' type (*see* p 88 for a definition). Each kiln is set at the downslope side of a shallow quarry, taking the limestone from the top 2m to 5m of the beds where it was naturally fractured and relatively easy to remove. As the working face moved away from the kiln a new one was eventually added closer to it and the old one abandoned. Thus, over time the quarrying complex slowly migrated across the landscape as more and more kilns were added. It was not until the late 18th century that lime producers started to move away from this kind of kiln and quarry, towards deep quarries with larger kilns where the greater investment in construction meant that they were 'permanent' features and stone was brought to them from the face over a long period, with quarries getting larger and deeper.

The early kilns cluster in specific places around the edge of the Peak's limestone plateau to allow the coal to be brought easily from local mines. The prime concentration developed around Grin Hill at Buxton, extending to Dove Holes and Peak Forest to the north and to Thirklow to the south; this general area was ideally placed as there was coal nearby and because, as the Industrial Revolution took hold, the kilns were well-sited for lime to be transported to the burgeoning Manchester area to the north-west (*see* Figs 6.1 and A1.4). Caldon Low at the south-western tip of the limestone plateau was similarly sited in relation to the Potteries. Other documented early sites to the north and east, at Bradwell and Calver, supplied lime to local markets.[3]

These proto-industrial kilns are recorded at Grin Hill, Dove Holes and Bradwell in the mid-17th century.[4] By the 1660s, at latest, the important limeburning centre at Grin Hill had been established, whilst kilns at Peak Forest were already in use by 1707 and some of the kilns at Thirklow are also likely to be this early. A turnpike branch to here was proposed in 1773, but this site was doomed to long-term commercial failure because its kilns were further away from the prime market around Manchester, making Grin Hill and kiln complexes further north more successful (Fig 7.1); it was not until the 1850s after a railway link existed that quarrying again extended south of Grin Hill with the start of deep quarrying at Harpur Hill.

Some places favoured what may have been 'permanent' kilns from an early date. At Stoney Middleton Dale the cliffs and steep slopes at the dale were the focus of limeburning from at least the 1690s, in which decade something like 1,000 tons (900 tonnes) of lime from here was used in rebuilding Chatsworth House.[5] Presumably 'intermittent' kilns were used, but in a limited number of locations due to the topography; unfortunately, nothing obvious from this period has survived as ongoing quarrying into the 20th century has removed the evidence.

Multi-kiln complexes were gradually superseded by banks of large 'continuous running' kilns between the late 18th and mid-19th centuries. Early change came about in response to the building of canals and tramways. Here it made sense to have permanent kilns where the lime could be loaded straight onto barges or waggons. The deep quarries at Dove Holes, and following expansion, those at Peak Dale, were developed following the building of the Peak Forest Tramway from 1794. Whilst there were some kilns within these quarries, at the bottom end of the tramway, at Bugsworth Basin, three large banks of tall, stone-faced kilns were built. Further banks of kilns were erected along the Peak Forest canal, as at Marple. To the south-east a large bank of kilns was erected in the 1790s close to the Cromford Canal at Bullbridge below quarries at Crich. Limestone from Caldon Low was burnt in banks against the terminal of the 1778 Caldon Canal at Froghall, with tramways and later a railway linking quarry with wharf. Near Buxton,

Fig 7.1
One of the kilns on Stanley Moor, where limeburning spread from Grin Hill in the 19th century before the takeover by Buxton Lime Company in 1857. Downslope from the obvious kiln at the centre of the photograph is a large flat-topped waste heap, while behind is the quarry. A second kiln can just be made out to the right, with an obvious waste heap below. [John Barnatt]

the quarries at Grin Hill were linked to the Cromford and High Peak Railway from 1831, whilst those nearby at Harpur Hill started in the 1850s. (*See also* 'Bulk production' on p 129.)

At Grin Hill two large banks of stone-faced and brick-lined kilns were built between 1858 and 1866. At Harpur Hill the earliest of three Hoffmann limekilns in the Peak was built in 1873. This massive kiln comprises a large oval tunnel, inside a stone-faced mound, which was divided into temporary compartments; whilst one part of the loop was being fired, others were being loaded and emptied, so that continuous firing could be achieved.[6]

Grin Hill

Limeburning here, for the Earls and later Dukes of Devonshire, is first recorded in 1662–3 and went on continuously well into the 20th century (Fig 7.2). Today 120 of the early type of kilns with waste heaps remain, mostly within the Country Park, some with clear barrow-runs for loading, all within a multitude of conjoined quarries. From the later 17th to earlier 19th century five to 10 kilns were probably in use in any given year. On top of the hill further kilns were removed by a deep quarry, now part-backfilled except at the main face. This was started in 1857 when Buxton Lime Company took over and started a deep quarry with 'permanent' kilns. This change-over was particularly late, for Thomas Boothman the previous tenant, who had had the site since 1826–7, had held production back in favour of his main business, the kilns at Bugsworth Basin near Whaley Bridge.

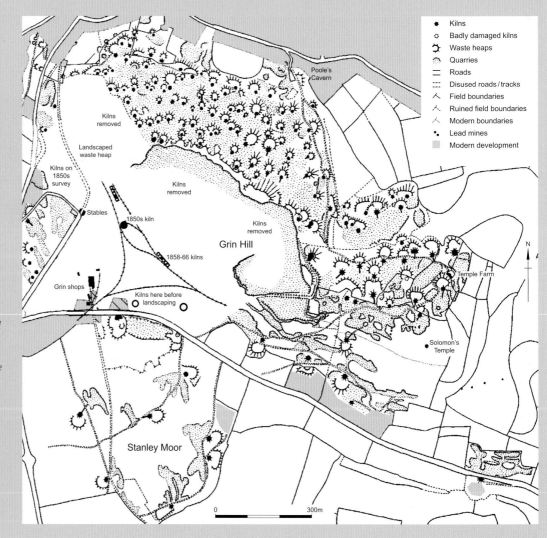

Fig 7.2
The limekiln complex on Grin Hill and the adjacent Stanley Moor. The 17th-century kilns are to the north, while gradual expansion upslope southwards and south-eastwards took place in the 18th and early 19th centuries. The kilns built on the south slope and on Stanley Moor date to the early to mid-19th century. The large 'permanent' quarry was started in 1857; an associated spoil heap to the north-west and ground to the south-west have now been landscaped.

Peak Forest kilns

A similar complex, but on private farmland, exists just west of Peak Forest, with five clusters of kilns to either side of the A623 (Fig 7.3). In total there are 129 to 138 kilns, with waste heaps, shallow quarries and access tracks. The earliest of these are likely to be 17th century in date and quarrying continued until 1823. In the early decades, in any given year between three and eight kilns were each rented out to individuals, some or all of whom were local farmers. They were only in use over the summer half of the year. A move towards industrial-isation came in 1767 after an assessment for the Duke of Devonshire. At that time the tools used by limeburners, who as was usual did their own quarrying, comprised only bars, picks, hammers, wedges, shovels, spades, baskets and wheelbarrows. After the assessment rents were increased and it seems limeburning at Peak Forest became more commercial, with regular production over six months of the year, with lime presumably available for sale rather than limestone being burnt on an ad-hoc basis by farmers as and when they needed lime.[7]

Fig 7.3
Part of the extensive 17th- to 19th-century limeburning complex west of Peak Forest, with shallow irregular quarries, each with small circular limekilns; to the top (north) there are several clear examples of late kilns with large circular waste heaps on the downslope sides. [© Crown copyright. Historic England Archive 17196_22]

Specialist products

Specialist products, eventually mined under-ground after limited surface outcrops were depleted, were worked from the later 18th century onwards.[8] Blocks of chert, a similar material to flint, were used as crushing stones by the potteries industry and these were mostly mined near Bakewell. At Ashford, a short distance west of Bakewell, a dark limestone, known as Ashford Black Marble, was mined from the 16th to 19th centuries for decorative polished items such as fireplaces, chequered floors and ornaments.[9] At Ricklow Dale near Monyash, highly fossiliferous limestone beds known as Grey Marble were used for polished paving slabs in the 18th and 19th centuries, with quarrymen again eventually following these beds underground.[10]

Chert

Holme Bank Chert Mine at Bakewell is a very extensive, labyrinth-like set of workings dating from the mid-19th century onwards (Figs 7.4 and 7.5); to the east side the chert was extracted under

land owned by Holme Hall rather than Chatsworth Estate and these workings were known as Holme Hall Mine, even though, except for one or possibly two brief periods in the 19th century, they were worked together. At both mines a bed of chert was extracted underground for use in the pottery industry.[11] The blocks were used in rotary mills to crushed burnt flint, with this added to clay by Wedgewood and others so that the resultant pottery resembled Chinese porcelain. At Holme Bank and Holme Hall the bed was wholly removed and waste stacked behind in large packs that supported the roof; roadways passing through these were used to take the chert blocks to surface. The workings can only be explored today with great care, for sections of the mine packs and roofs are collapsing; other parts became flooded when the pumps were turned off.

Fig 7.5
The earliest
underground workings
at Holme Bank Chert
Mine, and the adjacent
Holme Hall Mine to the
east side, were next to an
earlier small opencast
quarry to the south.
Extraction moved
northwards under the
hillside through time;
they eventually came
close to surface to the
north-west and here
chert was again worked
opencast in the 1940s
and 1950s. The face
dates given are derived
from surviving working
plans and other
documentation.

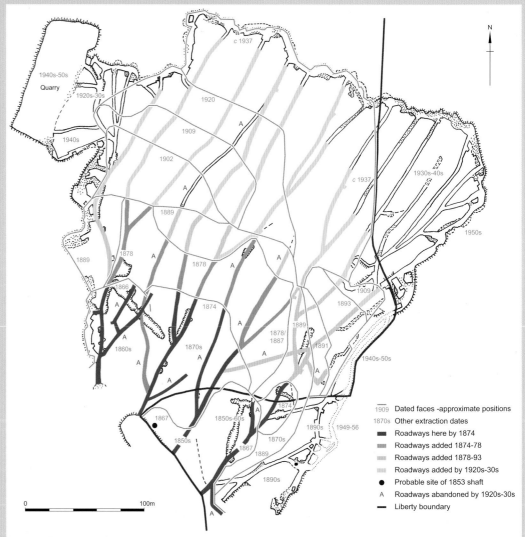

Sandstone

A coarse and hard-wearing sandstone, found widely across the Peak and often referred to as Millstone Grit, together with finer-grained sandstones, have been widely used for building and for architectural details such a roofing slates, quoins, sills and lintels. In addition, they have been used to produce specialist products, notably millstones and grindstones.

Millstone making

One traditional product from the Peak was millstones made in the local Millstone Grit.[12] The majority of sites where these were made are on the eastern gritstone upland, although small sites to the west include Cluther Rocks below Kinder Scout and the western side of Combs Moss. As with lead, those stones not for local use were shipped from Hull to places such as King's Lynn and London, coming from the quarries via inland ports such as Bawtry; hence this favoured production on the eastern side of the Peak. All millstones were made with a central hole, which can either be circular or square, but there are two basic types of stone. Individual 'domed millstones' have one flat face and a domed one with a rounded outer edge; they were used in pairs with the two flat faces placed together to mill flour (Fig 7.6). Stones of the other type have two flat faces and are cylindrical with a flat edge. These had a variety of uses. Some have a raised centre on one face and were millstones for cereals. Others, with two parallel faces, were used very differently. Some were grindstones used for initial grinding during manufacture of iron tools, before finishing was done with a finer-grained stone. Others of this type were 'edge-running' stones that revolved around a crushing bed (Fig 7.7); commonly these were employed in paper manufacture, used during pulp production to crush knots. Others, more occasionally, were used to crush such things as lead ore.

We know from documentation that millstone making in the Peak has been taking place from at least the 13th century and that these stones were used over large areas of eastern Britain. The stones were often made by masons working for themselves and each pair would take time and skill; when a stone broke during manufacture this was serious. It is believed that a collapse in the Peak millstone trade came with changes in fashion in bread making. Peak stones not only

left grit in the bread but also turned white bread to an unpalatable grey colour. They were fine for oats, barley and rye, hence later use of Peak stones was largely restricted to milling for coarse bread and animal feed. The domed millstones are thought to be 18th century and earlier in date; the flat-faced millstones, grindstones and 'edge runners' were mostly made in the 19th and earlier 20th centuries.

Millstone manufacturing sites are found intermittently all along the eastern gritstone scarps from Bamford Edge down to Fallinge Edge. Whilst some came from face-quarries at the scarp tops, the multitude of boulders below

Fig 7.6 (top)
An abandoned domed millstone at Great Tor on Bamford Edge.
[© Anthony Hammerton]

Fig 7.7 (bottom)
Flat-faced grindstones or 'edge runners' ready for removal, together with a small mason's trough for quenching tools after they were repaired, below Stanage Edge near its southern end.
[© Anthony Hammerton]

Fig 7.8
Quarry-related features
and agricultural enclosure
at Gardom's Edge, between
the scarp top and the main
road below. There are face-
quarries at the scarp top
and extensive areas where
large boulders have been
broken on the slope below.
Trackways lead away from
the production areas, going
both to the scarp top to take
stones eastwards for
shipping from Hull, and
downslope into the Derwent
Valley for more local use.
The illustration is based on
a rapid survey done in the
1990s and further examples
of broken products have
been found subsequently
in this bracken-and-tree
covered landscape.

the edges were also commonly targeted and here the distinctive archaeological signature comprises shallow pits where a boulder has been broken up, with waste stone left in heaps around the pit edges after shaping the rough-outs. In some cases parts of the boulders remain in the pits. It is believed that boulder breakage started in medieval times, whilst the larger face-quarries are mostly post-medieval in date. However, this started relatively early, for one of the quarries at Curbar Edge has a date of 1622 carved into the base of its disused face.

At the extraction sites, commonly we find unremoved boulders and outcrops that have slots and wedge-cuts where work was started but did not proceed. There is also a wide variety of stones abandoned during different stages of production, ranging from crudely shaped rough-outs with no chisel dressing, to others where the central hole was still to be made, and to some that are almost complete. Sometimes these stones are resting on the chock stones used to lift them up for dressing, abandoned because a crack appeared or a piece flaked off; after all the work done on each of these stones, no doubt the fatal blow was accompanied by profanities.

There are also stacks of stones ready for removal, which for reasons unknown were never taken away. Many stones have carved initials but it is unclear whether these signify the millstone makers or the buyer who had purchased them to transport them to Hull or other destinations. Readily identified trackways run through the boulder fields for moving finished stones, and nearby there are often small now-ruined sheds for shelter and repairing tools.

From the mid-18th century onwards, with the general improvement in the region's roads, finished stones were no doubt taken on carts. Earlier, ox-sleds were sometimes used, but it is noted by Defoe in the 1720s that stones were also moved across the moors by placing a timber 'axle' between a pair and rolling them as if they were wheels.[13] What he failed to note is how the edges were protected from damage.

There were two focal areas of particular importance where millstones were made, at Millstone Edge above Hathersage and Gardom's Edge at Baslow (Fig 7.8). At the other extreme are sites such as Carl Wark, where a small quarry in the cliff that partially defines the ancient hillfort has a scattering of abandoned

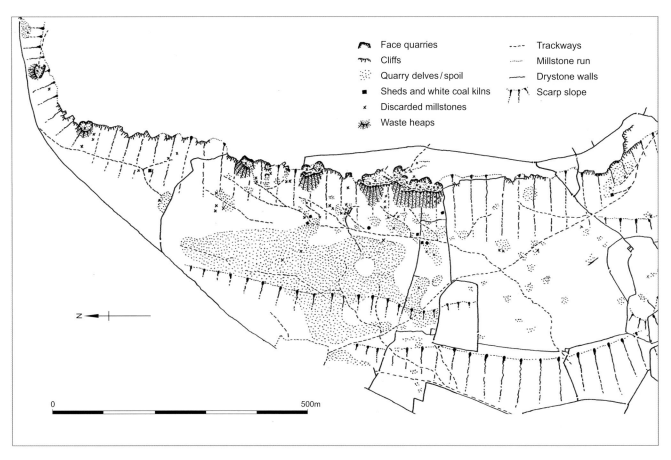

millstones nearby, both here and amongst broken boulders below. Just outside the rampart of the hillfort there is a ruined stone shed

against a boulder, with a trough which may have been used for quenching tools that were being repaired.

Millstone Edge and Bole Hill

Whilst the scarps above Hathersage were one of the main millstone production foci over several centuries, starting in the 14th century if not before, most of what can be seen today dates from the 18th to 20th centuries, with large-scale work presumably removing much that came earlier.

In the northern half of the area there is a series of quarries along the scarp top, for the most part with deep vertical faces; smaller quarries to the south may be earlier. A main access trackway leads to these following the top of their waste heaps. The faces and waste rock have good examples of wedge-slots, and also plug and feather holes, both used for splitting stone. Scattered nearby there are broken 'edge-runner' stones, grindstones, domed millstones, traces of small buildings and derrick bases, and burnt coal presumably from a smithy hearth. Hidden in the trees below the quarries, approached by a lower trackway, are concrete structures associated with a 20th-century crushing plant.

One of the main quarry faces has been reused for testing drill steels in the later 20th century, perhaps by the firm of Padley and Venables

based in Sheffield who made them. Whilst large and very long vertical shotholes, drilled in competent hard gritstone that is very thickly bedded, belong with the quarrying, there is a later array of horizontally drilled holes in tight clusters that cannot be explained in this way. Each of the latter is focused on a grid of red paint marks and clearly the accuracy with which a drill rig could be used was being demonstrated.

At Bole Hill to the south a straight embanked trackway, here by 1880, leads from the road southwards to a large quarry.[14] Much of what exists today dates to the early 20th century when the large quarry here provided stone for the Derwent and Howden dams and this is returned to in Chapter 8 (see pp 146–7). However, just before the quarry is reached, there is a large stack of finished 'edge runners'/grindstones of a variety of different sizes, placed here ready for sale and/or shipment. Nearby, on the down-slope side of the track, there is a smaller stack and several stones have rolled down the embankment. Over 375 stones in total have been counted. The most likely explanation for these is that they were products in stock at the time the quarry was taken over in 1901 by the Derwent Valley Water Board.

Other products and dayworking

The Millstone Grit beds were used for a variety of products as well as millstones; there are quarries that specialised in freestone for building and slabs for floors and roofs. A number of specific items that broke during manufacture also litter the moors, including troughs, gateposts and lintels. Whilst some came out of quarries, many items were made by breaking up scattered boulders. Some masons earned a living by paying landowners a day rate to allow them on their land to break scattered boulders in a type of quarrying known as 'dayworking'. Of the larger quarries producing freestone, noteworthy examples include those at Stanton and Birchover with high-quality sandstone used for decorative items such as fire surrounds. Others include quarries on the moors started in the 18th and 19th centuries above Beeley, at Brown Edge on

the Hallam Moors west of Sheffield, and those in Longdendale created when the reservoirs were built.

Slabs for roofs and floors

At specific places on the gritstone uplands, where the individual sandstone beds are thin, these have been targeted for the quarrying of stone suitable for roofing and paving slabs. These sites tend to be characterised by multiple interconnected pits rather than one large quarry with a vertical face. Good examples can be found beside the Wet Withens stone circle on Eyam Moor and across the valley on Abney Moor.

Very occasionally good beds of stone were followed underground to save having to remove excessive amounts of overburden: the classic Peak example is at Cracken Edge above Chinley, although a much smaller 19th-century example also existed at Longnor.[15]

Reeve Edge Quarries

Some of the most interesting old slab quarries are those in the Upper Dane Valley at Reeve Edge and across the river at Danebower.[16] The two sets of quarries were never linked; the river is the county boundary and the land to either side was owned by different estates, with Danebower in Cheshire belonging to the Earls of Derby and Reeve Edge in Derbyshire to the Dukes of Devonshire. Quarrying started long ago and stone pits on Reeve Edge are shown on an undated map which may date to the end of the 16th century;[17] it continued into the 20th century. At the heart of the Reeve Edge site there is a deep quarry, started before the late 1870s and the last area to be worked, with tramways leading from this to the 'finger tips' (Figs 7.9 and 7.10).[18]

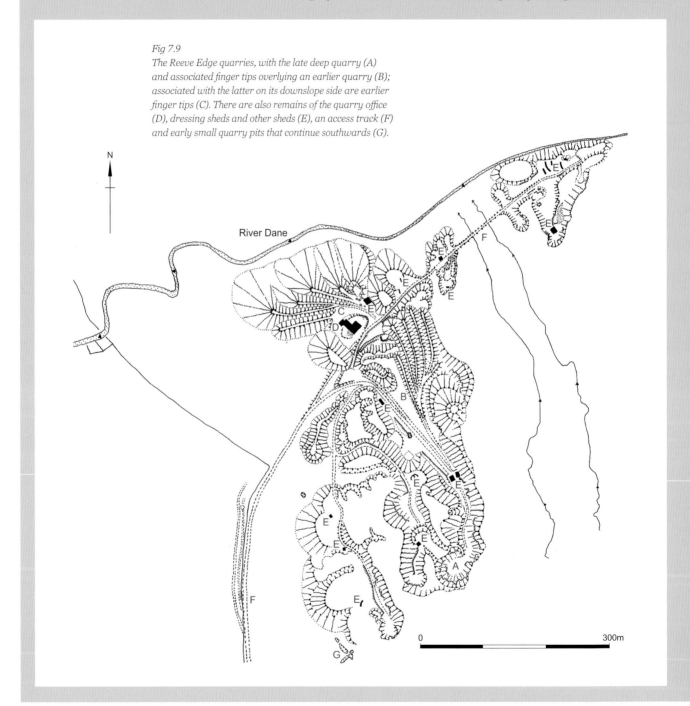

Fig 7.9
The Reeve Edge quarries, with the late deep quarry (A) and associated finger tips overlying an earlier quarry (B); associated with the latter on its downslope side are earlier finger tips (C). There are also remains of the quarry office (D), dressing sheds and other sheds (E), an access track (F) and early small quarry pits that continue southwards (G).

These overlie an earlier deep quarry to the north, of probable early to mid-19th-century date, with a second set of finger tips completed by the late 1870s, placed next to the ruins of the quarry office.[19] A piece of iron L-section tramway rail was found near here, probably of earlier 19th-century date. The quarries were accessed by a cart track that heads south rather than crossing the river to the nearby 1790 turnpike road to the north; it may be that agreement between the two estates could not be reached as their quarries were in competition. Throughout the main quarries there is a series of small ruined buildings, including open-fronted dressing sheds of 18th- to 20th-century date. To the south there is a series of smaller quarry pits; these are probably vestiges of earlier quarrying activities.

Fig 7.10
Finger tips next to the ruined office at Reeve Edge Quarry in the Upper Dane Valley south-west of Buxton. Across the river are the Danebower colliery trackways and shaft hillocks.
[John Barnatt]

Cracken Edge Quarries

The main quarries above Chinley follow the ridgetop. They closed in the 1920s, probably after hundreds of years of work but with the start date unknown. On the quarry floor there is a series of waste packs and ruined sheds. There are narrow ways to the face, with walled packs to either side, which led to now-collapsed adits into underground workings that dipped ever downwards to the west. Down the main slope, at a smaller set of quarried beds, there is a tramway or cart track heading south. There is also the brake drum of a certain tramway that took finished product diagonally down the steep eastern hillside (Fig 7.11, *see also* Fig 8.15). At the top of this incline a now-collapsed adit, in use in the early 20th century, led horizontally to late-phase workings in the upper band of dipping thin beds, reaching them at a point where they had already been followed a long way underground because they were ideal for good-quality slabs.

Fig 7.11
The brake drum at the top of the inclined tramway down the eastern hillside at the Cracken Edge quarries. [John Barnatt]

Bulk production

Deep limestone quarries started being dug at the turn of the 19th century and these became ever larger over the next two centuries; now cement and aggregates rather than lime are the most important products.[20] Today limestone extraction is one of the main industries in the Peak, with large quarries including that at the Hope cement works near the west end of the Hope Valley; Dove Holes Quarry and Tunstead Quarry north-east of Buxton; Hindlow and Dowlow quarries south-east of Buxton; and further south at Grange Mill near Aldwark, at Ballidon, and at Caldon Low (Fig 7.12).

Formerly there were further large quarries at Pin Dale near Castleton and in Bradwell Dale; at Eldon Hill near Peak Forest; near Peak Dale; at Grin Hill, Harpur Hill and Hillhead south-east of Buxton; in Millers Dale, Stoney Middleton Dale and at Backdale on Longstone Edge; and to the south at Dene Quarry above Cromford, Hall Dale Quarry in Matlock and several quarries around Wirksworth. Until recently, a high-grade limestone was mined underground at Middleton by Wirksworth from 1959.

Some quarries, such as those around Buxton, Dove Holes, Stoney Middleton and Caldon Low, developed from 17th- and 18th-century origins. Others were established in the 19th century, as with the Harpur Hill quarries in Buxton started in the 1850s against the Cromford and High Peak Railway. Elsewhere, two large quarries at Millers Dale in the heart of the limestone plateau were established after the Buxton to Rowsley railway was created in the 1860s. Similarly, large-scale quarrying at Wirksworth took off with the coming of the railway from Derby in 1867.

An important 19th-century development was the amalgamation of quarrying firms in the general vicinity of Buxton. Buxton Lime Company was established initially to work Harpur Hill, but soon acquired Grin Hill. Further consolidation took place, especially after the renaming of the firm to Buxton Lime Firms in 1891. The quarries south-east of Buxton, beyond Harpur Hill, were established in the 19th century. Dow Low Quarry, the furthest in the chain, was started in 1899. Buxton Lime Firms was absorbed into Brunner Mond in 1918 and this in turn became part of ICI when it was created in 1926. Both Hope cement works and Tunstead Quarry were begun in 1929, the

Fig 7.12 (above)
The active Dove Holes Quarry in bright sunshine with Beelow Quarry immediately behind. Beyond is the back of the disused Eldon Hill Quarry, where a sizeable piece of one of the highest hills on the limestone plateau was removed. In the foreground, just behind the Dove Holes houses to the left and hidden in shadow, are the much smaller 17th- to 18th-century limeburning heaps and quarries, which, in their day, were one of the most important sets of limestone workings in the region. [John Barnatt]

Fig 7.13 (left)
One of the largest modern limestone workings in the Peak, Tunstead Quarry, east of Buxton, has massive kilns for producing cement. [John Barnatt]

first by G & T Earl, the other by ICI (Fig 7.13). Eldon Hill Quarry was started in 1950 and this stands in strong contrast in terms of scale with late 18th- and early 19th-century limeburning quarries and kilns nearby to the west.

8

Travelling between places

People have always travelled, to visit markets, friends and family, transport goods for sale, or to search elsewhere for work. Sometimes the journeys were short but frequent, to reach local fields, quarries, mines and commons. Every now and again, people would go further afield, commonly visiting a local market town or to get together for family gatherings. Others made their living from transporting livestock, agricultural produce and manufactured goods across the country. Sometimes it was local products going outwards, as in the Peak with cheese and milk, or lead ore taken to smelters and then onwards to inland ports. There were also valuable commodities passing through, as with salt from Cheshire on its way to elsewhere in England, or desirable objects brought in for sale, such as pottery from the Stoke on Trent area or metal tools manufactured elsewhere such as in Sheffield and Chesterfield.

People have always walked between places, whilst horses and ponies have long been used by the wealthy and those needing to move heavy goods. Strings of packhorses would once have been a frequent sight, led by 'jaggers'. Waggons and carts, some with two wheels, others larger with four, have been used from at least Roman times for the heaviest of jobs. As amounts of traffic increased in the 17th and 18th centuries the roads struggled to cope; seeing a waggon bogged down would have been a common sight. Turnpike roads built from the 18th century onwards allowed goods traffic to move more successfully, and travellers who could afford the fare could easily go between cities by coach. Letters were delivered at surprising speeds over distances of tens or hundreds of miles. It was not uncommon for 19th-century businessmen to receive a letter one day with a reply returned to sender the next.

In the Peak there are roads and paths in use today with a variety of origins. A few can be recognised as going back to Roman times but many are of medieval or later date; some have changed beyond recognition as they have been adapted for ever-increasing traffic, with simple earthen paths overlain by cobbled surfaces and later replaced by tarmac; some narrow footpaths in use today were once more important highways. There are also vegetated-over hollow-ways, especially on the moors but with vestiges elsewhere, where routes have been abandoned leaving erosion scars where feet and hooves have worn a groove, sometimes metres deep, its downward path stopped only when intractable bedrock was reached. There are also paved packhorse tracks, commonly now often subsumed beneath heather and peat (Fig 8.1). Some abandoned trackways are specific to industrial enterprises and were only used over the time that stone was brought from the quarry or a mine from which lead was won. There is also road furniture, ranging from stone pillars known locally as 'guide stoups', which used carved hands to guide the early 18th-century traveller, through to stone milestones and cast-iron mileposts doing the same for late 18th- and 19th-century travellers along newly built turnpike roads. Where paths cross fields there are gateways and stiles, whilst on moors there is the occasional paved path across boggy ground, with only the odd stone to be seen, recognisable by the surface-wear made by generations of feet. The legacy of people moving through the land is rich and varied.[1] Routeways and specific places mentioned in Chapter 8 are given on Figure A1.5 (see p 231).

Whilst paths must have criss-crossed the Peak in prehistory, with people moving between house and spring, winter and summer pastures, and bringing valuable commodities such as flint and metals into the region, nothing now is clearly visible. Suggestions as to the exact routes for long-distance routeways, such as what had become named as the 'Portway', cannot be substantiated. The courses of Roman military roads are known whilst others have been postulated.[2]

However, often their lines are in part followed by modern roads and substantiated road earthworks of Roman date are rare. The bulk of today's roads and paths are likely to have medieval origins. In areas dominated by enclosed farmland it is easy to identify from maps those paths that went from a village into its surrounding fields, leading to and between cultivation strips. Villages and hamlets are also linked to neighbours with roads through fields and across what once were commons. Identifying medieval longer-distance routes, where following different lines from those just described, is more difficult although there is much potential for further study; roads exist that pass between villages rather than going via the local settlements, sometimes following parish boundaries. Some of those bypassing settlement foci are turnpike roads built from the 18th century onwards, but others may well be earlier; analysis of these could prove revealing.

In long-established farmland, particularly where enclosed into small fields, or where ways across open fields were carefully prescribed, then routes for travellers would be fixed; many of the sinuous walled lanes running through fields seen today across the Peak have such origins. Because people could not move sideways then mud would have been a problem. Where hard limestone or gritstone bedrock was close to surface this would have formed a hard substrate for traction, but where soils were thicker and the rocks friable or soft, then deep and constrained hollow-ways often formed. On open commons the restrictions did not apply and people had the freedom to spread out and roam at will but in places eroded routes that are still visible today were created (Fig 8.2).

Fig 8.1
This heavily worn paved path, known as Golden Carr Road, in parts restored in modern times, winds down Stanage Edge heading for North Lees below. Such paths can be medieval or later in date; in this case all we know is that it pre-dates the 19th century.
[John Barnatt]

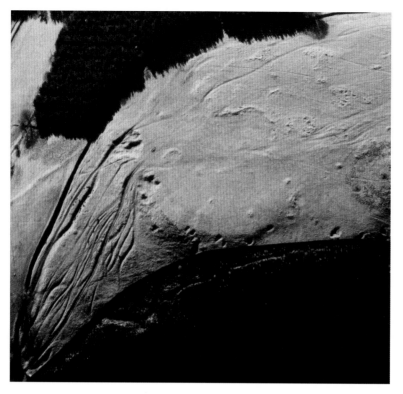

Fig 8.2
This hollow-way at Highlow Bank south-west of Hathersage, which pre-dates the improvement of the land when it was taken in from moorland, has deep braids where it comes up the steep slope (left). There are less obvious ones on flatter ground above (right), where the historic routeway passes through a small prehistoric cairnfield with the stone heaps created when the ground was cultivated. [© Crown copyright. Historic England Archive 17199_21]

Abandoned hollow-ways are most clearly seen on the Peak moorlands, with inter-linked, deeply cut braids visible, particularly on slopes, whilst on flatter land they tend to fade, sometimes to nothing. It is not so much the passage of feet that has led to the permanent scarring of the land, but that feet and hooves broke the vegetation cover. Once bare earth was exposed, it was run-off of water on slopes at times of rain that did the damage. Similarly, on moorland where travellers were funnelled together as they approached farmland and a bounded lane, or at specific points such as a stream crossing, then erosion was also severe. Because of the high density of traffic going in and out of Peak villages to the east, many braided hollow-ways are seen on the eastern moors.[3] They also occur to the west heading towards markets at Leek, Macclesfield and places in the direction of Manchester.[4] If you were a stranger passing through rather than knowing the local landscape intimately, then route-finding must have been a nightmare; in well-populated places, asking a local could be a good strategy. However, when away from the villages, especially on the extensive commons and moors, finding a safe way would be stressful. This was alleviated somewhat in the early 18th century when a series of stone 'guide stoups' were erected to show the way to named market centres (Fig 8.3).[5]

On the Peak's moorlands, at now long-abandoned hollow-ways, people often followed braids that were not unduly muddy, or would start new ones, stepping to one side if all ahead was a quagmire. When on horseback, the traveller would be less concerned about the mud, though hooves tend to do more damage than feet. In some instances, the traveller had choices of alternative routeways to reach their destination; sometimes this would be preference, but the bogginess of specific routes would change with the seasons, although if heavy raw materials or manufactured goods were being transported by cart then options were further restricted. Even on well-maintained routes with wide tracks where carts were catered for, sometimes these could only be passed in summer, whilst in winter the vehicle could become irrevocably stuck. With some of the most well-used routes, the braids can have a total width in excess of 100m. Whilst these would have formed major scars across the landscape at the time, significantly greater than the damage walkers have done more recently on routes such as the Pennine Way, after abandonment all is now vegetated over and healed, with the linear hollows adding to the interest of these moorland areas, telling how people once passed here.

For the most part what we see today on the moors may reflect only post-medieval use, when it is likely that much of the erosion occurred that makes the routes still visible today. This was as a consequence of increased movement of industrial products and because people had an ever-increasing capacity to buy goods as large-scale production brought down costs. It may be that many of the specific routes have much earlier origins but this is unknowable. Conversely, whatever the origin and purpose of routeways, it would be wrong to assume that routes were pickled in aspic; they were no doubt modified through time to meet changing needs from generation to generation. Thus, as settlements grew or shrunk the amounts of traffic on specific routes would change; where villages and hamlets had been abandoned, nobody went there. Similarly, specific mines and quarries would come and go.

In 1697 Celia Fiennes wrote 'all Derbyshire is full of steep hills, and nothing but the peakes of hills as thick as one by another is seen in most of the County which are very steep which makes travelling tedious and the miles long'.[6]

As just noted, the eroded hollow-ways we see today may reflect a time when long-established networks of routes were beginning to break down in post-medieval times due to significantly more traffic than previously. It led to unsustainable pressure on the system, with exponential erosion making the use of routes less and less tenable; this was the incentive for taking radical action by building turnpike roads.

As the Industrial Revolution was beginning, making mass production and distribution of goods possible, it became necessary to improve transport networks. Ensuring this happened was in the vested interests of industrialists and others who would benefit most, such as the landed gentry and large estate owners who had land with potentially profitable reserves of metal ores, coal and stone.[7]

Turnpike roads, built with funds raised by investors and gradually repaid by charging tolls for their use, were first built in the 18th century. In each case an Act of Parliament was sought that allowed the Turnpike Trustees to build the new roads, including branches from the main routes, across land owned by others. These routes were given firm footings and cobbled surfaces; where peaty ground was crossed they tended to be on low causeways. At first, where crossing moorland, they were normally unwalled. Whilst unauthorised access was thus easier, travelling any distance down the turnpike was not possible without paying tolls because a series of manned toll houses was erected, with 'bars' across the road to be opened by the toll keeper after money had changed hands. Many of the walls that now flank turnpike roads seem to have been built by landowners to keep people off their grouse moors (see Chapter 4). In the occasional instances where original 18th-century roads exist that have not been subsequently rebuilt, it is surprising how narrow they are. Often there was no room for large waggons to pass; they must have relied on occasional passing places. These 'state of the art' roads of their day must have been adequate for the traffic anticipated, demonstrating just how much things have changed between then and now.

The upland Peak District was not as suitable for canals and railways as the surrounding lowlands and the impact of these radical developments in methods for transporting goods in bulk was not as great. Canals had terminals at the lowland fringe of the Peak, whilst most railway links through the hills came relatively late. That said, important early remains, particularly of tramways and railways, have survived as the land here was not so radically improved later.

Fig 8.3
An 18th-century 'guide stoup' high on White Edge near its northern end, marking the way to the market centre at 'Dronfeild', and on the other faces to others at 'Sheffeild', 'Tidswall' (Tideswell) and 'Bakewell'. It has been utilised by the Ordnance Survey as a bench mark.
[© Anthony Hammerton]

Because of their character, the new rail lines across the landscape were difficult to construct due to the imperative to be relatively horizontal wherever possible; thus, the engineering was more ambitious, with cuttings and embankments being the norm.

No canals were ever built from one side of the Peak to the other, the hills were unsurmountable and cross-Pennine tunnels, such as the 5km-long examples at Standedge, running between Manchester and West Yorkshire just north of the Peak, were never driven.

Instead tramways with incline planes brought limestone, lime and other products out of the hills to canal wharfs at and near Whaley Bridge to the north-west and Cromford to the south-east (Fig 8.4).[8] The earliest schemes were the Peak Forest tramway and the shorter Butterley Gangroad from limestone quarries at Crich to the Cromford Canal at Bullbridge just outside the study area to the south-east, both built in the 1790s. These were followed in the 1820s and 1830s by the much more ambitious Cromford and High Peak Railway (Fig 8.5). This was first conceived as a tramway but was soon converted to a railway with steam locomotives. The line also had several inclines with haulage provided by large stationary steam engines. Other railways came later, first that to Matlock Bath and Rowsley in the 1840s, with Buxton connected to Manchester and Derby in the 1860s, with a second branch line from the Wye Gorge straight to Manchester via the Dove Holes Tunnel built in the same decade. The Buxton line has a noteworthy stretch between Bakewell and Buxton that passes along the Wye Valley Gorge through a series of tunnels. The river was crossed using the impressive Monsal Viaduct. The long Woodhead Tunnel allowed trains to run directly from Manchester to Sheffield from 1845, whilst the later Edale line, with two long tunnels, provided a second link from 1894.

Other late railways included the line from Ashbourne to Parsley Hay opened in 1899: the narrow-gauge line down the Manifold Valley from Hulme End to Leek opened in 1904: and a temporary line in the Derwent Valley that was used for building reservoirs in the early 20th century.

To the north-west there was also a series of small 19th-century industrial tramways, centred around Whaley Bridge in particular, created to bring coal from local mines down inclines to main railway lines, the canal and roads.

In the second half of the 20th century road transport rose to dominance, essential after the closing of railways, and because of the flexibility lorries offer when bringing goods in and out. Also of significance has been the radical rise in cars bringing visitors to the Peak. Main roads have been widened, tarmac is the norm and repaired constantly, and the ubiquitous car parks are often overflowing at peak times.

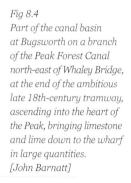

Fig 8.4
Part of the canal basin at Bugsworth on a branch of the Peak Forest Canal north-east of Whaley Bridge, at the end of the ambitious late 18th-century tramway, ascending into the heart of the Peak, bringing limestone and lime down to the wharf in large quantities.
[John Barnatt]

Fig 8.5 (opposite)
A high embankment on the 1830s' Cromford and High Peak Railway at Burbage, west of Buxton. The light is catching the slots for wooden sleepers that were laid to replace the original stone sleeper blocks.
[John Barnatt]

Roman and later straight roads

Many people believe if a road is straight it must be Roman. On occasion over the years this unfounded premise has led local researchers down a long straight garden path. Whilst some routes indeed have Roman origins, often straight roads were created in the 18th and 19th centuries during the enclosure of wastes and commons.

A network of Roman military roads has been suggested, linking the forts at Brough (Navio) in the Hope Valley and Melandra (Ardotalia) near Glossop; the baths and town at Buxton (Aquae Arnemetiae); and the postulated lead production centre of Lutudarum, now lost but most likely to have been near Carsington (see Fig 10.16 for the location of Roman places).[9] Whilst such roads must have existed, their exact lines are sometimes conjectural. Only at Batham Gate between Buxton and Brough are there unequivocal extant earth-works of Roman date.

The A515 running south-east out of Buxton towards Carsington has long straight stretches of road, which in most parts follow a post-medieval course, with sections turnpiked in 1738 and 1749. There is also a long straight line followed by parish boundaries running roughly parallel to the side; this has long been interpreted as following the line of a Roman road known locally as 'The Street'. Whilst there is almost certainly a Roman road somewhere here, identifying the exact line is problematic. In its favour the parish boundary line is marked on a parish map drawn as early as the late 16th century and it stands in strong contrast to all surrounding boundaries, which are sinuous; in parts, field walls lie above what have been interpreted as 'aggers'. However, excavations in 1991 close to Buxton in advance of pipeline construction showed that the earthwork here was a boundary bank, probably of medieval date rather than a Roman 'agger'.[10] Similarly, further to the south-east there are more than one parallel lines of slight earthworks and features visible from the air. It seems likely that when the parish boundary was marked with a permanent bank, there was rationalisation of the line. The known line stops to the south-east near Minninglow, at a point well short of the southern edge of the limestone plateau, although a possible continuation of the road can be traced as a slight terrace running diagonally down Carsington Pasture.[11]

Other postulated Roman roads have physical evidence indicating that a medieval date is likely. Across northern England several examples of cobbled roads once thought to be Roman can now be shown to be medieval or somewhat later constructions; the Doctor's Gate paved way crossing the moors east of Glossop may well fall into this category. The cobbling on this packhorse route may have been added by Doctor Talbot in the late 15th or early 16th century.[12]

On the crest of Stanage Edge there is short section of paved cartway with heavy wear grooves that has been interpreted as Roman; this is not to be confused with the paved road nearby that runs eastwards to Stanage Pole, which is known to have been created in the later 18th century (Fig 8.6).[13] From the worn paved way a sinuous hollow-way leads down towards the Hope Valley past the Buck Stone, where there is evidence for a packhorse overnight stopping place; this has all the characteristic of a medieval-type braided hollow-way.

In some cases, narrow archaeological excav-ation trenches have been placed across postulated Roman roads; if metalled surfaces were found they have been declared a Roman road; some-times this is wishful thinking, having found what the excavators expected to find. For instance, in the 1980s, this author re-excavated a trench near Carsington, at first interpreted as a Roman road. It turned out to have a cobble-like surface that was natural, which had been truncated to either side by medieval ploughing.

Often long and straight 18th- and 19th-century roads are clearly indicated on Parliamentary Enclosure Award plans drawn before they were built. Their design reflects the surveyor drawing the lines of roads and surrounding fields with a ruler. Often they rationalised earlier routes across the commons that were more sinuous. With all Parliamentary Enclosure Award roads, whether they had long straight sections or not, sometimes wide verges were incorporated because livestock were traditionally moved along the route (Fig 8.7).

Hollow-ways

As noted above, pre-turnpike roads are common in the Peak and today are especially visible on unenclosed land. This is illustrated here by a case study which looks at hollow-ways on the extensive Chatsworth Moorlands and their private and turnpike road replacements.

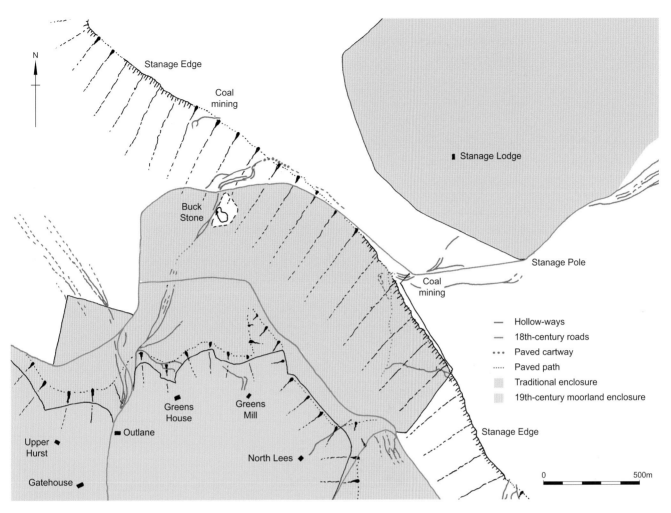

Legend:
— Hollow-ways
— 18th-century roads
••• Paved cartway
···· Paved path
▨ Traditional enclosure
▨ 19th-century moorland enclosure

Map labels: Stanage Edge, Coal mining, Stanage Lodge, Buck Stone, Stanage Pole, Coal mining, Greens House, Greens Mill, Outlane, Upper Hurst, North Lees, Gatehouse, Stanage Edge

0 500m

Fig 8.6 (above)
It is often claimed that a Roman road passed over Stanage Edge on its way from Brough in the Hope Valley to Templeborough between Sheffield and Rotherham. A paved cartway on the crest of the Edge is better interpreted as part of a sinuous medieval routeway, while the uninitiated have assumed that the straight 18th-century paved road passing Stanage Pole is much older than it is.

Fig 8.7 (left)
Horse Lane at Monyash, looking north-east, running over land first enclosed from common in the 1770s; the wide space between the flanking walls allowed for passage of livestock.
[John Barnatt]

Crossing the Chatsworth Moorlands

One area that has had braided hollow-ways and later roads that have been studied in some detail is the swath of moorlands of the Chatsworth Estate to the east of the house (Fig 8.8).[14] A large enough area has been surveyed to enable something of the destinations of early ways to be reconstructed and four surviving early 18th-century 'guide stoups' confirm routes to market centres. Some routes have braids that are deep and hard to miss, whilst elsewhere they are barely discernible, particularly when the heather is thick.

Although the Chatsworth Moors were unenclosed commons until the 19th century, and thus people could roam at will, only particular lines were routinely followed, whilst other moorland areas show no sign of heavy use. People took relatively straight-line routes from A to B to minimise time and effort. However, this was modified at a more local scale by zig-zagging up the steep scarp slopes, and avoiding obstacles such as bogs and scarp-top cliffs. Also, once a route was established and visible on the ground, there would be a natural tendency to follow this as it pointed the way. If people were heading to destinations such as the local market towns, often there were choices of viable routes according to the weather, season and preference.

The overall layout of pre-turnpike routes on the moorland shows that the main traffic was east–west. People, packhorses, carts and waggons came eastwards out of the Derwent Valley, some travelling from places further west, such as the market at Bakewell. Amongst the most important goods going east were lead ore and smelted lead from the Derbyshire orefield and salt from Cheshire. Crossing the moors, they were heading for markets at Sheffield, Dronfield, Chesterfield and Alfreton, and a variety of outlets beyond.

Fig 8.8
Traditional routeways, roads and drives on the Chatsworth Estate east of the River Derwent (for A–N see text). Abandoned hollow-ways and roads are particularly clear on the gritstone moorland.

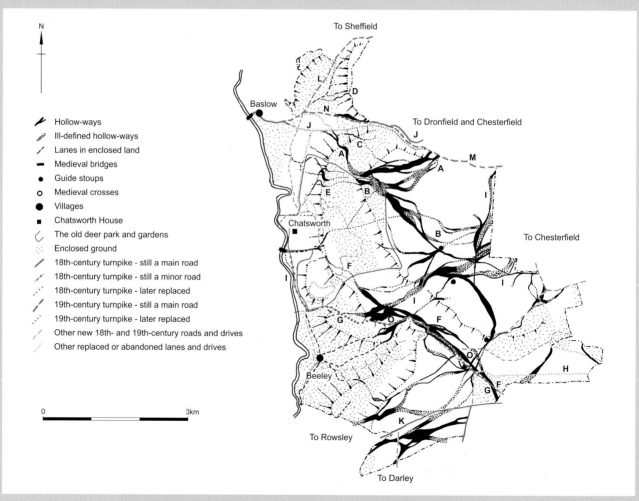

Similarly, goods came westwards from a variety of iron foundries, workshops and manufacturers. Earthenware pottery, stoneware and finer tableware came into the Peak from both west and east sides.

There is a network of interconnected hollow-ways. The pattern of routes seen on the moors is heavily influenced by crossing places on the River Derwent, with medieval stone bridges at Baslow, Chatsworth, Rowsley and Darley. Coming from the bridge at Baslow is a major braided hollow-way with alternative choices, probably in use from medieval times to the late 18th or early 19th century (A). Some braids are truncated by the boundary of Chatsworth Park (B), which has been on this line since before 1617, the date of the earliest map that survives.[15] In contrast, one hollow-way led specifically to early coal mines (C). Another route has been cut down to bedrock with rubble heaped to one side; this probably reflects 'King's Highway' maintenance after this was made a statutory part of parish duties in 1555 (D). A route coming through the northern end of Chatsworth Park from Chatsworth Bridge (E), again probably went out of use when the park was created in the 14th or 15th century. In contrast, a route coming from the bridge and going south-east through the Park and heading towards Alfreton was still in use in 1617 (F), but perhaps by then only by estate traffic; it passes a medieval cross base and

early lead-smelting boles. From the 16th to 18th centuries it was the way to the Cavendish family's other main seat, at Hardwick Hall, just over 15 miles away beyond Clay Cross. In 1710–11 it was improved to a coach road, which was partially superseded in 1739 when the early Bakewell to Chesterfield turnpike road was created on a more southerly line (G). Both were formally closed to non-estate traffic in 1759 when 'Capability' Brown's landscape park was created. The year before, a private carriage drive was created across the moors that made a more convenient continuation towards Hardwick (H). Another route from Chatsworth Bridge (I), perhaps with medieval origins, again avoided the old deer park by going south along the valley bottom before heading onto the moors towards Chesterfield, Dronfield and Sheffield, where there was a medieval cross on the scarp top. Other hollow-way routes further south came from the Rowsley and Darley bridges.

From the mid-18th century the modern road network across these moors was gradually created. The first wave of improvements, which followed traditional routes, comprised the 1759 Baslow to Chesterfield Turnpike (J) and the 1760 Rowsley to Stone Edge turnpike (K). Later, the Baslow to Sheffield road was authorised in 1803 (L), and a new route to Chesterfield was created in 1812 (M) and modified in the 1820s when the park was extended northwards (N).

Turnpike roads
Paying tolls

Three atypically early turnpikes were built that are worthy of note. The traditional main road from Manchester to Derby and ultimately London, passing through Buxton and from there in part following the approximate line of the Roman road south-east, had a section north-west of Buxton turnpiked in 1725, whilst a section south-east of the town following the pre-turnpike route was turnpike in 1752; a branch to Ashbourne, deviating from the old pre-turnpike route through Brassington, had previously been added in 1738.[16] What today is known as the Woodhead Pass, crossing the Pennine chain via Longdendale, was part of an ancient route, improved from Manchester to Woodhead after a 1731 Turnpike Act, with an eastern continuation authorised in 1741, which branched further east to both Doncaster

and Rotherham. The Bakewell to Chesterfield turnpike route, which went via Chatsworth, was authorised in 1739.[17]

It was not until the late 1750s to early 1760s that an integrated turnpike road network was developed in the Peak, which when completed linked all the main population centres fringing the region with the market towns in the Peak. Additions were made in the 1770s and 1780s. The trusts were seen as long-term investments, with the cost not expected to be recovered from tolls for several decades; some trusts never paid them off with the financial speculation being misplaced as not enough traffic was ever attracted. However, some of the investors presumably made much money elsewhere, because of the positive impacts made on their businesses and/or the incomes from their estates.

Where these roads crossed the Peak, in places there were problems with the routes chosen; after completion, with the original investor's money already spent, the Trusts realised that sections of road became impassable or were difficult in winter when there was snow and ice. In order to keep costs down, the original routes had followed relatively straight lines, which sometimes meant incorporating significant gradients. Over the years, when it could be afforded, minor diversions were made in order to bypass particularly problematic sections, with sinuous and somewhat longer routes added that followed the contour along more gentle gradients. Also, a second generation of trusts built new roads, mostly in the first two decades of the 19th century, replacing or supplementing old turnpikes. These again tended to be more sinuous; the lesson had been learned. Another significant difference is that unlike the earlier turnpikes, which rationalised well-established routes, these early 19th-century roads tended to follow new routes, shorter and more direct routes across moorlands, or for instance along

the limestone gorges between Bakewell and Buxton, where land had to be cleared of boulders and cuttings occasionally made through steep rocky spurs.

The turnpike roads in the Peak eventually lost much of the industrial customer base they relied upon. Sometimes alternative roads were competing for the same business. However, the coming of railways in particular dealt a hard blow when they eventually arrived. Several trusts were wound up in the 1870s; a few had folded long before. The duty of maintaining roads passed to local authorities after the Local Government Act of 1888.

Passable roads

As noted above, parts of turnpike roads were modified to take out steep gradients, following more sinuous routes that were easier to use. Two examples of diversions are illustrated here.

Long Hill

The A5004 'Long Hill road' from Buxton to Whaley Bridge has origins as the Manchester to Buxton Turnpike, large parts of which were made in about 1780 by the road builder John Metcalf as part of a diversion to the original 1725 turnpike road.[18] This diversion also had stretches that were hard to use and it was diverted again in about 1820. A classic example is where it descended into a steep-sided side valley at Rake End and then ascended the other side (Fig 8.9). The diverted route is about 1km longer and bends

sinuously around the head of this valley. Whilst the gradients were avoided and this solved the problem for waggons, it created an unanticipated problem that came to the fore in the late 20th century; this is one of the Peak roads that are notorious for motorcycle accidents on twisty bends. The old road is still used as a farm track.

A little further north the c 1780 road ran further up the hillside than that of c 1820, its line now identified on a map from the straight field wall to one side; today the original road survives as a disused, narrow, flat-topped causeway of single-waggon width.

Fig 8.9
This section of the Manchester to Buxton turnpike on Long Hill, north-west of Buxton, dating to about 1780, was abandoned some 40 years later due to the steep gradient and replaced by a more sinuous road that followed the contour; this lies below the skyline to the left of the earlier route but it is not easy to make out in this photograph.
[John Barnatt]

Robin Hood

Above Baslow around Robin Hood the situation is more complex than at Long Hill (Fig 8.10).[19] The original 1759 Chesterfield to Baslow Turnpike came up from Baslow, through what later became an extension to Chatsworth Park, where its now grassy course can still be traced as a slight linear terrace. Further east it crossed Heathy Lea Brook on a fine bridge that is now unfortunately collapsing and dangerous. It then ascended to the main scarp top and went straight ahead, passing a cottage at Robin Hood whose door originally opened onto the road, with a plaque above the door reading '1793, Buckles Made Repared, Knife Blades put in, By J Froggatt'. The route passing to the top of the upper scarp was subsequently moved to lessen the gradient. Beyond it went to 'New Bridge' going to Chesterfield via Old Brampton. Much of

this route where now moved is again clearly traced today as a linear terrace. Major changes came in the early 19th century. At Robin Hood a new turnpike route of 1812 followed the south side of the stream, leaving the old road next to the bridge, heading eastwards towards Chesterfield; this was short-lived and was replaced when another new road on the north side of the stream was created in the 1820s. To the west the creation of the new parkland at Chatsworth led to a new road being built to the north of previous routes so as to lie outside the new pleasure ground; this is the present A619 and is hidden from Chatsworth Park by tree screens. Further east, at Robin Hood, the 1820s' road ran close to the 1759 route and its late 18th-century diversion, but further east it took a new and more direct line towards Chesterfield, running much further south of the older road that followed the traditional hollow-way route.

Fig 8.10
Roads between Baslow and Robin Hood, showing pre-turnpike lanes and braided hollow-ways, 18th-century turnpike roads, 19th-century turnpike routes and drives from Chatsworth House. Routes that have been abandoned are shown dashed.

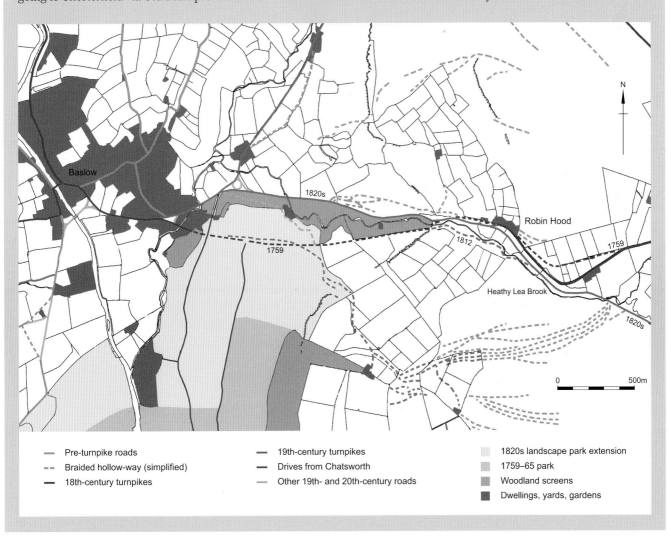

Pre-turnpike roads
Braided hollow-way (simplified)
18th-century turnpikes
19th-century turnpikes
Drives from Chatsworth
Other 19th- and 20th-century roads
1820s landscape park extension
1759–65 park
Woodland screens
Dwellings, yards, gardens

Guide stoups, milestones and mileposts

In 1697 an Act of Parliament was passed that instructed County Magistrates to erect guide stones on the King's highways where needed to aid travellers; this was first instigated in Derbyshire in 1709. A fine series of tall stone posts was erected, with others added through time (Fig 8.11).[20] Surviving examples are most common on the gritstone eastern moors but they can also be found elsewhere. Each is unique in that destinations are inscribed, the nearest local market centres given in a combination pertinent to the place erected. Usually they were placed at road junctions where the travelling stranger would need guidance. Depending upon how many choices a traveller was faced with, there are inscriptions on two to four faces of the pillar. Part of their particular charm is the non-standard spelling of place names, and the carved hands that pointed the way; to make carving easier they commonly only have three fingers! Dates and initials have also sometimes been added, some perhaps during highway inspections by official 'road surveyors'.

To the uninitiated how to use a 'guide stoup' can be downright confusing. Superficially, to our way of thinking, the faces state the wrong destinations. The unwritten rule, that all 18th-century travellers needed to understand, was that when looking towards a face of the stone, you should turn right to reach the destination indicated. However, to add to the confusion today, some stones have been re-erected after being taken down by the Home Guard in 1939–45, and their correct orientation was not retained.

When turnpike building began the designs for roadside stones changed; they were much shorter as people no longer needed the height to make them visible; the way ahead was clear for now a metalled surface was being followed. Posts were not placed at road junctions, but at regular intervals so that the mileage to places could be given; things were changing, time was precious and people wanted to know more precisely how far they still had to go. Each turnpike trust had their own standardised designs for posts, made under contract by stone masons or iron founders when each road was first constructed (Fig 8.12).

Fig 8.11
A fine 'guide stoup' at hollow-ways above Harland Edge on the Chatsworth Estate moors, erected in the early 18th century to indicate the direction to the market centres at Sheffield and Chesterfield for travellers coming from the Derwent Valley.
[John Barnatt]

Fig 8.12
A small selection of the various designs of milestones and mileposts in the region. The stone on the moors between Macclesfield and Buxton is on a 1759 turnpike (top left). The cast iron post near Alstonefield (bottom left) is on a road improved in the early 19th century, while the post between Ashford and Baslow (right) is on an 1812 turnpike; this lost its information on distances to local places when it was repainted a few years ago. [John Barnatt]

Eighteenth-century mileposts were made in hard-wearing sandstone, usually with carefully carved inscriptions, originally sometimes with paint added for readability. Nineteenth-century posts are often made in cast iron with embossed detail. Some have two angled faces that make them easier to see, whilst others are drum-shaped. The posts are usually painted black and white. The distances to market towns were stated on all; some also give the distance from London as stagecoach travellers would want to know how far they were from the civilised world.

With some of the iron posts, the places and mileages were not embossed but relied on them being painted on by a competent sign writer. Whilst there is often public pressure to retain mileposts as objects of interest, they are now irrelevant to modern road users when they pass at speed; once the signage is gone then, unless old photographs exist, future generations will be left guessing what was written. Not all mileposts have survived and over the years there has been a slow depletion; now in times of austerity many of the iron posts increasingly have flaking paint and rusty surfaces. Some people have thought they would make desirable garden ornaments; several years ago individuals were prosecuted when a post appeared in a local antique shop; the thieves had not realised that each is unique because of the distances given and the police were able to identify the perpetrators as the sub-contractors who had been doing the recent road repairs next to the post!

Rails and bulk transport

The Peak has two impressive sets of archaeological remains at important early rail lines, the first a tramway built in the 1790s; the other a railway built in the 1820s and 1830s.

Peak Forest Tramway

This was designed specifically for horse-drawn waggons used to bring out limestone from Lords Knoll, and later from Dove Holes Dale as the line was extended southwards.[21] This stone was burnt in limekilns at Bugsworth Basin on the Peak Forest Canal and at other places further along the canal. At various places along the line, parts of which have public access on footpaths, there remain visible stone sleeper blocks for L-section plateway rails. The original stones were laid by Benjamin Outram, the tramway's designer, of Butterley Iron Works fame. Part way along there was an inclined plane near Chapel en le Frith, which was of 'self-acting' type, with the weight of the loaded waggons pulling empty ones back up the incline, with a continuous cable and braking drumhouse at the top.[22] A short distance beyond the incline bottom the line passed into the short Stodhart tunnel built in 1795. One entrance has been buried and the other gated; within, the original sleeper blocks and horse-walk setts are well preserved. This was thought to be the oldest surviving railway tunnel in the world. But, recently the very short tunnel on the 1793 Butterley Gangroad, near Crich (but just outside the study area), again constructed by Outram, has been temporarily reopened and shown to be intact; for many years its entrances were blocked and it was unclear whether it survived. This was a 'cut and cover' tunnel, but is not the earliest of this type, as a 'cut and cover' colliery tramway tunnel at Flockton in West Yorkshire was built in the 1770s.[23]

Cromford and High Peak Railway

Much of this line is accessible to the public, including a long stretch from Cromford to just north of Hurdlow as the High Peak Trail for walkers and cyclists. Short parts near Harpur Hill and a long northern part in the Goyt Valley also have footpaths. These are to be found in Whaley Bridge, and from Fernilee southwards to a tunnel entrance south of Longhill Farm. This line is important to the early history of railways.[24] It was started after an Act of Parliament was passed in 1825, with the southern half opened in 1830 and the northern part in 1832. Horse-drawn waggons were used at first, but steam locomotives were introduced in 1841. The line's primary purpose was to transport industrial products such as coal from the Whaley Bridge area, with lime and limestone from the limestone plateau coming in the opposite direction, but from 1855 to 1877 passengers were also carried.

There were nine inclined planes on the route; except for one at Hurdlow, all were at the northern and southern ends of the route, where the line descended to lower ground and terminated at the Cromford Canal at Cromford Wharf and the Peak Forest Canal at Whaley Bridge. Both sites have extant canal/railway buildings. Eight of the inclines originally had a steam engine at its top used to haul waggons. The exception is a short one at Whaley Bridge that was counterbalanced and assisted by a horse gin. That steam engine at Middleton Top is intact, with its 1829 engine still within and open to the public. A short distance to the west, there is an in-situ 'waggon' boiler for a steam engine at the head of an early 19th-century branch line that ran down to limestone quarries at Hoptonwood. At Sheep Pasture above Cromford there is a now-empty engine house, whilst halfway up Bunsal Cob in the Goyt Valley there are footings of another. At the top of Bunsal Cob there is a reservoir for a second engine at the top of an upper incline. From 1857 the middle engine here was scrapped and the full length from the valley bottom to top was hauled from the top engine. Another fine conserved steam engine is that of 1849 at Leawood just south of Cromford, used to pump water up from the Derwent into the Cromford Canal at a point south of the railway wharf (Fig 8.13).

Other key archaeological features along the line include a series of bridges, cuttings and embankments. Noteworthy is the massive, stone-faced embankment at Minninglow (Fig 8.14). A particularly acute bend in the line at Harpur Hill was bypassed by building a high embankment with a gentler curve in 1875. Similarly, at Hurdlow the incline was bypassed in 1869 by building a long deviation. The Buxton Tunnel now has doors and there is no public access. When originally built the line had fish-bellied iron rails on stone sleeper blocks, and whilst these were later replaced by timber sleepers, displaced stone blocks can still be found incorporated in walls flanking the line, each with a distinctive central hole for the iron fastening pin. In some rock-sided cuttings, shothole scars in the rock sides illustrate where explosives were used when they were created or enlarged.

There were a number of sidings and short branches at industrial sites, including those at Harpur Hill where the large limestone quarry complex included a massive Hoffmann Kiln built alongside the line in 1872, now with only its oval base surviving. Two small similar examples near the line at Friden still exist, where the plant for making refractory bricks from local deposits of silica sands and gravels was started in 1892; they are still in use hidden within modern buildings. Further south-east a small quarry beyond the Minninglow Embankment still has an abandoned crane, whilst a little further along there are two conserved brick-making kilns.

The northern stretch of the line, from a point south of Buxton, was closed in 1892 when a new line into Buxton town centre was created. Shortly afterwards, what is now the Tissington Trail, leaving the High Peak Trail just south of Parsley Hay, was opened in 1899 as a line to Ashbourne. The southern half of the Cromford and High Peak Railway was last used in 1967 and was axed during the Beeching era.

Fig 8.13
The Leawood pumping engine south-east of Cromford was erected in 1849 to supply water to the late 18th-century Cromford Canal from the river below. This compensated for insufficient water taken from Cromford Sough and nearby streams. The vertical-cylindered engine is in the main building while the two boilers are in a one-storey building to the left. [John Barnatt]

Fig 8.14
This massive walled embankment was built in the 1820s north of Minninglow for the Cromford and High Peak Railway. The line is now a walking and cycle trail. [John Barnatt]

Other industrial lines

Quarry tramways include an impressive early 20th-century example at Bole Hill, where stone to build reservoir dams further up the Derwent Valley was acquired, whilst another smaller self-acting tramway near Chinley brought stone down from the Cracken Edge quarries (Fig 8.15) (*see* Chapter 7). Other industrial lines include those at coal mines, linking them with nearby roads, as at Burbage Colliery, or more commonly to the railway network.

Fig 8.15
At the Cracken Edge quarries, which produced sandstone slates, a narrow tramway leads in a straight line diagonally down from a small brake drum at the top. There are small earlier quarry workings here, but the incline dates to a late phase when a level led into the hill from here to the main dipping beds coming down from the quarries above that had been followed underground.
[John Barnatt]

Bole Hill

Spectacular archaeological remains, now largely hidden in birch woodland, exist at Bole Hill above Grindleford Railway Station (Fig 8.16).[25] Here there are large quarries created in the first two decades of the 20th century to provide the gritstone used in the construction of the Derwent and Howden reservoirs, located 13km to 15km further north in the Derwent Valley (*see* Chapter 9).[26]

In 1901 the reservoir builders took over a relatively small millstone and grindstone quarry at the scarp of the main eastern moors gritstone shelf here (*see* Chapter 7). This site was to be used to supply high-quality stone for the ambitious new reservoir venture and quarrying began in earnest in 1903. By the time extraction was completed, the quarry had produced over 1.2 million tons (1.1 million tonnes) of useable stone, and there was an in-part benched quarry face that was 600m long at the top of the site to the east; there also were part-filled quarries below to the west and at the southern end, dug earlier in the project. Large amounts of stone dressing waste were produced, which was dumped in the initial quarries, forming a series of flat-topped hillocks. Over the life of the quarry, the layout of faces, tips and railed routes was ever-changing as extraction proceeded.

Photographs of features taken whilst extraction was in progress are now sometimes hard to locate precisely.

To get building stone away from the faces, a complex standard-gauge railway line was installed, with waggons hauled by steam-powered tank-engines. Passing down through the quarry a 'permanent' zig-zag line was created, with two places where the direction of haulage was reversed. Near the top, the line passes through a cutting with bedrock to the sides, whilst lower down there are high heaps of waste to either side. It led down to a large flat hillock-top working area at the top of an incline, with a stone-built workshop and also a now-removed small brakeman's hut, a mess room and a locomotive shed.

In addition to the standard-gauge line, there were exceptionally wide lengths of temporary track, of 11ft (3.5m) gauge, that were laid to run parallel to active stretches of face, designed as stable 'platforms' for large mobile steam cranes used for loading waggons with stone; only slight possible traces of these survive. They also used smaller steam cranes on standard-gauge waggons. The waste heap tops have visible indicators of further temporary rail beds, used for taking stone in tubs for dumping. These lines were moved across the hillocks as dumping proceeded, to minimise the amount of movement of waste by hand.

At the south-western end of the site there was an impressive incline for a twin line leading down to the main Midland Railway Manchester to Sheffield line in the valley bottom that had been created in the 1890s. This steep incline took loaded waggons down and was of 'self-acting' type. Large stone piers can still be seen above the top of the incline that supported the vertical braking drum for the incline cable. These were once within a timber-framed, corrugated iron-sheeted drum house. Against the side of the incline there is a series of flat-topped plat-forms where temporary accommodation and a recreation hut with reading room, were provided for the quarry workforce.

From the siding at the base of the incline, beyond a road crossing the incline, the stone was transported partway to the reservoir dams on the main line. From a point at which the latter headed off towards Edale, a purpose-built line for the stone trains continued further up the Derwent Valley. In shallow water towards the west side of Derwent Reservoir, near the site of the navvy settlement at Birchenlee, stone pillars for a timber-framed viaduct can still be seen.

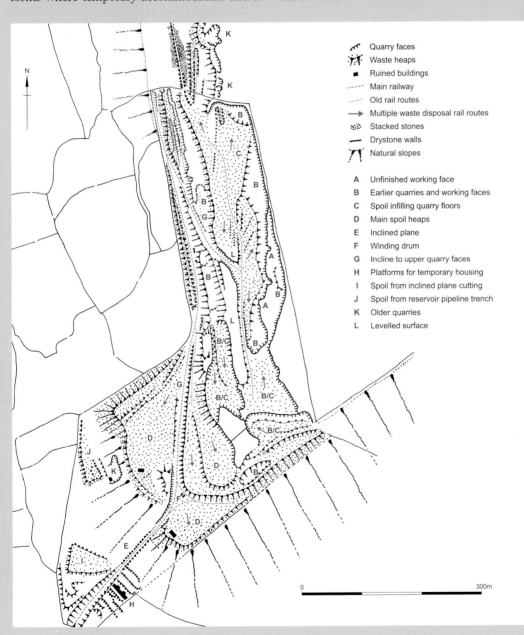

Quarry faces	
Waste heaps	
Ruined buildings	
Main railway	
Old rail routes	
Multiple waste disposal rail routes	
Stacked stones	
Drystone walls	
Natural slopes	

A   Unfinished working face
B   Earlier quarries and working faces
C   Spoil infilling quarry floors
D   Main spoil heaps
E   Inclined plane
F   Winding drum
G   Incline to upper quarry faces
H   Platforms for temporary housing
I   Spoil from inclined plane cutting
J   Spoil from reservoir pipeline trench
K   Older quarries
L   Levelled surface

0   300m

Fig 8.16
Bole Hill Quarry, showing the faces and waste heaps, together with the sites of the main railway lines, temporary lines for waste disposal, the incline to the valley below, and the site of temporary housing at a small navvy settlement in use when the quarry was active.

Burbage Colliery

A good example of a small colliery tramway is that built high on the moors above Buxton near the head of the River Dane on Axe Edge Moor. It was created in 1878–9 in the last phase of working at the Thatch Marsh Colliery complex, by that date known as Burbage Colliery (*see* the case study 'Thatch Marsh and Goyt's Moss

collieries' on pp 111–12).[27] Whilst most tramways built in the north-west Peak have only vestigial earthworks amongst farmland, which for the uninitiated are often hard to identify, that at Burbage Colliery is well preserved because of its isolated moorland site (Fig 8.17).

In order to mine the remaining coal reserves of the Duke of Devonshire's mine, at that date leased by Buxton Lime Company, a new colliery entrance was created. This was at the southern end of the mine, under desolate moorland. It comprised an underground inclined drift following the seam as it dipped westwards going ever deeper below the moor. Outside, at the crest of the hill, they installed a steam engine in a squat but sturdy engine house, with attached boiler house and chimney, and a shed nearby. The engine wound small tubs of coal up the narrow-gauge tramway in the drift to surface. Immediately beyond a flat area by the engine house the land fell away eastwards and the tubs were let down on a surface incline to a 'wharf' in Cisterns Clough just above the main road between Buxton and Leek. Here there was a small office, a store and sidings; coal was loaded onto horse-drawn carts, some belonging to local people who purchased the coal here, the rest presumably going to the Grin Hill limekilns.

The last accessible reserves were worked in 1915–16 and the mine closed in 1919 after a planned retreat towards surface robbing the pillars of coal that supported the roof.

All that remains today of the engine house are barely recognisable footings and a small reservoir pond nearby, with a bare spoil heap made up of waste shale dug out as the incline was sunk, and a collapsed entrance to the underground drift nearby. In contrast, the tramway incline leading south-east can be easily identified for much of its length as a narrow terrace, in one upper part in a shallow cutting and elsewhere on a low embankment; virtually all traces of the buildings at the roadside wharf were swept away by a flood several decades ago.

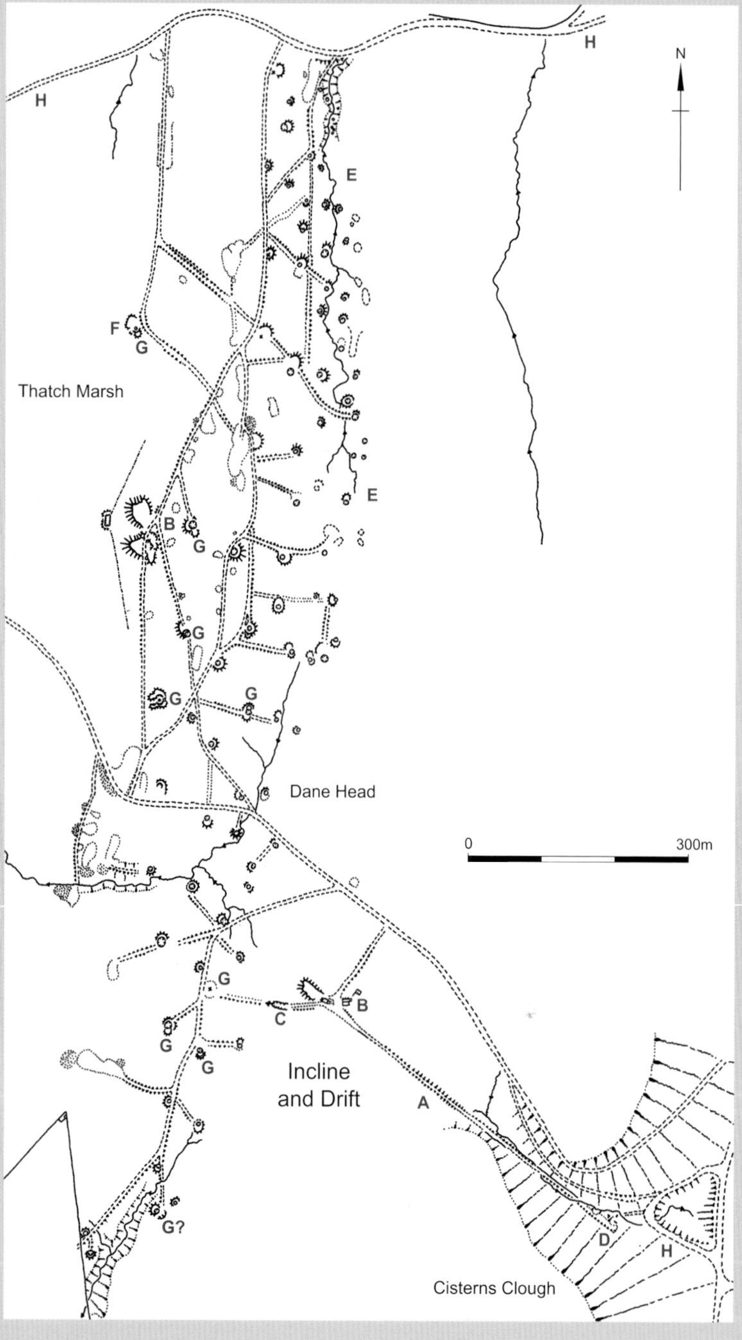

Fig 8.17
The southern part of Thatch Marsh Colliery, with sites of the tramway incline at what became known as Burbage Colliery (A), two later 19th-century steam engine houses (B), the entrance to the inclined drift (C), the wharf (D), early workings near outcrop (E), a ventilation shaft (F), two ventilation firehouses (G) and turnpike roads (H) (for a key, see Fig 6.24).

9

Using water

It rains in the Peak. Like any upland in Britain the rainfall is high and the plentiful water supply has been harnessed. For millennia rivers and streams have been used to power mills, traditionally for milling cereals, but in post-medieval times increasingly providing power for industrial processes such as cloth manufacture and pigment grinding.[1] Industrial-scale mills for cotton and silk manufacture, and for allied trades, led to places growing in importance, as at Cromford, Macclesfield, Bollington, New Mills and Glossop, with terraced housing being built to accommodate workers. As we saw in Chapter 3 (*see* p 56), in the north-western fringe of the Peak in particular the settlement was transformed at a landscape scale.

The other main use for water was as a drinking supply for surrounding towns and cities; large reservoirs started being built in the 1790s but this early example fed a canal, whereas those for drinking water came from the 1830s onwards (Fig 9.1).[2]

Fig 9.1
Ladybower Reservoir in the Upper Derwent Valley built in the 1930s and 1940s, with the high Dark Peak gritstone moorlands behind, viewed from Bamford Edge.
[© Anthony Hammerton]

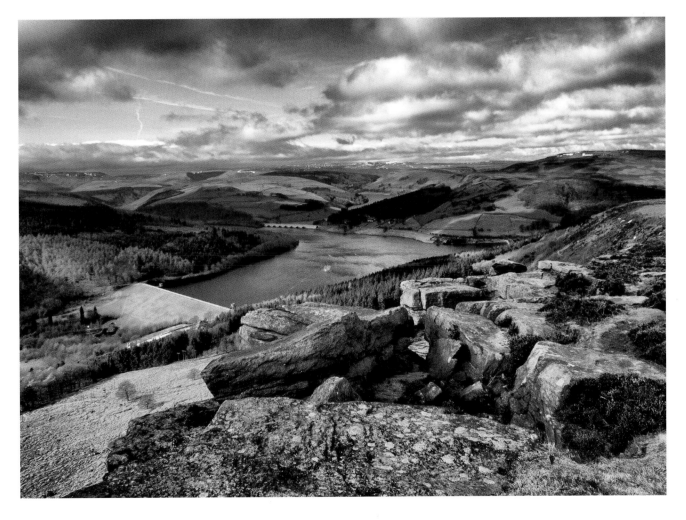

Mills for many purposes

Flour has been ground since Neolithic times, but the first evidence we have in the Peak for water-powered mills as opposed to hand-operated querns comes from the medieval period. There is documentation for a number of manorial mills. Domesday Book of 1086 records them at Bakewell, Ashford and Hope. Medieval mills were strung along the main rivers, particularly the Derwent and Wye, but also at less favourable places. Where possible each community needed to be self-sufficient, and sometimes the best site available was used even when not ideal because the water supply could dwindle in the summer. Places named in this section are given on Figure A1.6 (*see* p 233).

The old corn mills that survive today are mostly of 18th- or 19th-century date; the buildings often now converted to dwellings at best, with little but the waterwheel surviving. However, there are exceptions, with dilapidated privately owned buildings standing with all their internal machinery remaining. Caudwell's Mill at Rowsley is a conserved 1874 mill, powered by water turbines rather than a wheel, which is open to the public. The now-roofless mill at Edensor, at the

southern end of Chatsworth Park, is unusual in that it was designed by architect James Paine. It was built in the early 1760s in an austere classical design, as a working mill when the medieval mill near Chatsworth House was removed. More importantly, it stood as an eye-catching statement for visitors entering the park over Payne's Bridge, which told of style and prestige.

Silk manufacture on an industrial scale started in Macclesfield from the 1740s, with origins in home-production from the late 17th century. Mills were built for throwing, spinning and printing. Fine examples survive here at Chester Road Mill with its 1790 datestone, and at Paradise Mill built in 1862, which is open to the public. The impressive Clarence Mill nearby at Bollington, which is now apartments, was built in 1834 with additions to 1877.

The best-known cotton mills, those built for Richard Arkwright, the innovator of industrial-scale milling, at Cromford Mill and Masson Mill, are recognised as key sites in the development of the Industrial Revolution and these are returned to below. Whilst Arkwright started building at Cromford in 1771, by the 1780s cotton mills were springing up across the Peak, some built by him, some by other people who could see there

Fig 9.2
This fine architect-designed building of 1815, now luxury flats, is at Cressbrook Mill against the River Wye in the heart of the limestone plateau country. The mill was founded in the late 18th century, with its original building now demolished; the 1815 building was added to process a greater quantity of textiles when production was expanded.
[John Barnatt]

was money to be made. Other large standing mills are found, for example, at Edale on the Noe (1795), and at Bamford (1782, rebuilt 1791) and Calver (1785–6), both on the Derwent. Cressbrook Mill on the River Wye was started by Arkwright in 1783; the surviving building of 1815 has a fine 'Georgian' frontage (Fig 9.2). Further upriver Litton Mill (started 1782, rebuilt 1870s) is famous for the poor treatment in the late 18th century of apprentices brought from London as there was insufficient local workforce. Both mills are again now converted to luxury apartments.

In the north-western part of the Peak, industrial-scale mills again started in the late 18th century, with an exponential boom in the 19th century and decline in the 20th century. Mills here produced fine cotton and rougher calico, whilst finishing mills specialised in bleaching and textile printing. Although the rivers formed the focus which instigated the building of mills, as production increased it was necessary to supplement water power with steam engines. The latter had the iconic tall chimneys that were so characteristic of mill towns in northern England. The north-western Peak had a ready supply of local coal, mined in

places such as Whaley Bridge, whereas those mills in the heart of the Peak did not have coal nearby. Whilst many mills have been demolished and few chimneys are now to be seen, fine examples of converted mills remain, for instance in Glossop at Wren Nest (1815) and Howardtown (c 1830). At New Mills in The Torrs, a spectacular gritstone gorge with public access, the dilapidated Torr Vale Mill of 1788 still stands and there are ruins of others in the valley bottom (Fig 9.3).

Mills built for other purposes included those associated with lead processing, where colour works used for specialist products such as red lead found in paint manufacture were sometimes built close to the smelters. Similarly, barytes from Peak mineral veins was also milled for use in paint making, for example at mills around Chapel en le Frith and Whaley Bridge.[3] Paper was also made, which benefited from the availability of pure soft water, as at the now-ruined Greens Mill near North Lees built in 1792–3 on the site of an old lead smelting mill.[4] At Shacklow Wood, west of Ashford, a rare survival is a pair of small mills used from about 1870 for producing bobbins for the textile industry.

Fig 9.3
This workaday textile mill at Torrs Vale Mill, no longer used for its original purpose, was sited in a deep gorge that passes through New Mills.
[John Barnatt]

Cromford and Masson mills

At the northern end of the Derwent Valley Mills World Heritage Site are two of the most historically important mills in Britain, both partially open to the public.[5] Cromford Mill was Richard Arkwright's first industrial cotton mill, which was built in 1771. It formed the blueprint for factory production with its long-term global impacts, instigated during the Industrial Revolution here in Derbyshire. His Masson Mill was built in 1783 as his business expanded.

Today the Cromford Mill complex comprises three large mills of four to six storeys, various warehouses around a yard, footings of a barracks for the mill workers, a stables and coach house, and a defensible gate to the road outside, all built between 1771 and about 1790. Nearby are the mill manager's house of 1796, a loom shop and company cottages.

In Cromford village there is a market place with the Greyhound Inn in Georgian style, with surrounding shops, all built for Arkwright in about 1790 to provide facilities for his workers. Uphill there are rows of terraced housing built for the mill workers, the earliest of which date to 1776. Nearby, hidden behind houses is the Bear Pit, a 1785 entrance to the pre-existing Cromford Sough, from where water was culverted for the original mill.

The Cromford Canal, with its wharf near the mill, was built in the early 1790s by William Jessop and Benjamin Outram, who ran what later became the Butterley Company at Ripley. This canal allowed raw cotton to be more easily brought in and finished goods taken away southwards towards Derby. Across the river is Willersley Castle, a stately pile started in about 1790 as Arkwright's residence, designed in a plain but sturdy classical style, allowing the master to live in luxury, out of sight of his factories; he died in 1792 before it was finished. It replaced his first home at Rock House, a smaller plain house built in 1776 in Cromford itself, in an elevated position above the canal wharf overlooking the source of his wealth just across the road below. The parish church next to the river was built as a chapel for Willersley Castle but was opened for public worship in 1797 and Gothicised in 1858. A school house for young mill workers was erected in 1832.

About 0.5km upriver, Masson Mill stands five storeys high and is brick built. The original mill is designed in a tasteful style with classical details, reflecting Arkwright's growing wealth and confidence. A large addition to the south was created in the early 20th century and is more workaday in character, in what by then was typical mill style; it is now a retail centre.

Holding the water back

Turning now to dams to supply water, the earliest are the exceptional ponds added above Chatsworth from the 1690s onwards to supply the fountains and other features in the gardens.[6] Early reservoirs were also important for keeping canals from going dry and the distribution of these and drinking water supply reservoirs is given on Figure 9.4. The canal reservoirs lie to the west side of the Peak; that at Combs near Whaley Bridge was built in 1797 for the Peak Forest Canal (Fig 9.5). This was supplemented in 1831 by the Toddbrook Reservoir with its high embankment rising ominously above the town centre itself.

Perhaps the earliest water supply reservoir for drinking water, built at a larger scale than the many small stock ponds that provided water on farms, was a curious and now abandoned reservoir on Ollersett Moor near New Mills. This has an impressive circular embankment, now abandoned and dry, miles from anywhere on nearly flat, high moorland. It was built after an 1831 private Act of Parliament was passed for George W Newton, a local landowner, which allowed him to supply part of the town of New Mills and his own farms nearby.

Given the topography of the region, a more sustainable approach to storing large amounts of water was to build high dams across the deep upper valleys that dissect the gritstone upland, where settlement was sparse or non-existent. When dams were instigated to supply Sheffield, the first were the Redmires Dams of 1836–54, which have topographic similarities to Ollersett. But, in 1848 the Rivelin Dam was placed below in the deep valley of the River Rivelin.

Manchester and nearby places in Tameside started their quest for water from the Peak soon after Sheffield, building water supply dams in the Longdendale Valley at around the same time as Rivelin. Here there is an ambitious string of five reservoirs; to reach Manchester the water needed to be taken through the Mottram Tunnel driven in 1848 to 1850.

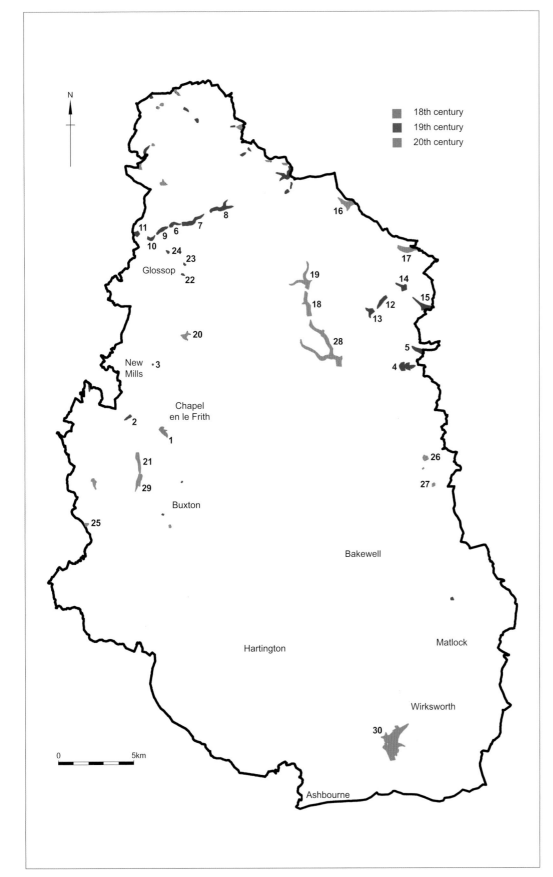

Fig 9.4
Peak reservoirs. Sites
mentioned in the text are:
1: Combs
2: Toddbrook
3: Ollersett Moor
4: Redmires
5: Rivelin
6: Rhodeswood
7: Torside
8: Woodhead
9: Valehouse
10: Bottoms
11: Arnfield
12: Dale Dike
13: Strines
14: Agden
15: Damflask
16: Langsett
17: Broomhead
18: Derwent
19: Howden
20: Kinder
21: Fernilee
22: Hurst
23: Mossy Lea
24: Swineshaw
25: Trentabank
26: Barbrook
27: Ramsley
28: Ladybower
29: Errwood
30: Carsington

153

The top three reservoirs came first, all started in 1848–9. Rhodeswood was finished in 1855, Torside in 1864 and Woodhead in 1877, the last delayed after the first dam, finished in 1854, was found to leak, hence a new dam had to be built in 1862 to 1877. The bottom two reservoirs were started later and were for 'compensation', filled in wet weather and then used to top up the River Etherow so that mills downstream always had water; Valehouse Reservoir was built in 1865 to 1869, whilst that at Bottoms took longer to complete and was finished in 1877. Arnfield Reservoir near the bottom of the string, but taking water from a side stream, was started in 1849.

As it grew, Sheffield needed ever more water. Reservoirs were placed in the River Loxley valley, a little further north and thus further from the city than the 1830s and 1840s dams, at Dale Dike in 1858 to 1864 and Strines in 1859. Confidence in such reservoirs was severely shaken in 1864 when the Dale Dike Dam failed

when it was first filled; the torrent of water flooded Sheffield with over 240 people killed. This forced a thorough review of dam-building techniques and Dale Dike Dam was rebuilt in 1875, following one built at Agden in 1869 and both were supplemented by that at Damflask in 1898. In the next valley north, that of the River Porter, the Langsett Reservoir was added in 1898 to 1904. Supply was further supplemented in 1929 at Broomhead Reservoir in the Ewden Valley. This reservoir had its own 'Tin Town' of temporary buildings for the workforce.

The most ambitious scheme of all came in the early 20th century, with the building of the Derwent and Howden dams in 1901 to 1919 in the Upper Derwent Valley. These supplied Derby, Nottingham and Leicester through a pipeline laid down the valley, with discreetly hidden pump houses and inspection hatches at set intervals that are still in use today. The dams also supply Sheffield via an ambitious tunnel driven under Bamford Moor and Stanage Edge.

Fig 9.5
Combs Reservoir south-east of Whaley Bridge was not built for drinking water, but is a header water supply for the Peak Forest Canal and was created in 1797 to keep the canal topped up.
[John Barnatt]

One side effect of damming the Derwent is that the reservoirs intercepted water when it rained heavily on Kinder Scout and Bleaklow; the river became less prone to flooding.

Stockport came late to the party, opening the Kinder Reservoir in 1912, and building the Fernilee Reservoir in 1932 to 1936. Smaller towns sometimes also had their own water supplies before water provision was planned at a national level. Glossop's water supply came very early, with Hurst Reservoir built in 1837, followed by that at Mossy Lea in 1840 and Swineshaw in 1864. Buxton started provision in the 1870s and eventually had three small reservoirs; they are now all emptied. Similarly, Macclesfield supplemented its water supply with Trentabank Reservoir in the 1920s. To the east, Chesterfield built Barbrook Reservoir in 1910, and then came Ramsley Reservoir after they acquired a large tract of land on the eastern moor from the Duke of Rutland in the 1920s. At the northern end of the Dark Peak there is a halo of about 20 small reservoirs, built from the later 19th century onwards, supplying towns in Tameside and in the Huddersfield area.

Later in the 20th century water provision for the Midlands cities was supplemented by Ladybower Reservoir in 1935 to 1944, followed by smaller reservoirs to the west, at Lamaload above Macclesfield in 1958 to 1964 and Errwood Reservoir in the Goyt Valley in 1964 to 1967. The latest grand scheme for Midlands' cities, which broke the mould in that a relatively shallow valley to the south was targeted, was Carsington Water. Construction began in 1979, with a significant delay after the first dam failed, and it was finally completed in 1992. This is a major tourist attraction, with people coming for the visitor centre, water sports and lakeside walks.

When constructing large reservoirs in the later 19th and early 20th centuries, farmsteads and even small villages were demolished or left in ruins as the water rose. In the Upper Derwent Valley when the Howden and Derwent reservoirs were built in 1901 to 1916 there were 11 farmsteads that had to be demolished, all close to or below the planned high water line; on the hillsides trees were planted to reduce stocking levels and help sterilise the water supply (Fig 9.6).[7] Later, when more water was needed and the Ladybower Reservoir was built immediately downstream in 1935 to 1944, the effect on settlement was more radical. By now there were no suitable places to build large reservoirs in

Fig 9.6
The impressive early
20th-century Derwent
Reservoir dam wall in
the Upper Derwent Valley.
[© Anthony Hammerton]

the Peak where there were few or no dwellings that would be affected. Thus, they had little choice but to displace a significant number of people; Derwent village, the hamlet at Ashopton, and a further 21 farmsteads were lost. People were rehoused in three terraces of typical 1930s' 'suburban' houses at Yorkshire Bridge just downriver from the dam. Today only eight farmsteads exist in the main Upper Derwent Valley and the tributary Woodlands Valley of the River Ashop.

Goyt Valley clearances

The solution in the Upper Goyt Valley at Errwood and Fernilee reservoirs was somewhat different to what happened in the Upper Derwent Valley (Fig 9.7). People were not wanted and

properties were removed even above the proposed water line, standing as a radical contrast with what happens today at the more recent Carsington Water where people are positively encouraged. The Fernilee Reservoir was built in 1932 to 1936 by Stockport Corporation; upstream the Errwood Reservoir was added in 1964 to 1967. In the Goyt Valley demolitions in the 1930s included virtually all dwellings in the catchment, removed primarily as a precaution against polluting the water supply.[8] In all 21 properties were destroyed, including eight farmsteads and five other dwellings scattered up the valley. Also removed was the small hamlet at Goytsbridge, and the small farmsteads and other houses at the head of the valley at the Derbyshire Bridge hamlet, which had grown up on the old Buxton to Macclesfield turnpike road at the heart of the isolated Goyt's Moss Colliery. Down in the valley, Errwood Hall, built in 1840–41 by Samuel Grimshawe, a wealthy Manchester business-man, was sold in 1930 and used by Stockport Corporation for four years as a youth hostel before it was demolished. Another site that disappeared under the water was the Fernilee gunpowder mills.[9] This was the Peak's only explosives works, producing 'black powder' from 1801 that was presumably made for use in the region's mines and quarries; it closed shortly after the 1914–18 war but stood in ruins until the 1930s. There was a series of distinctively wide-spaced buildings, designed so that if an explosion occurred the damage was minimised; several explosions, with a small number of fatalities, are recorded. Some of the buildings had machinery powered by water, and tramways covered the distances between them; presumably waggons were pushed slowly and carefully by hand.

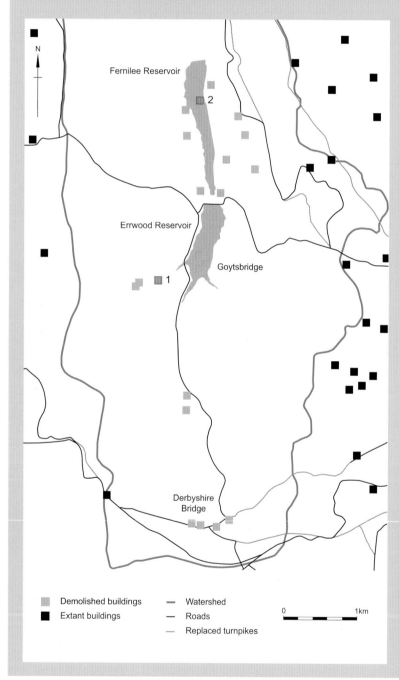

Demolished buildings — Watershed
Extant buildings — Roads
— Replaced turnpikes

0   1km

Fig 9.7

In the Goyt Valley, demolitions of many farmsteads and other dwellings took place in the 1930s with the building of Fernilee Reservoir; in contrast to these removals, dwellings survive to today close to and beyond the watershed. Also demolished were Errwood Hall (1) and the Fernilee Gunpowder Works (2). Much of the traditional road network survives, although some early turnpike routes were re-routed in the 19th century.

10

Past landscapes

The Peak has many ancient sites, ranging from those built in the Neolithic from about 5,500 years ago, onwards through to when the Romans arrived. These structures add to the overall richness of the historic landscape. They stand as vestiges within landscapes whose general character has been shaped more recently, and are found both in the enclosed farmed landscape and on moorlands.

Often the prehistoric monuments are large and have survived later farming in the enclosed landscapes because it was too much trouble to take away a large mound or a heavy stone, or they were in inaccessible locations. It may well be that some were recognised and respected over many generations. In contrast, on moorlands that have not been intensively used since pre-history, survival of slighter features is exceptionally good, with even round-house sites, field boundary banks and agricultural clearance cairns still remaining as upstanding structures. Here the governing factor is altitude. On the eastern grit-stone moorlands in particular there is much land that is high enough to have escaped intensive agriculture over many centuries, but low enough for extensive settlement and farming to have taken place in the last two millennia BC. They escaped 19th-century improvements because wealthy landowners developed a taste for grouse shooting and chose not to turn the moors to productive farmland. At the much higher Dark Peak areas to the north and west, people have done little except hunt and graze animals, walking through and leaving little trace of their presence, except for flints eroding from beneath the peat or an occasional round barrow looking over land below.

Although large areas of Peak commons, especially on the limestone plateau, were enclosed only 250 to 350 years ago, survival of earlier archaeological sites here is no better than in the former medieval open-field areas around each village where ploughing has taken place for over 1000 years. Even the fields on former commons have been ploughed several times, either for arable or reseeding. Survival of ancient features, except where they are large and hard to destroy, tends to be at rocky places in the enclosed farmland (Fig 10.1).

The land of the living

Overview

No prehistoric houses and outbuildings remain standing in the Peak; 'permanent' building for the most part had frames built of wood, wattle-and-daub walls and thatched roofs; all this has left for archaeologists are postholes and stakeholes where timbers were set in the ground, burning from hearths, scatters of artefacts and sometimes levelled platforms created when the buildings were made. In addition, it may well be that many generations of people spent long periods in tents, moving with livestock as they visited summer pastures on high ground; the evidence for this type of occupation is even slighter.

Fig 10.1
At Rainster Rocks, west of Brassington, medieval ridge and furrow stops short of the rock outcrop where there is a Romano-British settlement with possible prehistoric origins. All is overlain by post-medieval ruler-straight field walls and cut by two dew ponds.
[© Derrick Riley]

Except where investigated by archaeological excavation, as for example at Gardom's Edge above Baslow,[1] the sites of timber buildings and encampment are normally invisible, although their presence is attested by extensive waste from the making of stone tools that can be picked up in most ploughed fields in the region. In order to counter selective collection of fancy tools and more noticeable pieces, collection and study of lithics needs to be done systematically, using the same collection strategy over time. This has been done in a 6km-wide transect across the limestone plateau, Wye and Derwent valleys and eastern gritstone moors.[2] Lithics were found in all zones, but in greatest quantities on the limestone plateau. For the most part only a

broad brush picture is achieved, as details are obscured because many places were visited over and over again for thousands of years. Many flint and chert tools, and the debitage from their production, are not closely dateable, hence fine-grained pictures become clouded. The area around Arbor Low stood out as having a high density of material, some of which was exceptionally well-made, occasionally as elaborate tools, showing the importance of the high ridgetop pastures of the plateau. Interestingly, this started well before the long barrow and the henge were built.

In the Peak above-ground evidence for prehistoric settlement, fields and cairnfields is common on the eastern gritstone moors (Fig 10.2).[3] Here terraced house platforms have been identified amongst the many stone banks and cairns placed when ground was cleared for farming purposes. For the most part such evidence has been destroyed on the limestone plateau as farming has been more intense in historic times. Similarly, land at suitable altitudes on the western gritstone upland has been enclosed, whilst high moors there and to the north are too high to have ever been used for settlement.

The survival of prehistoric farming remains on the eastern gritstone moorlands is exceptional, matched in interest only in a few places elsewhere in England.[4] What makes them special is that we can get a picture of how the land was used over a relatively continuous stretch of moorland landscape with good survival of prehistoric features that is all at a similar altitude and over 25km long. Not only do we see the settlements and fields, but the spaces between that were used for open grazing, with stone circles and round barrows at and beyond the fields, which allows us to see how people organised themselves and their landscape. In other regions, all too often, what remains are small islands of surviving features surrounded by improved ground. On the eastern moorlands, in prehistory there were large swaths of farmed land in favourable locations, comprising low stone clearance features, sometimes found alone in cairnfields, but often the cairns are alongside low field banks and linear stretches of stone placed against the sites of hedges or fences; there are also terraces at the sites of circular timber buildings. At higher or otherwise less advantaged sites there are smaller areas with similar remains, some perhaps only used for short periods as the land proved unsuitable for sustained agriculture. Surrounding the

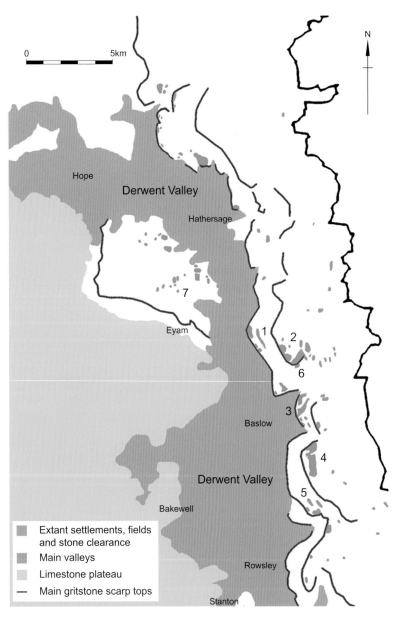

Fig 10.2
Prehistoric settlement and farmed areas with extant surface features on the eastern moors. Sites mentioned in the text are:
1: Stoke Flat
2: Big Moor
3: Gardom's Edge
4: Gibbet Moor
5: Beeley Warren
6: Swine Sty
7: Sir William Hill

agricultural areas, which are normally at places behind the scarps where originally there were good but stony light soils, with clay soils nearby avoided, there were extensive areas of upland grazing where the only built structures were scattered round barrows and smaller funerary cairns.

Today many of the features are hard for the uninitiated to locate as heather and coarse grasses tend to be higher than the heaps of stone and these are found with the feet rather than the eyes. The agricultural remains are located along the full length of the eastern gritstone upland wherever there is moorland as opposed to later improved fields in particular areas. The pre-historic farming concentrated on the main shelf between the scarp down to the Derwent Valley and an upper scarp to the east, and also where the upper scarp is breached by streams above Baslow. However, field evidence has been lost on the main shelf in those places where later farming has taken place. Evidence for prehistoric fields is also found west of the Derwent where there are smaller blocks of gritstone moorland above Eyam and Stanton. The largest, most complex and perhaps longest-used sites are found in the southern half of the eastern upland, on Stoke Flat, Big Moor, Gardom's Edge, Gibbet Moor and Beeley Warren, where the altitude is most advantageous. Here the moorland was retained for grouse shooting by the Dukes of Rutland and Devonshire rather than improved.

Dating and understanding these remains has long been one of the author's preoccupations. Close association of prehistoric fields with Earlier Bronze Age stone circles and barrows indicates use for farming at this date, whilst 1960s' excavations at Swine Sty on Big Moor found artefacts spanning the Earlier Bronze Age to Iron Age. Excavations at Gardom's Edge and pollen analysis at Stoke Flat have confirmed that much activity extended well into the Iron Age. The three excavated houses at Gardom's Edge belong to the Iron Age, but dating evidence for earlier agricultural remains here has proved elusive, although a percentage of the visible clearance features must be early, as witnessed by an excavated clearance cairn on Sir William Hill next to Eyam Moor that can be shown to have been created in the Late Neolithic. It is likely that in some places arable and livestock farming was practised for upwards of 2000 years, although the character of this no doubt changed through time.

Pollen analysis at deep peat bogs on the eastern moors has shown that trees were common here throughout prehistory.[5] Because different plants produce different amounts of pollen and this can travel very different distances according to species and how wooded the local environment is, only a general impression can be gained; the pollen does not give a clear picture that applies to specific places. In the Later Neolithic through to the Later Iron Age there were clearings and some cereals were being grown; it is likely that these focused on the areas with sandy soils where stone clearance features were created, whilst land with heavy clays and boulder-strewn slopes were more wooded. At around the time the Romans arrived most of the trees disappeared; taken at face value this would imply that settlement on the eastern gritstone upland increased exponentially. However, this did not happen, the archaeological evidence indicating that there was a significant contraction of settlement. Much more likely, but unprovably so, it was abandonment of large areas that led to tree loss; woodlands were a valuable resource that would have been carefully husbanded by local people. But, when many left and upland grazing became the norm, then non-selective but heavy grazing by livestock would have browsed out saplings.

Delving into the detail

The larger of the areas of prehistoric settlement and fields can each contain up to several hundred features. Most are made of stone cleared from the ground in preparation for, or during, cultivation. Many of the clearance heaps are placed on top of earthfast boulders, at spots that could not be cultivated. That these lie inside the small fields was not a problem for these areas; when cultivated intermittently they were not ploughed with a modern traction plough, but often hand dug much as an allotment is today. Linear clearance is intermittent and excavations have shown these stone heaps are not ruined walls but heaps of stone placed against now-lost boundaries such as fences or hedges. Potential timber house sites are seen as slight terraced platforms or have arcs of clearance stone following their edges. Excavations at Gardom's Edge have shown that not all houses are visible in these ways and not all potential sites with platforms turn out to be houses; the predicted success identification rate is perhaps only 50 per cent.[6]

Gardom's Edge

On the shelf above Gardom's Edge, mainly in its northern half (*see* Fig 2.16), there are many prehistoric remains.[7] Extensive excavations here have shown that most cairns overlie 'dead' ground with earthfasts underneath (Fig 10.3). Visible boundaries have stone features that accrued gradually. Three excavated houses have complex histories within the Earlier Iron Age. At one it was purposefully closed down by a bank built across the entrance after the house became disused. The largest house, once vacated became an atypical embanked enclosure of unknown purpose with a stone bank following the line of the house wall, entered by a narrow paved entrance of only half the width of the old porch. A large number of test pits across the shelf showed that artefacts are only found in small numbers except in the immediate vicinity of houses; one such house, on flat ground, was only found when an artefact cluster was investigated. Identifying phases of agriculture before the Iron Age proved an intractable problem due to lack of dating evidence; analogy with areas such as Big Moor and Sir William Hill suggest that some features are Bronze Age or earlier in date, but reconstructing the scale and character of this use at Gardom's Edge proved impossible.

Gardom's Edge is unusual in that there is the large Late Bronze Age scarp edge enclosure described below under 'Defending identity', in part overlain by clearance features, suggesting it did not retain its original purpose for many generations. Late in the overall sequence, a set of fields on a low back-ridge was bisected by two linear earthworks. The earlier of the two is a large stone bank, about 250m long, and excavation evidence suggested that adjacent cultivation continued despite its construction. In contrast, a short distance south, a pit alignment, about 330m long, cuts across everything. This curious monument comprises a large number of close-spaced small pits, each about 1m deep and clay-lined to hold water, with the upcast placed in low banks to either side. Both linears run across the ridge as if made to control movement of people who were passing through on a north–south route; breaks in the stone bank may well be prehistoric.

Fig 10.3
One of the many small clearance cairns on Gardom's Edge during excavation in the 1990s. This example includes large boulders in one half, some of which were earthfast, with smaller material placed between them and also in a more discrete later pile to the side.
[© Gardom's Edge Project]

Big Moor

A similar and instructive set of remains are found just over 1km to the north, to the west of Bar Brook. These show that interpretation needs careful thought (Fig 10.3).[8] On the crest of the main shelf there is good definition of earthen field boundaries. These banks have no ditches and are interpreted as the sites of hedges or fences that have trapped and dropped wind-blown soil coming from the adjacent fields. In contrast, the more sheltered area immediately downslope to the east has no visible boundaries, but this is very likely to have had fields in use longer than any other part of the shelf. Potential house sites are not scattered at random but are found at several clusters scattered amongst the fields and at two more sheltered locations with 'yards' and 'garden plots' below the scarp at the edge of wet ground below. One atypically small building at one of these areas, known as Swine Sty, had a stone bank interpreted as made to keep the timberwork off the ground, built as a shieling at a time late in the sequence when wetter conditions prevailed; it overlay the postholes of a larger house with timber posts but no stone bank. Whilst many of the visible features on Big Moor presumably accrued gradually as farming continued, in the central part of the shelf various linear features sit uncomfortably against others, suggesting that field layout was changed radically at some point in time. Three Earlier Bronze Age barrows, a freestanding stone cist and a ringcairn lie at the edge of the cultivation area, whilst two other barrows are in a central position. Such relationships demonstrate that this shelf was already used for farming when the monuments were built.

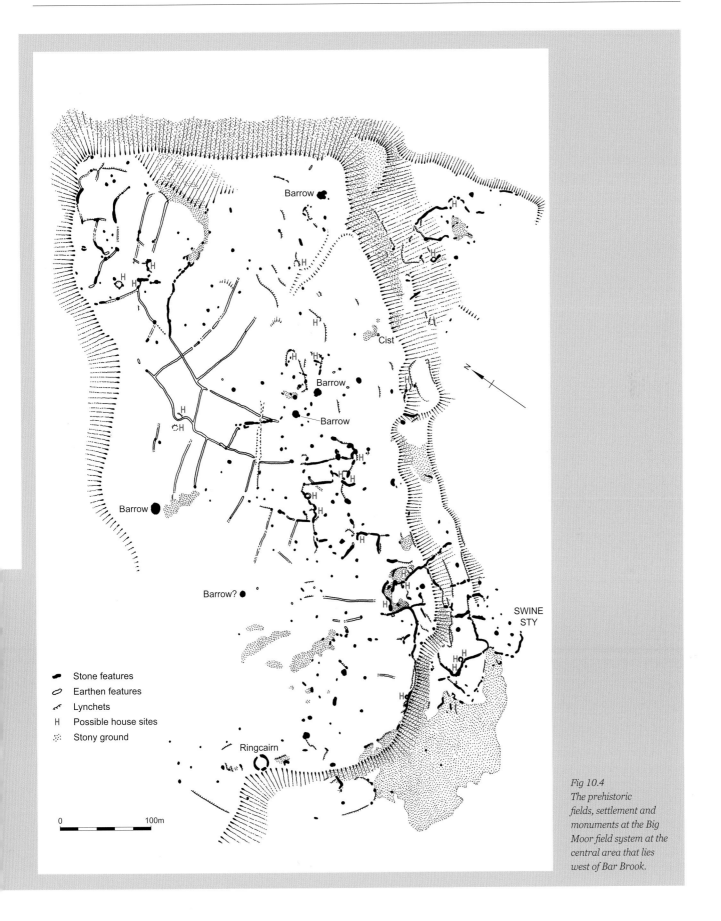

Barrow

Cist

Barrow

Barrow

Barrow

Barrow?

SWINE
STY

Ringcairn

Stone features
Earthen features
Lynchets
H   Possible house sites
Stony ground

0   100m

Fig 10.4
The prehistoric
fields, settlement and
monuments at the Big
Moor field system at the
central area that lies
west of Bar Brook.

161

Chatsworth moorlands

Further south, the remains on the Chatsworth moorlands, focused on Gibbet Moor and Beeley Moor, illustrate the relationships between field and monuments at a larger scale (Fig 10.5).[9]

Beyond the fields and associated round barrows and stone circles, there are funerary zones in the prehistoric open pastures with small cairns and low stone settings, together with larger barrows up near watersheds, but always sited so that views are directional across specific pastures.

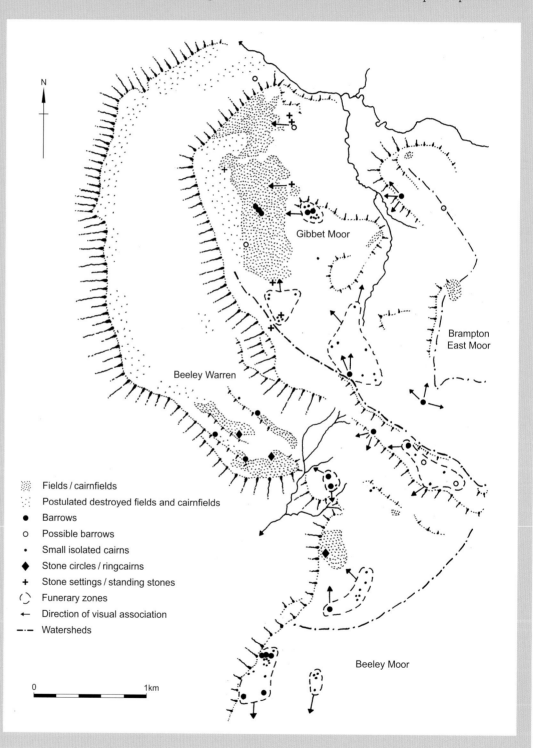

Fig 10.5
The gritstone upland east of Chatsworth, where there is good survival of prehistoric features on the moorlands, showing the inter relationships between fields, funerary zones and ceremonial monuments. The upland grazing areas of specific communities can be seen to be defined by watersheds.

Fields / cairnfields
Postulated destroyed fields and cairnfields
● Barrows
○ Possible barrows
· Small isolated cairns
◆ Stone circles / ringcairns
+ Stone settings / standing stones
◡ Funerary zones
← Direction of visual association
–·– Watersheds

0   1km

Gibbet Moor

Brampton East Moor

Beeley Warren

Beeley Moor

Monuments for all

The most widely known ancient sites in the Peak are the prehistoric ceremonial monuments built in the Neolithic and Earlier Bronze Age, which have long captured the public imagination and have been extensively studied by archaeologists and others. The location of those mentioned here are shown on Figure A1.7 (*see* p 235). Sometimes respect for these monuments has continued into the historic period, with names given such as 'Nine Ladies' or 'Hob Hurst House' appended.[10] These tell of now-obscure folk traditions or acknowledgement of the former importance of such places.

In some ways the most iconic prehistoric sites are the region's stone circles.[11] That at Arbor Low henge, probably built around 4,500 to 4,000 years ago, is by far the most impressive, sited high in the heart of the limestone plateau (Fig 10.6). Here a large bank with internal ditch, formerly with portal stones at the entrance, surrounds a sacred area containing a ring of stones and a central stone setting known as the cove. Most of the stones are flat to the ground and there have long been questions asked over whether the site was ever finished. This debate has been rather silly and should have been ended

decades ago, for even a cursory site visit reveals the stumps of some of the stones, set vertically. Instead, as often happens, authors who are not familiar enough with the site, trot out the same tired statements instead of going to look and think for themselves. The tall uprights have fallen or been felled. Long after the monument was first built a new generation stamped their authority by building a round barrow over the bank to overlook the interior. At a very similar monument long known as the 'Bull Ring', located nearly 17km away to the north-west as the crow flies at Dove Holes at the western edge of the limestone plateau, the bank and ditch remain, whilst the standing stones have now gone, although one was recorded as remaining in 1789 at a time when the land had been recently improved.

Both of these large henges were monuments built as places where people from broad areas of the Peak could come together seasonally for tribal ceremonies. For much of the year the people of the Peak in Neolithic times would have been scattered thinly across the landscape in small groups, at family dwellings in winter or tending livestock at upland pastures in summer. When they came together for communal ceremonies and festivities this allowed the

Fig 10.6
Part of the interior of Arbor Low, with the ring of now-recumbent upright stones and cove at the centre. A round barrow in the henge bank (right) was added later, with the bank to either side robbed to provide building material. [John Barnatt]

Fig 10.7
The Barbrook 2 stone circle, within the eastern Big Moor cairnfield, was restored in the 1990s and it now looks much as it did in prehistory, with small standing stones set on the inner edge of a retained rubble bank.
[John Barnatt]

Fig 10.8
The small Seven Stones of Hordron stone circle on the main gritstone shelf of Hordron Edge high above the Derwent Valley and Ladybower Reservoir, with Win Hill (left), Lose Hill (centre) and the Kinder Scout area (right) on the skyline.
[John Barnatt]

people to undertake other vital activities, such as discussions of farming strategies, exchanging goods and meeting prospective marriage partners. The act of erecting tall stones and creating high banks could have been instrumental in forging or strengthening tribal identity and people's relationship with the land; with subsequent generations seeing themselves as tied to the monument as their 'central place'.

There are a number of stone circles on the gritstone uplands to the eastern side of the Peak. These are very different in scale and character to the two henges. Typically, they are small in diameter and have low uprights set in the inner edge of a low rubble bank retained by drystone walls or vertical kerbstones; they were built in the Earlier Bronze Age. Fine examples include the well-known Nine Ladies on Stanton Moor and those on the moors just west of the main road between Baslow and Sheffield. Here the circle at Barbrook 1 is exceptionally well preserved, whilst Barbrook 2 nearby has been extensively restored in the 1990s after excavation in the

1960s (Fig 10.7).[12] There are variations to the design, as at the evocative Seven Stones of Hordron below Stanage Edge, where the stones are freestanding rather than set in a bank (Fig 10.8). Another freestanding ring is that at Nine Stone Close on Harthill Moor where the stones are much taller; perhaps this site was built in the Neolithic as part of an earlier circle building tradition. It is sited at a favourable location long in use, with other features nearby such as rock art, an Iron Age hillfort and two other enclosures of unknown date; one on Cratcliffe Rocks has been postulated to have been built in the Neolithic.[13] The circle lies close to Robin Hood's Stride, a visually striking natural outcrop with two 'pillars' where the full moon, at midsummer when low in the sky, passes between when viewed from the circle. The Peak also has the occasional single tall standing stone, as for example in fields just west of Wirksworth and at Old Woman's Stone on Bamford Moor, felled by a landowner during the access to moorland disputes in the 1930s.

In recent decades there has been controversy about the nature of the design of stone circles, with postulations that they were carefully laid out using a standard unit of measure to carefully designed geometric plans, with accurate astronomical alignments to distant stones and horizon features.[14] After starting as a supporter of such ideas in the 1970s, detailed research eventually led me to conclude that there was much wrong with the postulated ideas. The proposed geometric layouts, comprising a variety of near-circular flattened and egg-shaped designs, are better interpreted as circles laid out by eye to appear circular that are 'perfectly good' in these terms; it was easy to look along an arc of stones and iron out wobbles as these were being erected but impossible to assess overall circularity without the benefit of a bird's eye view. Experiments with building new circles by eye in the 1980s showed that geometric shapes could be fitted better to these than prehistoric stone circles.[15] Without the geometric constructs, the statistical evidence for standard units of length disappears. That said, it is certainly not the case that people in prehistory were incapable of sophisticated thought, but only that they chose to do things differently from us; interpretation in terms of high-precision geometric shapes is an imposition of modern ways of thinking. Similarly, it is now thought that whilst prehistoric peoples certainly had an interest in astronomy, it is impressive visual events, such as the sun rising from behind a sacred mountain, that work well, rather than high-precision alignments to distant points suitable for 'scientific' study of such things as eclipses.[16]

The distribution of stone circles on the eastern moors is such that it is clear that every farming group had its own monument, placed within or close by the most favourable areas for farming in their locality. Whilst the small stone circles in the Peak contain the occasional cremation burial, sometimes in urns, these are not funerary sites but ones where local farming communities are likely to have had ceremonies concerned with the seasons as well as birth, puberty, marriage and death; only the last leaves readily recognised deposits in the ground for archaeologists to find. It is ironic that at rescue excavations at Nine Ladies, a site which in recent years has attracted many people to practise 'alternative' rituals at solstices and other times, it was found that archaeological deposits at the centre had been wrecked by people 'respecting the site' by burying crystals![17]

Burying the dead

The commonest monument type in the Peak, of which there are several hundred, is the ubiquitous round barrow of Later Neolithic and Earlier Bronze Age date; there are also rarer Neolithic forms with long mounds and/or chambers.[18]

Neolithic chambered tombs and long barrows

In the Neolithic roughly 5,500 to 4,500 years ago, barrows have a variety of distinctive forms. The earliest are probably small round barrows that surround stone chambers, as at Green Low near Aldwark and Five Wells above Taddington (Fig 10.9). Later architectural forms diverged, with two main trends.

Firstly, a handful of mounds were enlarged significantly as further chambers were added. The classic example is Minninglow, west of Aldwark, where a large near-circular mound measures 45m by 38m across and has evidence for at least five chambers. Pea Low above Alstonefield is an intriguing site that is the same size as Minninglow and three or four other Neolithic mounds in the Peak, all of which are significantly larger than the Bronze Age round barrows; whilst there are no known chambers, the mound is high and well-preserved and I have long suspected it is actually the best-preserved chambered site in the Peak.

Secondly, the other architectural trend was for Neolithic mounds to be long as opposed to round; indeed Minninglow took on this form only to be enveloped in a later near-circular mound. Some long mounds, such as Gib Hill next to Arbor Low, are only short and have no stone chamber within them; analogy with excavated examples in other regions may indicate there was a timber chamber. The longest mound is the exceptional Long Low, south-east of Wetton. This 'bank barrow' is about 210m long with a bulbous north-east end under which there was a damaged 'closed' stone chamber with no entrance passage. This contained the jumbled bones of at least 13 individuals along with animal bones. Further human remains have been found along the mound, where a spinal drystone wall on the old ground surface had limestone slabs placed against either side to form the mound. This monument is comparable to the two henges in terms of the amount of labour involved in creating it, and it may be of comparable date; it seems they chose to do things differently in what later became Staffordshire!

Fig 10.9
The better-preserved of the two chambers at the Five Wells Neolithic tomb; its capstone was removed be wall builders and its two portals lie where a low approach passage came from the right. Close to the top of Taddington Moor, it was placed on a false crest to bring the extensive panorama northwards into view. Beyond is Tunstead Quarry; between the two is the almost invisible Wye Valley gorge, which for the prehistoric visitor unfamiliar with the place would have come as a great surprise, stopped by cliffs as they came towards the tomb they had glimpsed on the skyline.
[John Barnatt]

Fig 10.10
An excavated and restored, stone-built, round barrow at the edge of the Big Moor cairnfield on the eastern moors, with stones of the Barbrook 1 stone circle just visible behind on the slope down to Bar Brook.
[John Barnatt]

The chambers in the Neolithic mounds take on two basic forms: large closed boxes where entry would have been difficult without raising a capstone, and others that were approached by short and low entrance passages so that they could be entered with relative ease. This said, the entrances would no doubt be sealed with stones that prevented access by strangers and scavenging animals. It is likely that all these chambers each contained several bodies. However, in the Peak all had been disturbed before being archaeologically recorded, sometimes with scattered bones of several individuals left, so details cannot be reconstructed. There were few grave goods except for an occasional leaf-shaped arrowhead, either placed with the bodies or embedded in them and the cause of death or injury.

Round barrows

Many of the round barrows contain Earlier Bronze Age burials dating to roughly 3,500 to 4,000 years ago, as shown by the extensive diggings made by antiquarians and a small number of more careful, modern excavations. The most notable antiquarian was Thomas Bateman of Lomberdale Hall at Middleton by Youlgreave, who had a private museum and published details of his many excavations. A small number of burials found in small round barrows can be shown from their distinctive grave goods to be Later Neolithic in date made roughly 4,500 to 4,000 years ago. Graves of this date are probably more common than can be readily recognised, with a proportion of those with no dateable grave goods being of this early date.

Round barrows by definition have a similar architecture to each other, often seen today in the landscape as simple mounds of varied diameter and height but occasionally with visible traces of a kerb at the edge or a silted surrounding ditch (Fig 10.10). Many were built of surface-gathered stones and/or cut turves and only the largest had quarry ditches.

What lies within barrows is significantly more variable than their external appearance; whilst the outside could be copied by all and sundry, you needed to be invited to the funeral to witness how people were buried. Burials, for instance, were put into rock-cut pits under a mound, in small stone boxes known as cists under or within the mound, laid in the open before being covered by the mound, or placed in pits dug into the mound once built. Round barrows can have pre-mound enclosures defined by stone banks or timber fences, and later the mounds themselves were often enlarged through time. Burial rites include inhumations placed in graves, often with the body on its side with the knees contracted. In other instances there are calcined bones of people burnt on a pyre nearby or brought from elsewhere, sometimes placed in an urn, whilst in other instances cloth or hide bags, or wooden containers, were presumably used. Often scattered human bones are present within or under barrows and it is now unclear whether these were brought from elsewhere or were parts of early burials disturbed when further people were placed in the mound. In a few instances it can be shown that bodies were left in the open to rot or be carried away by crows and other scavengers; only small bones such as those from fingers and toes remain. Where round barrows have been fully excavated with care, it is the norm for there to be multiple burials, with in excess of 20 people in 40 per cent of cases; there is no evidence to support the idea that there is a primary burial of a 'chieftain' with the others being subsidiary. A range of grave goods is found, including weapons and tools in flint or bronze, pots of various types, and necklaces in jet or amber. There are also more mundane items, such as bone and bronze pins, whetstones, bone and faience beads, and jet buttons. The majority of bodies have no accompanying grave goods.

Monuments and people

Whilst the number of Neolithic sites is relatively small, these often impressive monuments are found scattered across the core limestone plateau and it is tempting to see them as being at foci that reflect the distribution of different small tribal groups.[19] Creating each large monument involved much work and no doubt they were built by the tribal communities to serve the needs of the group.

Later unchambered round barrows are very different, mostly built in the Earlier Bronze Age between 4,000 and 3,500 years ago. They are smaller, very numerous and found widely across the landscape, sometimes in small groups but often built singly. They are particularly common on the limestone plateau, which was the focal area for the people of the region. They are often located on hilltops and ridgetops but are also found elsewhere, with lower-lying surviving examples in good farmland showing that it is possible that many others here may have been destroyed. Mounds of good earth later made attractive quarries for 'fertiliser' that was spread on nearby fields once the soils here had been depleted of nutrients after millennia of farming.

As we have seen above, on the eastern gritstone moors survival of both prehistoric monuments and farming landscapes is exceptional. This allows original distribution patterns to be reconstructed; every small farming group had its own local monuments. Stone circles and barrows were built close to home on the best farming land, whilst barrows are also found at opposite points, at high places close to the edges of upland grazing areas. Here the barrows signalled that people had the traditional rights to use these pastures, for here were their ancestors.

Whilst Neolithic chambered sites had multiple burials and the emphasis seems to be on the community, by the Bronze Age this had mutated towards emphasis on individuals, lineage and users of specific locales. That said, at these later round barrows there are no fewer burials than at the earlier chambered sites. It is often said the round barrows across Britain contain tribal leaders and others with status; rare finds of goldwork and other prestigious items support this. However, this is a gross over-simplification. In the Peak, as shown on the eastern gritstone moors, every farming group, probably of little more than extended family size, had its own barrows. Thus, most if not all of the people buried were not of high status. Similarly men, women and children were buried, some with grave goods, many not. That said, we also know that the majority of people who lived and died in the region were not given burials in barrows, but were put in flat graves or disposed of in other ways that leave little archaeological trace. In any small community, at most, one person per generation was placed in the mound. Thus, it seems that people placed in barrows were representatives of the group, placed here for specific ritual or social reasons, perhaps buried at times of stress or change when group identity needed to be reaffirmed.

Throughout the Neolithic and Bronze Age human burial practice was very different to our own funerary rituals. Whilst dead relatives no doubt were normally shown respect, it was more than this, for rituals transformed them into ancestors. For the living their spirits were undoubtedly still present and played a role, with mediation by shaman or elders needed for the good of the community. The barrows would be special places that needed treating with care. Neolithic chambers would be liminal places that were respected and perhaps feared, where the dark and confined spaces that needed to be crawled into to reach the bones of the ancestors were conducive to altered states of consciousness and visions. It would have been a powerful and perhaps disturbing experience to enter with only a flickering tallow light, to commune with the dead.

Natural places and ancestors

In recent decades we have come to realise that prehistoric peoples did not make the same distinctions between made and natural that we do today; features such as rock outcrops were sometimes seen as the work of 'ancestors'. Whilst this is often difficult to prove, we occasionally get hints that this was the case in the Peak. Robin Hood's Stride and its connection with astronomical alignment from the Nine Stone Close stone circle has been mentioned above; the name itself tells of now-lost folk traditions associated with this place. A short distance to the east, on and near Stanton Moor, the Cork Stone is an obvious candidate, being a huge standing-stone-like pillar, which once apparently had a small setting of erected stones around it, whilst Rowter Rocks has prehistoric rock art in boulders near its summit. The Bawd Stone between the spectacular rock outcrops of The Roaches and Hen Cloud had folklore traditions that probably go back into the depths of time. Nearby a Bronze Age cremation burial with a collared urn, bronze awl and bone toggle, all in a pit below the main outcrop, have recently been found by accident during footpath work (Figs 10.11 and 10.12).[20]

Fig 10.11
The naturally placed Bawd Stone is sited between the rock outcrops at The Roaches (in background) and Hen Cloud (behind the photographer), both near Upper Hulme. It looks much like a portal dolmen type of chambered tomb and people in prehistory may well have venerated it; even in the early 20th century, local people processed to the stone and painted it white every year. [John Barnatt]

Now you see it – now you don't

With prehistoric monuments generally, often we are struck by particulars in their siting in the landscape and suspect the places chosen were special. Such factors are important, but one of the issues with attempting to assess this is to ask how readily they could be seen and what could be seen from them? In some places they may have been within glades in dense woodlands, in others they may have been in cleared agricultural land grazed by animals with only selected parts of the land beyond clearly seen, whilst elsewhere they may have been set amongst swaths of open grassland with uninterrupted views to the horizon. Similarly, whilst some sites have extensive long-distance views, these may have been inconsequential to the builders of specific monuments, whilst what lay within a kilometre or two was their concern. When we make assessments of place, the monumentality of structures or of astronomical connections, the 'now-unknowns' become caveats to our interpretations. However, we should also ask if such things as trees were irrelevant, for local prehistoric people would have had cognitive maps of where things were; a place did not need to be visible from a distance as they knew the way there and back.

Fig 10.12
Hen Cloud (right) and The Roaches (left) lie at the interface between rolling lowland behind the photographer and high gritstone lands beyond the outcrops. The rock outcrops form an impressive 'other world' that from time immemorial has undoubtedly been a special place.
[John Barnatt]

Arbor Low

Fig 10.13
The interior area of the Arbor Low henge, built in the Later Neolithic, photographed from the bank top. The impressive stones of the circle and central cove were originally upright. Before the eroding down of the outer bank and silting of the ditch, when stood inside much of the surrounding landscape would have been hidden except through the north-western entrance (seen to the left). Similarly nobody can see in unless the monument is approached by the correct route.
[John Barnatt]

This impressive henge has a high bank that prevents the visitor standing beyond the monument from seeing the interior except when stood outside either of the two entrances (Fig 10.13). From here, when the high stones of the cove were still standing, a view of rituals being performed at the very centre would still be hidden; perhaps only tribal members were allowed inside the monument, whilst strangers were barred from entry. The monument is sited on a false crest so that it overlooks extensive areas of lower ground to the north and north-west across a large upland basin at the head of Lathkill Dale and centred on Monyash; it may be that many of the users of the henge made extensive use of the grazing pastures here. When approaching the monument from this direction, whilst it is a skyline feature from a distance, as the base of slope is reached it disappears from view, to appear again just as the wide north-western entrance is reached, allowing the impressive circle of tall stones within to be seen clearly for the first time.

If leaving the monument from the opposite entrance to the south-east, which is half the width of the other, this leads to the flat ridgetop where there is the Gib Hill long barrow, which was the focal monument on the ridge long before the henge was built. Leaving the henge through the narrow gap was perhaps restricted to certain people, who were allowed to leave the land of the living and enter a world of ancestors beyond. It is hard to escape the conclusion that Arbor Low is carefully designed to control ranked access and for enhancement of the sense of theatre during rituals and ceremonies.

Later, an added element was created when a large round barrow was placed on the henge bank at the upslope side so that it dominated the interior. Similarly, the Gib Hill barrow was also overlain by a round barrow. Thus, whilst communal ceremonies continued, for such statements would not have been made at abandoned monuments, a specific group imposed their lineage and perhaps status on the people who gathered here.

Crow Chin

Another instructive example of the siting of monuments in the landscape is provided by two round barrows at Crow Chin on the crest of Stanage Edge. This scarp is one of the most impressive topographic features in the Peak, comprising a 5km-long cliff facing west, which can be seen for miles and dominates the lower gritstone moorland shelf below. Here there are extensive prehistoric settlements, fields and small monuments, centred on Bamford Moor. If the barrow builders had chosen to erect high 'bowl-shaped' mounds these would have been seen for miles. Instead, whilst of large diameter, they were created to be flat-topped and less than 1m high and they cannot be seen from anywhere below the edge. This suggests that the people who built the barrows, whose home base was almost certainly Bamford Moor, were not interested in visible barrows as reminders to themselves and strangers passing through that the land below the cliff was grazed. The crest of Stanage Edge lies at about 420 to 460m OD and is situated above the land used in prehistory for farming, in an upper liminal world perhaps seen as wilderness and a place for occasional forays to hunt game. It seems it was also an important place for spirits; Crow Chin was a place where ancestors could overlook the land of the living.

Big Moor

In strong topographic contrast to the last case study, on Big Moor to either side of the Bar Brook, there are two stone circles and a ringcairn lying on relatively flat shelves where there are extensive remains of prehistoric farming and settlement. These monuments are placed at the edges of the cultivated areas so that they were conveniently within five or ten minutes' walk from the heart of the fields. Despite the proximity, a careful study of what is visible from the monuments shows that they have restricted views that do not focus on the fields and none of the known possible house sites hereabouts are in view; the 'circles' are only clearly seen when stood close by.[21] Thus, whilst close to home they are set apart from the land of the living to allow ceremonies to take place in relative quiet.

Symbols in stone

Scattered in small numbers across the eastern gritstone upland there are prehistoric carvings pecked into the coarse sandstone outcrops and into portable stones found within prehistoric monuments (Fig 10.14).[22] These for the most part are typical examples of the abstract 'cup and ring' style found throughout Britain and commonly thought to be of Neolithic and Earlier Bronze Age date. One thing the Peak carvings have in common is that where found in reasonable condition they have long been protected by tree cover or have been buried under turf; this suggests that rock art was once more common locally and comparable with similar areas further north such as Ilkley Moor where it is plentiful. In the Peak the rock is perhaps a little softer or has had greater attack from acid rain and thus much has eroded away. Fine local examples include carvings on Gardom's Edge above Baslow, now buried with a replica placed to conserve the actual rock art, on Rowter Rocks at Birchover and at Ashover School.

How to interpret the meanings of the carvings is one of the most intractable problems in the study of British prehistory. The designs are too abstract to easily understand the symbols used. They are not 'Art' in the modern sense, with the carving to be viewed and judged on aesthetic grounds as if placed in an art gallery or museum. Some elements in the design appear overwritten by others. Similarly, when first created they may have been painted and later where not coloured could have become redundant and irrelevant. It may have been the act of carving and painting that was important, taking on meaning in conjunction with storytelling or ritual. It is suspected that the carvings are symbolic maps of selected meaningful places in the landscape but not drawn in literal fashion, telling of peoples' place in the world. But, when all is said and done, this is little more than guesswork.

Fig 10.14
A recently discovered example of prehistoric rock art on Dobb Edge high in the north-east corner of Chatsworth Park. The concentric rings have a shallow gutter coming in from the left. The earthfast boulder had been buried under turf until exposed through erosion by footfall on a concessionary path. Two large stones have been placed to either side to prevent future damage from footfall.
[John Barnatt]

Using caves

Whilst these places have long been occasionally occupied in prehistory, this was not the normal form of settlement, even in the Palaeolithic. In the earliest times caves were places of temporary shelter; however, often people would have been hunting well away from the nearest suitable caves, and tents were presumably the norm. In more recent times, caves were temporarily used as places of refuge for the dispossessed, as retreats where people could hide, and as special places to commune with spirits of the earth.

An exceptional place is Creswell Crags a few miles east of the Peak. Here, in a limestone gorge, several caves ideal for habitation were visited intermittently between about 50,000 and 11,000 years ago by people following migrating animals, first Neanderthals and then anatomically modern humans. There are large quantities of flint artefacts, others of bone, and many animal bones. Remarkable inscribed cave art, showing animals and birds, including a stag and an ibis, was first identified in 2003.[23] Perhaps they were once painted as with the well-known cave art of France where environmental conditions are more favourable for paint survival.

In the Peak, caves are largely confined to the limestone plateau and the gorges that pass through it, with a particularly high concentration in the Manifold Valley; occupation spans the Palaeolithic to medieval periods and a wide range of activities has taken place.[24] The deposits found in caves not only tell of the presence of people, but also are invaluable for the environmental data they contain, telling of ancient glacial and interglacial times as well as more recent changes in our present interglacial period. This material includes the bones of animals and birds that are now no longer found in the British countryside, some extinct such as mammoth, others such as hyena now resident in Africa.

Some caves are large and obvious, such as Thor's Cave in the Manifold Gorge.[25] The entrance is now largely devoid of cave sediments but past excavations within found evidence for Romano-British use and a contracted skeleton in a stone cist of Late Neolithic or Earlier Bronze Age date. Another obvious cave is Peak Cavern at Castleton, traditionally known as 'The Devils Arse'. Here the huge entrance chamber would have made an ideal prehistoric habitation site. However, archaeological excavations have never been allowed below the site of a row of post-medieval cottages and a ropewalk.

Not far from Thor's Cave, at the cliff top, is Elderbush Cave, which is a classic example of a cave rich in archaeological material.[26] Animal bones spanned the Palaeolithic to the present. There were Palaeolithic flints, a reindeer bone point and a cache of reindeer meat on the bone. Later, a Bronze Age beaker and arrowhead were deposited. In the Iron Age and Romano-British period people lit hearths and left potboilers, pottery and a metal brooch. Scattered human bones were either Bronze Age or later in date. In Wolfscote Dale, at the top end of the Dove valley gorge, the obvious but small entrances of Frank i' th' Rocks Cave leads to a comfortable chamber where early 20th-century excavations found Iron Age and Romano-British burials and artefacts, but little in the way of identifiable earlier material (Fig 10.15).[27] Fox Hole Cave at High Wheeldon near Earl Sterndale has a small and unobvious entrance near the top of this prominent symmetrical hill; taken together they feel almost like a massive but natural 'chambered tomb'. Inside there was skeletal evidence for occupation by bears, with claw scratching on the walls. Parts seem to have been paved, and there were Neolithic and Beaker pottery sherds on and under this, together with at least two hearths, animal bones and a few human bones. One of the hearths, in a low narrow part of the cave where crawling is the order of the day, had a smashed Bronze Age beaker next to it; this was a ritual deposit and one can speculate about people visiting caves to commune with the spirits of the earth.

Fig 10.15
In Wolfscote Dale, at Frank i' th' Rocks Cave, an easy step up at the base of a high limestone crag leads into a sheltered small cave chamber. Here, the bones of three adults and five children were found, along with artefacts including two bronze brooches and pieces of a torc, Roman coins and pottery, glass beads and bone objects. [John Barnatt]

Defending identity

From the Late Bronze Age into the Iron Age people built a small number of large enclosures in the Peak traditionally known as hillforts. These are a mixed bag of designs and sizes, and their distribution is shown on Figure 10.16.[28] All are monuments built by tribal societies with defence in mind, but whether they were used in earnest, or worked more in terms of deterrent and prestige, is often unclear. Recent excavations

at Fin Cop have shown that there are skeletons of women and children in the ditch, deposited at a time when the defences were being strengthened by adding an outer rampart. They are thought to have been dumped here after the hillfort was successfully attacked.

The four relatively large certain examples of 'hillforts' are located so that it is easy to access complementary landscapes with different resources. The classic example is Mam Tor at the western end of the Hope Valley (Figs 10.17 and 10.18).

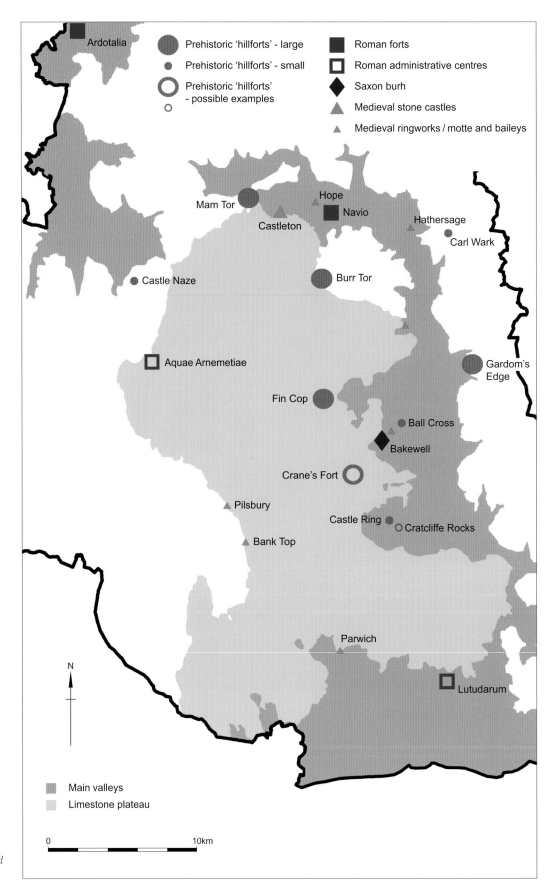

Prehistoric 'hillforts' - large

Prehistoric 'hillforts' - small

Prehistoric 'hillforts' - possible examples

Roman forts

Roman administrative centres

Saxon burh

Medieval stone castles

Medieval ringworks / motte and baileys

Ardotalia

Mam Tor

Hope

Navio

Castleton

Hathersage

Carl Wark

Castle Naze

Burr Tor

Aquae Arnemetiae

Gardom's Edge

Fin Cop

Ball Cross

Bakewell

Crane's Fort

Pilsbury

Castle Ring

Cratcliffe Rocks

Bank Top

Parwich

N

Lutudarum

Main valleys

Limestone plateau

Fig 10.16
The distribution of
prehistoric hillforts,
Roman forts and other
administrative centres, and
medieval defended sites.

0   10km

Fig 10.18 (below)
Mam Tor, with its impressive landslip cliff and hillfort above, lies at the western end of the sheltered Hope Valley and dominates the scene, at the interface between the high gritstone uplands (behind to the right) and the limestone plateau (behind to the left). From this direction the hill looks totally different from the view from the south-west [John Barnatt]

Fig 10.19
The enigmatic and undated Carl Wark hillfort seen from Higger Tor. Two sides of this triangular site have cliffs and precipitous boulder-strewn slopes, one with a defensive wall of boulders added, while to the west there is a high bank with a built face of gritstone boulders. The large boulders across the interior leave little room for buildings. [John Barnatt]

The hillfort, on an impressive and distinctively shaped hill known as 'the shivering mountain', is at the interface between this large sheltered valley, together with Edale nearby, the high northern limestone plateau and high gritstone upland around Kinder Scout. This hillfort has a large number of building platforms in its interior, accessed through two defended entrances through a sturdy rampart. In contrast, the scarp-edge enclosure at Gardom's Edge on the eastern gritstone moors has a low boulder-built bank with several entrances into this non-defensive site. There is a boulder-strewn interior with little room for houses. At one of the archaeologically excavated trenches here, the stone bank, placed on top of a line of sturdy posts, was built in two phases, the second comprising a doubling of the width when burnt stones with much charcoal had been placed to the inside of the original bank.[29] The monument is so unusual that it was thought to be Neolithic, having much in common with ceremonial 'causewayed enclosures' of that era, until radiocarbon dating showed it was Later Bronze Age in date. Burr Tor above Great Hucklow is in a similar topographical location, but overlooking the limestone plateau, and again has a relatively slight bank. The Fin Cop 'hillfort' has defences on a similar scale to Mam Tor, but with strengthening of these left unfinished, is again placed between the limestone plateau and a wide area of shale valleys.

Of five smaller 'hillforts', only that at Ball Cross above Bakewell is securely dated, whilst others at Castle Ring at Harthill Moor and Castle Naze above Chapel en le Frith are of typical Iron Age design. That at Carl Wark above Hathersage and another at Cratcliffe Rocks at Harthill are atypical and could be of any date from the Neolithic to Iron Age (Fig 10.19).

11

Roman occupation and medieval elites

Important archaeological sites survive from the time when the Romans were in occupation and from after the Anglo-Saxon kingdoms were established. Roman features include earthworks at forts and military roads, as well as many settlements occupied by the local population. In a few of the medieval villages in the Peak the earliest visible feature is the Anglo-Saxon cross erected in the churchyard.

Features built in the 1000 years from the Norman Conquest onwards, of medieval and later date, are for the most part covered elsewhere in this volume. However, medieval castles built by secular lords and parish churches and chapels erected in villages by the powerful Catholic Church are included below. For the overall distribution of forts and castles see Figure 10.16, whilst all places mentioned below are shown on Figure A1.8 (see p 237).

The Peak in Roman times

In Britain the Romans arrived to stay in AD 43, after a temporary incursion by Julius Caesar in 55–54 BC, reaching northern England three decades later. The Roman military left Britain in the early fifth century AD after which the administrative systems the Romans had established gradually fragmented. Whilst the governance of much of Britain ultimately came from Rome, with administrators and military personnel drawn from across the empire, the bulk of the population were native peoples descended from the tribal groups that were here before the invasion. Whilst they assimilated such things as better pottery, in many ways life for them continued much as before.

Roman governance

With the coming of the Romans, things were done very differently to how the political elites of the Iron Age used defended places of power, with new forts placed at the heart of valleys with population concentrations (see Fig 10.16).[1] Here civil settlements grew up outside their gates. The forts were linked by military roads (as discussed in Chapter 8). Navio, at Brough in the heart of the Hope Valley, was built in the AD 70s to 80s shortly after Roman troops arrived in the Peak and was re-established after a period of abandonment in the AD 150s. It lies on an east–west route across the Pennines, and is at the northern edge of the limestone plateau. Another fort, of similar date, at Ardotalia at Melandra near Glossop, lies in the north-western valleys at the Peak fringe. The outlines of both forts can still be traced on the ground. Nothing can now be seen at two other important Roman settlements. Aquae Arnemetiae, now known as Buxton, grew up around the warm springs here; there may have been a fort nearby but this has never been found. At the southern end of the limestone plateau, the lost Lutudarum was an administrative centre for lead production. It seems most likely to have been near modern Carsington, where an atypical but badly damaged settlement and a small villa nearby have been excavated, although alternative locations around Wirksworth and Matlock have also been suggested.

Farming

Across the limestone plateau, and also flanking the Derwent Valley at Ladybower and North Lees, there are between 26 and 65 places with earthworks at sites of settlements and fields that date to Romano-British times, lived in by local people during the Roman occupation.[2] Often they have survived in isolated places or on patches of ground which are rocky and thus have not been improved later.

The settlements, best described as farmsteads and small hamlets, each have up to a handful of building platforms, some for houses, others presumably outbuildings, and not all are certainly in use at any one point in time. The houses were often built using timber rather than stone and thus sometimes it is difficult to distinguish between building platforms and garden plots, pens and yards. It is thought that in some cases at least they have Iron Age origins. A series of examples of settlements and fields is now described to illustrate the range of sites to be found.

Whilst small excavations have been undertaken at several settlement sites only those at Roystone Grange, north of Ballidon, and Staden, south-east of Buxton, have been adequately published. At the former there are four or five house platforms, one of which has been fully excavated. This was a large aisled hall of at least three bays, with an outer wall on drystone footings with curved ends. Later, stone paving was placed around the central rectangular space defined by the aisle posts.[3] At Staden small

trenches were dug over several years. There were three house platforms, two smaller platforms, pens and small irregular enclosures, with artefacts showing that occupation started in the Iron Age and continued until at least the end of the second century AD.[4] At Chee Tor above the Wye Valley gorge near Blackwell there have been unpublished excavations at a fine site with four clusters of house sites and yards, with an associated lane passing through, and surrounded by small sub-rectangular garden plots (Fig 11.1).[5] At The Warren at North Lees a small unpublished excavation produced Romano-British pottery and a flat quern. Here there are a series of narrow co-axial terraces on a slope with yard and garden plot boundaries, where there must have stood at least one and probably more houses. All are surrounded by small irregular fields, with co-axial fields of unknown date nearby.[6]

Fig 11.1
The Romano-British settlement at Chee Tor near Blackwell, with visible house, garden plot and yard sites that have survived later ploughing because of the site being on a narrow promontory above the River Wye gorge.
[© Derrick Riley]

Dating of the sites in general is often not secure, relying on occasional finds of Roman-period pottery, often the durable Derbyshire Ware, picked up from mole hills and livestock scrapes. Sometimes it is just the morphology of the earthworks or their location which suggests a Roman date. At Cow Low east of Buxton above the Wye Valley gorge there are several small sub-rectangular platforms at the top end of fields where flat and beehive querns have been found.[7] At Rainster Rocks west of Brassington, a settlement tucked below a limestone crag, with medieval ridge and furrow coming up to it from flatter ground below, has small sub-rectangular revetted enclosures and house sites that have produced Roman material (*see* Fig 10.1).[8]

The associated fields take on two basic forms. Commonly at the settlements there are irregular layouts of small sub-rectangular parcels, although here it is usually hard to distinguish between yards, garden plots, paddocks and fields for cultivation. The other form that fields take is rectangular co-axial plots. Sometimes these are directly associated with the settlements, as at Cow Low[9] and Banktop.[10] Elsewhere all that survives are small areas of co-axial fields and these are usually hard to date, as at Waterlees near Taddington.[11] At Dam Cliff near Peak Forest there is a small patch of similar surviving straight-edged fields on a different alignment to the post-medieval walled fields; given what we know of the history of enclosure here the earlier fields are likely to be pre-medieval in date. At Chee Tor in an area of ancient fields to the east of the settlement, there are several large co-axial lynchets that look much like medieval open-field features (Fig 11.2). However, they are overlain by a layout of sub-rectangular fields that is Romano-British in character.

Fig 11.2

Extract from the author's 1989 survey of Blackwell Hall Farm, showing Romano-British and other ancient features, including the settlement at Chee Tor (A) and fields to the east (B). While some of these fields superficially look like medieval strip lynchets (C), they are overlain by the sub-rectangular fields and neither of the sets of features fit with the documented medieval layout of field strips nearby, nor with the present post-medieval fields and thus are likely to be earlier.

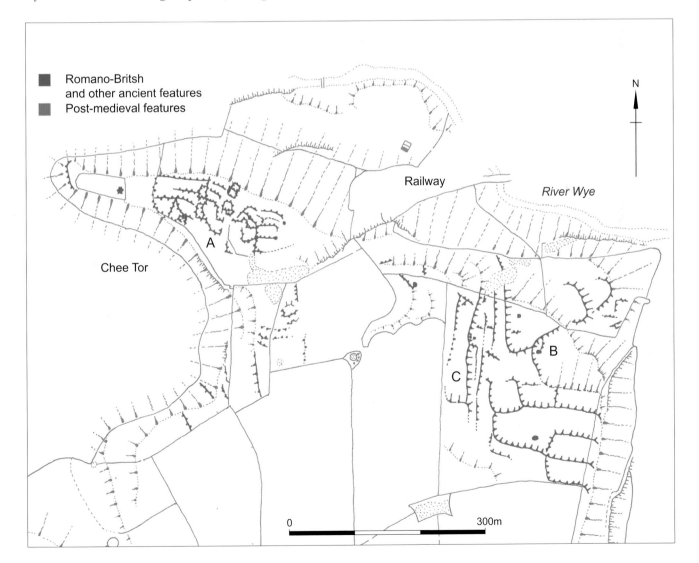

179

At Thorpe Pasture to the east of the southern end of Dove Dale there is a multi-period palimpsest of ancient farming remains (Fig 11.3). To the eastern and southern sides there are extensive medieval and undated cultivation earthworks, whilst at a dry valley at the centre of the medieval common there is an isolated area of small co-axial and rectangular fields, with two platforms that may once have contained buildings. Surrounding this area there are stony banks that appear to define property boundaries contemporary with the Romano-British farm, one on a ridgetop, another on the opposite valley side and a third crossing the valley between the other two.[12] 'Ranch-like' property boundaries can also be identified elsewhere, for example at Deep Dale between Sheldon and Taddington where one follows the base of the valley.[13]

Elsewhere there is confusion as to whether examples of co-axial fields are of Romano-

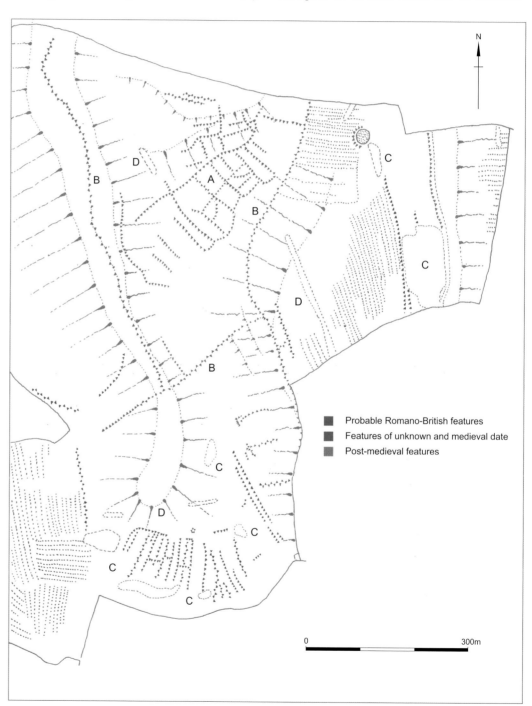

Fig 11.3
Thorpe Pasture, showing features of probable Romano-British date and others of unknown or medieval date. These include an area with building platforms within small fields (A) and 'property boundaries' (B). There are also later quarries (C) and lead mining (D).

Probable Romano-British features
Features of unknown and medieval date
Post-medieval features

0   300m

British or medieval date. A well-preserved layout within a large irregular boundary east of the settlement at Roystone Grange was interpreted as being of Romano-British date but has now been re-evaluated as more likely to be medieval.[14] At Carsington Pasture an extensive area of strip fields within enclosing banks is again likely to be medieval. At The Liffs south of Biggin the situation is more ambiguous and the only available dating evidence is a few scraps of Romano-British pottery, which could be residual. Two well-defined rectangular house platforms, perhaps of Romano-British type, overlie cultivation strips and lynchets with a superficially medieval appearance, whilst to the north and west there are small rectangular fields (Fig 11.4).[15] Research to further our understanding of the date and context of farming at such sites in badly needed.

Romano-British and/or medieval features
Post-medieval features

Fig 11.4
Extract from the author's 1990 survey of Biggin Grange, showing Romano-British and/or medieval features at The Liffs, including house platforms (A), sub-rectangular fields (B) and cultivation strips (C). There are also post-medieval quarries with limekilns (D) and a field barn complex (E).

State and Church in medieval times

The medieval hierarchy in the Peak, including secular lords of the manor and priests, the foot-soldiers of the powerful Christian Church, instigated the erection of castles and churches across the Peak.

Defending new political masters

After the Roman administration left, there were no fortifications in the Peak until after the Norman Conquest, with the exception of the burh at Bakewell built in AD 920 when King Edward of Wessex came here as part of his campaign to unify England. With the coming of the Normans, castle building came to the fore, initially at least because the ruling elite felt the need to defend themselves against the native populace and rival lords (*see* Fig 10.16). Several motte-and-bailey castles and ringworks were built, the finest surviving example being that at Pilsbury in the Upper Dove Valley.[16] In the Hope Valley a motte and bailey was built at Hope just over 1km from Navio; later the local focus moved westwards with the building of the planned town at Castleton and the building of the Peak's only stone castle on the steep hill above (Fig 11.5).

Fig 11.5
The 12th-century Peveril Castle was built around the same time as the planned 'town' of Castleton, sited close to the head of the Hope Valley. The castle is sited on a spur at the edge of the high limestone plateau, while the medieval core of the village mostly lies out of sight in a sheltered valley location at the base of the steep slope up to the castle.
[John Barnatt]

Medieval churches

Many of the villages of the Peak have medieval churches, although in a significant number of cases these were restored or rebuilt in the 19th century.[17] An extreme case is the church built by Giles Gilbert Scott for the Duke of Devonshire at Edensor in 1867 to 1870, with its exceptionally tall spire seen from all over Chatsworth Park, which replaced a much smaller and less grand medieval church. The medieval churches are typically small with towers that sometimes are rather squat, with highlights including Norman sculptural work as found for example at Tissington, Parwich and Alsop le Dale, the broach spire at Baslow and large later tower at Youlgreave. The noteworthy exceptions are the large churches at market centres at Bakewell, Tideswell, Wirksworth and Ashbourne (Fig 11.6). Some parishes were very large, such as at Bakewell and Hartington; technically even what are relatively large churches in subsidiary villages within these ecclesiastical parishes, as at Baslow for example, were technically classed as chapels.

A very different type of chapel is the non-conformist chapels, found in many villages, which were built after the Reformation by sectors of communities that broke away from the Church of England. The majority are of 19th-century date, but some are earlier.

Fig 11.6
Tideswell Church, known as 'The Cathedral of the Peak', is a fine example of a large Gothic church, built in 14th-century 'Decorated' style, standing within the large market centre at the heart of the northern limestone plateau.
[John Barnatt]

Reminders of pre-Norman Christianity

At a small number of churchyards with post-Norman Conquest churches, except that at Bradbourne which has pre-Conquest fabric, there are fragments of earlier crosses.[18] These crosses were redundant when the present churches were built and often the fragments were found during Victorian restorations either incorporated into the church fabric or buried in the graveyard. In some instances, the crosses have been brought from remote moorland locations where they marked roads or boundaries. In the case of One Ash near Monyash two cross head fragments were found in 1983 in drystone walls close to the site of a now-abandoned medieval village.

At the manorial centres at Hope, Eyam, Bakewell and Bradbourne, there are large churchyard crosses of late eighth- to tenth-century date, that pre-date the surviving Norman and later church fabrics.[19] This said we know from documentation that there were pre-conquest churches at Hope, Bakewell, Darley, Wirksworth and Ashbourne, whilst the church at Bradbourne has long and short quoins of early date in the nave.

There are two styles of carvings on the crosses. One, which is characteristically Mercian, includes twisted vine scrolls and stylised figures, as found on the large cross in the churchyard at Bakewell and on fragments in the church porch, and at a handful of other churchyards at important settlements elsewhere. The other style, which is locally more common, is dominated by abstract interweaved knotwork. Traditionally the first style has been interpreted as late eighth and early ninth century in date and the other as late ninth century onwards; alternatively, both may be of the later date.

Bakewell is exceptional as a large number of cross fragments exist; there was a monastery recorded here in the mid-10th century but perhaps already long established (Fig 11.7). Bakewell was also the centre of a large royal manor, and it has been suggested that many of the crosses throughout the manor were collected up and brought back to the churchyard once they became redundant. A second important place is Alstonefield where there are fragments of several crosses, again found during church restoration. The original church was dedicated in AD 892 during a visit to Alstonefield by St Oswald, Archbishop of York.

Fig 11.7
A large number of broken pieces from Anglo-Saxon crosses were found in the medieval fabric of Bakewell church when it was restored in the 19th century. Many of these were placed in the porch for safekeeping and display a range of styles, with stylised people, vine scrolls and knotwork.
[John Barnatt]

12

Polite landscapes

The Crown, aristocracy and landed gentry have had a significant effect on the landscape over the centuries, not only on how and where their tenants lived, worked and worshipped, but also by creating distinctive landscapes dedicated to their pleasure.

In the medieval period there were both royal and private hunting forests in and around the Peak. These areas were governed by forest laws designed to protect deer and the hunting environment. In the uplands the forests were dominated by open moorland rather than trees; 'Forest' originally was a specific term for a hunting preserve rather than a heavily wooded area. In the Peak deer were encouraged and wolves still inhabited the land. However, from the mid-13th century onwards the forests were little used by the Crown and their nobility and encroachments by people carving out new farmland led to their slow decline; by the mid-17th century all were moribund. Within forests and elsewhere in the Peak, there were also private parks, generally smaller areas enclosed within a pale, used for hunting and other purposes. Here there were no feudal tenants and thus their owners had more freedom to use them for pleasure and profit in ways that were constrained by feudal traditions in the landscapes beyond.

In post-medieval times fashions changed; mansions and halls built in stone proliferated from the 16th century onwards, at first as sturdy buildings with mullioned windows, and then from the 18th century in classical and then more eclectic 19th-century styles. Early halls, following the fashion of the day, had formal gardens but a more naturalistic approach was adopted later. In the 18th century landscape parks became the fashion, with mansions surrounded by seas of grass with carefully arranged scattered trees and woodland plantings as well as decorative buildings such as lodges. However, gardens were never abandoned, they were too well-loved, and these were reinvigorated in the 19th century.

All places mentioned in Chapter 12 are given on Figure A1.9 (*see* p 239).

Whilst many halls, parks and gardens were strictly private places, Chatsworth was somewhat different; created as an ambitious palace built to be seen, but to be visited only by the right class of people (Fig 12.1). The main road up the valley was moved to the other side of the river when the landscape park was built to keep all but welcome visitors at arm's length.

Fig 12.1
The East Front of Chatsworth House built in the 1690s, with the Salisbury Lawn in the foreground, which although often said to have been laid by 'Capability' Brown in about 1760, was perhaps created by William Kent in the 1730s. It appears on a painting of 1743 by Thomas Smith. The lawn, which allows an uninterrupted view of the house for visitors to the grounds, replaced a geometric garden layout of hedges, paths and flowerbeds that had fallen out of fashion.
[John Barnatt]

From the mid-18th century onwards the upland landscape of the Peak began to be increasingly valued for its picturesque qualities, with artists and visitors alike flocking here in ever-increasing numbers. For some it was natural rugged places such as Dove Dale that were attractive, whilst others came for the polite society and cures to be had at the thermal baths at Buxton and Matlock Bath. The owners of halls did not confine themselves to decorating their parks and gardens, but in subtler ways their taste spread across the countryside; estate buildings were often erected in fashionable if vernacular styles as higher-quality builds than otherwise would have occurred. Plantation woodlands were a long-term cash crop for those who could afford to wait for a return, and in the 18th and 19th centuries these were often placed strategically to decorate the landscape (Fig 12.2). For instance, the Devonshire Estate planted rectangular copses at regular intervals along the road from Bakewell to Buxton, whilst various hilltop prehistoric barrows across the Peak have small stands added for decorative effect. In the 19th century, as discussed in Chapter 4 (*see* pp 70–1), landowners even had a radical effect on the Peak's moorlands, privatising the commons and turning these over to grouse shooting rather than enclosing them and improving the land as profitable farmland. At the Duke of Rutland's estate at Longshaw, lodges for guests and gamekeepers were built.

Forests in the Peak

Approximately half of the Peak was set aside as large hunting forests in the medieval period, often known locally as 'Friths'. The largest was the Royal Forest of the Peak, which occupied a large tract of north-west Derbyshire.[1] Its boundary was for the most part defined by rivers, with the Etherow to the north, Derwent to the east, Wye to the south and Goyt to the west. To the west of the Goyt, in Cheshire, Macclesfield Forest took in all the Peak upland and foothills in this county.[2] South of the Dane on the Staffordshire side of the river was Alstonefield Frith, also known as Malbanc Frith, which covered the parishes of Quarnford, Heathylee, Fawfieldhead and Hollinsclough. The adjacent land to the south-west, including the present parish of Leek Frith, was also a forest.[3] The possibility of another Frith at Hartington is discussed in Chapter 14 (*see* pp 216–7). At the south-eastern fringe of the Peak was yet another, that of Duffield Frith.[4]

The Royal Forest of the Peak was created by the Normans and was held by the Crown (Fig 12.3). Although it includes large areas that were unenclosed 'empty' upland, such as the high gritstone areas around Kinder Scout and Bleaklow, and the high parts of the limestone plateau between Castleton and Buxton, there were also areas that had long-established settlement, there since before the Norman

Fig 12.2
The crest of Minninglow is surmounted by a large Neolithic chambered tomb, currently not visible because of a low modern planting of trees. On the tomb there is an ornamental planting of tall beech trees, now over-mature and gradually dying. These have been visible from places across the Peak for many decades and form a distinctive skyline feature that was added with this in mind. Because the mound is a Scheduled Monument and new tree planting here would do damage, trees were planted in a ring around the site; eventually these will hopefully be thinned and the mound will be opened up to the landscape again. [John Barnatt]

Conquest. These included the manorial centre of Hope and a series of settlements around the Forest's south-east fringe, with more to the north-west in and around Longdendale. There were also scattered farmsteads in Edale, the Upper Derwent Valley, and around Chapel en le Frith, Hayfield and Glossop. Some had early origins, others were assarts created during the lifespan of the forest, sometimes on land granted by the Crown or settled illegally with trespass fines paid; further properties were owned by the Crown and leased to tenants. It seems hunting and management for deer only took precedence on the large expanses of higher land, mostly comprising open moorland rather than being wooded.

The Forest was divided into three wards, named Longdendale (north-west), Hopedale (north-east) and Campana (south). A series of places were important for the management of the Forest; the forester's chamber was at the heart, at what is now the village of Peak Forest. The main administrative centre and lock-up was the Peak's only stone castle, at Castleton, with a market and fair in the planned town below. Other markets were held at Tideswell, Chapel en le Frith, Charlesworth and Glossop. The main forest courts or 'eyres' were held at Tideswell, with lesser courts or 'swainmotes' held in a variety of places.

After more than 150 years of hunting, with Norman and then the first Plantagenet kings coming to the Peak regularly, by the mid-13th century this had ceased and the forest laws were relaxed. Settlement seems to have increased exponentially in favourable areas until the Black Death of the mid-14th century. In 1579 the Crown erected a fence around what is now the parish of Peak Forest to create a deer park at the heart of the original medieval forest, in a final attempt to retain something of the old Forest, albeit at a much-reduced scale. By the mid- to late 17th century, after the Civil War, the Forest had effectively ceased to exist and it was disafforested.[5]

Macclesfield Forest was established by the Earls of Chester who were granted much of Cheshire soon after the Norman Conquest, but this reverted to the Crown in 1237 when the earldom was disbanded; again by the later 17th century the Forest had gone. The small hamlet of Macclesfield Forest is thought to be the site of the forest chamber, whilst the forest courts were held in Macclesfield where there was also a market.

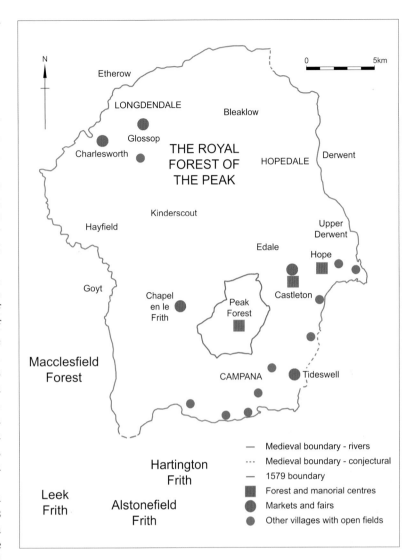

Alstonefield Frith existed by the 12th century but was moribund by the 17th century when there was only memory of the deer here; it was a private forest held by the Malbanc family as sub-tenants of the Earls of Chester until 1176.

Leek Frith existed by about 1170 and was again held by the Earls of Chester who owned the manor of Leek in 1086, whilst from about 1230 land in the Forest was granted by them to Dieulacres Abbey. By the late 15th century the whole of the Frith was used as livestock pasture.

Duffield Frith to the south-east fringe of the Peak was initially held by the de Ferrers family and then the Duchy of Lancaster, but reverted to the Crown in 1399. Thick woodlands within parts of the forest were decimated in the later 16th century, whilst other areas had become private parks in the medieval period. Surviving remnants of the Forest were disafforested in 1630.

Fig 12.3
The Royal Forest of the Peak, showing its medieval extent and the contraction in 1579, the forest administrative centres and markets, as well as villages with open fields within the forest.

187

A walk in the park

There are not many known medieval deer parks in the Peak and it seems they were never common, in contrast to the land immediately to the south-east where the hunting forest of Duffield Frith had several,[6] with more along the southern fringe of the Peak going westwards,[7] and also in north-east Derbyshire just beyond the Peak.[8]

Medieval parks were enclosed areas created by the wealthy as private reserves. Whilst some are early, most were created after mid-14th-century Black Death depopulations. They were islands in the landscape where different rules applied as there were no feudal tenants. Where lords of the manor found themselves with few or no people on their land, one sensible option was to create a park. Although they are generally known as deer parks, the keeping of deer for hunting was just one of their functions; they were food stores, with deer, rabbits and other live-stock commonly kept and wildfowl encouraged.

Similarly, they were exploited for their industrial resources, with coal and iron worked where it was present, whilst mature trees were a useful cash crop and resource for construction materials, and woodland was also coppiced for charcoal.

The park at Chatsworth comprised a large walled area running eastwards from the Elizabethan hall onto a high shelf above the steeply sloping Stand Wood (Fig 12.4). The fine hunting tower, 'The Stand', still remains overlooking the high land and mansion below, built on the scarp top from where all the park could be seen. The deer park itself was lost when it was enclosed in the decades either side of 1800, well after the completion of 'Capability' Brown's 1759 landscape park that fills the Derwent Valley west of the house. Today there are fine veteran oak trees along the western edge of the old deer park, in the area where it overlapped with the landscape park, some of which date to the later medieval period (Fig 12.5).[9]

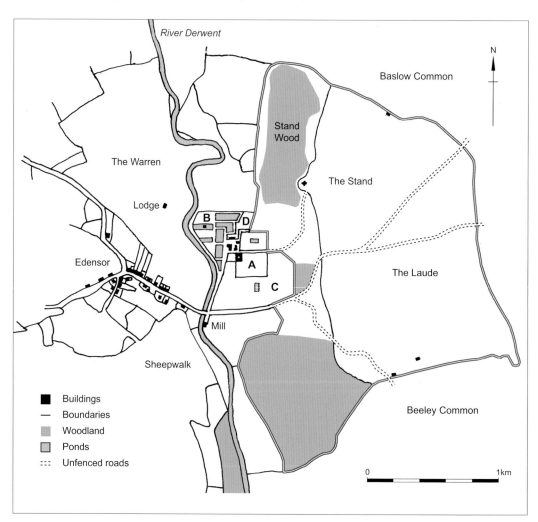

Fig 12.4
Chatsworth in the early 17th century, based on Senior's survey of 1617, showing the main deer park outlined in red, as well as the warren and sheepwalk, together with the house and garden (A), formal ponds and garden orchards (B), and small enclosures called the 'New Park' (C) and 'Roe Park' (D).

Fig 12.5
On the slopes of the present Chatsworth Park to the north and south of the house there are surviving veteran oak trees, some of which started growing in late-medieval times and are upwards of 500 years old. While they now stand in the landscape park designed by 'Capability' Brown in 1759, before this date they lay within the lower part of the much older Chatsworth deer park, which extended to the scarp top high above the house.
[John Barnatt]

There was another large deer park relatively close by, created in 1330 surrounding the important medieval hall at Haddon. This covered much of the ground between the top of Calton Pasture and the River Wye; adjacent to the park, there was a large 'sheepwalk' by the 18th century at latest, extending from the old village of Nether Haddon across Haddon Fields to the River Lathkill, whilst the site of the medieval village was known as the 'Little Park' (see Fig 2.13).

The ruined medieval hall at Upper Padley lay within a small park walled out in 1499, which was described as 'ould' in 1598. At Tissington there was a medieval park south of the village and its 17th-century hall; it existed by the late 13th century but had probably gone by the late 15th. Another smaller park at Harthill existed by the 16th century.[10]

At Rowsley, a large bank with ditch on the upslope side, running around the north side of Peak Tor, has long defied interpretation. Whilst it has been tentatively suggested to be a pre-Norman estate boundary,[11] it seems more likely to be medieval in date and is possibly a park pale that defines a small area between here and the river. Another park, identified from field names on historic maps, with some high deer-proof walls remaining, existed at Snitterton in the Derwent Valley, but whether this was medieval in date or goes with the fine 17th-century hall is unclear. Similarly, at Broadlowash there was a deer park in the 17th century.

In the South-West Peak a park is known to have existed at Blore, at the edge of the limestone plateau.[12] The now-ruined hall at Throwley was started in 1503 and at that time stood within a deer park which in parts had been cultivated earlier (Fig 12.6). The top of Ecton Hill was also possibly a park but the case for this is not strong.[13] On the western fringe of the Peak there was a large 14th-century deer park, of similar importance to those at Chatsworth and Haddon, surrounding the mid-16th-century mansion at Lyme in Cheshire.[14] The tower known as 'The Cage', dating to about 1580, was built as a hunting lodge and stand. Further south, an early park at Quarnford within Alstonefield Frith is documented as fenced in the early 1200s but the owner was made to remove the pale in 1227.[15] Further to the north there may have been a small park at Hayfield, the only one within the Royal Forest.

Why so few private parks appear to have existed in the Peak as a whole is in need of detailed analysis.

Fig 12.6
Medieval strip lynchets near Throwley Hall in an area that became a deer park in late medieval times.
[John Barnatt]

Ideal landscapes

Fig 12.7

Chatsworth Park in about 1860, showing features still here today and others now gone or disused. The features include the river widened to a 'lake' (A), Paine's two bridges (B), his mill (C), the boundary of Brown's 18th-century park (D), the 1820s' turnpike road (E), lodges (F), the 1850s' serpentine drives (G) and the Great Conservatory (H).

In the 18th century the traditional idea of how deer parks should look was transformed, with 'landscape parks' being created that were, fundamentally, landscapes that were designed to form a backdrop to stately homes. Whilst they often had deer, these were seen as 'nature idealised' and although they can be of great beauty, they are far from what the landscape would look like if nature was left to its own devices.

An archetypal landscape park designed by the landscape designer 'Capability' Brown was created around Chatsworth House from 1759, with work continuing into the 1760s (Fig 12.7).[16] Unusually, it was laid out at a new site rather than being redesigned at a much older deer park. Field hedges were removed wholesale but some of their oak trees were retained, allowing a 'ready-made' parkland effect; this was enhanced both by planting a scattering of beech trees and retaining decorative stands of trees added three decades before by the architect William Kent. The river was widened to be lake-like, held back by a weir, and two fine bridges over the river, together with a new mill, were designed by the architect James Paine. The park was enlarged significantly in the 1820s to 1830s, with farmland

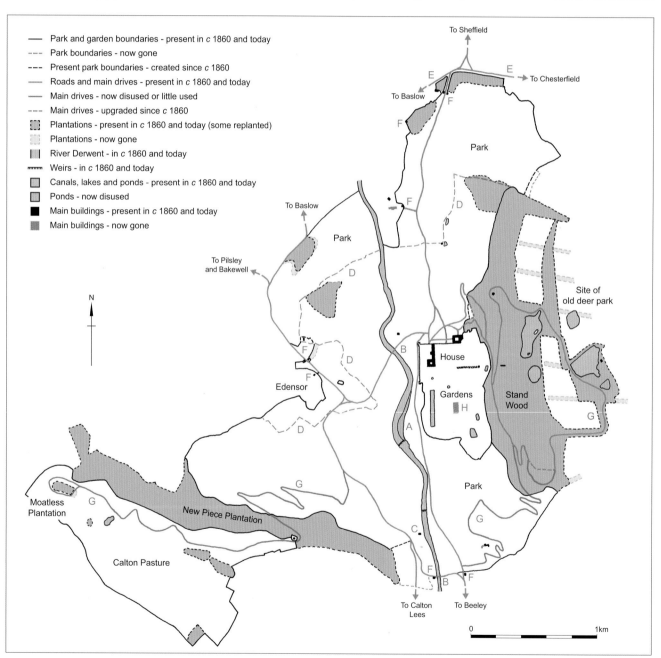

around Edensor taken in, done in advance of the transformation of the upper half of Edensor into a model village in the 1830s to 1840s (Fig 12.8). Creation of a larger area of new park going northwards on the east side of the river became possible after exchanging land with the Duke of Rutland in the 1820s; a turnpike road was moved to keep the park private. Lodges at park entrances were built and scenic drives added to take visitors in coaches around the park and to an outer park at Calton Pasture beyond the New Piece Plantation tree screen. The park as it looks today, with close-cropped grass but large numbers of trees, owes much to plantings made by Joseph Paxton, the well-known garden designer and architect who was based at Chatsworth for many years in the mid-19th century; Brown's original concept was more open.

Lyme Park, in contrast with Chatsworth, started life as a medieval deer park; this was altered over the centuries according to then current fashion, with avenues of sycamore and lime planted in the 17th century, and more informal plantings made later.

In the 18th century Haddon Hall was little used by its owners, the Dukes of Rutland, and the old deer park was fully enclosed as farmland, probably in about 1770; no attempt to create a fashionable landscape park was made. What is seen today is a 19th-century creation.[17]

Smaller parks exist elsewhere. At Hassop Hall there was a small park mapped in 1751, but this had been significantly enlarged by 1831 at the latest, perhaps when the hall was rebuilt in the later 18th century.[18] The new park was a typical one of its day, with privacy protected by a high boundary wall. Within this was a small area of decorative parkland in front of the house where the formal drive approached, but elsewhere it contained arable farmland surrounded by extensive tree plantings. Unusually, there is a 19th-century 'prospect mount', a large mound near the south-west corner of the park, where the family could picnic and view the surrounding landscape; here the nearby park wall was placed in a ha-ha to make this possible.

Swythamley Park, surrounding the late 18th-century hall, also has a high wall. The estate was broken up in 1975 and today the whole is used as farmland but still has a scattering of parkland trees, whereas in 1831 it is documented as being stocked with deer.

Fig 12.8
The archetypal 'model village' of Edensor was transformed in the 1830s and 1840s to architectural designs by Joseph Paxton and his assistant John Robertson. One half of the village had been demolished in the 1830s. However, in the other half, most of the houses were remodelled in an eclectic mixture of architectural styles.
[John Barnatt]

Houses with style

Most villages in the Peak have at least one manor house, hall or stately residence, usually built by lords of the manor or sometimes wealthy industrialists. Today's buildings are very variable in date, size and style; a few are open to the public but most are not.[19] What follows is a brief review of highlights.

The earliest halls date to the medieval period, with the grand hall at Haddon being one of the most important survivals in Britain, mostly dating from the 12th to 14th centuries and built on a low crag beside the river. There are two courtyards surrounded by buildings, with the great hall at the centre. Haddon was long the home of the Vernon family, but eventually passed to the Dukes of Rutland and after being long neglected was restored in the early 20th century. A similar if somewhat smaller and now-ruined house belonging to the Eyre family stood at Upper Padley and was built in the 13th century. A medieval gatehouse tower remains at Fenny Bentley. Slightly later are the impressive ruins of Throwley Hall, where the present house was started in 1503, and a remaining cross-wing of Hazlebadge Hall, dating to 1549, is now a farmhouse.

In 1549 work started on the grand mansion at Chatsworth built by Sir William Cavendish and his wife Elizabeth, better known as 'Bess of Hardwick'; it was as exceptional then as it is today. However, the sturdy house with many mullioned windows was taken down and rebuilt wing by wing between 1687 and 1707, to give it the classical look fashionable at the time; this still stands today.[20]

Only Lyme, built by the Legh family from the mid-16th century, came close to Chatsworth in terms of grandeur; parts of the Elizabethan house remain, but it is much-altered and again has impressive classical frontages (Fig 12.9).[21] A much smaller house, at North Lees, was built in 1594 by Robert Smythson, the architect of grand dwellings at Hardwick Hall and Bolsover Castle in north-east Derbyshire and Wollaton Hall near Nottingham.

One of the highlights of the Peak is the large number of later 16th- and 17th-century halls built by the gentry and yeoman farmers, with over 35 remaining. These typically are sturdy stone dwellings with H-shaped plans, mullioned and transomed windows, string courses and stone-slate roofs, built to last in a period when there was much wealth in the region from the blossoming lead trade, especially from the late

Fig 12.9
The south front of Lyme Park, designed by Giacomo Leoni in the 1720s; the ornamental lake came later.
[John Barnatt]

16th century onwards.[22] To mention a few: Eyam Hall, built sometime in the early 17th century, is open to the public; Offerton Hall (1658) is a classic H-plan house; Holme Hall (1626) is an impressive square house still with gardens behind a high wall and outbuilding ranges; Hartington Hall (pre-1611) is now a youth hostel. Tissington Hall, long the home of the FitzHerberts, was started in 1609 but much enlarged over the centuries; it is open to the public and overlooks a fine example of an estate village surrounded by decorative parkland. Snitterton Hall (1631) is another fine but private example, with restored gardens and two small pavilions, all hidden behind a high wall. Smaller 17th-century houses include one at Beeley Hilltop now a farmhouse, and a picturesque early 17th-century example at Hazleford near Hathersage. Hazleford was one of the houses built by the prolific Eyre family, whose other houses include an earlier one nearby at Highlow, probably built in the late 16th century (Fig 12.10; *see also* Fig 3.1).

Turning now to the 18th century and houses built in the classical style, paramount for splendour is Chatsworth as always. Smaller well-proportioned stone-built halls are found for example at Winster (probably early 18th century), Stoke Hall (1757), Holt House at Two Dales (c 1777–80) and Ashford (late 1770s), whilst those at Great Longstone (1747) and Parwich (1747) stand out as brick built (Fig 12.11). The grand Hassop Hall, often said to have been built for the Earl of Newburgh in a rather uninspiringly heavy classical style in the 1820s, is now thought to date to the 1770s.

The 19th century brought houses that were more eclectic in design; for example at Churchdale Hall (1831), which is in Jacobean style, as is Thornbridge Hall across the road, an impressive rebuild of the 1870s, enlarged from 1902. Burton Closes at Bakewell, built in the later 1840s to a design by Joseph Paxton and his assistant John Robertson, is in Tudor Gothic (*see* Fig 3.22). The rather plain Stancliffe Hall (late 1860s to 1885), built for the industrialist Joseph Whitworth, again has Jacobean details. Although its land is much built over, as you pass down the A6 there are distinctive signs of the estate influence, such as the expensively detailed Whitworth Institute and well-made roadside wall copings.

Fig 12.10
The picturesque Hazleford Hall near Hathersage was built in the early 17th century for the prolific Eyre family, who were landowning gentry with several houses in the area.
[John Barnatt]

Fig 12.11
Stoke Hall, in the Derwent
Valley between Calver
and Grindleford, is a fine
example of an 18th-century
house in Palladian classical
style. It was built in 1757 by
James Booth, who worked
closely with the architect
James Paine, and replaced
an earlier hall here.
[John Barnatt]

Chasing the picturesque

In 1697 Celia Fiennes, who wrote of her tours around Britain, said of Derbyshire 'you see neither hedge nor tree but only low drye-stone walls round some ground, else its only hills and dales as thick as you can imagine, but tho' the surface of the earth looks barren yet those hills are impregnated with rich Marbles Stones Metals Iron and Copper and Coale Mines in their bowells' which made up for 'the deficiency of a place'.[23] Her tour, and that of the author Daniel Defoe in the 1720s, extolled the virtue of places such as Chatsworth House whilst the landscape around was not seen as attractive. Defoe, commenting on travelling across the moors above Chatsworth, with him 'beaten out with the fatigue of' crossing 'a comfortless, barren' and as he thought 'endless moor'.[24] However, this commonly held view was to be radically transformed from the mid-18th century onwards.[25] One of the key factors was a growing interest amongst artists in depicting landscape, with this discipline gradually being seen as of great value rather than as an impoverished cousin of portraiture, culminating in the work of artists such as Turner and Constable in the first half of the 19th century. Hand in hand with this was an interest in the picturesque and depicting a romanticised landscape. Ironically, as is often the case with such things, people began to appreciate the traditional landscape at a time when it was first

coming under threat from the effects of the industrialisation of Britain. Places such as Dove Dale, the Matlock tors and Castleton became iconic picturesque places that had to be visited; this provided a cheaper option than the Grand Tour (Fig 12.12).

The first tourists were of the 'polite class', with gentlemen and their ladies coming to particular places from the 18th century onwards, notably Buxton and Matlock Bath where they took the waters. Buxton, whose thermal waters had been popular from the 16th century, was promoted by the Duke of Devonshire who owned much land here, improving the facilities with the building of The Crescent and its grand stables in the 1780s. Matlock Bath, with its impressive backdrop of limestone tors, was on the tourist trail from the 1730s when the Old Bath was improved. In the 18th century one of the more curious tourist attractions at Buxton was a visit to gape at the lime workers at the Grin Hill limekilns who lived in the waste heaps; in the 19th century this went out of fashion and the traces of industry were hidden behind a plantation so as not to offend genteel tastes.

From the late 18th century onwards a series of published tourist guides extolled the virtues of the Peak and brought in more visitors.[26] In the mid-19th century the situation started to change with the coming of railways into the Peak. People from the 'lower classes' came on outings, firstly using the 1849 line through Matlock Bath that at first terminated at Rowsley, and from the 1860s lines to other parts such as Buxton. Over the next 150 years the number of visitors expanded exponentially. Tastes also changed, with more demand for access to the high moorlands by the working people of Sheffield and Manchester, with walking groups publishing guides such as the Sheffield Clarion Ramblers handbooks from 1902, leading to the well-known mass trespass of 1932 and other less-publicised fights for access. From the 1950s staff of the national park brokered many access agreements onto the moorlands, which were replaced in 2000 by the Countryside and Rights of Way Act that gave statutory access to open land.

The value of the Peak landscape was affirmed at the beginning of the 1950s when much of the region was made into Britain's first national park. Areas around Buxton and on the southern limestone plateau around Wirksworth and Cauldon were left out because of the active quarries there, whilst the Whaley Bridge to New Mills and Glossop areas were also excluded because of mills and other factories. Most mills have now closed and whilst some quarries are still active, the boundaries, particularly around Buxton, have proved restrictive. Tunstead Quarry east of Buxton, one of the largest limestone quarries in Britain, has encroached into the national park as it has expanded. If the park boundary was being defined for the first time today, it is a moot point whether it would have been drawn in exactly the same place; as many people in recent decades have come to appreciate the relics of old industry as having their own landscape value, perhaps the excluded areas would have been included with modern industry also accommodated.

Fig 12.12
The entrance to Dove Dale where the river flows out of its gorge at the edge of the limestone plateau, with Thorpe Cloud to the right. This entrance has been the beginning of a popular visitor trek into the gorge, now heavily wooded, from the 18th century onwards. [John Barnatt]

13

Conflict landscapes

Although the Peak was far away from foci of wartime conflicts in the 20th century these have still left their traces that again add to its character. They take on two basic forms; structures and scars left from military training, and others that were part of the defence of Britain, built to protect against air raids or invasion.

As often happens with archaeological studies, researchers have become interested at a point in time when it is, or is almost, too late to ask questions of those involved; this is compounded by a common lack of documentation of the structures we now find, for military activities at the time were regarded as 'secret', and if anything was ever written down it seems not to have survived. We are left with the physical remains and the clues they give to build interpretations and reconstruct details.

Amongst the most interesting are 1914–18 practice trenches and moorland training relics for more mobile warfare in 1939–45 with remaining slit trenches, gun platforms, tank

stands and scars from bullets and mortars. Similarly, there are surviving earthworks for 1939–45 anti-aircraft batteries across the Peak and defended munitions storage at Harpur Hill above Buxton (Fig 13.1).

There is also an assortment of more minor features such as: a 'starfish' site where fires were lit on Houndkirk Moor above Sheffield to confuse German bombers into thinking this was their target; a sturdy metal hook in Bradwell Dale, which once had a cable crossing the road, erected as a tank trap; circular bases for spigot mortars in Bole Hill Quarry above Hathersage and at Windy Knoll at the head of the Winnats; and concrete platforms around Langsett, Midhope and Underbank reservoirs that supported metal pylons holding up catenary wires to prevent low-flying German bombers attacking the dam, placed here after our own Dambusters raids.[1] There are no doubt other structures, probably known about by local people, which otherwise are currently unrecognised. Places mentioned in this chapter are shown on Figure A1.10 (*see* p 241).

Practice in remote places

Two places in the Peak have silted or backfilled 1914–18 trenches where the British Army practiced trench warfare before going to France. Both sets tell a similar story, of training for what proved to be a futile way of fighting where stalemate was the order of the day.

There are extensive remains of 1914–18 training trenches at Redmires on high ground north-west of the dams, which were first identified two decades ago and are now a Scheduled Monument.[2] Many of these trenches were dug by the Sheffield City Battalion before going to France, possibly with later digging by the Sherwood Foresters and Royal Engineers. Details of a second similar site above Burbage are given below.

Fig 13.1
On High Edge above Harpur Hill near Buxton, an elevated ridge with natural limestone pavement, there are two World War II pill boxes that were part of the defences around the Harpur Hill munitions storage facilities. This one was built into, and partially hidden, by a Bronze Age round barrow, presumably with its contents dug out without a second thought.
[John Barnatt]

There are several places on the Peak moors with indications that later military training has taken place. On Big Moor between Baslow and Sheffield there are many bullet and distinctive mortar-bomb scars on boulders and rock outcrops; these are associated with one-man trenches, often in clusters.[3] To the south, on Gardom's Edge the wartime remains are different, with four low platforms for artillery guns, whilst on Gibbet Moor, the presumed target area, large shells have been found over the years and bomb disposal called; after 1945 the gamekeepers here, when burning the heather, used to light the fires and then run. Nearby there are the earthworks of a fortified command post and an observation station.[4] Below Burbage Moor near Fox House and nearby around Carl Wark, there are again numerous bullet and mortar scars on rocks.[5]

A far from complete picture exists as to who exactly was practising on the eastern moors. Much, and probably all, we see belongs to 1939–45; dated .303 bullet cases and fins from mortar-bombs littered the ground for decades afterwards. We know that British and overseas troops were here, possibly Canadian and/or American, as were the Home Guard, whilst at Burbage, amongst others, the 2nd Battalion Rifle Brigade were there in 1941.

Further north, on Ewden Height, there are vehicle emplacements and brick-built target bays at the Midhope Armoured Vehicle Firing Range, used by tanks, armoured vehicles and field guns.[6]

Burbage

A recently discovered example of training trenches on the moors above Burbage near Buxton has a variety of slight earthworks dug over a broad area (Fig 13.2).[7] These include crenellated 'fire trenches' dug in straight lines following the contours as front-line earthworks, each with a series of shooting 'bays' separated by 'traverses'. The latter were designed as barriers to stop enemy fire reaching all troops along the trench when the trench was stormed. There are also 'communication trenches', approaching the 'fire trenches' from behind; what can be interpreted as forward 'machine gun emplace-ments' or 'observation trenches'; and two examples of oval 'redoubts' with crenellated trenches. The last were designed as strong points within trench networks for front-line command, field kitchens and supply depots. Many visible features at Burbage Edge are defined today by shallow ditches, often only partially visible, along the lines of presumably largely backfilled trenches. The impression gained is that the earthworks accrued gradually, with new ones dug after others were abandoned, rather than the whole representing a single mock battlefield. In contrast to what remains at Burbage Edge, a solitary 'fire trench' on Watford Moor, just over 1.5km to the north, was never backfilled. It is believed that all these trenches were dug by the British army's Royal Engineers, from 1915 to 1918, who were billeted at the Empire Hotel and elsewhere in Buxton.

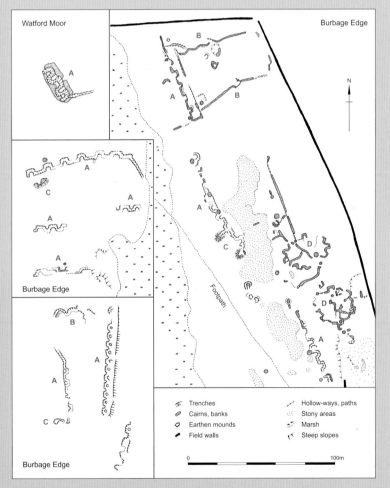

Fig 13.2
Plan of the main World War I trenches on Burbage Edge moorland, with insets showing parts of others nearby and that at Watford Moor. Features include fire trenches (A), communication trenches (B), forward posts for machine guns or observation (C) and redoubts (D).

Lighting the sky

At least seven sites of 1939–45 light anti-aircraft searchlight batteries still have surviving earthworks in the Peak.[8] Another four are recorded in archaeological databases but are in improved farmland.[9] It may be that more sites await discovery. Archaeologically, the distinctive features are circular banks, which originally in some cases were built as sandbag walls around searchlights and/or anti-aircraft guns, and sites of barrack blocks. Three sites are described below as examples.

It is recorded that at least some of the Peak batteries were under the command of 353 Searchlight Battery based at Leek, and under the command of 38 Searchlight Regiment Okeover Hall, but no systematic assessment has been published and much needs to be done to understand how each searchlight battery was used; despite physical similarities current interpretation at the two sites is very different. Presumably, the majority were primarily designed to intercept enemy aircraft on their way to and back from Manchester and other industrial targets to the west.

Bailey's Tump

Earthworks here, above Matlock to the east of the town, have been conserved by the local community (Fig 13.3). Here there are three large circular rings said to have been built around sites of a searchlight, a generator and a sound locator. A small central mound with sunken centre is interpreted as the command centre, and there is also an earthwork at the site of three small anti-aircraft machine guns and an oval embankment with a concrete 'Stanton Shelter' within for use when under attack. Nearby are the footings of a rectangular toilet block and an ammunition store. Interpretation was provided by someone, then a boy, who remembered the site in use during the war.

Fig 13.3
The searchlight battery earthworks at Bailey's Tump above Matlock. The lobate earthwork in the foreground is thought to have surrounded three machine guns, while at least one of the big rings behind surrounded a searchlight.
[John Barnatt]

Biggin

On high ground east of the village, there are exceptionally well-preserved earthworks of three large circular structures, defined by banks with external ditches, one with a central mound. Nearby there is a rectangular earthwork, whilst to one side there is a rectangular footing for a barrack block, smaller mounds and an open-sided trapezoidal bank.

Nearby, on the other side of the old railway line, there was a camp for Italian prisoners of war, with five 'huts' still standing, built of concrete and brick with corrugated asbestos roofs, and concrete platforms for at least two more now-removed buildings.

Edale

In the valley bottom near its western end, there is another set of well-preserved earthworks; in 1993 the elderly farmer, Mr Cooper, remembered the site in use in the 1939–45 war and was able to identify the component parts (Fig 13.4). There are circular banks that he remembered to be the sites of three searchlights set in a triangle, originally with sandbag walls, two with penannular internal rings and the third now badly damaged. To the north was another circular wall surrounding listening apparatus, with a small platform nearby built of bricks, of unknown purpose. The only guns on site were two small machine guns, each position now marked by a small mound. Against the lane there are the sites of eight small buildings in a row, each visible as a platform; these were the barracks for officers, NCOs and men, with toilet blocks. High on the hillside above to the west, there was a command/observation point from where operations were directed.[10]

This site may have functioned differently from the norm. It is recorded that it was on the fighter patrol ring around Manchester and Liverpool, marked for night fighters by electric flares at node points such as Edale. The Edale site was also part of the 'Sandra' lights system, which was designed to direct lost aircraft back to airfields. A published first-hand account by someone stationed here from 1940 also records that the huts were wooden, and that the searchlights, of American-built Sperry Corporation type with 150cm reflectors, were powered by a Lister diesel generator on a truck.[11]

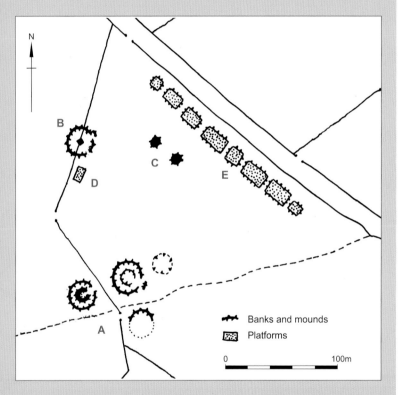

Fig 13.4
The searchlight battery earthworks south of Upper Booth in Edale. These define three embanked searchlight sites (A), an embanked listening device (B), sites of two machine guns (C), a brick platform (D) and a line of eight platforms for wooden buildings (E).

Storing munitions

A single 'permanent' storage depot has been identified at Harpur Hill near Buxton. This facility was one of many large permanent storage bases across Britain used in 1939–45 by either the British Army and RAF, including the stone mines at Corsham in Wiltshire. These were supplemented by ammunition parks, for example under the trees of Sherwood Forest in Nottinghamshire. The now most-infamous underground storage depot was the RAF depot at the Fauld alabaster mine in the Trent Valley, which exploded in 1944 in what was the largest explosion ever to have taken place in Britain.

Harpur Hill

On high ground south-west of Harpur Hill, there is the site of an extensive munitions storage base (Fig 13.5).[12] This was set up by the RAF Maintenance Unit as a Reserve Depot. A large quarry here was bought in 1938; a two-tiered store was built in concrete and then buried. The site finally came into use in March 1940 for bomb and other munition storage; until 1942 this included mustard gas bombs. Because of fears about the stability of the buried store, after a similar construction collapsed at Llanberris Quarry in North Wales in January 1942, its

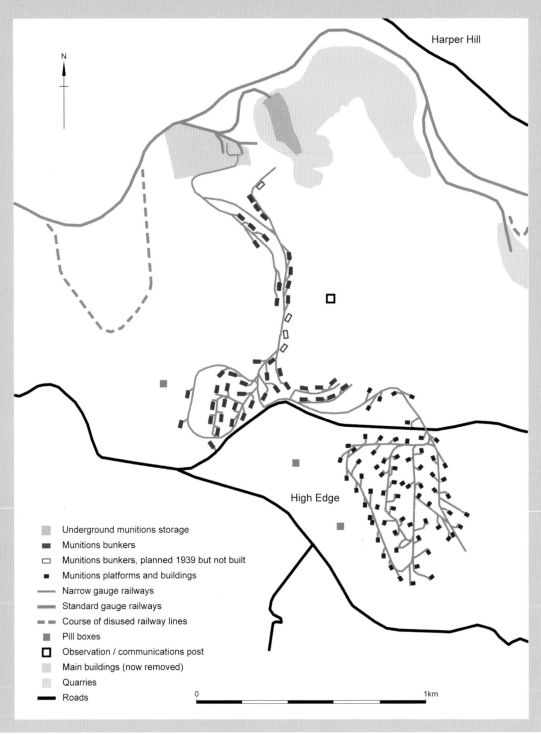

Fig 13.5
The World War II munitions facility at Harpur Hill. This included underground storage buried in a disused quarry, linked to the Cromford and High Peak Railway by a siding. Also, on the high limestone plateau to the south, there was a large number of bunkers and platforms, linked by narrow-gauge railways. The northernmost ones were erected shortly before the war, but most were added during the conflict years.

Underground munitions storage
Munitions bunkers
Munitions bunkers, planned 1939 but not built
Munitions platforms and buildings
Narrow gauge railways
Standard gauge railways
Course of disused railway lines
Pill boxes
Observation / communications post
Main buildings (now removed)
Quarries
Roads

Harper Hill

High Edge

0   1km

contents were moved outside. At Harpur Hill these and other ordnance were stored over a wide area to the south in 45 individual rectangular bunkers, some roofed and part-buried, others now-open standings and surrounded by blast-banks (Fig 13.6). To the east of High Edge over 60 smaller rectangular platforms, each with six stacks, were still in use and are visible on an RAF aerial photograph taken shortly after the war; some still survive. There were three pill boxes nearby, two inserted into Bronze Age barrows.

Shortly after the war, Harpur Hill, along with storage facilities at Bowes Moor in County Durham and at Rhydymwyn in North Wales that had the main wartime production factory for mustard gas, were the main centres for its disposal. At Harpur Hill some of the gas bombs were burnt on site, whilst much eventually was taken away to be put into ships and either dumped or scuppered at sea. The underground storage at Harpur became a mushroom farm and is now a storage facility; there is no public access. Other parts became the Mines Research Laboratory and later the Health and Safety Laboratory. The covered bunkers are again private, but to the south other features can be viewed from a footpath.

Fig 13.6
Below the northern end of High Edge, at the southern end of the Harpur Hill RAF facility, there is a series of hard standings with blast banks in case of accidental explosion, where munitions were stored in World War II. [John Barnatt]

14

Inhabited places

This last chapter returns to where we started in Chapter 2 – the dominant character of today's Peak historic cultural landscapes – but it takes a different perspective. We now take a broader view and consider landscapes according to how they were traditionally used by local people; again vignettes are given to illustrate similarities and differences.

The traditional ways of presenting historic landscape character, as a series of maps showing designated character of specific parcels of land (*see* Appendix 2 for examples), whilst useful for landscape managers with an interest in making sustainable conservation decisions, is in some ways flawed. It is over-simplistic as it does not allow for multiple functions of parcels of land, such as mining in the same field as grazing. More importantly, it does not look at the dynamics of how people lived in the land.

By the high medieval period occupation in the Peak was essentially sedentary with long-established patterns of settlement that have come through to today. At earlier dates, before the pattern established over the last thousand years was in place, more radical transformations have been discussed in Chapters 10 and 11 but are not considered further here. These include change from the transhumant ways of the Mesolithic and Neolithic to the adoption of more sustained settled farming by the Iron Age. A second significant transformation is the change from predominantly dispersed settlement across the Peak to nucleation into villages, implemented by feudal lords in the centuries around the Norman Conquest on the limestone plateau and the main shale valleys.

Even in medieval times, community boundaries were not quite set in stone; trans-humance between summer and winter pastures perhaps still took place and certainly high commons were shared between adjacent communities, governed by informal inter-commoning agreements. This said, the long-established township boundaries in use through to today, but now called civil parishes, have long been vital building blocks in defining local identity. Often these include varied topography and complementary or contrasting resources, which allowed local people for the most part to be self-sufficient. Similarly, manors and ecclesiastical parishes were important, as were the positions of market centres. As we have seen, often villages and markets were sited at interfaces between different resource areas. Ideally, local communities needed sheltered places to live, good arable land, extensive pastures, stone, wood and peat for building and fuel, mineral resources to supplement income, and good points of access to the outside world. Places at topographical interfaces take on particular importance.

Larger divisions of the landscape are not considered here; these include county bound-aries, District Council boundaries and those of the traditional county divisions called 'hundreds'. Similarly, there were complex divisions of land between royal and private estates. Some estates have existed for hundreds of years, but often they have been significantly modified through time as land was bought and sold, as families transferred land through marriage, and as the fortunes of the nobility and landed gentry waxed and waned. Such matters are important to the study of history but often not to the physical appearance of the land and how local communities used it. The major exception to this was at the large estates of the nobility, as at Chatsworth, Haddon and Lyme, where radical changes were implemented, such as the creation of parks and replacing fields with new layouts that were in keeping with fashionable views as to how agriculture should be practised.

In Chapter 2 the emphasis in describing the historic landscape was on zones defined by geology and topography, with distinctions drawn between limestone plateau, shale valleys and gritstone uplands. Cultural landscape zones are redefined here in this chapter to include land used by each community within their townships. The resulting zones comprise 'the valley heartlands', 'the limestone core', 'the south-west landscape' and 'remote places' (Fig 14.1).

Some areas at the edges of the region to the east and west of the high moorlands are parts of foothill zones outside the remit of this book and are not considered here. Places mentioned in this Chapter are shown on Figure A1.11 (*see* p 243).

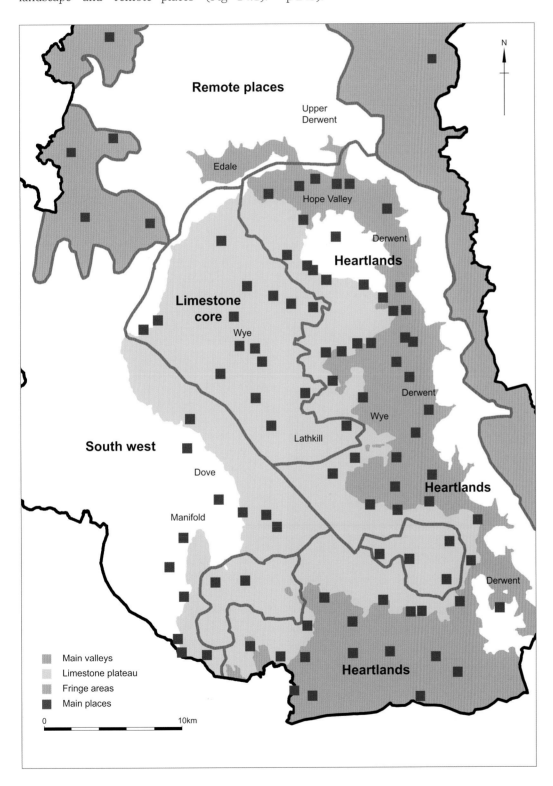

Fig 14.1
The community landscape zones of the Peak.

The valley heartlands

The traditional key areas for settlement in the Peak have long been the deep shale valleys to the north, east and south of the central limestone plateau. Here were the main market centres and strings of villages sited to take advantage of the shelter they provided. These made good places to live and farm, which also had access to extensive areas of limestone plateau and gritstone uplands; areas vital to their prosperity as they provided a wide range of resources. In the high medieval period there was greater emphasis on arable farming than today. However, population loss caused by the Black Death in the mid-14th century, and subsequent climate fluctuations, led to livestock becoming more important.

To the north the wide Hope Valley has focal places, including: Hope, long an important royal manorial centre; Castleton, a planned 'town' dominated by its stone castle; and Hathersage, another long-established centre (*see* the case study on pp 22–3). In the western half of the valley there were places with extensive medieval open fields and rich lead mines, and administrative

emphasis was focused here rather than towards Hathersage to the east. The main villages are often on the south-facing slopes and in the valley bottom.[1] The main exception is Bradwell, which was strategically placed in relation to the mines. The north-facing slopes further east have only a few smaller places, some shrunk to nothing more than isolated farmsteads (Fig 14.2).[2]

Going downriver, after a narrow section of the Derwent Valley between Hathersage and Calver where the settlements are small,[3] the valley opens up before reaching Matlock (Fig 14.3). It then runs southwards through a limestone gorge. In this central heartland part of the valley there is a ribbon of villages.[4] To the south both Darley and Matlock were medieval royal manorial centres. Further north the main royal centres were at Bakewell and Ashford (*see* the case study on p 55); these lie on the lower stretch of the River Wye above the confluence with the Derwent. This gave them access to the adjacent limestone plateau. Those villages on the east side of the Derwent had access to the gritstone eastern moors. Between the two rivers there is a triangle of land with low shelves containing a high density of villages, with the principal ones nestled below the edge of the limestone plateau (Fig 14.4).[5] An atypical topographical situation occurs further north where a string of villages and hamlets occupies the interface between the limestone plateau and a high gritstone block of moorland west of the Derwent.[6] Going south, beyond the River Lathkill, there is another string of settlements following the limestone plateau edge or lying close by, with Youlgreave and Winster the most important.[7]

South of the limestone plateau, the valleys at the edge of the limestone plateau contain the market towns of Wirksworth and Ashbourne. Both lie at the centre of medieval royal manors, whilst between the two are villages that took advantage of the sheltered land suitable for arable in the lee of higher land to the north.[8] Some but not all of these are at the plateau-edge springline (*see* the case study on p 35). Those to the east were close to rich lead mines that made them prosperous.[9] Wirksworth, as well as having mines, was also the administrative centre where the main miners' Barmote Courts for the Low Peak were traditionally held.

To the west, whilst the limestone plateau again drops off steeply into the upper part of the Dove Valley, this area is more isolated and the settlement pattern is predominantly dispersed; this area is discussed below under 'The south-west landscape'.

Fig 14.2
Offerton Hall, built in 1658 on the site of an earlier house and presumably a small village or hamlet, stands at the southern side of the Hope Valley opposite Hathersage. From here sinuous braided hollow-ways ascend out of the valley up the steep slope onto the high gritstone moor above, allowing the complementary resources these provided to be easily accessed.
[John Barnatt]

Fig 14.3
The Derwent Valley
between Bamford and
Matlock is dominated
by the main scarp of the
eastern gritstone upland,
as here at Curbar Edge
(left) and Baslow Edge
(right). Between the two lies
Curbar Gap, the target of
traditional hollow-ways
and a 1759 turnpike road
out of the valley. Below the
Gap are ancient irregular
enclosures and the small
village of Curbar, with the
large early 19th-century
Calver Mill built for textile
spinning by the river below,
with Calver village in front.
[John Barnatt]

Fig 14.4
Between the rivers Wye
and Derwent north of their
confluence there are low-
lying gritstone shelves and
ridges, as here at Handley
Bottom between Bakewell
and Pilsley. Unlike the higher
gritstone uplands to the
east of the Derwent, they
are all fully enclosed and
have attracted settlement
over many centuries.
[John Barnatt]

Castleton, Hope and Bradwell

The deep and sheltered Hope Valley has long been a focal point for settlement, probably from prehistory onwards (*see* also the case study on p 22). It lies relatively cut-off from the rest of the Derwent Valley heartland downriver to the south-east, nestled between the highermost parts of the limestone plateau to the south and even higher and much bleaker Dark Peak moorlands to the north (Fig 14.5).

The Hope Valley has long been a focus of administration and power. Forts and castles mostly lie in the western half and locations have migrated through time according to need and preference.[10] In the valley bottom, at Hope there is a Norman motte at the heart of the royal manor, whilst nearby, again close to the River Noe, is the Roman fort at Brough with civil settlement outside its walls. Hundreds of years before the Romans arrived the inhabitants of the valley were overlooked by the Mam Tor hillfort

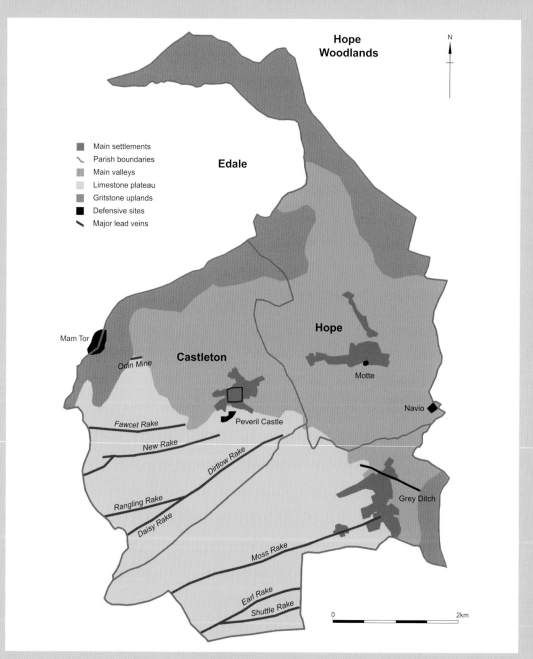

Fig 14.5
The parishes of Castleton, Hope and Bradwell, showing the relationship with limestone plateau, gritstone uplands, defensive sites and major lead veins.

high at the west end of the valley, an impressive symbol of the power of the community and its leaders (Fig 14.6). Roman power was based on its military and administrative organisation; thus, a fort at Navio at the heart of the valley made more sense. After the Romans left, the Grey Ditch was built to separate the heart of the Hope Valley from the limestone plateau to the south; this hints at different political imperatives, perhaps with a small British enclave in the valley, at or near the boundaries of the kingdoms of Mercia and Northumbria, separated from Anglo-Saxon dominated lands on the plateau. A motte-and-bailey castle was built at Hope after the Normans arrived. In the 12th century the focus of power in the valley shifted to Castleton with the building of Peveril Castle and a planned defended town below, these last two being symbols of lordly power, built to control people living within the Royal Forest (*see* Chapter 12).

Further access to land outside the valley is illustrated by the positions of township boundaries; all three villages have valley land with medieval open fields and uplands with complementary resources. Both Castleton and Bradwell have

extensive areas on the limestone plateau, useful for grazing, but with parts of the Bradwell open field also extending upslope onto limestone land. Most important of all, from medieval times onwards, were the rich veins of lead ore found on the limestone commons of Castleton and Bradwell. In contrast, Hope had extensive lands on the gritstone upland and its narrow dissecting valleys. Today's detached Hope Woodlands parish reflects this, and Edale was also once part of the manor of Hope. In the Norman period the royal manor of Hope, which extended well beyond the township, included large tracts on both limestone and gritstone. Land on the limestone included Tideswell to the south, whilst to the north Edale and parts of the Hope Valley further east were included. The manor had been even larger before the Conquest, but places such as Castleton and Bradwell had been granted to a variety of lords in the late Anglo-Saxon period.

The people of Castleton, Hope and Bradwell are reported to have long been rivals; whilst living in places with similar resources and lifestyles, no doubt differences were played upon to strengthen local identities.

Fig 14.6
The western end of the Hope Valley, west of Castleton, is one of contrasts, with ancient enclosures in the valley bottom and former commons starting on the steep edge of the limestone plateau above. Winnats Pass (left) leads up to the plateau top and to Mam Tor (right) and the high gritstone moors beyond. [John Barnatt]

The Derwent Valley from Froggatt to Beeley and sandstone ridges around Hassop and Pilsley

This stretch of the Derwent Valley is one with great contrasts (Fig 14.7). The valley has fertile areas and therein lie the villages of Froggatt, Curbar, Baslow, Bubnell, Edensor and Beeley (*see also* the case study on p 24). To the west the villages of Hassop and Pilsley on the sandstone shelves are smaller. At less fertile parts are the hamlets of Calton Lees and Birchills, once matched on the other side of the river by Chatsworth, Langley and Besley, now lost, all subsumed within Chatsworth Park. This spectacular parkland landscape was created as a statement of idealised nature and the power of the Cavendish family, and it is wonderfully different from surrounding agricultural and wooded areas. A smaller park around Hassop exists to the north-west. The townships on the east bank of the Derwent extend upwards to include large tracts of gritstone moorland with scattered long-established farmsteads such as at Moorside, Harewood Grange, Beeley Hilltop and Fallinge. West of the river the townships extend over more dissected sandstone shelves and ridges, the upper parts of which were fully enclosed in post-medieval times, whilst the older settlements lie in more sheltered parts.

Much of the land in the valley comprises hedged and walled fields, often with vestiges of former medieval open fields identifiable as enclosed strips, but with extensive areas modified over the centuries of continuous use. Enclosures on the upland shelves can also be ancient but others are post-medieval in date. The central area of the valley was transformed, firstly by the creation of a deer park at Chatsworth in late medieval times, and then from the mid-18th century with the making of the huge landscape park in the valley below with the sweeping away of miles of hedges (*see* Chapter 12).

The townships in this part of the Derwent Valley are all arranged so that they include both

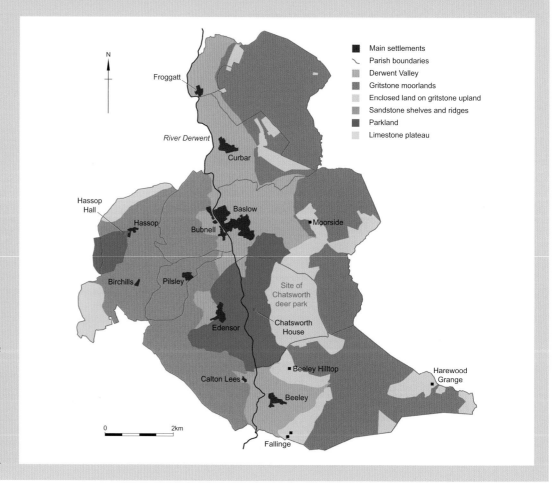

Fig 14.7
The Derwent Valley from Froggatt to Beeley and sandstone ridges around Hassop and Pilsley, showing the relationship between shale valley villages, western sandstone shelves and eastern gritstone uplands.

good valley farmland and uplands. The latter were important to communities for the resources they provided, including open grazing, peat and furze, good building stone and coal. Baslow and Beeley were the principal settlements east of the river and the moorlands of the former extend above Froggatt, Curbar and Chatsworth. Between the Derwent Valley bottom lands and the uplands, the upper steep slopes were also once important for their woodlands and the firewood, charcoal and timber they provided. These steep areas have been much modified in post-medieval times, some woods being felled and others made into plantations; those flanking Chatsworth Park also have a decorative landscape purpose.

Bradbourne, Brassington, Ballidon and Aldwark

Three of these villages lie in the sheltered clayland valleys beyond the southern edge of the limestone plateau; in contrast the small settlement at Aldwark lies high on the limestone plateau (Fig 14.8). All of the valley settlements have good valley-bottom land with extensive survival of ridge and furrow indicating the former importance of arable here. Fossilised open-field strips are also present, and are particularly evident around Brassington.

Bradbourne is small but was a medieval manorial centre, with Anglo-Saxon cross and early church. Brassington grew to be the largest village because of rich lead mines on the limestone plateau nearby. In contrast, Ballidon is shrunken, with earthworks of former houses and yards still evident in pastures near the three surviving farmsteads.[11] Aldwark, which today has only four farmsteads, was first recorded in 1142 and its township boundary has Brassington land to the north and south indicating it was a subsidiary settlement.

Brassington and Ballidon have access to extensive tracts of limestone plateau as well as sheltered valley-bottom land. On the plateau there are farmsteads with origins as monastic granges, as well as later farmsteads added after the commons were enclosed. The lead mines in this part of the orefield have long been worked. The veins are plentiful but relatively narrow and shallow and were ideally suited for early working; this was certainly taking place in medieval times and may well have origins in the Roman period. Brassington has a large parish, whilst that of Ballidon is small, squeezed between Parwich and Brassington. Thus, it never had the capacity to be a large place; now, a significant part of the limestone land here has been quarried away over recent decades and lorries regularly pass through the village. Bradbourne is different again. Whilst it occupies a good focal position overlooking valleys to the east and west, and this no doubt in the past made it an important 'mother village', there is no extensive limestone plateau land within the township. Thus, although an early manorial centre, the village's raison d'être later was essentially agricultural and this restricted its capacity for growth.

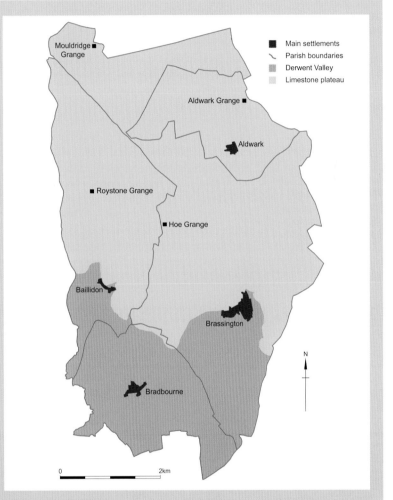

Fig 14.8
The parishes of Bradbourne, Brassington, Ballidon and Aldwark, showing the relationship between the southern valley landscape and the limestone plateau.

The limestone core

At the heart of the limestone plateau are villages with medieval origins whose townships were confined to the limestone rather than including complementary resource areas. For many villages their siting was determined by spring lines and good agricultural land that was located in favourable areas suitable for large open fields, whilst the extensive commons beyond were used for grazing. For some places an additional factor was the presence of lead mines. From the Black Death onwards, the altitude and upland climate made the villages at the heart of the plateau relatively sleepy places where villages continued in relative seclusion to modern times. With the coming of tourists and commuters all have been smartened up and now are picture-postcard perfect.

To the north two key areas with core villages flank the gorges of the Wye and Lathkill, both comprising shallow upland basins that provide good land. At the heart of the former, on the north side of the Wye gorge is the market village of Tideswell, with other villages and hamlets running both west and east.[12] To the south side a matching large village is Taddington, with a complex medieval street layout with back lanes (*see also* the case study on p 15). Again there are further settlements to the west and east.[13]

To both sides of the river, to the west there is a tendency for the places to be smaller as altitude rises and areas of suitable land get smaller. At the heart of the Lathkill basin is the market village of Monyash, with other villages nearby.[14] The Tideswell and Monyash markets were the only two in the heart of the plateau, filling the gap between centres such as Hartington and Bakewell that were at topographical interfaces and accessed complementary resources.

To the far north, Peak Forest is an atypical settlement (*see* the case study on p 48). As well as nucleation around the turnpike road, which follows an earlier route through the village, there was a loose concentration of hamlets and farmsteads of different dates in a small upland basin largely surrounded by high parts of the plateau (Fig 14.9). This place had origins at the focal point for the foresters who policed the Royal Forest of the Peak and who had their chamber here.

To the south there are two islands of limestone core. At the south-east there are a series of shelves with villages and hamlets above the Via Gellia gorge (Fig 14.10). The largest places are Bonsall and Middleton by Wirksworth, whilst there are again smaller places upstream to the west.[15]

To the south-west there is another area of shelves above the gorges of the Dove and Manifold. Here the focal place is the ancient manorial

Fig 14.9 (below)
The higher parts of the limestone plateau, as here just east of Peak Forest, have scattered post-medieval farmsteads and fields.
[John Barnatt]

Fig 14.10 (opposite)
A typical ancient limestone plateau landscape, near Middleton by Wirksworth, looking south-east from above the Via Gellia. The walls enclose medieval open-field strips, some of which are also defined by lynchets. Narrow walled access paths lead from the village to the fields.
[Derrick Riley]

centre of Alstonefield; in medieval times its parish included a large part of the Staffordshire Peak extending northwards to take in a large hunting forest (*see* the case study on pp 19–20). Whilst the area occupied by the forest is poor upland terrain, Alstonefield itself is on good land and is a focal point for hamlets nearby.[16] Not far away, the village of Wetton stands out as a place with a planned medieval layout with a grid of streets. It never reached its expected potential, remaining relatively small (*see* the case study on p 46). It was founded long after Alstonefield and the two were too close together for both to thrive as anything other than villages.

At the western edge of the zone, Buxton and Fairfield do not quite fit comfortably into the four-fold division of the Peak landscape used in this chapter. These occupy the same topographical niche as Hartington in the south-west zone in the sense that they lie near the interface with the limestone plateau and a shale valley to the west, but here the latter is small and isolated. This said, the old village of Fairfield had much in common with limestone core agricultural villages to the east in the Wye basin before it was subsumed by Buxton. The town of Buxton had a market charter granted in 1813, although an informal market probably existed long before. It grew rapidly in post-medieval times, largely because of the spa waters here.

Monyash and One Ash

Monyash is a vibrant village at the heart of the limestone plateau, standing close to the head of Lathkill Dale, at the most advantaged part of the Lathkill basin farmland (Fig 14.11).[17] It contrasts with its sister settlement a short distance to the south-east, which now has only the single Chatsworth Estate farmstead of One Ash Grange. The place-name 'ash' is thought to derive from Anglo-Saxon words for water (*eas*), springs (*aesce*) or ash trees (*aesc*). Both places were recorded in Domesday in 1086 as subsidiary settlements of Bakewell.[18] Later, one was to take on added importance as a market grew up there, whilst the other eventually waned.

The five natural meres at Monyash made it an ideal spot for a local market where stock could be watered in numbers when brought for sale (Fig 14.12). A charter for a market and fair was granted in 1340. Monyash was strategically place midway between other medieval markets at Bakewell, Hartington and Tideswell; the last is also in the heart of the plateau but with the barrier of the Wye valley gorge no doubt forming the boundary between their respective catchments. Whilst the market at Monyash no longer occurs, the green where it was held, with its medieval cross, remains.

Although people no doubt came to market from a wide swath of the central part of the limestone plateau, Monyash was also a large agricultural village, surrounded by big open fields where farmers concentrated their efforts, with their everyday lives focusing on Monyash township rather than the wider landscape. Beyond the fields were extensive commons, which ran uninterrupted to those of surrounding communities (*see* Fig A2.8). It may well be that some parts were grazed by people from more than one village. Sometimes things were acrimonious; a dispute over rights of turbary on Monyash commons came to court in the 1270s.[19]

Fig 14.11
The upper River Lathkill basin photographed from above Flagg, looking south across mine workings associated with the rich Hubbadale Pipe. This is a high but relatively fertile area that has always attracted settlement, such as at Monyash hidden by trees in the middle distance, surrounded by higher land that for centuries was commons.
[John Barnatt]

Fig 14.12
At the heart of the upper River Lathkill basin, near the head of the Lathkill gorge, lies the tree-shrouded village of Monyash. It is sited around rarely occurring natural ponds for watering stock and once had its own market.
[John Barnatt]

The villagers of Monyash could graze all their commons freely, but the people of Taddington, Priestcliffe and Ashford also had rights of pasture, turbary and heath over some parts.[20] Ongoing disputes rumbled on until 1776 when the Monyash commons were enclosed following an Act of Parliament. Water for grazing local stock, except in the village, would have been in short supply, but it may be that cattle were herded every day into the top end of Lathkill Dale to Lathkill Head Cave, which issues a plentiful supply except in dry conditions. Today the cave lies just within the corner of Over Haddon parish, which bends to take it in, and again this valuable resource may well have been disputed.

One Ash has a very different history. Before the Norman Conquest it must have been of relative importance for there was a stone cross of ninth- to tenth-century type, two fragments of which have been recovered from a drystone wall.[21] In the second half of the 12th century, the land was granted to the Cistercian abbey of Roche near Maltby in what is now South Yorkshire. When the land was surveyed in the early 17th century, the farmstead known today as One Ash Grange was the only settlement here; it was surrounded by early rectangular fields and had its own common to the south. However, in the fields a short distance south of this farmstead, there are earthworks that may be the site of the village; when in the medieval period it was last occupied is unclear (see pp 50–1).

Tideswell, Wheston and Litton

Tideswell was the other medieval market centre in the heart of the plateau, which judging from its two surviving market places was intensively used.[22] Its charter for market and fair was granted in 1251 and it probably served people over much of the limestone plateau from the Wye gorge northwards. Its sheltered location makes an ideal focal point, hidden in a flat-bottomed section of the steep-sided Tideswell Brook, where a stream runs down the alluvial-filled base of the valley from springs above lava beds to the north-west.

In 1086 Tideswell was a subsidiary settlement of the Royal Manor of Hope, whereas the adjacent Litton was privately held by William Peveril (Fig 14.13). Unlike the two settlements just mentioned, the village of Wheston does not appear in records until 1225. There is extensive good farmland on rolling ground in this part of the Wye basin. Fossilised medieval open-field strips run continuously between the three villages, with extensive commons beyond to the north and the Wye valley gorge to the south. The parish boundaries indicate a strong contrast between Litton and Wheston. The former had a clear-cut line with Tideswell, whereas Wheston had a complex arrangement of parcels interspersed with land within Tideswell parish. This reflects the late foundation of Wheston, probably as a settlement that grew because of the long distances between Tideswell and the furthermost open fields to the west; people presumably moved to Wheston to make tending these fields more convenient.

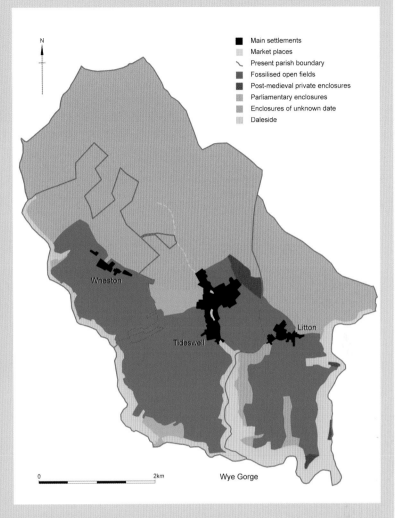

Fig 14.13
Tideswell, Wheston and Litton, showing modern parish boundaries and the relationship between the market centre and nearby settlements.

The south-west landscape

This large area is relatively remote and includes all the gritstone upland west and south of Buxton, the upper valleys of the rivers Dane, Dove and Manifold, and the limestone shelves flanking the Dove to the east side. Traditionally people have used this landscape differently from the limestone core and valley heartlands. As a result, the settlement pattern is predominantly dispersed, commonly comprising isolated farmsteads and hamlets spread across upland valleys, shelves and ridges (Fig 14.14). Serving these scattered communities were two market centres with medieval origins, at Longnor and Hartington.

There is a transitional zone as the limestone is reached. Above Hartington, as well as dispersed farmsteads on the high plateau, there are also small villages on shelves.[23] Similarly, further south there are villages at the limestone/shale interface above the gorges of the Manifold and Hamps, running from Warslow southwards.[24]

In the medieval period much of the area was so remote that large tracts were set aside as 'forests', with these hunting preserves held both by the Crown and the nobility. These included Macclesfield Forest in Cheshire, Alstonefield Forest and Leek Frith in Staffordshire and probably an area north-west of Hartington in Derbyshire (*see* Chapter 12).

Fig 14.14
In the higher parts of the farmed landscape to the west, as here in the Dane Valley at Knar below Cut-thorn Hill in the background, there are scattered farmsteads surrounded by irregular enclosures interspersed with high moorland and similar land that was enclosed and 'improved' into rectangular fields in the 18th and 19th centuries. [John Barnatt]

Throughout the area its main resource was rather poor upland grazing, together with peat and coal for fuel. Specific places were important for copper, lead and zinc ores, notably at Ecton in the 18th and 19th centuries, with copper also coming from Mixon further west in the19th century.

This south-western landscape was a backwater, remote from both the core areas of the Peak to the east and the lowlands of Staffordshire and Cheshire to the west. For instance, in 1781 a trial venture for copper ore at Mixon, made by the well-known Derbyshire smelting business of Barker and Wilkinson, was 'abandoned because it was at too great a distance & for want of a proper person to conduct it'.[25] Even today in this era of globalisation Staffordshire hill farmers are renowned as hardy individuals who have their own ways.

Longnor and its hinterland

The village of Longnor, the only settlement of any size in the northernmost part of the Staffordshire part of the Peak, was a market centre, with its charter granted in 1293 (*see* Chapter 2). Running west from this central place a large swath of landscape, between the upper valleys of the Manifold, Dove and Dane, has scattered farmsteads and hamlets, except at the high western ridges where moorland survives or was enclosed in the 18th and 19th centuries (Fig 14.15). Adjacent to Longnor township, all the land to the west within Staffordshire, running from Quarnford through Hollinsclough, Heathylee and Fawfield-head, once lay within the large medieval forest of Alstonefield Frith (*see* Chapter 12). Although the Frith was hunting preserve, a number of the scattered farmsteads are documented from the beginning of the 14th century and may have earlier origins, some potentially ancient and here before the Norman Conquest. This said, by the 14th century, as with other forests, they were little used and new settlement was quietly established, with fines often paid to the forest courts to secure their establishment. From time immemorial the emphasis in this upland corner of Staffordshire was on livestock farming, with the exception of Longnor itself, which had large open fields, intact in fossilised form on the Longnor ridge but now only partially visible in the valley land next to the River Dove.

In the scattered farmsteads little arable was undertaken above and beyond that for family consumption; yield would not have been good because of high altitude and acidic soils. Without Longnor, local people would have had to travel miles to obtain goods they could not produce themselves.

Much of today's historic agricultural landscape around the scattered farmsteads comprises sub-rectangular and irregular fields of unknown date. However, across the River Dove on the Derbyshire side there are parcels of fields of similar type running from Brandside southeastwards, where an early estate map of Hartington manor allows identification of pre-17th-century enclosure as well as later fields.

It is not known whether the people here chose to cross the county boundary at the river and use the market of Longnor or travel further to the one at Hartington at a distance to the south-east.

Longnor was formally established as a market centre in 1293 to serve the needs of the local farming population, presumably superimposed by the Lord of Alstonefield.[26] This large area within the manor of Alstonefield had an otherwise dispersed settlement pattern. Alstonefield village lay on rich limestone plateau ground over 10km to the south-east, well away from the farmers who lived around Longnor and there may have been an informal market centre at the latter well before the late 13th century.

Fig 14.15 Longnor and its hinterland within Alstonefield Frith.

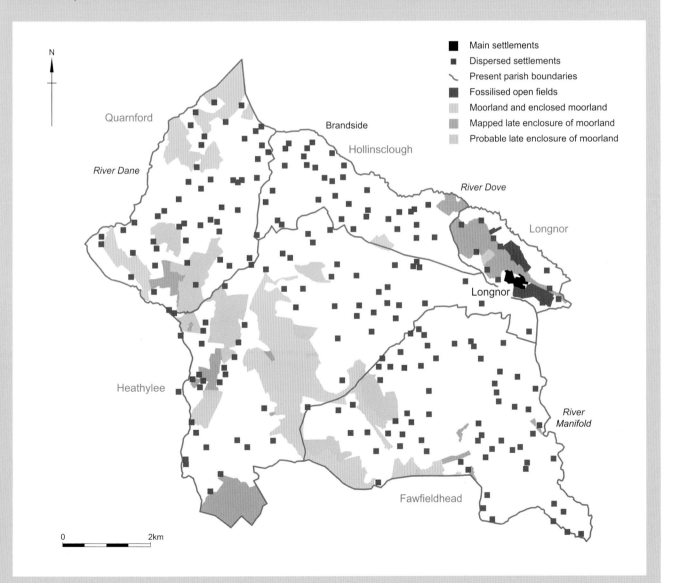

Hartington and its quarters

The Upper Dove Valley flanking the western edge of the limestone plateau, with Hartington at its heart, is isolated from the rest of the Derbyshire Peak by the highest parts of the plateau, leaving the village and a number of medieval hamlets and farmsteads up the valley divorced from communities to the east (*see* the case study on pp 16–17) (Fig 14.16). Whilst the River Dove is the boundary between Derbyshire and Staffordshire, nearby places across the river within Staffordshire presumably saw Hartington as their market centre although it lay in Derbyshire.

When Hartington rose to dominance in the valley is open for debate; its medieval market charter dates to 1203 and by then it was undoubtedly sufficiently important to draw people in from the high limestone areas to the east and shale valleys and gritstone lands to the west (Fig 14.17). It made an obvious focal point, at the interface between resource zones, in a sheltered riverside location, next to a dry valley that rose gently deep into the limestone plateau.

However, in the centuries immediately prior to 1203 things may have been different. Before the Norman Conquest there had been four small settlements of similar size spaced along the valley, at Hartington, Ludwell, Pilsbury and Soham.[27] By the time of Domesday in 1086 all the land in what became the four Hartington Quarters had been granted to the powerful De Ferrers family; it was described as 'waste' at this date.[28] Why this was so is unclear; the 'harrying of the north' of 1069–70 seems unlikely to be the reason, as settlements nearby were untouched. It may be that people had left the settlements in the valley, which then were probably small and poor, for more attractive prospects elsewhere. Or, people were moved by the lord as part of planned reorganisation, perhaps with the aim of creating a large private hunting forest north of Hartington; an area towards the north-western end of the parish is still known as the Frith. Later this area acquired a scatter of farmsteads wherever the land was favourable enough. Throughout the central and southern parts of the parish hamlets were allowed to grow up, and some had small open fields.[29] Monastic granges were also founded high on the limestone plateau (*see* Chapter 3). The De Ferrers may also have developed manorial sheep farms known as 'bercaries', but the earliest surviving documentation for these is the mid-14th century.[30] Later, when the commons on the limestone plateau were enclosed in the early 19th century, new farmsteads were placed amongst new fields.

Fig 14.16

In the upper reaches of Hartington parish to the north-west, once within the Frith, there are scattered post-medieval farmsteads below the high moors, as here looking south-east over the low gritstone ridges in the Brandside area near the head of the River Dove in Hartington Upper Quarter. To the left, running south-eastwards, are the limestone ridges at the plateau edge, including the distinctive knife-edge ridge of Chrome Hill. [John Barnatt]

Fig 14.17
On the high limestone ridges above Hartington, there are scattered post-medieval farms with ruler-straight enclosures on the former commons, as here to the north-east of the market centre at the Lean Low farmstead with its prominent prehistoric round barrow on the hilltop. [John Barnatt]

It may be that an initial focal point for the De Ferrers land in the Dove valley was at Pilsbury, about 3.5km up the valley from Hartington, where there is a motte-and-bailey castle; why there is a second and apparently unfinished castle, where only the motte was built, placed halfway between Pilsbury and Hartington, is not known. Later, as Hartington was in the obvious place for a large settlement to develop, the De Ferrers must have been instrumental in promoting this at the expense of Pilsbury.

Whatever the details, Hartington manor was clearly an isolated fiefdom that the De Ferrers family had a large hand in reshaping. However, decades after the general pattern of settlement in the valley was set, in 1266 the De Ferrers, Earls of Derby from 1138, had all their lands confiscated after a failed rebellion against Henry the Third.

Flash and upland coal mining

This area, despite being high and with heavy rainfall, has more farmsteads than most other parts of the Peak at comparable altitude (Fig 14.18). These lie scattered across several upland valleys and shelves, bounded by the high moors at and to the west of Axe Edge to the north and the high Roaches ridge to the south. The 'hamlet' of Flash with its sturdy post-medieval dwellings has a reputation for outsiders coming in the summer, buying a house and staying only one winter.

Each farmstead is surrounded by small irregular and rectangular fields, interspersed with a patchwork of small enclosed moors. They lie in Quarnford township and were once part of the medieval Alstonefield Forest. The rainfall is high, the land is poor with peaty soils, and the pastures are mostly hard to sustain, with a tendency for coarse moorland grasses and rushes to take over. The peat has its uses, for small disused peat cuts can still be found close to many dwellings; one was still in use when archaeological mapping of the area was undertaken in 1987.[31]

It may be that one reason so many farms, small holdings and cottages exist is because of the many small coal mines across this area (see Chapter 6). The coal mines at Goldsitch Moss are documented as working in 1401 and mining across the zone was common into the 19th century (Fig 14.19).[32] Thus, the pattern we see reflects a dual economy, mining and upland farming, which together supported the local population over several centuries. This probably peaked economically in the 18th and earlier 19th century when the local demand for coal was greatest, but tailed off after better-quality coal from elsewhere became more readily available with improvement in road and rail networks.

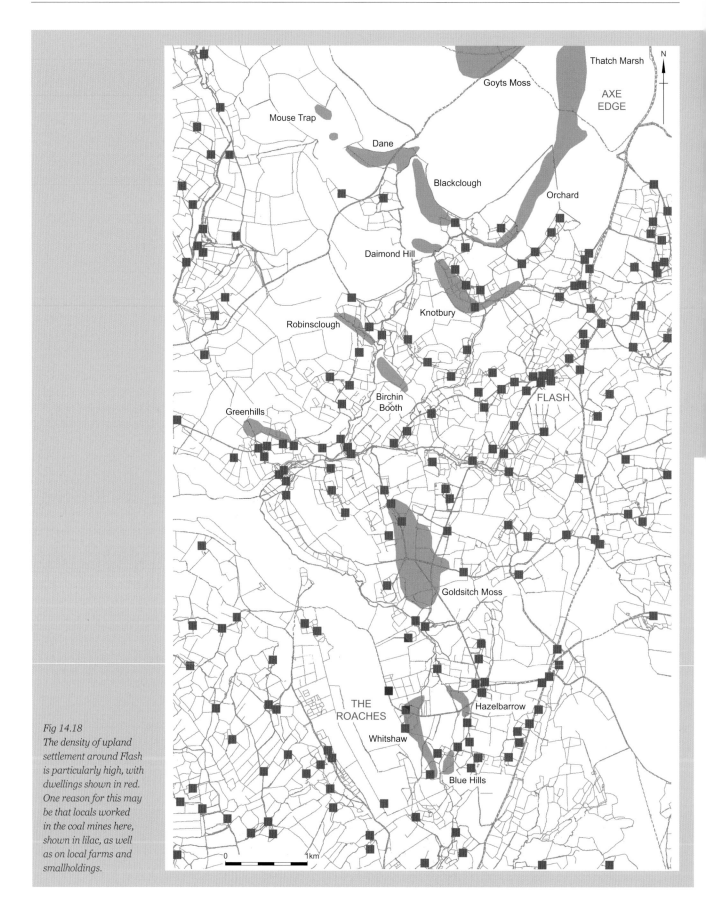

Fig 14.18
The density of upland
settlement around Flash
is particularly high, with
dwellings shown in red.
One reason for this may
be that locals worked
in the coal mines here,
shown in lilac, as well
as on local farms and
smallholdings.

Fig 14.19
At Goldsitch Moss, mining took place from medieval times to the 19th century. The shallow basin, with mining remains, has a scattering of farmsteads, smallholdings and cottages. It is likely that the density of scattered settlement here, with 11 dwellings visible in shot, was influenced by the opportunities for mining as well as farming. [John Barnatt]

Remote places

Some parts of the Peak are inherently remote, with moorland dominating the scene. This is particularly true to the north and this is identified as the fourth main Peak landscape area. Here the high gritstone moors run uninterrupted except for deep and narrow-bottomed valleys that cut into them. The isolated farms strung along the valleys have provided a hard living over the centuries. The main valleys include those of the upper reach of the River Derwent, and its tributaries the Alsop and Ashop further west (*see* the case study 'Parwich and Newton Grange' on p 35). Another important valley is Longdendale flanking the River Etherow to the far north-west. An atypical valley is that of the River Noe in Edale; this is wide-bottomed and has attracted more settlement, but all dispersed in character, contrasting strongly with the nearby and larger Hope Valley where villages were the predominant form.

Other northern valleys, to the west around Chapel en le Frith, Whaley Bridge, New Mills, Hayfield and Glossop, are now heavily populated because of post-medieval industrial developments,

commonly associated with textile mills. These are not considered further in this chapter as they are part of a much larger zone running north from here at the western fringe of the Southern Pennines, rather than being specific to the Peak. Similarly to the north-east a large area centred on Bradfield is part of another Peak foothills zone that extends beyond the remit of this book.

The valleys of the upper Derwent and Longdendale have had their traditional settlement patterns severely truncated by the creation of large reservoirs with concomitant demolitions and flooding. In contrast, the dispersed farmstead distributions around the rivers Alsop, Ashop and Kinder are intact. The farms here were remote and often the only people you would have seen day to day would be relatively close neighbours. Before the advent of modern roads, it would have been hard work for anyone to get anywhere beyond their valley. Life would have been inward-looking, constrained by the expanses of moorland beyond the valley. In Longdendale this changed after 1740 with the building of the turnpike road through the Woodhead Pass, whilst another, the Snake Pass road, was built through the Ashop Valley after 1818.

Edale and its Booths

Fig 14.20
The two peat-cutting
areas on the high moor
between Upper Booth
and Grindsbrook Booth
in Edale, with a strip
of intact peat between
them. Going uphill the
hollow-ways and tracks,
used by sleds, spread out
across the steep slopes to
reach different parts of
the peat-cutting areas
on the flat land above.

The traditional settlement pattern of Edale, which revolved around five medieval hamlets known as 'booths', has been discussed in the case study on pp 22–3. Here we turn to traditional local links between this large isolated valley to and over gritstone uplands and ridges.[33] Some hollow-ways lead to surrounding places, down the valley to Hope and over ridges to Alport, Castleton, Peak Forest, Chapel en le Frith and Hayfield. One of these is documented as a coffin road, taking Edale's dead for burial in Castleton. Other routes have specific purposes, for instance in two cases leading to stone quarries.

Notable are the hollow-ways coming up the steep valley sides that lead specifically to peat cuts; these were well used into the 19th century, with coal only being commonly adopted for domestic use with the coming of the railway in 1894 (Fig 14.20). These routes may well have medieval origins as the main ones lead up from the Booths. For the most part each of these places had their own specific moors to use. In the case of the Upper Booth and Grindsbrook Booth routes, they braid and head for specific parts of the cuts and were presumably created over time as cutting developed. Both come to the same moor but still have discrete cuts, with a band of uncut peat between the two.

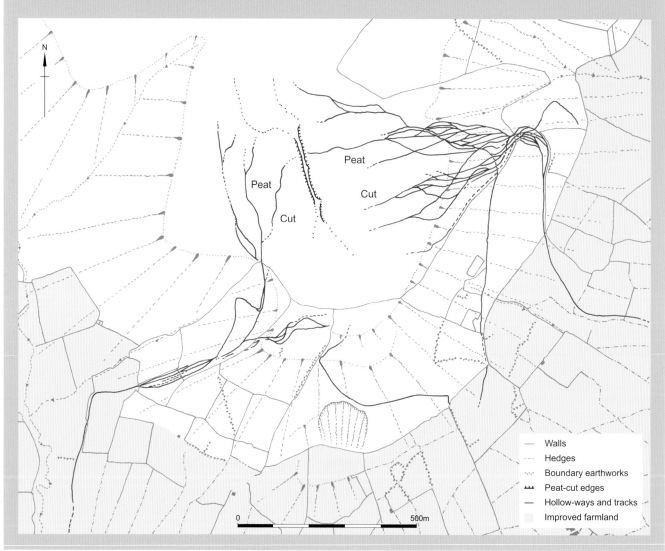

Peat

Peat

Cut

Cut

—	Walls
---	Hedges
⋅⋅⋅	Boundary earthworks
ᴛᴛᴛ	Peat-cut edges
—	Hollow-ways and tracks
▨	Improved farmland

0   500m

15

Postscript – People, place and archaeology today

There is a lot we do not know about the archaeology and historic landscapes of the Peak. Some aspects may become clear with further research and new fieldwork; both academics and local people have a part to play. Other aspects may be truly lost. Much valuable information on sites and how they were used is known about by local people; often they assume, wrongly, that everyone else knows; there is a huge amount of recording for future generations still to do. The role of communities in studying their own place and building upon the outline given here is vital. Doing the work now is particularly apposite, especially in a time of contracted resources, but also while members of long-standing local families retain their traditional knowledge; with every passing generation information is lost. It is often incomers who kindle interest because they do not take their recently adopted place for granted.

Hopefully the ideas presented in this book will promote ways of seeing and thinking about the Peak, and local people and others will build upon this, arriving at their own and perhaps more vibrant visions of the time depth of this special place. As time goes by, new generations will undoubtedly ask different questions of the data and reach new insights. Our knowledge of a place is often governed, and in some ways limited, not by what data are available, but what questions it occurs to us to ask. No matter how objective we try to be, questions about the past are governed by our experiences in the present; as society changes then new perspectives and insights will inevitably follow.

All this said, for many it is enough to visit or inhabit the Peak landscapes. This is a place where the contrasting landscapes are all within easy reach; there is always somewhere different to suit the mood, ranging from the busy limestone landscape with its many miles of walls, to the bleak moorland vistas. Things change with the seasons. Features such as low ridge and furrow only become visible with a light dusting of snow, especially on those crisp winter days with raked sunlight. In the spring when the cattle are let out from their winter sheds, sometimes looking in a field can be hazardous when a herd of bullocks are charging round full of new-found joys, examining an ancient field system that lies beneath their hooves can be foolhardy. In the summer there is nothing better than wandering in the sultry sun to old haunts or finding new and unexpected details. Sitting quietly at Arbor Low in midweek, listening to skylarks singing, can evoke visions of the past. Similarly, the haunting call of the curlew on the moors can take you straight to mysterious lost times. In the autumn, during the rutting season, sitting in the Barbrook I stone circle shortly after dawn and listening to the red deer stags barking around you can make you temporarily forget the meaning of the stones but at the same time transport you back to a distant past. The Peak is an upland place where you can be basking in the richness of the landscape when the fog comes down or you suddenly find yourself in a blizzard. On the moors it is easy to become disoriented and sometimes you find new and exciting places by accident. In some harsh winters much can disappear from sight under a deep blanket of snow reaching to above the wall tops; the landscape becomes a blank canvas.

The author has led archaeological guided walks in the Peak for several decades, and as we walked around one thing I commonly said was 'you can see Minninglow from here'; this distinctive hill can be seen on the skyline from a surprising number of places across the Peak. After a while I started receiving anonymous postcards from all over the world where all it said on the reverse was 'you can see Minninglow from here'; they still occasionally arrive. It is these 'off the wall' happenings that have added to my joy of sharing what I know of this wonderful landscape.

It is hoped this book has helped people reach a deeper understanding of the Peak's rich tapestry that they walk amidst.

Appendix 1: The locations of Peak District places referred to throughout the book

This appendix gives a series of Peak District maps that show the locations of the many places referred to in the book:

- Fig A1.1 The Peak District, showing historic character areas, main rivers, A-roads and places mentioned in Chapter 1.
- Fig A1.2 Places mentioned in Chapters 2 and 3.
- Fig A1.3 Places mentioned in Chapters 4 and 5.
- Fig A1.4 Places mentioned in Chapters 6 and 7.
- Fig A1.5 Roads, canals and railways mentioned in Chapter 8 (tunnels shown as dashed lines).
- Fig A1.6 Peak District mills mentioned in Chapter 9.
- Fig A1.7 Prehistoric monuments, rock art and caves mentioned in Chapter 10.
- Fig A1.8 Roman and medieval places mentioned in Chapter 11.
- Fig A1.9 Places mentioned in Chapter 12.
- Fig A1.10 Places mentioned in Chapter 13.
- Fig A1.11 Places mentioned in Chapter 14.

Fig A1.1 The Peak District, showing historic character areas, main rivers, A-roads and places mentioned in Chapter 1

1: Calton Pasture
2: Harthill Moor
3: Stanton Moor
4: Edale
5: Kinder Scout
6: Bleaklow
7: Abney, Offerton and Eyam Moors
8: Hope Valley
9: Watergrove Mine
10: Cressbrook Dale
11: Parsons House
12: Tideslow Rake
13: Stanage Edge
14: Barbrook I
15: Foolow
16: Longstone Edge
17: Flagg

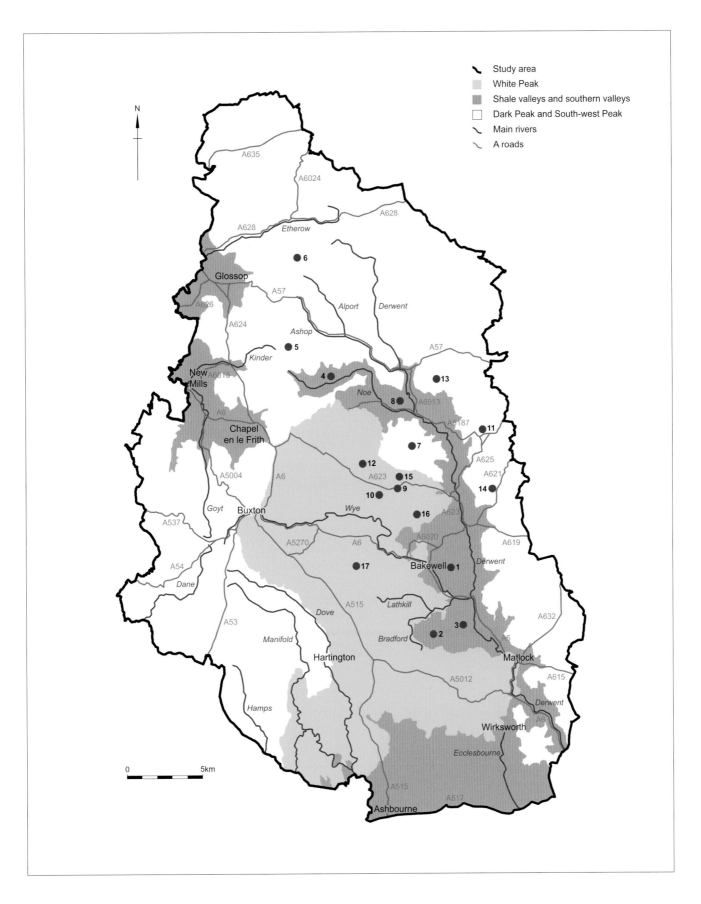

Fig A1.2 Places mentioned in Chapters 2 and 3

Main settlements

1: Alderwasley	49: Hassop
2: Aldwark	50: Hathersage
3: Alstonefield	51: Heathcote
4: Ashbourne	52: Hognaston
5: Ashford	53: Hope
6: Aston	54: Hopton
7: Bakewell	55: Ible
8: Ballidon	56: Ilam
9: Bamford	57: Kirk Ireton
10: Baslow and Bubnell	58: Kniveton
11: Beeley	59: Little Hucklow
12: Biggin	60: Little Longstone
13: Birchover	61: Litton
14: Blackwell	62: Longnor
15: Bonsall	63: Mappleton
16: Bradbourne	64: Matlock Churchtown
17: Bradfield	65: Matlock Bank
18: Bradwell	66: Matlock Bath
19: Brassington	67: Middleton by Wirksworth
20: Brushfield	68: Middleton by Youlgreave
21: Butterton	69: Monyash
22: Buxton	70: New Mills
23: Calton	71: Over Haddon
24: Calver	72: Parwich
25: Carsington	73: Peak Forest
26: Castleton	74: Pilsley
27: Cauldon	75: Priestcliffe
28: Chapel en le Frith	76: Rowsley
29: Charlesworth	77: Sheldon
30: Chelmorton	78: Snitterton
31: Cromford	79: Stanton
32: Curbar	80: Stoney Middleton
33: Darley Churchtown	81: Taddington
34: Edensor	82: Thornhill
35: Elton	83: Thorpe
36: Eyam	84: Tideswell
37: Fairfield	85: Tissington
38: Fenny Bentley	86: Wardlow
39: Flagg	87: Warslow
40: Foolow	88: Waterfall
41: Froggatt	89: Waterhouses
42: Glossop	90: Wensley
43: Great Hucklow	91: Wetton
44: Great Longstone	92: Whaley Bridge
45: Grindleford	93: Winster
46: Grindlow	94: Wirksworth
47: Grindon	95: Wormhill
48: Hartington	96: Youlgreave

Other places

97: Abney Moor	146: Nether Bradbourne
98: Alsop le Dale	147: Nether and Upper Padley
99: Alton	148: Newton
100: Atlow	149: Northwood
101: Bamford Moor	150: Offerton
102: Birchills	151: Offerton Moor
103: Uppertown Birchover	152: One Ash
104: Bleaklow	153: Organ Ground
105: Blore	154: Padfield
106: Bradley	155: Peak Dale
107: Broadlowash	156: Pikehall
108: Burbage	157: Revidge
109: Burton	158: Roaches
110: Callow	159: Shatton
112: Castern	160: Sheffield Plantation
113: Chatsworth	161: Shottle
114: Chunel	162: Shutlingsloe
115: Cold Eaton	163: Slaley
116: Combs Moss	164: Smerrill
117: Conksbury	165: South Carolina Farm
118: Coplow Dale	166: Staden
119: Cowlow	167: Stanage Edge
120: Cronkston Lodge	168: Stanshope
121: Darley Dale	169: Swythamley Hall
122: Derwent Reservoir	170: Three Shires Head
123: Dove Holes	171: Throwley
124: Eyam Moor	172: Tunstead
125: Fivewells Farms	173: Upper Elkstone
126: Gardom's Edge	174: Upper Town Bonsall
127: Goyt's Moss	175: Via Gellia
128: Gratton	176: Wetton Hill
129: Haddon Hall	177: Wincle
130: Hanson	178: Windmill
131: Harthill	
132: Hazlebadge	
133: Highlow Hall	
134: Holme	
135: Howden Reservoir	
136: Kinder Scout	
137: King Sterndale	
138: Lawrence Field	
139: Lea Hall	
140: Longdendale	
141: Lower Green Farm	
142: Lyme Hall	
143: Middle Hills	
144: Morridge	
145: Musden	

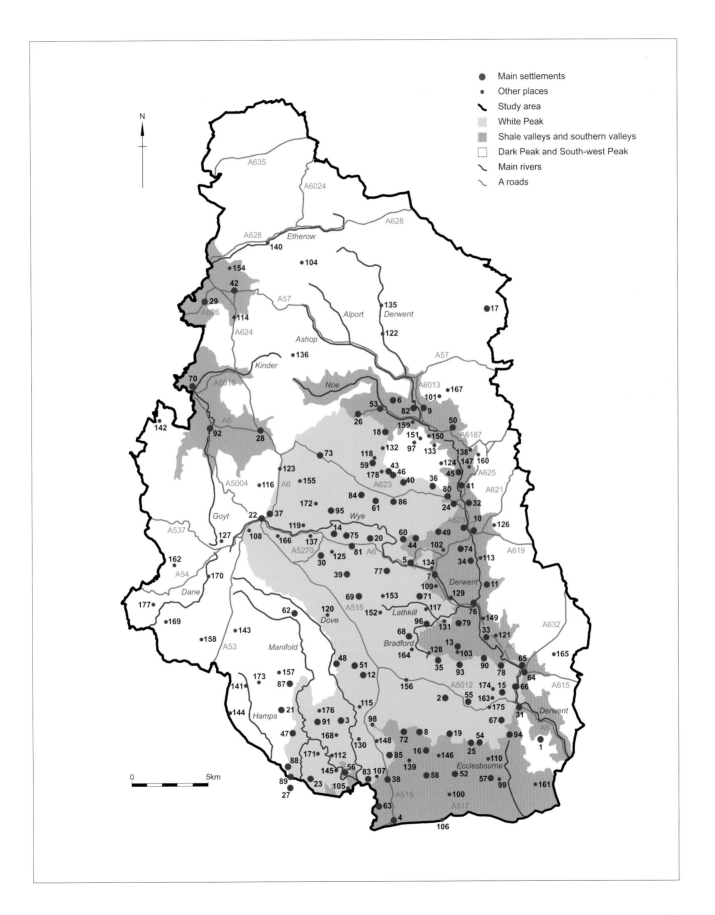

Fig A1.3 Places mentioned in Chapters 4 and 5

Villages and their fields		Sheepwalks	Other fields	Parks and warrens	Grouse shooting
1: Litton	16: Bradwell	29: Thorpe Pasture	34: Haylee Farm	46: Haddon	54: Chatsworth moorlands
2: Bakewell	17: Castleton	30: Carsington Pasture	35: Rodknoll	47: Chatsworth Old Park	55: Longshaw
3: Flagg	18: Hope	31: Chatsworth	36: Roystone Grange	48: Harthill	
4: Wheston	19: Thornhill	32: Calton Pasture	37: Needham Grange	49: Blore	
5: Tideswell	20: Fawfieldhead	33: Cracknowl Pasture	38: Cronkston Grange	50: Edensor	
6: Foolow	21: Upper and Lower Elkstone		39: Pilsbury Grange	51: Nether Haddon	
7: Eyam	22: Onecote		40: Mouldridge Grange	52: Chatsworth New Park	
8: Chelmorton	23: Edale		41: Biggin Grange	53: Lyme	
9: Taddington	24: Bradfield		42: Bamford Common		
10: Priestcliffe	25: Edensor		43: Castleton Commons		
11: Monyash	26: Hartington		44: Edale		
12: Elton	27: Baslow		45: Lathkill Dale		
13: Winster	28: Brushfield				
14: Bonsall					
15: Ible					

Walls and wall furniture	Field barns	Ridge and furrow	Meres and dew ponds	Limekilns
56: Roystone Grange	59: Gateham	64: Ashford	77: Taddington	80: Grin Hill
57: Gardom's Edge	60: Wetton	65: Priestcliffe	78: Heathcote	81: Mixon
58: Ramshaw Rocks.	61: Edensor	66: Youlgreave	79: Pilsbury	82: Upper Elkstone
	62: Bakewell	67: Wensley		83: Goyt Valley
	63: Foolow.	68: Snitterton		84: Litton Edge
		69: Bakewell		
		70: Chatsworth Park		
		71: Carsington		
		72: Bradbourne		
		73: Parwich		
		74: Tissington		
		75: Brassington		
		76: Ballidon		

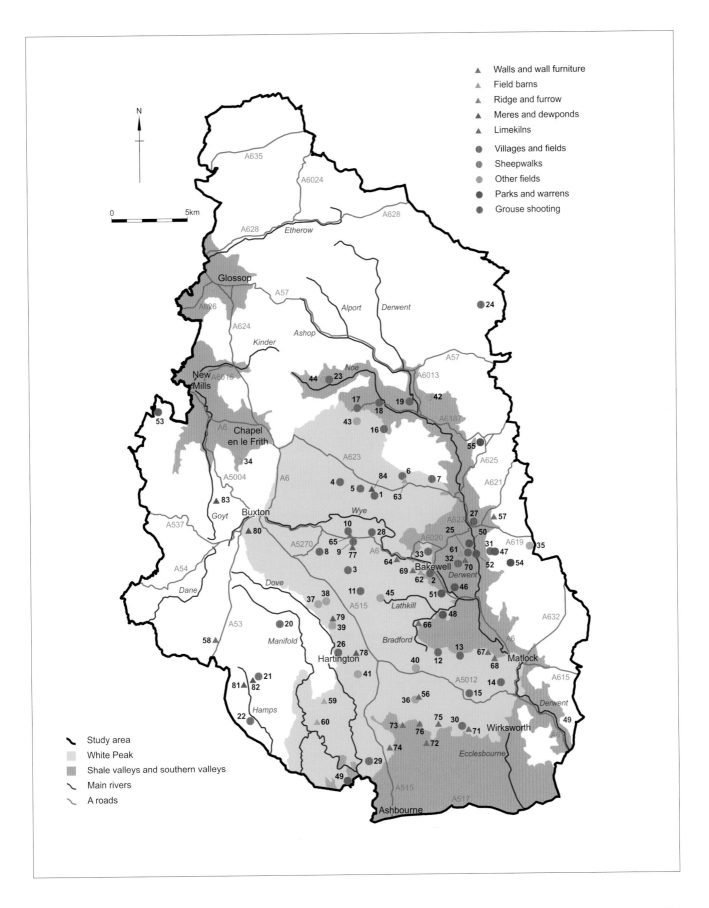

Fig A1.4 Places mentioned in Chapters 6 and 7

Lead and copper mines		Soughs	Coal mines	Smelting and fuel production	Early limestone quarries
1: Wellfield Rake	13: Mandale	25: Magpie	30: Ollersett Moor	43: Gradbach	60: Grin Hill
2: Ecton	14: High Rake	26: Stoke	31: Combs Moss	44: Upper Derwent Valley	61: Dove Holes
3: Ashton's Mine	15: Tideslow Rake	27: Hillcarr	32: Goyt's Moss	45: Linch Clough	62: Peak Forest
4: Millclose Mine	16: Oxlow Rake	28: Meerbrook	33: Thatch Marsh	46: Stone Edge	63: Caldon Low
5: Blue John Mine	17: Dirtlow Rake	29: Cromford	34: Orchard Common	47: Alport	64: Thirklow
6: Odin Mine	18: Moss Rake		35: Danebower	48: Brough	65: Bradwell
7: Coalpit Rake	19: How Grove		36: Goldsitch Moss	49: Crich	66: Calver
8: Old Millclose	20: Hazard Mine		37: Ringinglow	50: Whiston	67: Stanley Moor
9: Nestus Pipes	21: Bonsall Lees		38: Owler Bar	51: North Lees	
10: Old Ash	22: Dunnington		39: Baslow Colliery	52: Froggatt Wood	
11: Watergrove	23: Carsington Pasture		40: Beeley Moor	53: Cromford	
12: Magpie	24: Speedwell Mine		41: Oaking Clough	54: Whatstandwell	
			42: Stanage	55: Gardom's Edge	
				56: Padley Wood	
				57: Shacklow Wood	
				58: Burbage Brook valley	
				59: Moscar	

Later limestone quarries and kilns	Specialist products	Millstone making	Sandstone quarries	Modern quarries	
68: Harpur Hill	76: Bakewell	79: Cluther Rocks	88: Stanton	96: Hope	107: Eldon Hill
69: Stoney Middleton	77: Ashford	80: Combs Moss	89: Birchover	97: Dove Holes	108: Grin Hill
70: Dove Holes	78: Ricklow Dale	81: Bamford Edge	90: Beeley Moor	98: Tunstead	109: Harpur Hill
71: Peak Dale		82: Stanage Edge	91: Brown Edge	99: Hindlow	110: Hillhead
72: Bugsworth		83: Fallinge Edge	92: Eyam Moor	100: Dowlow	111: Millers Dale
73: Marple		84: Curbar Edge	93: Abney Moor	101: Grange Mill	112: Backdale
74: Bullbridge		85: Millstone Edge	94: Cracken Edge	102: Ballidon	113: Dene Quarry
75: Froghall		86: Gardom's Edge	95: Reeve Edge	103: Caldon Low	114: Hall Dale
		87: Carl Wark		104: Pin Dale	115: Wirksworth
				105: Bradwell Dale	116: Middleton by Wirksworth
				106: Stoney Middleton	

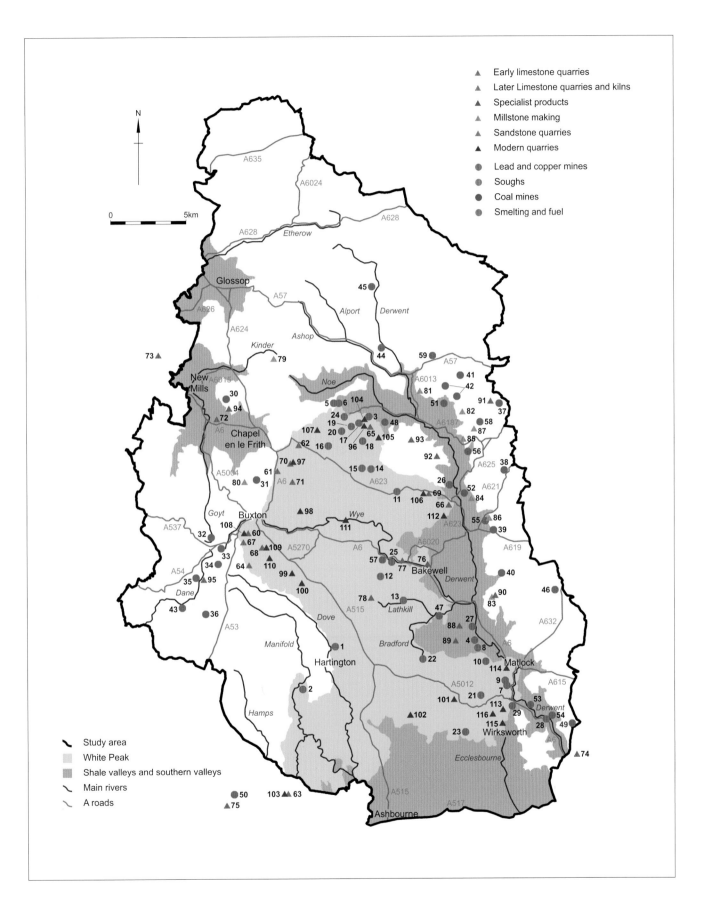

Fig A1.5 Roads, canals and railways mentioned in Chapter 8

Roman roads	*Medieval and later roads*	*Early turnpike roads*
1: Batham Gate	3: Doctor's Gate	8: Manchester to Buxton 1725, the 1752 extension to Hurdlow and the 1780 diversions (both dashed)
2: The Street	4: Stanage Edge and Golden Carr Road	9: Hurdlow to Ashbourne 1738
	5: Horse Lane	10: Woodhead Pass 1731 and 1741
	6: Highlow Bank	11: Bakewell to Chesterfield 1739
	7: White Edge	

The Robin Hood case study together with guide stoup and guide stones	*Canals*	*Tramways and railways (tunnels shown as dashed lines)*
12: Robin Hood	17: Peak Forest Canal	25: Peak Forest Tramway
13: Harland Edge	18: Cromford Canal	26: Cromford and High Peak Railway
14: guide post between Macclesfield and Buxton	19: Caldon Canal	27: Matlock to Buxton
15: guide post near Alstonefield	20: Whaley Bridge	28: Wye Gorge to Manchester
16: guide post between Ashford and Baslow	21: Bugsworth Basin	29: Buxton to Manchester
	22: Cromford Wharf	30: Manchester to Sheffield via Woodhead
	23: Leawood pumping engine	31: Manchester to Sheffield via Edale
	24: Froghall Wharf	32: Parsley Hay to Ashbourne
		33: Hulme End to Leek
		34: Derwent Valley reservoirs line
		35: Dove Holes Tunnel
		36: Woodhead Tunnel
		37: Minninglow Embankment
		38: Harpur Hill diversion
		39: Hurdlow diversion
		40: Buxton tunnel
		41: Harpur Hill kilns
		42: Friden kilns
		43: Cracken Edge incline
		44: Bole Hill incline
		45: Burbage Colliery incline

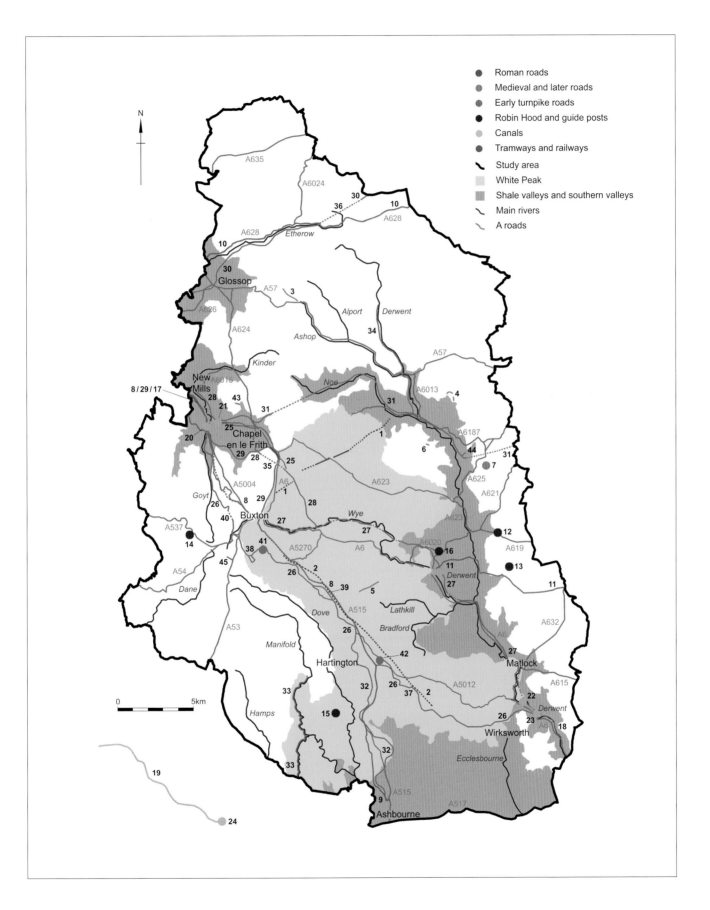

Fig A1.6 Peak District mills mentioned in the text

Textile mills	_Mineral processing mills_	_Manorial mills_	_Corn mills_
1: Cromford	12: Whaley Bridge	16: Bakewell	19: Caudwell's Mill
2: Macclesfield	13: Chapel en le Frith	17: Ashford	20: Edensor
3: Bollington	14: Greens Mill	18: Hope	
4: New Mills	15: Shacklow Wood		
5: Glossop			
6: Masson			
7: Edale			
8: Bamford			
9: Calver			
10: Cressbrook			
11: Litton			

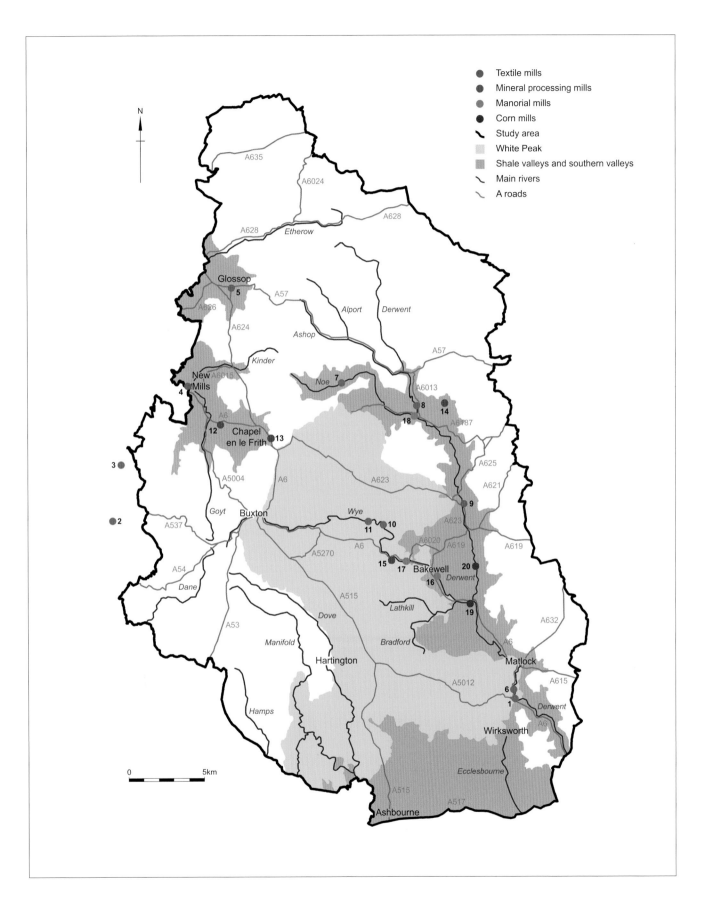

Fig A1.7 Prehistoric monuments, rock art and caves mentioned in Chapter 10

Henges and stone circles	Standing stones	Barrows and chambered tombs	Natural places	Rock art	Caves
1: Arbor Low	7: stone near Wirksworth	9: Big Moor	18: Robin Hood's Stride	22: Gardom's Edge	24: Thor's Cave
2: Bull Ring	8: Old Woman's Stone	10: Crow Chin	19: Cork Stone	23: Ashover school	25: Peak Cavern
3: Nine Ladies		11: Green Low	20: Rowter Rocks		26: Frank i' th' Rocks Cave
4: Barbrook		12: Five Wells	21: Bawd Stone, The Roaches and Hen Cloud		27: Fox Hole Cave
5: Seven Stones of Hordron		13: Minninglow			
6: Nine Stone Close		14: Pea Low			
		15: Arbor Low			
		16: Long Low			
		17: Hob Hurst House			

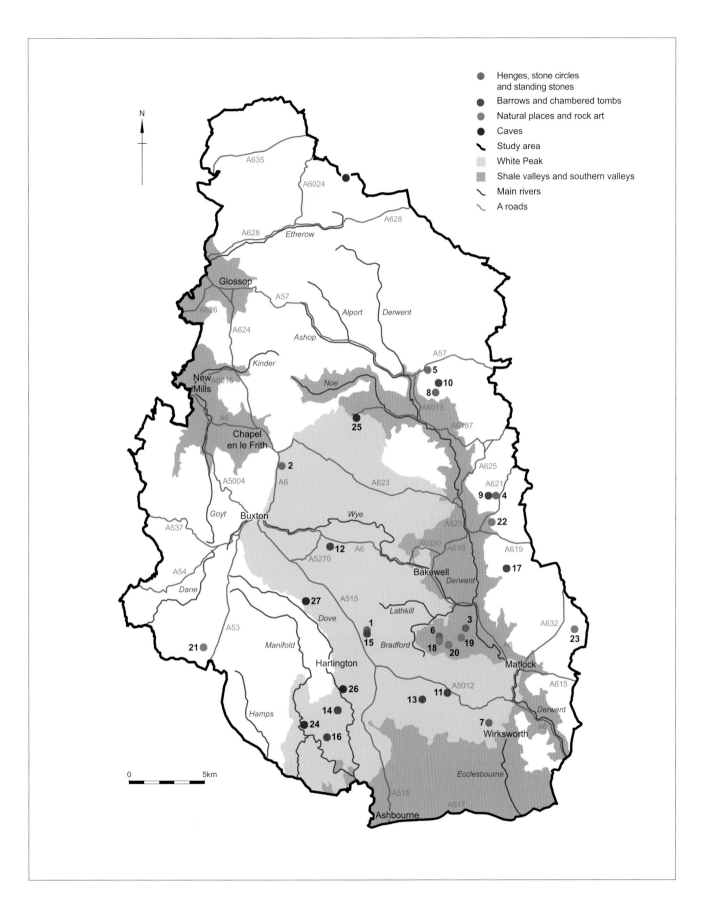

Fig A1.8 Roman and medieval places mentioned in Chapter 11

Roman centres	Romano-British settlements and fields	Medieval defensive sites	Medieval churches and crosses
1: Navio	5: Roystone Grange	18: Bakewell	22: Tissington
2: Ardotalia	6: Staden	19: Pilsbury	23: Parwich
3: Aquae Arnemetiae	7: Chee Tor	20: Hope	24: Alsop le Dale
4: Lutodarum	8: The Warren	21: Castleton	25: Bakewell
	9: Cow Low		26: Tideswell
	10: Rainster Rocks		27: Wirksworth
	11: Banktop		28: Ashbourne
	12: Waterlees		29: Baslow
	13: Dam Cliff		30: Youlgreave
	14: Thorpe Pasture		31: Hartington
	15: Deep Dale		32: Hope
	16: Carsington Pasture		33: Darley
	17: The Liffs		34: Bradbourne
			35: Alstonefield
			36: One Ash

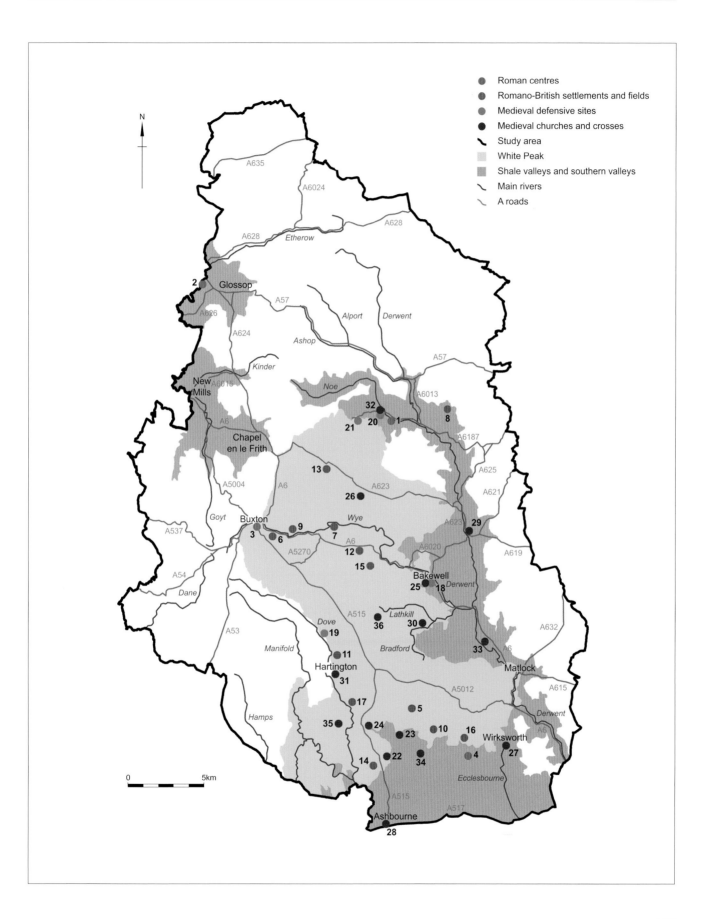

Legend:
- Roman centres
- Romano-British settlements and fields
- Medieval defensive sites
- Medieval churches and crosses
- Study area
- White Peak
- Shale valleys and southern valleys
- Main rivers
- A roads

Fig A1.9 Places mentioned in Chapter 12

Parks	Halls and houses	Picturesque places	Quarries
1A: Chatsworth landscape park	16: Chatsworth	44: Dove Dale	51: Buxton
1B: Chatsworth old deer park	17: Haddon	45: Matlock tors	52: Wirksworth
2: Haddon	18: Upper Padley	46: Matlock Bath	53: Cauldon
3: Tissington	19: Fenny Bentley	47: Castleton	54: Tunstead
4: Harthill	20: Throwley	48: Rowsley	
5: Upper Padley	21: Hazlebadge	49: Buxton	
6: Peak Tor	22: Lyme	50: Minninglow	
7: Snitterton	23: North Lees		
8: Broadlowash	24: Eyam		
9: Blore	25: Offerton		
10: Throwley	26: Holme		
11: Ecton Hill	27: Hartington		
12: Lyme	28: Tissington		
13: Hayfield	29: Snitterton		
14: Hassop	30: Beeley Hilltop		
15: Swythamley	31: Hazleford		
	32: Highlow		
	33: Winster		
	34: Stoke		
	35: Holt		
	36: Ashford		
	37: Great Longstone		
	38: Parwich		
	39: Hassop		
	40: Churchdale		
	41: Thornbridge		
	42: Burton Closes		
	43: Stancliffe		

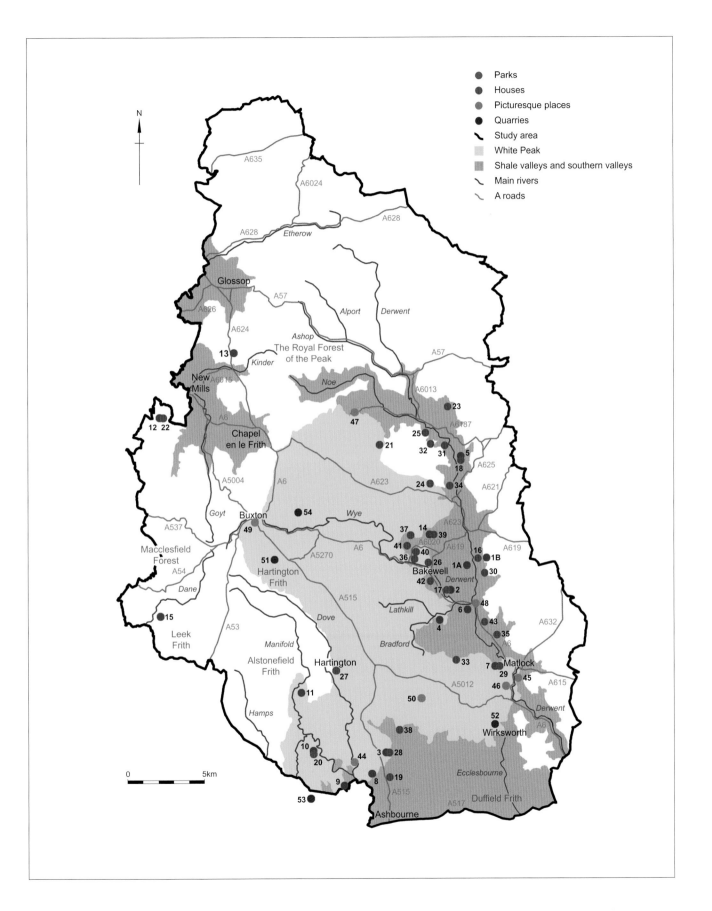

Fig A1.10 Places mentioned in Chapter 13

1: Harpur Hill
2: Houndkirk Moor
3: Bradwell Dale
4: Bole Hill
5: Windy Knoll
6: Langsett, Midhope and
   Underbank reservoirs

7: Burbage
8: Redmires
9: Big Moor
10: Gardom's Edge
11: Gibbet Moor
12: Burbage Moor

13: Ewden Height
14: Bailey's Tump
15: Biggin
16: Edale

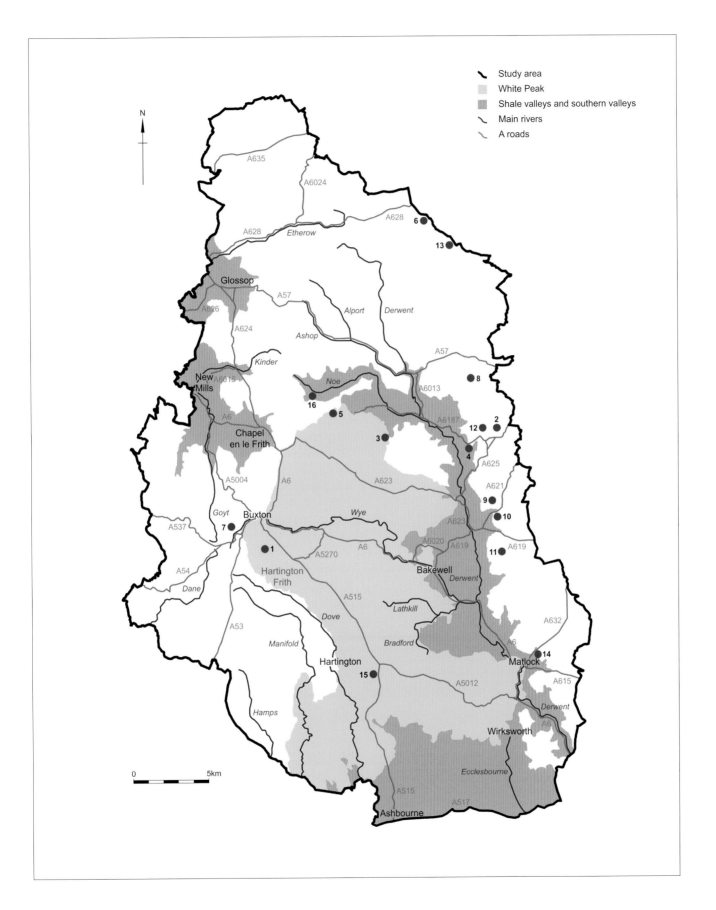

Fig A1.11 Places mentioned in Chapter 14 and other main settlements shown on Fig 14.1

Main settlements

Other places

1: Castleton
2: Hope
3: Aston
4: Thornhill
5: Bamford
6: Bradwell
7: Hathersage
8: Abney
9: Froggatt
10: Stoney Middleton
11: Calver
12: Curbar
13: Bubnell
14: Baslow
15: Pilsley
16: Edensor
17: Beeley
18: Rowsley
19: Darley
20: Matlock
21: Bakewell
22: Ashford
23: Little Longstone
24: Great Longstone
25: Rowland
26: Hassop
27: Little Hucklow
28: Great Hucklow
29: Grindlow
30: Foolow
31: Eyam
32: Middleton by Youlgreave
33: Youlgreave

34: Stanton
35: Birchover
36: Elton
37: Winster
38: Wensley
39: Cromford
40: Wirksworth
41: Alderwasley
42: Hopton
43: Carsington
44: Ballidon
45: Bradbourne
46: Parwich
47: Tissington
48: Fenny Bentley
49: Thorpe
50: Ilam
51: Mappleton
52: Ashbourne
53: Kniveton
54: Hognaston
55: Hulland
56: Kirk Ireton
57: Idridgehay
58: Tideswell
59: Buxton
60: Fairfield
61: Wormhill
62: Wheston
63: Litton
64: Wardlow
65: Taddington
66: Chelmorton

67: Blackwell
68: Priestcliffe
69: Monyash
70: Flagg
71: Sheldon
72: Over Haddon
73: Peak Forest
74: Bonsall
75: Middleton by Wirksworth
76: Aldwark
77: Ible
78: Alstonefield
79: Wetton
80: Hartington
81: Longnor
82: Earl Sterndale
83: Heathcote
84: Biggin
85: Sheen
86: Warslow
87: Butterton
88: Grindon
89: Waterfall
90: Waterhouses
91: Calton
92: Chapel en le Frith
93: Whaley Bridge
94: New Mills
95: Hayfield
96: Glossop
97: Bradfield

98: Chatsworth
99: Offerton
100: Handley Bottom
101: Mixon
102: Ecton
103: Ludwell
104: Pilsbury
105: Soham

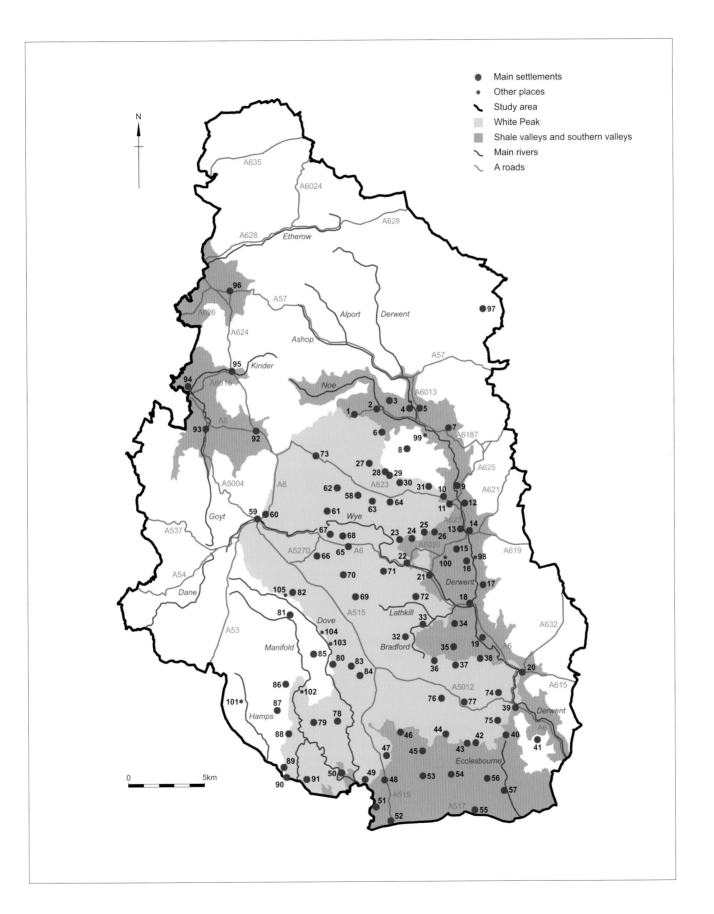

Appendix 2: Historic landscape character assessment in the Peak District

In the 1990s, the National Park Authority undertook an historic landscape character assessment for the Peak District National Park, which was later complemented by work done in other parts of Derbyshire.[1] The first study contributed to a more generalised landscape character assessment for the national park which was designed to underpin policy and planning that was sensitive to the varying character areas.[2] All in turn refine even broader-brush mapping at a national level undertaken by Natural England.[3]

The 'historic landscape character assessment' has finely tuned polygon boundaries determined on an individual field parcel basis when plotting the 19 land-use categories identified and listed below, whereas the 'landscape character assessment' for the national park took a broader approach for plotting 20 categories based on a variety of present-day landscape characteristics.[4]

The 'historic landscape character assessment' was part of a suite of such studies carried out for English Heritage from the 1990s onwards; the Peak assessment was one of the first, done at a time when various methodologies were being experimented with. The approach adopted here was based on assessment of estate, enclosure award, tithe and Ordnance Survey maps, which were used to build up a picture through time. This was possible from 1600 to the present, with time-slice maps at 50-year intervals produced showing how the landscape has changed (Figs A2.1– A2.6). This method had the advantage that it was firmly based on data, with clear patterns objectively identified. In the Peak there are large swaths of landscape where the dominant character is agricultural and clearly identified distinctive field patterns are readily interpreted as belonging to distinct phases of farming activity.

As historic character assessment became more widely adopted, second and subsequent generation studies for counties across England went in a different direction. The Peak method proved difficult elsewhere and often impossible to apply successfully. Not only were data time-consuming to compile when time-slice maps were produced, but for many regions there was not the wealth of surviving historic maps spanning several centuries that we are lucky to have for much of the Peak; indeed, we encountered the same problem over significant parts of the South-West Peak where the method gave results that were not as useful as elsewhere in the national park. Across England, where patterning is sometimes less distinctive, the majority of historic character assessments have concentrated on the present landscape and field-shape morphology, sometimes with results based on field shape and size that have poorly understood explanations in terms of historic landscape development; their value is contested by some landscape archaeologists and historians.

The following table shows the historic landscape character types that were identified and used for the cultural mapping; outline definitions are given below, while detailed discussion of the main agricultural categories has been included in Chapter 4 (*see* p 63). When mapped, basic character types were each given a different colour, while differences within each type were given identifiable shades and hues to distinguish one from the other.

Landscape category	Basic colour	Shades/Hues
ANCIENT ENCLOSURE (pre-1650)	Green	
Medieval open fields – traditional strips		Blue green
Medieval open fields – fossilised strips		Dark green
Rectangular and/or irregular fields		Yellow-green
Form unknown		Pale green
POST-MEDIEVAL ENCLOSURE (post-1650)	Blue	
Parliamentary Enclosure Award		Dark blue
Formal private enclosure agreement		Mid-blue
Private enclosure – no details		Pale blue
Form unknown		Lilac
ENCLOSURE OF UNKNOWN DATE	Blue/Green	Green hatching on blue background
UNENCLOSED LAND	Yellow	
Wastes and commons/private moorland		Bright yellow
Open pasture/enclosed moorland		Pale yellow
Daleside enclosure		Yellow-brown
INDUSTRIAL	Purple	
URBAN	Red	
RECREATION	Crimson	
PARKLAND	Pink	
WOODLAND	Brown	
Well-established woodland or plantation		Brown
Daleside scrub or open woodland		Brown stripe
RESERVOIR OR ORNAMENTAL LAKE	Black	Black hatching

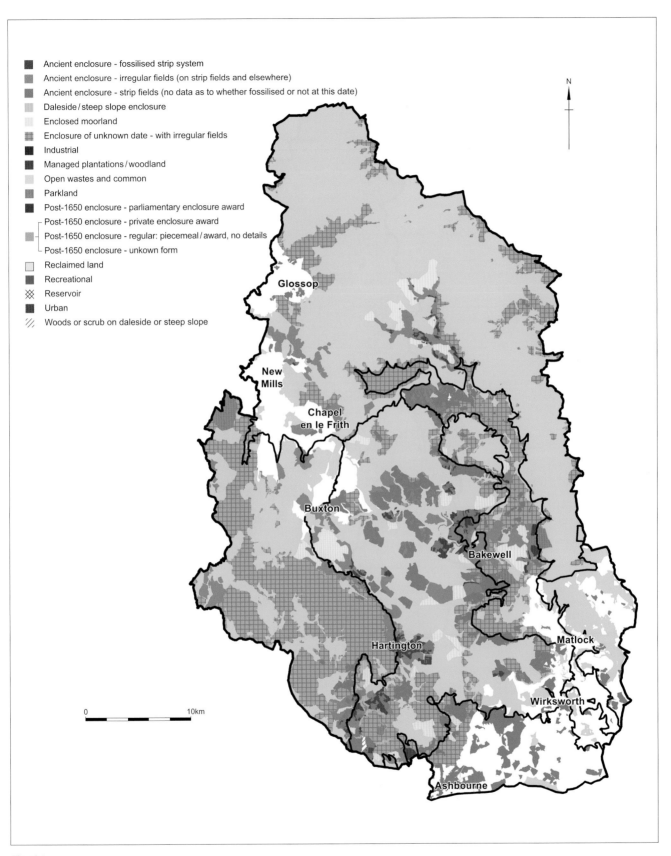

Ancient enclosure - fossilised strip system
Ancient enclosure - irregular fields (on strip fields and elsewhere)
Ancient enclosure - strip fields (no data as to whether fossilised or not at this date)
Daleside / steep slope enclosure
Enclosed moorland
Enclosure of unknown date - with irregular fields
Industrial
Managed plantations / woodland
Open wastes and common
Parkland
Post-1650 enclosure - parliamentary enclosure award
Post-1650 enclosure - private enclosure award
Post-1650 enclosure - regular: piecemeal / award, no details
Post-1650 enclosure - unkown form
Reclaimed land
Recreational
Reservoir
Urban
Woods or scrub on daleside or steep slope

N

Glossop

New Mills

Chapel en le Frith

Buxton

Bakewell

Hartington

Matlock

Wirksworth

Ashbourne

0   10km

Fig A2.1
Overview of the dominant historic character in the Peak landscape in 1650.

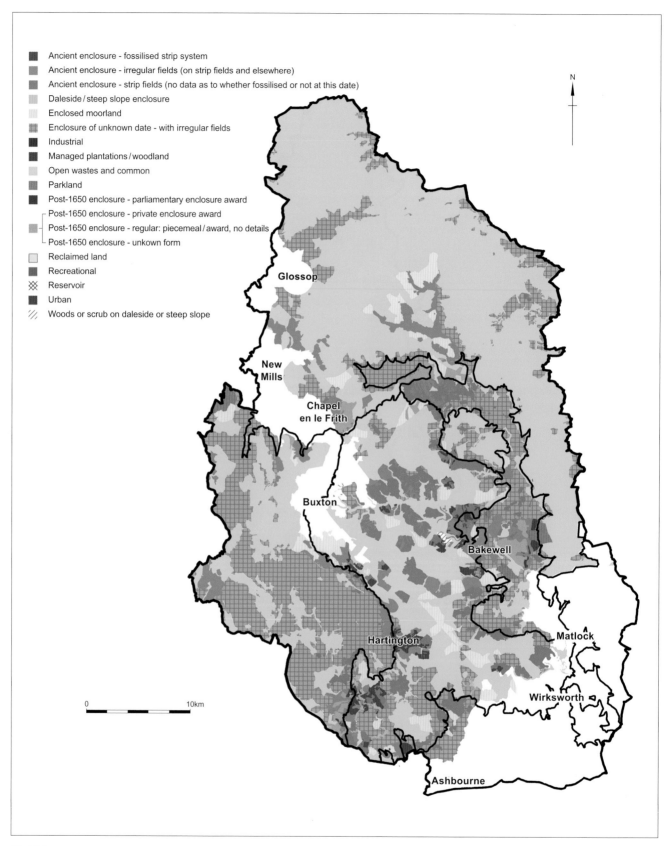

Fig A2.2
Overview of the dominant historic character in the Peak landscape in 1750.

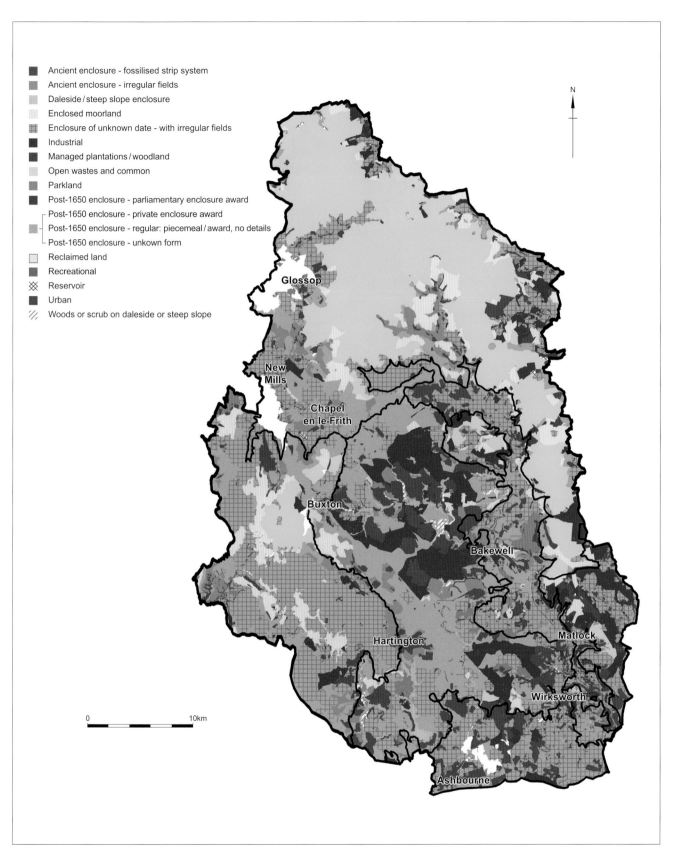

Ancient enclosure - fossilised strip system
Ancient enclosure - irregular fields
Daleside / steep slope enclosure
Enclosed moorland
Enclosure of unknown date - with irregular fields
Industrial
Managed plantations / woodland
Open wastes and common
Parkland
Post-1650 enclosure - parliamentary enclosure award
Post-1650 enclosure - private enclosure award
Post-1650 enclosure - regular: piecemeal / award, no details
Post-1650 enclosure - unkown form
Reclaimed land
Recreational
Reservoir
Urban
Woods or scrub on daleside or steep slope

Glossop

New Mills

Chapel en le Frith

Buxton

Bakewell

Hartington

Matlock

Wirksworth

Ashbourne

0   10km

Fig A2.3
Overview of the dominant historic character in the Peak landscape in 1850.

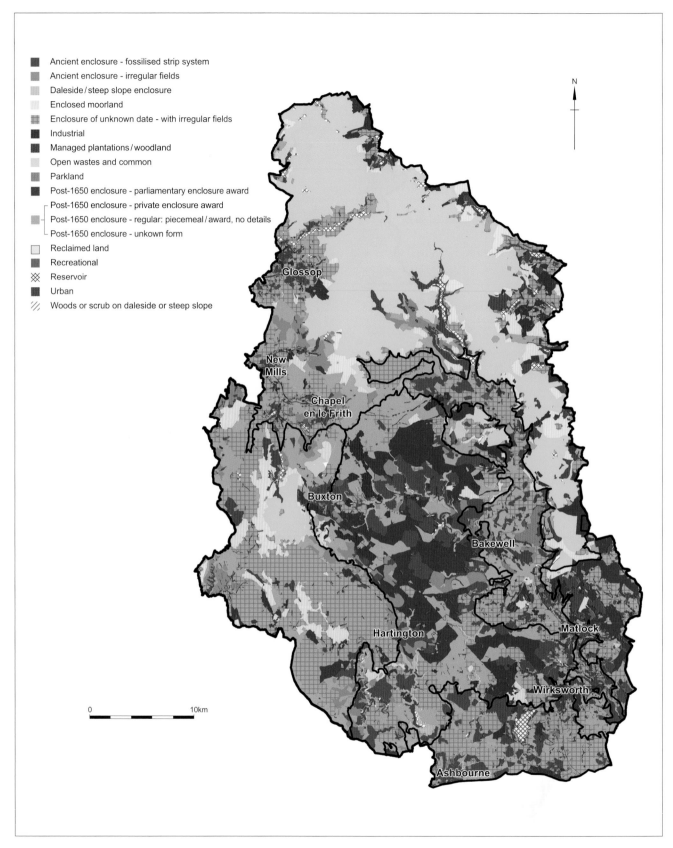

Fig A2.4
Overview of the dominant historic character in the Peak landscape in 2000.

Fig A2.5
An example of detailed historic landscape character mapping with present land boundaries shown. In this case it shows the shale valley landscape in the western half of the Hope Valley, with parts of the Dark Peak upland to the north and south-east, and White Peak plateau land to the south-west (for a colour key see Figs A2.1 to A2.4; the edges of the shale valley character area are shown as red lines).

Fig A2.6
An example of detailed historic landscape character mapping with present land boundaries shown. In this case it shows the southern valleys landscape at its western end, centred on Parwich and Fenny Bentley, with the edge of the White Peak limestone plateau to north and west (for a colour key see Figs A2.1 to A2.4; the edge of the southern valleys character area is shown as a sinuous red line).

Ancient enclosure

The date of 1650 was chosen as a cut-off, primarily because the first commonly surviving estate maps date to the first half of the 17th century and thus a distinction is drawn between enclosure shown on these maps and what came later. Four types of 'ancient enclosure' are identified. Firstly, strips still used in the traditional way within large 'open fields' enclosed by a boundary bank that separates them from the wastes and commons; none of these survive today but in some places they were present up to the early 19th century. Secondly, former strips within open fields that have been 'fossilised' into small narrow permanent fields with sinuous boundaries. Thirdly, rectangular or irregular fields that also existed by 1650. Lastly, 'form unknown' was used where there is historic map evidence that the land was not open common, often labelled 'ancient enclosures' on maps, but where the layout of the fields was not shown.

Post-medieval enclosure

All bounded fields where historic map evidence shows they were created after 1650 are placed here. Four sub-divisions are identified. Firstly, Parliamentary Enclosure Award fields that were created by commissioners following an Act of Parliament for the township in the later 18th or earlier 19th century; award maps usually survive that identify these. Secondly, rare formal private agreements with maps also survive and these are distinguished on the historic landscape character maps. Thirdly, most privately undertaken enclosures have no surviving agreement or mapping, and sometimes were added piecemeal, and these are again mapped differently; this category includes areas where there are no pre-1650 maps but the fields are clearly not 'ancient' as they have ruler-straight boundaries. The fourth category is used where historic mapping coverage is inadequate and it is unknown whether large ownership parcels shown on historic maps were enclosed into fields soon after they were allocated to farmers, or if this came significantly later.

Enclosure of unknown date

When there are no historic maps to elucidate their date, and the fields are irregular to sub-rectangular in shape, they are placed here.

Unenclosed land

The majority of land categorised here is open moorland, now all privately owned but in the past manorial 'wastes and commons'. Two other less common types are included. Firstly, in some cases moorland is divided into large grazing parcels by walls that are significantly larger than fields in the vicinity; these were not necessarily ever 'improved'. Secondly, the steep-sided dales and dry valleys on the limestone plateau are often divided into large grazing parcels which again are much larger than the fields on flatter land above.

Other

Six categories are identified to cover non-farming or atypical aspects of the landscape; with the exception of woodland they are confined to specific small areas. Most terms are self-explanatory. 'Industrial' was only used when whole parcels were used in this way; old lead-mining hillocks crossing fields or coal-mining remains on moorland, both on land having primary farming function, were ignored; fine-grained mapping with individual fields was not practical within the financial and time constraints imposed, plus and more problematically, as the assessment was based on historic maps, many industrial sites are not consistently shown on these. Thus, industrial sites are significantly under-represented on the 'predominant character' mapping. 'Urban' was only used for towns; villages were ignored as having a spatially small footprint within the agricultural landscape. This decision was again governed by financial and time constraints and it worked for the Peak District National Park as the size of villages for the most part has changed little over the last 500 years. However, when the industrial areas of Derbyshire outside the national park were mapped, this proved an untenable approach; even some large towns effectively did not exist in 1650 and even small settlements needed to be mapped to demonstrate settlement growth through time. On the 'present-day' map several areas of 'parkland' are mapped and these are all landscape parks around mansions and halls created as aesthetic statements by designers such as 'Capability' Brown. However, on earlier time-slice maps the parkland comprises deer parks of medieval type. With 'woodland' it is often impossible on the basis of map evidence to distinguish ancient deciduous woodland from plantations where only specific deciduous and/or conifer species may be present. Consequently, these are lumped together, while, in contrast, land can be identified that had open woodland, sometimes of great age, and/or scrubland that has self-seeded on dale sides in recent times.

Mapping

The detailed unpublished historic landscape character mapping that underpins Chapters 2, 4 and 14, comprised a series of time-slice maps at 50-year intervals from 1600 onwards. However, that for 1700 was abandoned at an early stage because there were too few historic maps in the 50 years to either side to make this viable. One for 1950 was never digitised because, in terms of dominant character, it would have been virtually identical to those for 1900 and 2000.

The detailed mapping is all digital, with extracts illustrated in this appendix, held within the National Park Authority's 'geographical information system' database. Two sets of maps are available for the national park.[5] The first maps only those polygons with 'known' data derived from extant historic maps in the 50-year blocks to either side of the date of the character map in question; the second also fills all blank spaces, which are found especially on character maps of 1800 and earlier; these have been filled by 'extrapolation'.[6] This was done in three ways; the most common was where the same 'known' basic character was identified on historic maps at least a hundred years apart in date and it was assumed that the same applies for the intervening time-slice map(s). Secondly, where there are no early historic maps, it is assumed that if the land on one of the later time-slices is known to be moorland then it has been so since prior to 1650.

Thirdly, if the land was enclosed, then mapping its form on earlier time-slice maps was determined according to the type of fields present and thus whether they are likely to have 'ancient' origins or not. When looking at change over centuries across wide areas, then short-lived or local changes are inconsequential and, where historic map coverage is good, they can be shown to be rare. If the three infilling options just noted were unavailable, which was only the case over small- to moderate-sized areas for the 1750 and 1800 maps, then professional judgement was used to make an interpretation based on topography and similarities or differences with adjacent areas where data were 'known'.

Digital mapping presents new opportunities when compared with traditional paper maps. It is now easy to combine data layers at will and to alter the scale at which the mapping is viewed to achieve overviews or burrow into local detail. However, with the latter there is always a danger that if you zoom too close then the data are not accurate enough to be reliable. In this sense digital maps still have

appropriate scales for viewing in terms of sensible amounts of detail examined and what minutiae should be ignored. In the case of the historic landscape character mapping of the Peak, the basic unit used was a single farmer's field as shown on Ordnance Survey maps. Anything within a field, such as a corner with a quarry or mine is ignored if the predominant character in terms of extent is agricultural.

Of the seven time-slice maps produced for the whole national park, the most useful for showing basic landscape changes through time are those for 1650, 1750, 1850 and 2000. The first is the earliest with good reliable data over significant areas, largely due to the wealth of historic maps that survive for the 1610s to 1630s (Fig A2.7). Those for 1750 and 1850 show the start and end of the main period of radical landscape transformation with the enclosure of wastes and commons, while the 1650 and 1750 maps show a slower pace of early enclosure of what had been open land in the medieval period. The 1850 and 2000 maps show that in terms of the dominant character, there has been little change (Fig A2.8).

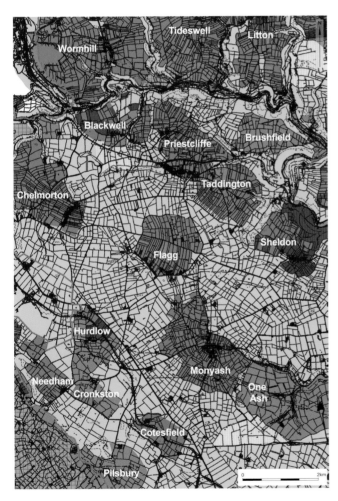

Fig A2.7
An example of detailed historic landscape character mapping with present land boundaries shown. The historic landscape character of a typical White Peak landscape in 1650, contrasting with the present-day landscape shown in Figure A2.8, showing the extensive commons that existed 350 years ago (for a colour key see Figs A2.1 to A2.4).

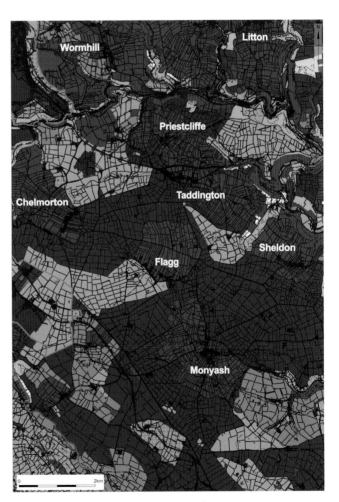

Fig A2.8
The historic landscape character of a typical White Peak landscape, showing how this landscape had changed since the situation shown for 1650 illustrated in Figure A2.7 (for a colour key see Figs A2.1 to A2.4).

Notes

Chapter 1

1 Barnatt and Smith 2004.
2 Notably summarised in Barnatt and Bannister 2009; Barnatt and Smith 2004; Bevan 2004; 2007a; Cooper 1991; Edmonds and Seabourne 2001; Hart 1981; Heath 1993; Hey 2008; 2014; Hodges 1991; Pevsner 1978; Wood 2007.
3 Barnatt and Smith 2004, 63–5; Cameron 1959.
4 Barnatt and Smith 2004, 2–7; Ford 2002.
5 The approach adopted for drawing each boundary line, as best suited for individual places, leads to inconsistencies. For instance, in the case of the limestone plateau, and much of Edale and the Hope Valley, the base of slope is chosen. In contrast, further down the Derwent Valley going southwards, the tops of the main scarps are chosen as enclosure extends towards the tops of the valley sides. Also, just beyond the edge of the 'White Peak' to the south there are four small outliers of outcropping limestone that are not topographically distinct from other parts of the 'Southern valleys', thus they are included in the latter.
6 At altitudes between approximately 470m and 220m OD.
7 The latter is relatively wide but its altitude means that it only ever attracted settlement in a series of hamlets rather than having a focal village.
8 Between the north and south areas there is a relatively narrow stretch between Hathersage and Curbar. From Matlock southwards, the Derwent enters the Matlock Bath limestone gorge, downstream of which it again runs through a relatively narrow valley.
9 With the northern tops at mostly between about 635m and 400m altitude OD and the eastern moors mostly between about 420m and 240m altitude OD. To the south-east, a large area outside the national park, included here under 'Dark Peak', is today very different from the eastern moors in that the land has for the most part been enclosed. However, topographically they go together and before the large-scale enclosure from the18th century onwards they had much in common. Thus, they are treated together here.
10 Between about 560m and 350m altitude OD.
11 These fringes are mostly relatively small in extent within the landscape considered and mapped here, but include larger areas around Chapel en le Frith, Whaley Bridge, Hayfield and Glossop to the north-west and Bradfield to the north-east.

Chapter 2

1 These include: Peak Forest on the northern plateau; Tunstead, Wormhill, Tideswell, Litton, Wardlow, Chelmorton, Blackwell, Priestcliffe, Taddington, Brushfield and Sheldon in the Wye basin; Flagg, Monyash and Over Haddon in the Lathkill basin; Pikehall, Aldwark, Ible, Slaley, Bonsall and Middleton by Wirksworth on shelves to the south-east above the Via Gellia; and Wetton, Alstonefield, Hope, Stanshope and Calton on the shelves of the south-western plateau.
2 Settlements to the east include Castleton, Bradwell, Stoney Middleton, Calver, Hassop, Great Longstone, Little Longstone, Ashford, Bakewell, Youlgreave, Middleton by Youlgreave, Elton, Winster, Wensley, Snitterton and Cromford. Those to the south include Ilam, Blore, Thorpe, Tissington, Parwich, Ballidon, Brassington, Carsington, Hopton and Wirksworth.
3 These include Hazlebadge, Coplow Dale, Little Hucklow, Windmill, Great Hucklow, Grindlow, Foolow and Eyam.
4 These include Dove Holes, Peak Dale, Cowlow, King Sterndale and Staden.
5 These include Earl Sterndale, Hurdlow, Heathcote and Biggin.
6 Settlements including Warslow, Butterton, Grindon, Waterfall, Waterhouses and Cauldon.
7 Taddington 1794, Chelmorton and Flagg 1809.
8 Between Taddington and Chelmorton the private enclosures were here by 1794 at the latest in the former parish and by 1809 in the latter. Those south-east of Flagg were here by 1809, and those north-east of Flagg by 1794.
9 Cameron 1959, 74.
10 Barnatt and Manley 2006, 19–26.
11 Nichols with Wiltshire and Woore 2012, 123–4.
12 Featherstone 1998; Porter 2012; Taylor 1998; Weston 2000.
13 At Biggin, Heathcote, Stanedge, Pilsbury, Cotesfield, Cronkston and Needham.
14 Wiltshire and Woore 2011.
15 Barnatt and Manley 2006, 39–45.
16 The workhouse is now a private residence with little to indicate its former purpose.
17 These include Castleton, Bradwell, Stoney Middleton, Calver, Hassop, Great Longstone, Little Longstone, Ashford, Bakewell, Youlgreave, Middleton by Youlgreave, Elton, Winster, Wensley, Snitterton and Cromford.
18 These include Hope, Thornhill, Aston, Bamford, Hathersage, Padley, Froggatt, Curbar, Baslow, Pilsley, Edensor, Beeley, Rowsley, Stanton, Birchover, Darley, Matlock Churchtown and Tansley.
19 Those centred at Chatsworth House, Haddon Hall and Hassop Hall; see Barnatt and Bannister 2009; Barnatt 1993c.
20 Barnatt 1993b.
21 Bevan 1995, 5–7, 25, Figs 11–13, 16.
22 The parish boundaries shown on Fig 2.13 for Nether Haddon and adjacent parishes held by the Duke of Rutland are those of the 1790s; that for Nether Haddon was later modified.
23 Here by the early 18th century at latest, the date of the first available detailed maps – Nichols with Wiltshire and Woore 2012, 121–2.
24 Hey 2014b.
25 Barnatt and Smith 2004, 76, 78, Fig 39; Bevan 2004, 76–90, 98–117.
26 Ainsworth and Barnatt 1998a; Barnatt 2000a; Barnatt 2008; Barnatt et al 2002; 2017; RCHME and PPJPB 1993.
27 Bound volume of maps at Haddon Hall showing land belonging to the Duke of Rutland.
28 Of a long but narrow type illustrated in Dyer 1995.
29 Williams and Martin 1992, 742.

Chapter 3

1 Craven and Stanley 2001.
2 Barnatt and Bannister 2009, 100–1.
3 For example, see Caird 1852, letters XLIV and XLV.
4 Brumhead and Weston 2001; Cameron 1959; Dodgson 1970; Greenslade 1996; Horovitz 2005; Williams and Martin 1992.

5   And conversely there may be errors of detail in Fig 3.2, as sometimes place-name evidence can be misleading in that the names do not necessarily relate to settlement and the original medieval documents need returning to in order to seek clarity.

6   Hey 2014b.

7   Barnatt and Smith 2004, Fig 38.

8   Beswick and Merrills 1983, Fig 15.

9   Makepeace 1995.

10 Cameron 1959, 101, 176; Williams and Martin 1992.

11 Roffe 1986.

12 Barnatt and Smith 2004, 61.

13 Most of those named below had medieval royal charters for markets and often also fairs. However, this is not the case at Winster, which was not granted until 1711, although the market hall is of 15th- or 16th-century date. Buxton's charter dates to 1813 but Senior's plan of the town of 1631 shows what may well be a market place. In both cases there may have long been markets here.

14 Roberts 2008.

15 Hart 1981, Fig 10.3.

16 Barnatt and Smith 2004, Fig 35.

17 Hart 1981, Fig 10.10.

18 Barnatt and Manley 2006, 115–21.

19 Horovitz 2005, 571.

20 Wetton Hill lies just north of the area shown on Figs 3.9 and 3.10.

21 Barnatt and Smith 2004, Figs 33, 34.

22 Further small surviving examples of greens also exist at Great Longstone, Eyam and Beeley, with infilled examples at Fairfield and possibly Great Hucklow, Youlgreave and Slaley.

23 Barnatt and Smith 2004, Figs 33, 34.

24 Beswick and Merrills 1983, Fig 32.

25 For Burton see: Barnatt 2002b, 12–13, 144, 147–8, Fig 12b; For Ballidon see: Hart 1981, Fig 10.2; Hodges 1991, 113–7.

26 Myers and Barnatt 1984.

27 As at Birchills, Gratton, Snitterton, Cold Eaton, Broadlowash, Swinscoe, Lea Hall, Uppertown at Birchover, Nether Bradbourne, Callow, Bradley, Atlow and Shottle.

28 A few other farmsteads with the 'grange' name have no medieval origins but are of 19th-century date.

29 Barnatt and Smith 2004, 74.

30 Midmer 1979, 62, 128; Tomkinson 2000, 89–99.

31 Hodges 1991, 92–121; Hodges and Wildgoose 1991.

32 Hart 1981, Fig 10.19.

33 Barnatt and Bannister 2009, 62–3.

34 1796 and 1799 maps in the Bakewell Conservation Area Appraisal, Sections 3–4, at www.peakdistrict.gov.uk (accessed 24 July 2018); Ordnance Survey 25 inch to a mile map for 1898; modern Ordnance Survey mapping.

Chapter 4

1   Barnatt and Smith 2004, 54–88; Barnatt and Bannister 2009, 44–128; Bevan 2004, 76–139.

2   Carr 1963; Jackson 1962; Wightman 1961.

3   However, when parcels were still mapped as shared it may be that this related to grazing rights rather than arable cultivation. For example, see Barnatt and Bannister 2009, 109.

4   Barnatt 2002b, 33–7, Fig 4b.

5   Barnatt and Bannister 2009, 73–9; Barnatt and Williamson 2005, 81–5.

6   Now both partially within the landscape park.

7   Barnatt and Bannister 2009, 73–9.

8   Devonshire collection at Chatsworth House; Welbeck Abbey collection; Fowkes and Potter 1988.

9   Barnatt 2002b, 13–37, Figs 2–4b.

10 Milford, ed. 1924.

11 Barnatt and Williamson 2005, 102–25, 157–81, 197–222.

12 Barnatt 1993a, 6–7, Figs 20–24b.

13 Pollard, Hooper and Moore 1974, 79–85.

14 Barnatt and Bannister 2009; Barnatt and Williamson 2005.

15 This map is in a volume of early 17th-century multicoloured maps on vellum done for the Cavendish Family by William Senior and still in Chatsworth House.

16 Again mapped by Senior in 1617.

17 Barnatt and Smith 2004, 71–6.

18 At Pilsbury, Cotesfield, Needham and Cronkston.

19 At One Ash, Calling Low and Meadow Place.

20 At Heathcote, Biggin and Stanedge.

21 At Mouldridge, Roystone, Hoe, Aldwark, Ivonbrook and Griffe.

22 At Earl Sterndale, Hurdlow, Biggin, Heathcote and Ible.

23 As at Blackwell, Needham and probably Roystone Grange.

24 Barnatt 2000c; Chadwick and Evans 2000; Hodges 1991, 84.

25 As at One Ash, Pilsbury, Blackwell and Aldwark.

26 Barnatt 1990b, 3–4, Fig 2; Hodges 1991, 27–34, 109–13.

27 Brumhead and Weston 2001.

28 Barnatt and Bannister 2009, 113–4.

29 Nichols with Wiltshire and Woore 2012, 52–3.

30 Brumhead and Weston 2001; Nichols with Wiltshire and Woore 2012, 63–4, 222–5.

31 Buckingham *et al* 1998.

32 Beckett and Heath (eds) 1995, 17–9. Turnips 20 acres, potatoes 10 acres, cabbages 1 acre, seeds 75 acres, dead fallow 45 acres.

33 Following Beckett and Heath (eds) 1995. The Edale, Hope and Derwent valleys with 2,120 acres arable out of 15,602 enclosed acres (Edale, Brough and Shatton, Bamford, Nether Padley, Bubnell, Pilsley, Edensor, Great and Little Rowsley and Darley); the limestone shale interface with 867 acres arable out of 14,612 acres (Castleton, Bradwell, Hazlebadge, Foolow, Eyam, Stoney Middleton, Holme, Ashford, Buxton); the limestone plateau with 1,376 acres arable out of 13,837 acres (Fairfield, Wheston, Tideswell, Blackwell, Taddington and Priestcliffe, Brushfield, Sheldon); the southern valleys with 717 acres arable out of 6,086 acres (Tissington, Fenny Bentley, Bradbourne, Hognaston, Carsington).

34 Buckingham *et al* 1999, 40, 42.

35 Standing mature trees, referred to as 'timber', were normally reserved for the Lord, while 'brushwood' could be collected; peat cutting came under 'rights of turbary'.

36 In addition, there are a few earthworks that could be earlier, including a linear terrace that could mark the line of the Roman road from Buxton (Stewart Ainsworth, pers comm).

37 Barnatt 2006, 32–49.

38 Barnatt 2005, 17–76.

39 Barnatt and Bannister 2009, 15–39, 125–6; Barnatt and Smith 2004, 13–40; Hey 2007; 2014a, 138–51.

Chapter 5

1   Hodges 1991, 26–43; Wildgoose 1991.

2   Chadwick and Evans 2000.

3   Barnatt and Bannister 2009, 116.

4   Barnatt *et al* 2017, 63–90.

5   Farey 1811–17 (Vol 2 1813), 92–3.

6   For examples see Barnatt and Bannister 2009, 120–2.

7   Barnatt and Bannister 2009, 118–20; Hine 2013.

8   Barnatt with Stroud 1996, 31–3, Fig 23.

9   Barnatt and Bannister 2009, 119.

10 Very narrow forms of early date, known as 'cord rig', as found in the Cheviots for example, have not been identified in the Peak.

11 The first edition Ordnance Survey 25 inch to a mile maps, which in the Peak were surveyed in late 1870s, show that most but not all known dew ponds were in place by then.

12 Farey 1811–17 (Vol 1 1811), 492–3.

13 Farey 1811–17 (Vol 1 1811), 493–5.

14 Today the lime that is spread on fields is not burnt limestone, but crushed limestone, a change made possible in the 20th century with advances in technology that allowed limestone to be crushed much more finely than previously.

15 Farey 1811–17 (Vol 2 1813), 436–7.

16 Wood and Black 2013–14.
17 Johnson 2010; Leach 1995; David Kitching at: www.brocross.com/industrial%20history/limekilns.htm (accessed 24 July 2018).
18 Leach 1999; 2000; Trueman 2000.
19 Locally known in the Peak as 'pudding pies', but this was also applied to other types of clamp kiln.
20 The advantages of application of lime in agriculture had been known since at least the 16th century, as indicated by an account by Fitzherbert in his 'Boke of Husbandry' published in 1523 and thus some examples within pre-enclosure fields may be earlier; similarly, small kilns of this type have been used since at least medieval times for the production of lime for lime mortar.
21 Farey 1811–17 (Vol 2 1813), 435.
22 Although still a type of running kiln.
23 Farey in 1813, followed by Leach in 1995, termed these 'pye kilns', noting they were 'boat-shaped', but this is potentially confusing as it is thought that the traditional term 'pudding pies' was also used for 'circular clamp kilns'.
24 Farey 1811–17 (Vol 2 1813), 440–1.
25 Leach 1995.

Chapter 6

1 Barnatt 2002a; 2003; 2011; 2012; in prep; Barnatt and Penny 2004; Barnatt and Rieuwerts 1998, Barnatt and Worthington 2006; 2007; 2009; Barnatt et al 2013; Ford and Rieuwerts 2000; Kiernan 1989; Rieuwerts 2007; 2008; 2010; 2012; 2013; Willies and Parker 1999; Willies 1979; 1986; 1999; Wood 1999.
2 Except under churchyards, Kings' highways and orchards.
3 Rieuwerts 1998.
4 Crossley and Kiernan 1992; Kiernan 1989; Willies 1991.
5 Willies, Gregory and Parker 1989; Rieuwerts 2015.
6 Barnatt and Penny 2004; Barnatt et al 2013.
7 Ford 2000.
8 Barnatt 2013; 2016; Barnatt et al 1997; Barnatt and Thomas 1998; Porter and Robey 2000; Timberlake 2014.
9 The other being at Alderley Edge in Cheshire.
10 As did the nearby Clayton Mine in the early 19th century when taken over by the Duke of Devonshire.
11 Barnatt 2014b; Brumhead 2012; Leach 1992; 1996b; Rieuwerts and Barnatt 2015.
12 To the east in the Yorkshire and Derbyshire coalfields, and to the west around Manchester and in the Cheshire, North Staffordshire and Cheadle coalfields.
13 Battye 2004.
14 Bevan 2004, 131–4.

15 Crossley and Kiernan 1992; Kiernan 1989, 140–5.
16 Barnatt 2003a; 2011; in prep; Barnatt and Penny 2004; Barnatt and Rieuwerts 1998, Barnatt and Worthington 2006; 2007; 2009; Barnatt et al 2013; Ford and Rieuwerts 2000; Rieuwerts 2007; 2008; 2010; 2012; 2013.
17 Galena (lead sulphide) is the principal lead ore, with an oxidised form, cerrusite (lead carbonate), also relatively common; Ford, Searjeant and Smith 1993.
18 Investigated by explorers with specialist equipment; recent collapses, not far inside the entrance, make this a very dangerous place that should not be entered.
19 These mines, where not open as tourist attractions, should only be explored with specialist equipment and in the company of experienced explorers. There are societies to join who enter mines, such the Peak District Mines Historical Society and various local caving clubs.
20 Rieuwerts 2007; 2008; 2010; 2012.
21 Barnatt 2018.
22 Barnatt 2013, 192–208.
23 Barnatt 2016.
24 Barnatt 2011.
25 Willies 2003; Rieuwerts 2008, 44–8.
26 The brick top of the former was added in the 1860s after the original chimney had developed a lean.
27 Barnatt 2000b; Barnatt and Penny 2004, iv, 4.22.
28 With the key players being Historic England, Natural England and the Peak District National Park Authority, with support from Peak District Mines Historical Society and local wildlife trusts.
29 Some of which also have accessible underground interest.
30 Barnatt and Penny 2004; Barnatt et al 2013.
31 Barnatt 2011.
32 Barnatt 2002a.
33 Barnatt 2003a; Barnatt and Rieuwerts 1998; Flindall and Hayes 1976.
34 Barnatt and Worthington 2006.
35 Rieuwerts and Ford 1985.
36 Barnatt 2013, 81–93, 288–95; 2015a.
37 Barnatt 2014b; Brumhead 2003; 2012; 2013; Leach 1992; 1996b.
38 There are also many smaller concentrations on the moors, together with sites of deeper collieries around Whaley Bridge, New Mills and Poynton, where there are interesting archaeological survivals such as engine houses, but much has been destroyed as these mines lay in agricultural land or at urban locations.
39 Heathcote 2006b, 24–9; 2008.
40 Rieuwerts and Barnatt 2015.
41 Barnatt with Rieuwerts and Roberts 1996, 8–16, 25–8; Crossley and Kiernan 1992;

Ford and Rieuwerts 2000; Kiernan 1989; Willies 1969; 1990; 1991; Willies, Gregory and Parker 1989.
42 Bevan et al 2004.
43 But see Ecton below.
44 The impressive remains at Alport are in strictly private woodland, whereas flues at Brough are next to a public footpath and those at Crich on the land of the Crich Tramway Museum have recently been cleared and displayed.
45 Barnatt 2016.
46 Crossley and Kiernan 1992, 6–9; Kiernan 1989, 140–5.
47 And there are one to four possible smaller heaps.
48 Bevan 1994, 6–7, 10–1, 13, 15, 17, Figs 11–14; Bevan 2004, 131–4.

Chapter 7

1 Harris 1971, 60–92.
2 Barnatt 2014b; Barnatt and Dickson 2004; Harris 1971, 60–4; Leach 1996a.
3 But with the first definite evidence for Calver in the mid-18th century.
4 With no early kilns now obvious at Bradwell; presumably these have been quarried away.
5 With some of this lime also coming from Ashover and Crich, with the last used for plasterwork.
6 Johnson 2003, 22–3.
7 This compared with a seven-month season at Grin Hill in the same period, but where production was controlled by one family from the 1660s; whether they rented individual kilns to others is not known.
8 Barnatt and Worthington 2017; Bowering and Flindall 1998.
9 Tomlinson 1996.
10 Barnatt 2005, 69–70, 85–90, 92–4, Figs 9–11.
11 Barnatt and Worthington 2017; Bowering and Flindall 1998.
12 Harris 1971, 81–4; Polak 1987; Tucker 1985.
13 Defoe 1724–6, Vol 3, 476.
14 Barnatt 1993d, catalogue 1–3, Fig 1d.
15 Harris 1971, 88.
16 Unpublished surveys of Danebower Quarry 2007–9 and Reeve Edge Quarry 2010–2 by Margaret Black and Eric Wood.
17 Or possibly dating to the later 17th century.
18 With this quarry shown on the first edition 25 inch to a mile Ordnance Survey map.
19 Both shown on the same late 1870s' Ordnance Survey map.
20 Barnatt and Dickson 2004, 195–9; Boyes and Lamb 2012, 90–3, 122–30; Harris 1971, 66–74; Hudson 1989, 183–90; Jeuda 2000; Leach 1996a; Marshall 2011, 17–32; Peak Dale Local History Group 1989; Rimmer 1985.

Chapter 8

1 Dodd and Dodd 1980; Hey 1980; Radley 1963; Radley and Penny 1972.
2 Wroe 1982.
3 Barnatt and Bannister 2009, 148–53; Barnatt and Smith 2004, 103–10; Bevan 2004, 115–7.
4 Dodd and Dodd 1980, 45–129; Wood 2007, 50–80.
5 Smith 2009.
6 Morris (ed) 1995, 104.
7 Barnatt and Bannister 2009, 153–60; Dodd and Dodd 1980, 130–81; Radley and Penny 1972; Roberts 1992; Wood 2007, 143–66.
8 Boyes and Lamb 2012; Harris 1971, 65–8, 167–71; Marshall 2011; Rimmer 1985.
9 Hart 1981, 83–94; Wroe 1982.
10 Guilbert and Challis 1993.
11 Stewart Ainsworth, pers comm.
12 Bevan 2004, 115–6.
13 Barnatt 1991b, catalogue 1–2, Figs 1, 10b.
14 Barnatt 1998b; Barnatt and Bannister 2009, 148–53.
15 Drawn by William Senior, reproduced in Barnatt and Williamson 2005, 31–2. While the park has existed since at least the 15th century, there is what may be a park pale earthwork below the braided ways, which indicated the park boundary was moved uphill, probably in 1504 or shortly before.
16 Radley and Penny 1972, 94; Roberts 1992, 9–28.
17 Barnatt and Bannister 2009, 154–7.
18 Roberts 1992, 9–28.
19 Barnatt and Bannister 2009, 148–53.
20 Smith 2009.
21 Barnatt and Dickson 2004, 195–9; Boyes and Lamb 2012, 90–3, 122–30.
22 Mountford 2013.
23 Ian Castledine, pers comm.
24 Marshall 2011; Rimmer 1985.
25 Barnatt 1993d, catalogue 1–3, Fig 1d.
26 Robinson 1993.
27 Barnatt 2014b.

Chapter 9

1 Cooper 1991, 52–108, 131–5; Gifford 1999; Harris 1971, 95–118; Lewis 2014; New Mills Local History Society 1997; Quayle 2006a; Roberts 2010.
2 Edwards 1974, 184–94; Quayle 2006b; Robinson 1993.
3 Heathcote 2006a.
4 Barnatt 1991b, catalogue 3–4, Fig 1b.
5 Derwent Valley Mills Partnership 2001.
6 Barnatt and Williamson 2005, 74–8.
7 Bevan 2004, 141–59; Bevan 2006; Robinson 1993.
8 Barnatt 1994a.
9 Winfield 1996.

Chapter 10

1 Barnatt et al 2017.
2 Barnatt and Edmonds 2014.
3 Ainsworth 2001; Ashmore et al 2010; Barnatt 1986; 1991c; 1994; 1999; 2000; 2001; 2008; Barnatt et al 2002; Barnatt et al 2017; Barnatt and Bannister 2009, 15–39; Bevan 2007b; Edmonds and Seabourne 2001; Machin 1971; Machin and Beswick 1975; Richardson and Preston 1969; Wilson and Barnatt 2004.
4 Notably on Dartmoor and Bodmin Moor in the South-West, and Cumbria and the Cheviots in the north.
5 Hicks 1972; Long et al 1998.
6 Barnatt 2017.
7 Barnatt 2000a; 2008; Barnatt et al 2002; 2017; Barnatt and Smith 2004, 9, Fig 4.
8 Barnatt 2000a; 2001; 2008; Machin and Beswick 1975.
9 Barnatt and Bannister 2009, 36–9.
10 The name 'Hob Hurst House', an unusual square barrow with central cist and surrounding ditch and outer bank, means the dwelling of the hobgoblin of the wood.
11 Barnatt 1990a; 1996a; 1996b; 1996c; 1999; 2000; Barnatt and Bannister 2009, 30–3; Bevan 2007b, 38–41, 50–6, 59–61, 65–82; Edmonds and Seabourne 2001, 147–69; Gray 1903; Guilbert and Garton 2010.
12 The Barbrook 1 stone circle is illustrated at Fig 1.10.
13 Hart 1981, 79, Fig 7.5; Makepeace 1999.
14 Eg Thom 1967.
15 Barnatt and Herring 1986.
16 But specific instances of these 'impressive visual events', as at Robin Hood's Stride noted above, are often hard to prove because there are many potential celestial and landscape targets to choose from.
17 Guilbert and Garton 2010.
18 Ashbee and Ashbee 1981; Barnatt 1986; 1994b; 1996a; 1998; 1999; 2000; Barnatt and Bannister 2009, 24–30; Barnatt and Collis 1996; Barnatt and Manley 2006, 34, 50, 63–6; Bateman 1848; 1861; Bevan 2007b, 34–8, 43–9, 61–3, 79, 80–2; Collis 1983; Edmonds and Seabourne 2001, 123–42; Harding and Beswick 2005; Last 2014; Marsden 1963; 1970; 1976; 1982; Riley 1966; 1981.
19 At Tideslow; Ringham Low and Bole Hill nearby; Minninglow and Stoney Low nearby; and Pea Low. To this list can be added sites with different types of impressive monument, such as the Long Low bank barrow and the henges at Arbor Low and Bull Ring, which may have emerged later as particularly important locales.
20 Barnatt 2017.
21 Barnatt 1998a.
22 Barnatt 2014a; Barnatt and Reeder 1982; Barnatt and Robinson 2003; Edmonds and Seaborne 2001, 107–18; Guilbert et al 2006.
23 Bahn and Pettitt 2009.
24 Barnatt and Edmonds 2002; Bramwell 1973; Branigan and Dearne 1992; Edmonds and Seabourne 2001, 99–108.
25 Barnatt and Manley 2006, 135; Bramwell 1973, 65.
26 Bramwell 1964.
27 Palmer and Lee 1925.
28 Ainsworth and Barnatt 1998a; Barnatt et al 2002; 2017; Coombs and Thompson 1979; Hart 1981, 73–82; Hart and Makepeace 1993; Makepeace 1999; Stanley 1954; Waddington 2012.
29 Barnatt et al 2017, 39–58.

Chapter 11

1 Dearne 1993; Dearne et al 1995; Drage 1993; Hart 1981, 83–108; Jones 1967; Jones and Wild 1968; Ling and Courtney 1981; Ling et al 1990; Webster 1971.
2 Beswick and Merrills 1983; Bevan 2005; 2007b, 114, 121–6; Hart 1981, 84, 94–105; Hodges 1991, 70–91; Hodges and Wildgoose 1981; Makepeace 1998. There is a significant number of uncertainly dated sites in the absence of archaeological excavation.
3 Hodges and Wildgoose 1981; Hodges 1991, 74–81.
4 Makepeace 1983; 1987; 1989; 1995.
5 Barnatt 1989, catalogue 1–3, Figs 1–2, 5, 7–9; Bevan 2005; 2007b, 120–2; Hart 1981, 99.
6 Barnatt 1991b, catalogue 3, Figs 1, 6b; Bevan 2005; Hart 1981, 97; Makepeace 1998, 127, Fig 24.
7 Bevan 2005; Hart 1981, 104.
8 Hart 1981, 101; Makepeace 1998, 127–8, Fig 9.
9 Hart 1981, 104.
10 Barnatt 1991a, catalogue 2–3, Figs 1–2c; Beswick and Merrills 1983, 41, Fig 29; Makepeace 1998, 119–20, Figs 31–2.
11 Beswick and Merrills 1983, 39, Fig 26.
12 Makepeace 1998, 130, Fig 15; Ullathorne 2004 49–52, Fig 38. Data in Fig 11.3 are from the Ullathorne report.
13 Bevan 2005.
14 Barnatt 2000c; Chadwick and Evans 2000; Hodges 1991, 26–43, 81–91; Hodges and Wildgoose 1981.
15 Barnatt 1990b, 2–3, Figs 1–2; Makepeace 1998, 123, Fig 19.
16 Hart 1981, 143–9; Landon et al 2006.
17 Cox 1875–79; Leonard 1993; Pevsner 1967; 1971; 1974; 1978.
18 Bevan 2007b, 131–40; Myers and Barnatt 1984; Sidebottom 1999; Sharpe 2002.
19 Barnatt and Smith 2004, 57–9; Sidebottom 1999; Sharpe 2002.

Chapter 12

1 Burton 1966.
2 Husain 1973, 61.
3 Greenslade 1996, 5–6, 197.
4 Wiltshire *et al* 2005.
5 For detail of the process to the north-west around Chapel en le Frith and Hayfield, see Brumhead and Weston 2001.
6 Wiltshire *et al* 2005; with the nearest to the Peak District study area at Hough, Champion at Windley, Postern and Shottle.
7 At Atlow, Bradley and Ashbourne.
8 Wiltshire and Woore 2009; with the nearest at Holmesfield Park.
9 Barnatt and Williamson 2005, 24–125.
10 Saxton 1579.
11 Hart 1981, 118.
12 Saxton 1579.
13 Barnatt 2013, 24.
14 Saxton 1579.
15 Greenslade 1996, 51–52.
16 Barnatt and Williamson 2005, 91–125.
17 Barnatt 1993b.
18 Barnatt 1993c, 2–4, 15–22, Figs 2, 9.c.
19 Craven and Stanley 2001; Pevsner 1971; 1974, 1978.
20 Thompson 1949; Barnatt and Williamson 2005, 33–75.
21 Rothwell 1998; Groves 2004, 50–7.
22 Kiernan 1989; Ford and Rieuwerts 2000, 31.
23 Morris (ed) 1995, 104.
24 Defoe 1724–26, Vol 3, 476–7.
25 Brighton 2004.
26 For example Adam 1838 (which went to a sixth edition by 1857); Bray 1783; Jewitt 1872; Moore 1819; Pilkington 1789; Ward 1827.

Chapter 13

1 Barnatt 2007, 18, Fig 1; Handley and Rotherham 2011; Payne 2006.
2 Ullathorne, H with Stirling, C (2006) 'Training Trenches at Redmires, Sheffield: The Great War Remembered'. www.pals.org.uk/sheffield/redmires.pdf (accessed 24 July 2018).
3 Ainsworth and Barnatt 1998b, National Monuments Record, NMR nos. SK27 NE 1, 13, 18, 19, 28, 35, 41, 53, 54, 78–98.

4 RCHME 1990, National Monuments Record NMR no: SK 27 SE 22; RCHME and PPJPB 1993, National Monuments Record NMR no; SK 27 SE 98.
5 Bevan 2007a, 53–60.
6 Handley and Rotherham 2011.
7 Barnatt 2015b.
8 The three detailed below and also at Brassington, Coplow Dale, Holt in the Upper Dane valley and at Stone Ruck Moss at the head of Longdendale.
9 At Grindon, Over Wheal near Taddington, Stanton in Peak and Thorpe.
10 Barnatt 1993a, 7–12, Fig 3, 56–60.
11 Bamford and Collier 2005, 56-60.
12 McCamley 2004, 13–5, 48–56, 70–1, 150–1, 158.

Chapter 14

1 At Hope, Aston, Thornhill, Bamford and Hathersage.
2 At Brough, Shatton and Offerton.
3 Notably at Padley, Grindleford, Froggatt and Stoke.
4 Including Stoney Middleton, Calver, Curbar, Baslow, Bubnell, Pilsley, Edensor, Beeley, Rowsley, Darley and Matlock.
5 At Little and Great Longstone, Rowland and Hassop.
6 At Little and Great Hucklow, Grindlow, Foolow and Eyam.
7 Also at Middleton by Youlgreave, Elton and Wensley, with Stanton and Birchover on the gritstone nearby.
8 At Ilam, Thorpe, Fenny Bentley, Tissington, Parwich, Bradbourne, Ballidon, Brassington, Carsington, Hopton and Wirksworth.
9 At Brassington and Wirksworth in particular.
10 The only exception is the Norman ringwork at the manorial centre of Hathersage.
11 Hart 1981, Fig 10.2.
12 Including Fairfield, Wormhill, Wheston, Litton and Wardlow.
13 Including Chelmorton, Blackwell and Priestcliffe.
14 At Flagg, Sheldon and Over Haddon.
15 Including Aldwark and Ible.
16 At Hope and Stanshope.

17 Johnson and Johnson 2010.
18 Williams and Martin 1992, 742.
19 Cox 1906.
20 This presumably included people from the subsidiary settlements of Flagg and Sheldon.
21 Myers and Barnatt 1984.
22 It may be that other parts of the original market place have been built upon and it was once larger and perhaps ran continuously through the heart of the village.
23 At Earl Sterndale, Heathcote and Biggin.
24 At Warslow, Butterton, Grindon, Waterfall, Waterhouses and Calton.
25 Barnatt 2015c.
26 Hugh le Dispenser, later made Earl of Winchester.
27 The last lost but near Earl Sterndale.
28 Landon *et al* 2006, 95–101; Weston 2000, 29–38.
29 As at Earl Sterndale, Hurdlow, Heathcote and Biggin.
30 Weston 2000, 39, 48–52.
31 Barnatt 1987.
32 Barnatt 2014b, 98, Fig 22.
33 Barnatt and Smith 2004, Fig 58.

Appendix 2

1 Barnatt 2003b; Barnatt, Johnson and May 2001.
2 PDNPA 2009
3 At www.gov.uk/government/publications/national-character-area-profiles-data-for-local-decision-making/national-character-area-profiles (accessed 24 July 2018).
4 'Historic landscape character' mapping using the same methodology as employed in the national park and Derbyshire has not been carried out for adjacent areas, in Staffordshire, Cheshire, Greater Manchester and Yorkshire, thus the mapping presented throughout the volume, and the definition of the area to be studied here, stops at the park boundary for these counties.
5 But outside the national park only one set – 'known' data – was mapped.
6 To be technically correct: 'interpolation', 'extrapolation' and 'interpretation'.

Bibliography

General reading

Barnatt, J 1990a *The Henges, Stone Circles and Ringcairns of the Peak District*. Sheffield: Sheffield Archaeological Monograph 1.

Barnatt, J 2013 *Delving Ever Deeper: The Ecton Mines Through Time*. Bakewell: Peak District National Park Authority.

Barnatt, J and Bannister, N 2009 *The Archaeology of a Great Estate: Chatsworth and Beyond*. Bollington: Windgather.

Barnatt, J, Bevan, B and Edmonds, M 2017 *Upland Biographies: Landscape and Prehistory on Gardom's Edge, Derbyshire*. Oxford: Windgather.

Barnatt, J and Collis, J (eds.) 1996 *Barrows in the Peak District: Recent Research*. Sheffield: Sheffield Academic Press.

Barnatt, J, Huston, K, Mallon, D, Newman, R, Penny R and Shaw, R 2013 'The lead legacy: an updated inventory of important metal and gangue mining sites in the Peak District'. *Mining History* **18.6**, 1–112.

Barnatt, J and Smith, K 2004 *The Peak District; Landscapes Through Time*. Bollington: Windgather.

Barnatt, J and Williamson, T 2005 *Chatsworth: A Landscape History*. Bollington: Windgather.

Bateman, T 1848 *Vestiges of the Antiquities of Derbyshire*. London.

Bateman, T 1861 *Ten Years Diggings in Celtic and Saxon Grave Hills in the Counties of Derby, Stafford and York*. London and Derby.

Bevan, B 2004 *The Upper Derwent: 10,000 Years in a Peak District Valley*. Port Stroud: Tempus.

Bevan, B 2007a *Sheffield's Golden Frame: The Moorland Heritage of Burbage, Houndkirk and Longshaw*. Wilmslow: Sigma.

Bevan, B 2007b *Ancient Peakland*. Wellington: Halsgrove.

Boyes, G and Lamb, B 2012 *The Peak Forest Canal and Railway: An Engineering and Business History*. Derby: Railway and Canal Historical Society.

Brighton, T 2004 *The Discovery of the Peak District*. Chichester: Phillimore

Burton, I E 1966 *The Royal Forest of the Peak*. Bakewell: Peak Park Planning Board.

Cooper, B 1991 *Transformation of a Valley: The Derbyshire Derwent*. Cromford: Scarthin Books.

Craven, M and Stanley, M 2001 *The Derbyshire Country House* (2 Vols). Ashbourne: Landmark.

Dodd, A E and Dodd, E M 1980 *Peakland Roads and Trackways* (2nd edn). Ashbourne: Moorland.

Dodgson, J McN 1970 *The Place-Names of Cheshire; Part 1*. Cambridge: Cambridge University Press.

Edmonds, M and Seabourne, T 2001 *Prehistory in the Peak*. Port Stroud: Tempus.

Farey, J 1811–17 *The Agriculture and Minerals of Derbyshire* (3 Vols). London: Board of Agriculture.

Flindall, R and Hayes. A 1976 *The Caverns and Mines of Matlock Bath*. Hartington: Moorland.

Ford, T D 2002 *Rocks and Scenery of the Peak District*. Ashbourne: Landmark.

Ford, T D and Rieuwerts, J H 2000 *Lead Mining in the Peak District* (4th edn). Matlock Bath and Ashbourne: Peak District Mines Historical Society and Landmark Publishing.

Harris, H 1971 *Industrial Archaeology of the Peak District*. Newton Abbot: David and Charles.

Hart, C 1981 *The North Derbyshire Archaeological Survey*. Chesterfield: North Derbyshire Archaeological Trust.

Heath, J 1993 *An Illustrated History of Derbyshire*. Derby: Breedon Books.

Hey, D 1980 *Packmen, Carriers and Packhorse Roads*. Leicester: Leicester University Press.

Hey, D 2008 *Derbyshire: A History*. Lancaster: Carnegie.

Hey, D 2014a *A History of the Peak District Moors*. Barnsley: Pen and Sword.

Hine, S 2013 *Field Barns of the Peak District*. Leek: Churnet Valley Books.

Hodges, R 1991 *Wall-to-Wall History: The Story of Roystone Grange*. London: Duckworth.

Hudson, B 1989 *Through Limestone Hills: The Peak Line – Ambergate to Chinley*. Sparkford: Haynes.

Kiernan, D 1989 *The Derbyshire Lead Industry in the Sixteenth Century*. Chesterfield: Derbyshire Record Society, 14.

Marshall, J 2011 *The Cromford and High Peak Railway* (revised edition). Privately published.

Pevsner, N 1978 *The Buildings of England: Derbyshire* (2nd edition). Harmondsworth: Penguin.

Porter, 2012 *The Duke's Manor: Georgian Hartington and Buxton under the Dukes of Devonshire*. Ashbourne: Landmark.

Porter, L and Robey, J 2000 *The Copper and Lead Mines Around the Manifold Valley, North Staffordshire*. Ashbourne: Landmark.

Rieuwerts, J H 2007 *Lead Mining in Derbyshire: History, Development & Drainage. 1: Castleton to the River Wye*. Ashbourne: Landmark.

Rieuwerts, J H 2008 *Lead Mining in Derbyshire: History, Development & Drainage. 2: Millers Dale to Alport and Dovedale*. Ashbourne: Landmark.

Rieuwerts, J H 2010 *Lead Mining in Derbyshire: History, Development & Drainage. 3: Elton to the Via Gellia*. Ashbourne: Horizon Press.

Rieuwerts, J H 2012 *Lead Mining in Derbyshire: History, Development & Drainage. 4: The area south of the Via Gellia*. Matlock Bath: Peak District Mines Historical Society.

Robinson, B 1993 *Walls Across the Valley: The Building of the Howden and Derwent Dams*. Cromford: Scarthin Books.

Sharpe, N T 2002 *Crosses of the Peak District*. Ashbourne: Landmark.

Willies, L and Parker, H 1999 *Peak District Mining and Quarrying*. Stroud: Tempus.

Wiltshire, M and Woore, S 2009 *Medieval Parks of Derbyshire*. Ashbourne: Landmark.

Wood, A 1999 *The Politics of Social Conflict: The Peak Country 1520-1770*. Cambridge: Cambridge University Press.

Wood, E 2007 *The South-West Peak: A Landscape History*. Ashbourne: Landmark.

In addition, there are a large number of other papers in the many volumes of the *Derbyshire Archaeological Journal*, the *Proceedings of the Hunter Archaeological Society*, and *Mining History* published by the Peak District Mines Historical Society.

Other published texts referred to in the chapters

Adam, W 1838 *Gem of the Peak, or Matlock Bath and its Vicinity*. London.

Ainsworth, S 2001 'Prehistoric settlement remains on the Derbyshire gritstone moors'. *Derbyshire Archaeological Journal* **121**, 19–69.

Ainsworth, S and Barnatt, J 1998a 'A scarp-edge enclosure at Gardom's Edge, Baslow, Derbyshire'. *Derbyshire Archaeological Journal* **118**, 5–23.

Ainsworth, S and Barnatt, J 1998b, 'An Archaeological Survey of the Scheduled Landscape on Big Moor and Ramsley Moor, Baslow and Holmesfield, Derbyshire'. Unpublished report.

Ashbee, P and Ashbee, R 1981 'A cairn on Hindlow, Derbyshire: Excavations 1953'. *Derbyshire Archaeological Journal* **101**, 9–41.

Ashmore, P, Barnatt, J and Wilson, A 2010 'The Sir William Hill prehistoric cairnfield, Eyam Moor, Derbyshire: Excavations 2007-2008'. *Derbyshire Archaeological Journal* **130**, 63–77.

Bahn, P and Pettitt, P 2009 *Britain's Oldest Art: The Ice Age Cave Art of Creswell Crags*. Swindon: English Heritage.

Bamford, J and Collier, R 2005 *Eyes of the Night: The Air Defence of North-Western England 1940-43*. Barnsley: Pen and Sword.

Barnatt, J 1986 'Bronze Age remains on the East Moors of the Peak District'. *Derbyshire Archaeological Journal* **106**, 18–100.

Barnatt, J 1987 'A Preliminary Survey of Archaeological Remains within the Warslow Moors Estate, Staffordshire'. Bakewell: Peak District National Park Authority, Cultural Heritage Team archive – unpublished report.

Barnatt, J 1989 'Blackwell Hall Farm, Blackwell, Derbyshire: Archaeological Survey 1989'. Bakewell: Peak District National Park Authority, Cultural Heritage Team archive – unpublished report.

Barnatt, J 1990b 'Biggin Grange, Hartington Nether Quarter, Derbyshire'. Bakewell: Peak District National Park Authority, Cultural Heritage Team archive – unpublished report.

Barnatt, J 1991a 'Bank Top Farm, Hartington Town Quarter, Derbyshire, Archaeological Survey 1991'. Bakewell: Peak District National Park Authority, Cultural Heritage Team archive – unpublished report.

Barnatt, J 1991b 'The North Lees Estate, Outseats, Derbyshire: Archaeological Survey 1991'. Bakewell: Peak District National Park Authority, Cultural Heritage Team archive – unpublished report.

Barnatt, J 1991c 'The prehistoric cairnfield at Highlow Bank, Derbyshire: A survey of all remains and excavation of one of the cairns, 1988'. *Derbyshire Archaeological Journal* **111**, 5–30.

Barnatt, J 1993a 'The Edale Valley Archaeological Survey', 6–7. Bakewell: Peak District National Park Authority, Cultural Heritage Team archive – unpublished report.

Barnatt, J 1993b 'Haddon Park, Nether Haddon, Derbyshire: Archaeological Survey 1993'. Bakewell: Peak District National Park Authority, Cultural Heritage Team archive – unpublished report.

Barnatt, J 1993c 'Hassop Estate, Hassop and Rowland, Derbyshire: Archaeological Survey 1993'. Bakewell: Peak District National Park Authority, Cultural Heritage Team archive – unpublished report.

Barnatt, J 1993d 'Greenwood Farm, Hathersage, Derbyshire: Archaeological Survey 1993'. Bakewell: Peak District National Park Authority, Cultural Heritage Team archive – unpublished report.

Barnatt, J 1994a 'The Goyt Valley, Hartington Upper Quarter, Derbyshire: Archaeological Survey 1994 (2 Vols)'. Bakewell: Peak District National Park Authority, Cultural Heritage Team archive – unpublished report.

Barnatt, J 1994b 'Excavation of a Bronze Age unenclosed cemetery, cairns and field boundaries at Eaglestone Flat, Curbar, Derbyshire, 1984, 1989–90'. *Proceedings of the Prehistoric Society* **60**, 287–370.

Barnatt, J 1996a 'Moving between the monuments: Neolithic land use in the Peak District', in P Frodsham (ed) *Neolithic Studies in No-Man's Land: Papers on the Neolithic of Northern England, from the Trent to the Tweed. Northern Archaeology* **13/14**, 45–62.

Barnatt, J 1996b 'Recent research at Peak District stone circles; including restoration work at Barbrook II and Hordron Edge and new fieldwork elsewhere'. *Derbyshire Archaeological Journal* **116**, 27–48.

Barnatt, J 1996c *Arbor Low: A Guide to the Monuments*. Bakewell: Peak National Park.

Barnatt, J 1998a 'Monuments in the landscape: thoughts from the Peak', in A Gibson (ed) *Prehistoric Ritual and Religion: Essays in Honour of Aubrey Burl*. Stroud: Sutton, 92–105.

Barnatt, J 1998b 'The Chatsworth Estate Historic Landscape Survey – Chatsworth Moorlands – Archaeological Survey 1997–98 (2 Vols)'. Bakewell: Peak District National Park Authority, Cultural Heritage Team archive – unpublished report for Chatsworth Estate and English Heritage.

Barnatt, J 1999 'Taming the land: Peak District farming and ritual in the Bronze Age'. *Derbyshire Archaeological Journal* **119**, 19–78.

Barnatt, J 2000a 'To each their own: later prehistoric farming communities and their monuments in the Peak'. *Derbyshire Archaeological Journal* **120**, 1–86.

Barnatt, J 2000b 'Lead Rakes in the Peak: Hillock Today, Gone Tomorrow'. Bakewell: Peak District National Park Authority, Cultural Heritage Team archive – unpublished report.

Barnatt, J 2000c 'Oldfields Farm, Ballidon, Derbyshire'. Bakewell: Peak District National Park Authority, Cultural Heritage Team archive – unpublished report.

Barnatt, J 2001 'Trial excavations of prehistoric field boundaries on Big Moor, Baslow, Derbyshire, 1983'. *Transactions of the Hunter Archaeological Society* **21**, 63–77.

Barnatt, J 2002a 'Excavations and conservation at How Grove, Dirtlow Rake, Castleton, Derbyshire'. *Mining History* **15.2**, 1–40.

Barnatt, J 2002b 'The Bakewell Archaeological Survey'. Bakewell: Peak District National Park Authority, Cultural Heritage Team archive – unpublished report.

Barnatt, J 2003a 'A Landscape Through Time: The Historic Character of the Peak District National Park Landscape – Aims, Methods and User Manual'. Bakewell: Peak District National Park Authority, Cultural Heritage Team archive – unpublished report for English Heritage.

Barnatt, J 2003b 'The Lower Nestus Pipe re-entered'. *Mining History* **15.3**, 15–21.

Barnatt, J 2005 'Lathkill Dale National Nature Reserve: Over Haddon, Monyash and Youlgreave Parishes, Derbyshire: Archaeological Survey 2005'. Bakewell: Peak District National Park Authority, Cultural Heritage Team archive – unpublished report for Natural England and English Heritage.

Barnatt, J 2006 'The Deep Dales: Shaded Natural Woodland Survivals or a Long-Maintained Resource. An Historical Land-Use Survey of the Peak District Dales Special Areas of Conservation Woodland'. Bakewell: Peak District National Park Authority, Cultural Heritage Team archive – unpublished report for the Ravine Woodlife Project.

Barnatt, J 2007 'Bradwell Dale, Bradwell and Hazlebadge Parishes, Derbyshire: Archaeological Field Survey 2007'. Bakewell: Peak District National Park Authority, Cultural Heritage Team archive – unpublished report.

Barnatt, J 2008 'From clearance plots to "sustained" farming: Peak District fields in prehistory', in A M Chadwick (ed) *Recent Approaches to the Archaeology of Land Allotment*. Oxford: British Archaeological Reports, International Series 1875.

Barnatt, J 2011 'High Rake Mine, Little Hucklow, Derbyshire: Excavations and Conservation at an Important Nineteenth Century Mine'. *Mining History* **18.1/2**, 1–217.

Barnatt, J 2012 'Silence Mine, Grindlow, Derbyshire: investigating an 1870s' steam engine house'. *Mining History* **18.4**, 1–55.

Barnatt, J 2014a 'Prehistoric rock art, Dobb Edge, Baslow'. *Derbyshire Archaeological Journal* **134**, 78–80.

Barnatt, J 2014b 'Coal mining near Buxton: Thatch Marsh, Orchard Common and Goyt's Moss'. *Mining History* **19.2**, 17–107.

Barnatt, J 2015a 'Underground electric lighting in the 1880s: Clayton Mine, Ecton, Staffordshire'. *Industrial Archaeological Review* **37.1**, 20–32.

Barnatt, J 2015b 'Discovery and survey of World War I practice trenches, Burbage, Derbyshire'. *Derbyshire Archaeological Journal* **135**, 82–98.

Barnatt, J 2015c 'Eighteenth-century mining at Mixon Mine, Staffordshire'. *Newsletter of the Peak District Mines Historical Society* **156**, October 2015, 6.

Barnatt, J 2016 'The 1788 Boulton and Watt Engine House at Ecton: Archaeological Excavations 2012-14'. *Mining History* **19.5**, 38–76.

Barnatt, J 2017 'A Bronze Age flat grave at The Roaches, Staffordshire'. *Staffordshire Archaeological and Historical Society Transactions* **49**, 1–27.

Barnatt, J 2018 'Watergrove Mine, Foolow, Derbyshire: excavating a 1794–95 Newcomen engine house and a history of the mine'. *Mining History* **20.2**, 1–95.

Barnatt, J, Bevan, B and Edmonds, M 2002 'Gardom's Edge: a landscape through time'. *Antiquity* **76**, 50–6.

Barnatt, J and Dickson, A 2004 'Survey and interpretation of an early limeburning complex at Peak Forest, Derbyshire'. *Derbyshire Archaeological Journal* **124**, 141–215.

Barnatt, J and Edmonds, M 2002 'Places apart? Caves and monuments in Neolithic and Earlier Bronze Age Britain'. *Cambridge Archaeological Journal* **12.1**, 113–29.

Barnatt, J and Edmonds, M 2014 'Walking the furrows: a lithics transect across the Peak'. *Derbyshire Archaeological Journal* **134**, 1–77.

Barnatt, J and Herring, P 1986 'Stone circles and megalithic geometry: an experiment to test alternative design practices'. *Journal of Archaeological Science* **13**, 431–49.

Barnatt, J, Johnson, M and May, R 2001 'The Derbyshire Historic Landscape Character Assessment: Aims, Methods and Definitions of Character Types'. Bakewell: Peak District National Park Authority, Cultural Heritage Team archive – unpublished report for English Heritage.

Barnatt, J and Manley, R 2006 *In the Footsteps of the Ancestors: Heritage Walks*. Bakewell: Peak District National Park Authority.

Barnatt, J and Penny, R 2004 *The Lead Legacy: The Prospects for the Peak District's Lead Mining Heritage*. Bakewell: Peak District National Park Authority.

Barnatt, J and Reeder, P 1982 'Prehistoric rock art in the Peak District'. *Derbyshire Archaeological Journal*, **102**, 33–44.

Barnatt, J and Rieuwerts, J 1998 'The Upper Nestus Pipes: an ancient lead mine in the Peak District of Derbyshire'. *Mining History* **13.5**, 51–64.

Barnatt, J with Rieuwerts, J H and Roberts, J G 1996 'The Lead Mine Related Landscape of the Peak District, Part 1 – Smelting Sites, Fuel Sources and Communications'. Bakewell: Peak District National Park Authority, Cultural Heritage Team archive – unpublished report.

Barnatt, J, Rieuwerts, J and Thomas, G H 1997 'Early use of gunpowder in the Peak District: Stone Quarry Mine and Dutchman's Level, Ecton'. *Mining History* **13.4**, 24–43.

Barnatt, J and Robinson, F 2003 'Prehistoric rock art at Ashover School and further new discoveries elsewhere in the Peak District'. *Derbyshire Archaeological Journal* **123** 1–28.

Barnatt, J with Stroud, G 1996 'The Lead Mine Related Landscape of the Peak District, Part 2 – Settlement, Population and Miner/Farmers'. Bakewell: Peak District National Park Authority, Cultural Heritage Team archive – unpublished report.

Barnatt, J and Thomas, G H 1998 'Prehistoric mining at Ecton, Staffordshire: a dated antler tool and its context'. *Mining History* **13.5**, 72–8.

Barnatt, J and Worthington, T 2006 'Using coal to mine lead: firesetting at Peak District mines'. *Mining History* **16.3**, 1–94.

Barnatt, J and Worthington, T 2007 'Post-medieval firesetting in British metal mines: the archaeological evidence'. *British Mining* 83, 4–20.

Barnatt, J and Worthington, T 2009 'Metal mines through time: Unravelling archaeological evidence at long-worked mines in the Peak District'. *Mining History* **17.3**, 1–124.

Barnatt, J and Worthington, T 2017 'Quarrying chert at Bakewell: a detailed archaeological survey of Pretoria Mine and observations on Holme Bank, Holme Hall and Endcliffe Mines'. *Mining History* **19.6**, 1–119.

Battye, R 2004 The Forgotten Mines of Sheffield. Privately published.

Beckett, J V and Heath, J E (eds) 1995 *Derbyshire Tithe Files 1836-50*. Chesterfield: Derbyshire Records Society.

Beswick, P and Merrills, D 1983 'L H Butcher's survey of early settlements and fields in the Southern Pennines'. *Transactions of the Hunter Archaeological Society* **12**, 16–50.

Bevan, B 1994 'Hagg Side, Lee Wood, Fearfall Wood, Rough Wood, Grimbocar; Hope Woodlands, Derbyshire'. Bakewell: Peak District National Park Authority, Cultural Heritage Team archive – unpublished report.

Bevan, B 1995 'Haddon Fields, Nether Haddon, Derbyshire: Archaeological Survey 1995'. Bakewell: Peak District National Park Authority, Cultural Heritage Team archive – unpublished report.

Bevan, B 2005 'Peaks Romana: The Peak District Romano-British rural upland settlement survey 1998-2000'. *Derbyshire Archaeological Journal* **125**, 26–58.

Bevan, B 2006 'Village of the Dammed: Upper Derwent's tin town and planned navvy settlement'. *Derbyshire Archaeological Journal* **126**, 103–26.

Bevan, B, Doonan, R, and Gale, R 2004 'Medieval rural lead working: excavations at Linch Clough, Upper Derwent Valley, 2000-2001'. *Derbyshire Archaeological Journal* **124**, 113–40.

Bowering, G and Flindall, R 1998 'Hard times: a history of the Derbyshire chert industry'. *Mining History* **13.5**, 1–33.

Bramwell, D 1964 'The excavations at Elder Bush Cave, Wetton, Staffs'. *North Staffordshire Journal of Field Studies* **4**, 46–59.

Bramwell, D 1973 *Archaeology in the Peak District: A Guide to the Region's Prehistory*. Hartington: Moorland.

Branigan, K and Dearne, M J 1992 *Romano-British Cavemen: Cave Use in Roman Britain*. Oxford: Oxbow.

Bray, W 1783 *Sketch of a Tour into Derbyshire and Yorkshire* (2nd edn). London.

Brumhead, D 2003 'The coal mines of New Mills'. *Derbyshire Archaeological Journal* **123**, 146–94.

Brumhead, D 2012 *Coal Mining in Marple and Mellor*. Marple Local History Society.

Brumhead, D 2013 *The Coal Mines of New Mills*. New Mills Local History Society.

Brumhead, D and Weston, R 2001 'Seventeenth-century enclosures of the commons and wastes of Bowden Middlecale in the Royal Forest of the Peak'. *Derbyshire Archaeological Journal* **121**, 244–86.

Buckingham, H, Chapman, J and Newman, R 1998 *Meadows Beyond the Millennium: The Future of Hay Meadows in the Peak District National Park* (amended reprint). Bakewell: Peak District National Park Authority.

Buckingham, H, Chapman, J and Newman, R 1999 *Hidden Heaths: A Portrait of Limestone Heaths in the Peak District National Park*. Bakewell: Peak District National Park Authority.

Caird, J 1852 *English Agriculture in 1850–51*. London.

Cameron, K 1959 *The Place-Names of Derbyshire* (3 Vols). Cambridge: Cambridge University Press.

Carr, J P 1963 'Open field agriculture in mid-Derbyshire'. *Derbyshire Archaeological Journal* **83**, 66–76.

Chadwick, A, M and Evans, H 2000 'Reading Roystone Rocks: landscape survey and lithic analysis from test pitting at Roystone Grange, Ballidon, Derbyshire, and its implications for previous interpretations of the region'. *Derbyshire Archaeological Journal* **120**, 87–100.

Collis, J 1983 *Wigber Low, Derbyshire: A Bronze Age and Anglian Burial Site in the White Peak*. Sheffield: University of Sheffield.

Coombs, D G and Thompson, F H 1979 'Excavations of the hill fort of Mam Tor, Derbyshire 1965-69'. *Derbyshire Archaeological Journal* **99**, 7–51.

Cox, J C 1875–9 *The Churches of Derbyshire* (4 Vols). Chesterfield: Palmer and Edmonds.

Cox, J C 1906 'The church and village of Monyash'. *Derbyshire Archaeological Journal* **28**, 1–20.

Crossley, D and Kiernan, D 1992 'The lead smelting mills of Derbyshire'. *Derbyshire Archaeological Journal* **112**, 6–47.

Dearne, M J (ed) 1993 *Navio, the fort and vicus at Brough-on-Noe, Derbyshire*. Oxford: Tempus, British Archaeological Report, British Series 234.

Dearne, M J, Anderson, S and Branigan, K 1995 'Excavations at Brough Field, Carsington, 1980'. *Derbyshire Archaeological Journal* **115**, 37–75.

Defoe, D 1724–6 *A Tour Through the Whole Island of Great Britain*. London (Penguin edition – edited Rogers, P).

Derwent Valley Mills Partnership 2001 *The Derwent Valley Mills and their Communities*. Matlock: Derwent Valley Mills Partnership.

Drage, C 1993 'Brough-on-Noe, Derbyshire: excavations on the Vicus 1983-84', in M J Dearne (ed) 1993 *Navio, the fort and vicus at Brough-on-Noe, Derbyshire*. Oxford: Tempus, British Archaeological Report, British Series 234.

Dyer, C 1995 'Sheepcotes: evidence for medieval sheep farming'. *Journal of Medieval Archaeology* **39**, 136–64.

Edwards, K C 1974 *The Peak District* (2nd edn). London: Bloomsbury Books.

Featherstone, P 1998 *Biggin and Hartington Nether Quarter*. Privately published.

Ford, T D 2000 *Derbyshire Blue John*. Ashbourne: Landmark.

Ford, T D, Sarjeant, W A S and Smith, M E 1993 'Minerals of the Peak District of Derbyshire'. *Bulletin of the Peak District Mines Historical Society* **12.1**, 16–65.

Fowkes, D V and Potter, G R (eds) 1988 *William Senior's Survey of the Estates of the First and Second Earls of Devonshire c. 1600-1628*. Chesterfield: Derbyshire Records Society 13.

Gifford, A 1999 *Derbyshire Watermills: Corn Mills*. Midland Wind and Water Mills Group.

Gray, St G H 1903 'On the excavations at Arbor Low, 1902-3'. *Archaeologia* **58**, 461–98.

Greenslade, M W (ed) 1996 *A History of the County of Stafford: Volume 7, Leek and the Moorlands*. Oxford: Oxford University Press.

Groves, L 2004 *Historic Parks & Gardens of Cheshire*. Ashbourne: Landmark.

Guilbert, G and Challis, K 1993 'Excavations across the supposed line of "The Street" Roman road south-east of Buxton, 1991'. *Derbyshire Archaeological Journal* **113**, 45–60.

Guilbert, G and Garton, D 2010 'Nine Ladies, Stanton Moor: surface survey and exploratory excavations in response to erosion 1988-2000'. *Derbyshire Archaeological Journal* **130**, 1–62.

Guilbert, G, Garton, D and Walters, D 2006 'Prehistoric cup and ring art at the heart of Harthill Moor'. *Derbyshire Archaeological Journal* **126**, 12–30.

Handley, C and Rotherham, I 2011 *Hills, Dykes and Dams: Moor Memories in the Bradfield, Midhope and Langsett Areas*. Sheffield: Wildtrack Publishing.

Harding, P and Beswick, P 2005 'Excavations at a Bronze Age barrow on Carsington Pasture by Time Team 2002'. *Derbyshire Archaeological Journal* **125**, 1–20.

Hart, C R and Makepeace, G A 1993 '"Cranes Fort", Conksbury, Youlgreave, Derbyshire: A newly discovered hillfort'. *Derbyshire Archaeological Journal* **113**, 16–20.

Heathcote, C 2006a 'Barytes Mills at Shallcross, Cadster and Barmoor Clough, North-West Derbyshire'. *Mining History* **16.4**, 1–5.

Heathcote, C 2006b 'The coal mine soughs draining into the Rivers Goyt and Sett in North-West Derbyshire'. *Mining History* **16.4**, 21–35.

Heathcote, C 2008 'Coal mining in the hamlets of Beard and Bugsworth in Northwest Derbyshire 1650-1926'. *Mining History* **17.1**, 1–17.

Hey, D 2007 'The grouse moors of the Peak District', in P S Barnwell and M Palmer (eds) *Post-Medieval Landscape*, 68–79. Bollington: Windgather.

Hey, D 2014b 'The medieval origins of South Pennine farms: the case of Westmondhalgh Bierlow, South Yorkshire'. *Agricultural History Review* **14.1**, 23–39.

Hicks, S P 1972 'The impact of man on the East Moors of Derbyshire from Mesolithic times'. *Derbyshire Archaeological Journal* **129**, 1–21.

Hodges, R and Wildgoose, M 1981 'Roman or native in the White Peak: the Roystone Grange Project and its regional implications'. *Derbyshire Archaeological Journal* **101**, 42–57.

Hodges, R and Wildgoose, M 1991 'Roystone Grange: excavations of the Cistercian Grange 1980-87'. *Derbyshire Archaeological Journal* **111**, 46–50.

Horovitz, D 2005 The Place-Names of Staffordshire. Privately published.

Husain, M C 1973 *Cheshire Under the Norman Earls*. Chester: Cheshire Community Council.

Jackson, J C 1962 'Open field cultivation in Derbyshire'. *Derbyshire Archaeological Journal* **82**, 54–72.

Jeuda, B 2000 *The Limestone Quarries of Caldon Low*. Leek: Churnet Valley Books.

Jewitt, L (ed.) 1872 *Black's Tourist Guide to Derbyshire*. Edinburgh: Adam and Charles Black.

Johnson, D 2003 'Friedrich Edouard Hoffmann and the invention of the continuous kiln technology: the archaeology of the Hoffmann lime kiln and 19th-century industrial developments (Part 2)'. *Industrial Archaeology Review* **25.1**, 15–30.

Johnson, D 2010 *Limestone Industries of the Yorkshire Dales* (2nd edn). Stroud: Amberley.

Johnson, R and Johnson, S 2010 *Monyash: The Making of a Derbyshire Village*. Ashbourne: Landmark.

Jones, G D B 1967 'Manchester University Excavations, Brough on Noe (Navio) 1967'. *Derbyshire Archaeological Journal* **87**, 154–8.

Jones, G D B and Wild, J P 1968 'Excavation at Brough on Noe (Navio) 1986'. *Derbyshire Archaeological Journal* **88**, 89–93.

Landon, N, Ash, P, Payne, A and Phillips, G 2006 'Pilsbury; a forgotten castle'. *Derbyshire Archaeological Journal* **126**, 82–102.

Last, J 2014 'The excavation of two round barrows at Longstone Edge, Derbyshire'. *Derbyshire Archaeological Journal* **134**, 81–172.

Leach, J T 1992 *Coal Mining Around Whaley Bridge*. Matlock: Derbyshire Library Service.

Leach, J T 1995 'Burning lime in Derbyshire pye kilns'. *Industrial Archaeology Review* **17.2**, 145–58.

Leach, J T 1996a 'Grin Hill, Buxton: a major Derbyshire limestone quarry'. *Derbyshire Archaeological Journal* **116**, 101–34.

Leach, J T 1996b 'Coal mining around Quarnford'. *Staffordshire Studies* **8**, 66–95.

Leach, J 1999 'A proposed limekiln typology'. *Industrial Archaeology News* **110**, 5–7.

Leach, J 2000 'Final word on kilns'. *Industrial Archaeology News* **113**, 9.

Leonard, J 1993 *Derbyshire Parish Churches from the Eighth to the Eighteenth Centuries*. Derby: Breedon Books.

Lewis, S 2014 *Cotton Mills and Printworks on the River Goyt and its Tributaries*. High Peak: Florence Publishing.

Ling, R and Courtney, T 1981 'Excavations at Carsington, 1979-80'. *Derbyshire Archaeological Journal* **101**, 58–87.

Ling, R, Hunt, C O, Manning, W H, Wild, F and Wild, J P 1990 'Excavations at Carsington, 1983-84'. *Derbyshire Archaeological Journal* **110**, 30–55.

Long, D J, Chambers, F M and Barnatt, J 1998 'The palaeoenvironment and the vegetation history of a later prehistoric field system at Stoke Flat on the gritstone uplands of the Peak District'. *Journal of Archaeological Science* **25**, 505–19.

Machin, M L 1971 'Further excavations of the enclosure at Swine Sty, Big Moor, Baslow'. *Transactions of the Hunter Archaeological Society* **10**, 5–13.

Machin, M L and Beswick, P 1975 'Further excavations of the enclosure at Swine Sty, Big Moor, Baslow, and report on the shale industry at Swine Sty'. *Transactions of the Hunter Archaeological Society* **10**, 204–11.

Makepeace, G A 1983 'A Romano-British settlement at Staden, near Buxton'. *Derbyshire Archaeological Journal* **103**, 75–86.

Makepeace, G A 1987 'The Romano-British settlement at Staden, near Buxton: the 1983 excavations'. *Derbyshire Archaeological Journal* **107**, 24–34.

Makepeace, G A 1989 'The Romano-British settlement at Staden, near Buxton: the 1984 and 1985/86 excavations'. *Derbyshire Archaeological Journal* **109**, 17–33.

Makepeace, G A 1995 'The Romano-British settlement at Staden, near Buxton: the 1987-88 and 1989-90 excavations and final report'. *Derbyshire Archaeological Journal* **115**, 107–35.

Makepeace, G A 1998 'Romano-British settlements in the Peak District and North-East Staffordshire'. *Derbyshire Archaeological Journal* **125**, 95–138.

Makepeace, G A 1999 'Cratcliff Rocks - a forgotten hillfort'. *Derbyshire Archaeological Journal* **119**, 12–8.

Marsden, B M 1963 'The re-excavation of the Green Low, a Bronze Age barrow on Alsop Moor, Derbyshire'. *Derbyshire Archaeological Journal* **83**, 82–9.

Marsden, B M 1970 'The excavation of the Bee Low round cairn, Youlgreave'. *Antiquaries Journal* **50**, 186–215.

Marsden, B M 1976 'The excavation of Snelslow and Lean Low round cairns, Derbyshire'. *Derbyshire Archaeological Journal* **96**, 5–14.

Marsden, B M 1982 'Excavations at the Minninglow Chambered Cairn (Ballidon 1), Ballidon, Derbyshire'. *Derbyshire Archaeological Journal* **102**, 8–22.

McCamley, N J 2004 *Disasters Underground*. Barnsley: Pen and Sword.

Midmer, R 1979 *English Medieval Monasteries 1066-1540*. London: Heinemann.

Milford, H (ed) 1924 *Travels Through Several Parts of England in 1782 by Carl Philipp Moritz*. Oxford: Oxford University Press.

Moore, H 1819 *Picturesque Excursions in the High Peak*. Derby.

Morris, C (ed) 1995 *The Illustrated Journeys of Celia Fiennes 1685-c. 1712*. Stroud: Alan Sutton.

Mountford, C E 2013 *Rope and Chain Haulage: The Forgotten Element of Railway History*. Melton Mowbray: Industrial Railway Society.

Myers, A M and Barnatt, J 1984 'Pre-Norman cross fragments from Monyash, Derbyshire'. *Derbyshire Archaeological Journal* **104**, 5–9.

New Mills Local History Society 1997 *New Mills: A Look Back at its Industrial Heritage*. New Mills: New Mills Local History Society.

Nichols, H, with Wiltshire, M and Woore, S 2012 *A Catalogue of Local Maps of Derbyshire c. 1528-1800*. Chesterfield: Derbyshire Records Society 37.

Palmer, L S and Lee, L S 1925 'Frank i' th' Rocks Cave and other northern caves in relation to the Ice Ages'. *Proceedings of the University of Bristol Speleological Society* **2.3**, 244–60.

Payne, A 2006 *Houndkirk Decoy: A Survey and Interpretation*. Sheffield: Scaramouch Books.

Peak Dale Local History Group 1989 *More than Just Dust*. Privately published.

Peak District National Park Authority 2009 'Landscape Strategy and Peak District National Park Action Plan 2009–2019'.

Pevsner, N 1967 *The Buildings of England: Yorkshire West Riding* (2nd edition). Harmondsworth: Penguin.

Pevsner, N 1971 *The Buildings of England: Cheshire*. Harmondsworth: Penguin.

Pevsner, N 1974 *The Buildings of England: Staffordshire*. Harmondsworth: Penguin.

Pilkington, J 1789 *A View of the Present State of Derbyshire*. Derby.

Polak, J P 1987 The production and distribution of Peak millstones from the sixteenth to the eighteenth centuries. *Derbyshire Archaeological Journal* **107**, 55–72.

Pollard, E, Hooper, M D and Moore, N W 1974 *Hedges*. London: Collins.

Quayle, T 2006a *The Cotton Industry in Longdendale and Glossopdale*. Stroud: Tempus.

Quayle, T 2006b *Manchester's Water: The Reservoirs in the Hills*. Stroud: Tempus.

Radley, J 1963 'Peak District roads prior to the turnpike era'. *Derbyshire Archaeological Journal* **83**, 39–50.

Radley, J and Penny, S R 1972 'The turnpike roads of the Peak District'. *Derbyshire Archaeological Journal* **92**, 93–109.

Richardson, G G S and Preston, F L 1969 'Excavations at Swine Sty, Big Moor, Baslow 1967–8'. *Transactions of the Hunter Archaeological Society* **9**, 261–3.

Rieuwerts, J H 1998 *Glossary of Derbyshire Lead Mining Terms*. Matlock Bath: Peak District Mines Historical Society.

Rieuwerts, J H 2013 *Adventurer in the Lead Trade: Being an Account of the Mining Interests of the Thornhill Family of Stanton Hall near Bakewell, Derbyshire*. Great Hucklow: Hucklow Publishing.

Rieuwerts, J H 2015 *Mill Close – the Last Great Lead Mine; the History of Mill Close Mine in the Liberties and Manors of Wensley, Birchover, Stanton and Great Rowsley*. Great Hucklow: Hucklow Publishing.

Rieuwerts, J H and Barnatt, J 2015 'Coal mining on the Peak District's uplands during the 16th to early 20th centuries'. *Mining History* **19.4**, 1–49.

Rieuwerts, J H, and Ford, T D 1985 'The mining history of the Speedwell Mine or Oakden Level, Castleton, Derbyshire'. *Bulletin of the Peak District Mines Historical Society* **9.3**, 129–70.

Riley, D N 1966 'An Early Bronze Age cairn on Harland Edge, Beeley Moor, Derbyshire'. *Derbyshire Archaeological Journal* **86**, 31–53.

Riley, D N 1981 'Barrow no. 1 on Ramsley Moor, Holmesfield, North-East Derbyshire'. *Transactions of the Hunter Archaeological Society* **11**, 1–13.

Rimmer, A 1985 *The Cromford and High Peak Railway*. Oxford: Oakwood Press.

Roberts, A F 1992 *Turnpike Roads Around Buxton*. Privately published.

Roberts, A F 2010 *Water Mills on the Derbyshire Wye*. Privately published.

Roberts, B K 2008 *Landscapes, Documents and Maps: Villages in Northern England and Beyond, AD 900–1250*. Oxford: Oxbow.

Robinson, B 1993 *Walls Across the Valley: The Building of the Howden and Derwent Dams*. Cromford: Scarthin Books.

Roffe, D 1986 *The Derbyshire Domesday*. Darley Dale: Derbyshire Museums Service.

Rothwell, J 1998 *Lyme Park*. National Trust.

Royal Commission on the Historic Monuments of England 1990 'Gibbet Moor, Derbyshire'. Unpublished report. National Monuments Record NMR no: SK 27 SE 22.

Royal Commission on the Historic Monuments of England and Peak Park Joint Planning Board 1993 'An Archaeological Survey of the Northern Halves of Gardom's and Birchen Edges, Baslow, Derbyshire'. National Monuments Record NMR no; SK 27 SE 98. Unpublished report: RCHME/PPJPB.

Saxton, C 1579 *Atlas of the Counties of England and Wales*.

Sidebottom, P C 1999 'Stone crosses in the Peak and "the sons of Eadwulf"'. *Derbyshire Archaeological Journal* **119**, 206–19.

Smith, H 2009 *Guide Stoups of Derbyshire*. Ashbourne: Landmark.

Stanley, J 1954 'An Iron Age fort at Ball Cross Farm, Bakewell'. *Derbyshire Archaeological Journal* **74**, 85–99.

Taylor, H 1998 'A Report on the 1614 Survey of the Lordship of Hartington, Derbyshire'. Bakewell: Peak District National Park Authority, Cultural Heritage Team archive – unpublished report.

Thom, A 1967 *Megalithic Sites in Britain*. Oxford: Clarendon Press.

Thompson, F 1949 *A History of Chatsworth: Being a Supplement of the Sixth Duke of Devonshire's Handbook*. London: Country Life.

Timberlake, S 2014 'Prehistoric Copper Extraction in Britain: Ecton Hill, Staffordshire'. *Proceedings of the Prehistoric Society* **80**, 159–206.

Tomlinson, J M 1996 *Derbyshire Black Marble*. Matlock Bath: Peak District Mines Historical Society.

Tompkinson, J L 2000 *Monastic Staffordshire: Religious Houses in Medieval Staffordshire and its Borderlands*. Leek: Churnet Valley Books.

Trueman, M 2000 'Lime kilns – modelling their technological development'. *Industrial Archaeology News* **112**, 4–5.

Tucker, G 1985 'Millstone making in the Peak District of Derbyshire: the quarries and the technology'. *Industrial Archaeology Review* **8.1**, 42–58.

Ullathorne, A. 'National Trust South Peak Estate: Area 3, Archaeological Survey 2004'. Bakewell: Peak District National Park Authority, Cultural Heritage Team archive – unpublished report for the National Trust. Data in Fig 11.4 are from the Ullathorne report.

Waddington, C 2012 'Excavations at Fin Cop, Derbyshire: An Iron Age hillfort in conflict?' *Archaeological Journal* **196**, 159–236.

Ward, Revd R 1827 *A Guide to the Peak of Derbyshire*. Birmingham: Ward.

Webster, P V 1971 'Melandra Castle Roman fort: excavations in the civil settlement, 1966-9'. *Derbyshire Archaeological Journal* **91**, 58–118.

Weston, R 2000 *Hartington: A Landscape History from the earliest times to 1800*. Matlock: Derbyshire County Council Libraries and Heritage Department.

Wightman, W E 1961 'Open field agriculture in the Peak District'. *Derbyshire Archaeological Journal* **81**, 111–25.

Wildgoose, M 1991 'The drystone walls of Roystone Grange'. *Archaeological Journal* **148**, 205–40.

Williams, A and Martin G H (eds) 1992 *Domesday Book: A Complete Translation*. London: Penguin.

Willies, L 1969 'Cupola lead smelting sites in Derbyshire, 1737-1900'. *Bulletin of the Peak District Mines Historical Society* **4.1**, 97–115.

Willies, L 1979 'Technical development in Derbyshire lead mining, 1700-1880'. *Bulletin of the Peak District Mines Historical Society* **7.3**, 117–51.

Willies, L 1986 'Prosperity and decline in Derbyshire lead mining'. *Bulletin of the Peak District Mines Historical Society* **9.5**, 251–82.

Willies, L 1990 'Derbyshire lead smelting in the eighteenth and nineteenth centuries'. *Bulletin of the Peak District Mines Historical Society* **11.1**, 1–19.

Willies, L 1991 'Lead Ore Preparation and Smelting', in J Day and R F Tylecote (eds) *The Industrial Revolution in Metals*, 84-130. London: Institute of Metals.

Willies, L 1999 'Derbyshire lead mining in the 18th and 19th centuries'. *Mining History* **14.2**, 31–3.

Willies, L 2003 *Magpie Mine* (revised edition). Peak District Mining Museum: Peak District Mines Historical Society.

Willies, L, Gregory, K and Parker, H 1989 *Millclose, the Mine that Drowned*. Cromford: Scarthin Books.

Wilson, A and Barnatt, J 2004 'Excavation of a prehistoric clearance cairn and ritual pits on Sir William's Hill, Eyam Moor, Derbyshire, 2000'. *Derbyshire Archaeological Journal* **124**, 13–63.

Wiltshire, M and Woore, S 2011 '"Hays" possible early enclosures in Derbyshire'. *Derbyshire Archaeological Journal* **131**, 195–225.

Wiltshire, M, Woore, S, Crisp, B and Rich, B 2005 *Duffield Frith: History & Evolution of the Landscape of a Medieval Derbyshire Forest*. Ashbourne: Landmark.

Winfield, J 1996 *The Gunpowder Mills of Fernilee*. Privately published.

Wood, E and Black, M 2013–14 'Surviving Limekilns of the South West Peak' (3 Vols). Bakewell: Peak District National Park Authority, Cultural Heritage Team archive – unpublished report.

Wroe, P 1982 'Roman roads in the Peak District'. *Derbyshire Archaeological Journal* **102**, 49–73.

Index

Page numbers in **bold** refer to figures and tables.

A

Abney (Derbys) 42–3, 51–2, **242–3**
Abney Grange (Derbys) 51–2
Abney Moor (Derbys) 9, 27, 125, **222–3, 224–5, 228–9**
Agden Reservoir (Yorks) 154
agricultural landscape
  arable crops 73, **74**
  changes over time 63
  Chatsworth Estate 68–9, **69**
  commons see commons
  dew ponds and meres 86–7, **87**
  enclosure see commons, enclosure of
  field barns **17, 81–3, 81, 82, 87, 226–7**
  field kilns 88–90, **89, 90**, 118, **226–7**
  field walls 65, 67–8, **67**, 72, 79, **226–7**
  hedges 65–8, **66, 67**
  limestone commons 73–4
  locations **226–7**
  meadows 73
  monastic granges 18, **18**, 27, 50, 51–3, **51, 52, 53**, 70
  ridge and furrow field systems 83, **84**, 85, **85**, 86, **226–7**
  sheepwalks 63, 75, **226–7**
  strip lynchet field systems 83, **84**, 85, **85**
  wall furniture 80–1, **80, 226–7**
agricultural practices 11–12
Alderwasley (Derbys) 27, **224–5, 242–3**
Aldwark (Derbys) 40, 209, **209, 224–5, 242–3**
Allcard, John **56**
Alport (Derbys) 25, **25**, 220
Alport mines (Derbys) **97**, 115, **228–9**
Alport, River 9, 27, 117, **223**
Alsop le Dale (Derbys) 35, 183, **224–5, 236–7**
Alstonefield Forest (Staffs) 213, 217
Alstonefield Frith (Staffs) 186, 187, **187**, 189, 214–15, **215**

Alstonefield (Staffs)
  agricultural landscape **19**
  Anglo-Saxon crosses 19, 47, 184
  field systems 19–20, **20**
  location **224–5, 230–1, 236–7, 242–3**
  manorial centre and market 40, 42, 210–11, 215
  milepost **143**
  settlement 19–20, **19**, 47
  surrounding area 20
Alton (Derbys) 34, **224–5**
Amber, River 115
Aquae Arnemetiae Roman centre (Derbys) 136, 177, **236–7**
arable crops 73
Arbow Low stone circle/henge (Derbys) 158, **163**, 163, 165, 170, **170, 234–5**
Ardotalia Roman fort (Derbys) 136, 177, 236–7
Arkwright, Richard 150, 151, 152
Arnfield Reservoir (Derbys) 154
Ashbourne (Derbys)
  church 183, 184
  field systems 34
  location **224–5, 230–1, 236–7, 242–3**
  manorial centre and market 34, 41–2, 45, 54, 204
  railway 134, 145
  settlement 34, 45
  turnpike road 139
Ashford (Derbys)
  Black Marble 118, 121
  field systems 212
  hall 193
  location **224–5, 226–7, 228–9, 232–3, 238–9, 242–3**
  mill 150
  settlement 21, 40, 41, 47, 204
Ashop, River 9, 27, 155, 219
Ashopton (Derbys) 155
Ashover (Derbys) 99, 171, **234–5**
Ashton's Mine (Derbys) **93, 228–9**
Aston (Derbys) 22, **224–5, 242–3**

B

Backdale Quarry (Derbys) 129, **228–9**
Bailey's Tump (Derbys) 198, **198, 240–1**
Bakewell (Derbys)
  Anglo-Saxon cross fragments 47, 184, **184**
  Anglo-Saxon defences 182
  Bakewell Chert 118, 121, 122, **122**
  Burton Closes **55**, 56, **56**, 193, **238–9**
  church 47, 183
  development of town 54, 55–6, **55, 56**
  field barns 82
  field systems 57, 58, 64, **64, 65**, 85, **85**
  location **224–5, 226–7, 228–9, 230–1, 232–3, 236–7, 242–3**
  manorial centre and market 21, 41, 204, 211
  mill 150
  topographical zone, relationship to 42
  turnpike road 139, 140
Ball Cross hillfort (Derbys) 176
Ballidon (Derbys) 50, 85, **86**, 129, 209, **209, 224–5, 226–7, 228–9, 242–3**
Bamford Common (Derbys) 70, **226–7**
Bamford (Derbys) 23, 151, **224–5, 232–3, 242–3**
Bamford Edge (Derbys) 123, **123**, 228–9
Bamford Moor (Derbys) 27, 154, 164, 171, **224–5**
Bank Top Farm, Hartington (Derbys) **17**
Barbrook Reservoir (Derbys) 155
Barker and Wilkinson smelting company 214
barrows and chambered tombs
  Arbor Low 163, **163**, 170
  Big Moor 160, **161, 166**, 171
  burial practices 167–8
  Chatsworth moorlands 162, **162**

Crow Chin 171
Five Wells 165, **166**
forms 166
Gardom's Edge **29**
Gib Hill 165, 170
Green Low 165
Lean Low 217
locations **234–5**
long barrows 165–6
Long Low 165
Minninglow 165, **186**
modern reuse of **196**, 201
organisation in prehistoric landscape 158, 167
Pea Low 20, **20**
round barrows 166–7
barytes mines 5, 95, 103, 151
Baslow Colliery (Derbys) 113, **228–9**
Baslow (Derbys)
  church 183
  field systems 24, **24**, 71
  land lost to Chatsworth 69
  location **224–5, 226–7, 236–7, 242–3**
  settlement 208, 209
  thatched roofs 37
  turnpike road 124, 139, 141, **141**
Baslow Edge (Derbys) **205**
Bateman, Thomas 166
Batham Gate Roman road 136, **230–1**
Bawd Stone (Staffs) 168, **168, 234–5**
Beauchief Abbey (Yorks) 51, 53, **53**
Beeley (Derbys) 37, 47, 208, 209, **224–5, 242–3**
Beeley Hilltop (Derbys) 193, 208, **238–9**
Beeley Moor (Derbys) 113, **162**, 162, **228–9**
Beeley Warren (Derbys) 159, **162**
Big Moor (Derbys)
  location **234–5, 240–1**
  military sites 197
  prehistoric sites 159, 160, **161**, 164, **166**, 171
Biggin (Derbys) 17, 48, **49**, 52, 70, 199, **224–5, 240–1, 242–3**
Biggin Grange (Derbys) 52, 181,

181, **226–7**
Birchills (Derbys) 24, 208, **224–5**
Birchover (Derbys) 42, 125, 171, **224–5**, **228–9**, **242–3**
Black Marble 118, 121, **228–9**
Blackwell (Derbys) 42, 52, **224–5**, **242–3**
Blackwell Hall Farm (Derbys) 179, **179**
Bleaklow (Derbys) 9, 26, 155, 186, **222–3**, **224–5**
Blore (Staffs) 34, 50, 63, 189, **224–5**, **226–7**, **238–9**
Blue John Mine (Derbys) 93, **228–9**
bole hearths 114, 115
Bole Hill Quarry (Derbys) 125, 146–7, **147**, 196, **230–1**, **240–1**
Bollington (Cheshire) 149, 150, **232–3**
Bonsall (Derbys) 40, 62, 82, 83, 210, **224–5**, **226–7**, **242–3**
Bonsall Lees (Derbys) 103–4, **104**, **228–9**
Booth, James **194**
Boothman, Thomas 120
Booths of Edale (Derbys) 23, 220, **220**
Bottoms Reservoir (Derbys) 154
Boulton and Watt engine designers 98–9, **99**
boundaries, local 6
Bradbourne Brook 34, 35, **35**
Bradbourne (Derbys) 34, 85, 184, 209, **209**, **224–5**, **226–7**, **236–7**, **242–3**
Bradfield (Yorks) 27, 39, 219, **224–5**, **226–7**, **242–3**
Bradford Dale 42
Bradford, River **223**
Bradwell (Derbys)
　field systems 21, 22, 62, 207
　limestone kilns 118, 119
　location **224–5**, **226–7**, **228–9**, **242–3**
　mines 207
　settlement 42, 204, **206**, 207
Bradwell Moor (Derbys) 73, 103, **103**
Bronze Age sites
　Big Moor 159, 160
　caves 172
　funerary rights 167–8
　Gardom's Edge 160
　hillforts 173, 176
　mines 104
　natural places, revered 168, **168**
　rock art 171
　round barrows 166–7, **166**, **196**, 201
　stone circles 164, **164**
Broomhead Reservoir (Yorks) 154
Brough (Derbys) 22, 115, **115**, 136, **137**, 177, 206, **228–9**

Brown Edge (Yorks) 125, **228–9**
Brown, Lancelot 'Capability' 65, **66**, 68, 69, 139, **185**, 188, **189**, 190
Brushfield (Derbys) 50, 71, **224–5**, **226–7**
Bubnell (Derbys) 24, **24**, 208, **224–5**, **242–3**
Bugsworth and Bugsworth Basin (Derbys) 118, 119, 120, **134**, 144, **228–9**, **230–1**
Bull Ring henge/stone circle (Derbys) 163, **234–5**
Bullbridge (Derbys) 119, 134, **228–9**
Bunsal Cob (Derbys) 144
Burbage Brook valley 40, 117, **228–9**
Burbage Colliery (Derbys) 146, 148, **148**, **230–1**
Burbage (Derbys) 14, 17, **111**, 112, **135**, **224–5**, **240–1**
Burbage Moor (Derbys) 197, **197**, **240–1**
burhs, Anglo-Saxon 47, **174**, 182
Burr Tor hillfort (Derbys) 176
Burton Abbey (Staffs) 35
Burton Closes, Bakewell (Derbys) **55**, 56, **56**, 193, **238–9**
Burton (Derbys) 50, **55**, 64, **64**, **224–5**
Butterley Gangroad (Derbys) 134, 144
Butterton (Staffs) 30, 32, 33, **224–5**, **242–3**
Buxton (Derbys)
　collieries 111–12, **111**, 148, **148**
　exclusion from National Park 195
　First and Second World Wars **196**, 197, **197**, 199, 200–1, **200**, **201**
　Grin Hill kiln 88, 118, 120, **120**
　location **224–5**, **230–1**, **238–9**, **242–3**
　manorial centre and market 42, 211
　picturesque spa town 186, 194
　quarries 118, 119–20, 129, **129**, 195
　railways and tramways 134, 144–5, 148, 148, 195
　reservoirs 155
　Roman period 136, 177
　settlement 14, 211
　topographical zone, relationship to 42
　turnpike road 139, 140, **140**
　urbanisation 17, 54, 55, 56
Buxton Tunnel (Derbys) 144, **230–1**

C

cairns, prehistoric **29**, **30**, **78**, **132**, 157, 158–9, 160, **160**, 161, 162, **162**, 171
calcite mines 5, 95
Caldon Canal 115, 119, **230–1**
Caldon Low (Staffs) 118, 119, 129, **228–9**
Callow (Derbys) 34, **224–5**
Calton Lees (Derbys) 208, **208**
Calton Pasture (Derbys) 9, 63, 69, **69**, 190, 191, **222–3**, **226–7**
Calton (Staffs) 43, **224–5**, **242–3**
Calver (Derbys) 118, 151, **205**, **224–5**, **228–9**, **232–3**, **242–3**
canals 118, 119, 134, **134**, 144, **145**, 152, **154**, **230–1**
canals, underground 107, **107**, 112
Carl Wark (Derbys) 124–5, 176, **176**, 197, **228–9**
Carsington (Derbys) 34, 85, 136, 177, **224–5**, **226–7**, **242–3**
Carsington Pasture (Derbys) 63, 75, **75**, 104, 136, 181, **226–7**, **228–9**, **236–7**
Carsington Water (Derbys) 155, 156
Carter's Mill (Derbys) 76
Castern (Staffs) 50, **224–5**
Castle Naze hillfort (Derbys) 176
Castle Ring hillfort (Derbys) 176
castles, medieval
　Bakewell **55**, 56
　Bradford 27
　Castleton 36, 42, 45, 182, **182**, 187, **206**, 207
　development of 182
　Hathersage 22
　Hope 22, 41, 182, 207
　locations **174**, **236–7**
　Pilsbury 18, **18**, 182, 217
Castleton Commons (Derbys) 71, 72, **72**, **226–7**
Castleton (Derbys)
　caves 172
　coffin road 220
　field systems 21, 22, 62–3
　grazing land 207
　location **224–5**, **226–7**, **236–7**, **238–9**, **242–3**
　manorial centre and market 21, 42, 45, 204, 206–7, **206**
　mines and quarries 93, 96, 107, **107**, 129, **206**, 207
　Peveril Castle 36, 42, 45, **182**, 182, 187, **206**, 207
　picturesque 194
　topographical zone, relationship to 42
　view from Winnats Pass **22**
Caudwell's Mill (Derbys) 150, **232–3**

Cauldon (Staffs) 30, 195, **224–5**, **238–9**
Cavendish family *see* Devonshire, Earls/Dukes of
Cavendish, Sir William 192
caves
　mines in 95, 96, **96**, 105–6, **105**, **106**, 107, **107**
　prehistoric use of 172, **173**, **234–5**
Chapel en le Frith (Derbys)
　enclosure of common 72
　location **224–5**, **232–3**, **242–3**
　manorial centre and market 39, 42, 45, 187
　mills 151
　railways and tramways 144
　topographical zone, relationship to 42
　urbanisation 54, 56, 219
chapels, non-conformist 183
charcoal production/use 95, 114, 115, 116, 117, **117**, 188
Chatsworth Estate (Derbys)
　Chatsworth Park Colliery 113
　deer park 50, 63, 71, 188, **188**
　field systems 63, 65, **66**, 68–9, **69**, 85
　grange 53
　hedges 65, **66**
　House 116, 119, 185, **185**, 192, 193, 194
　incorporation of surrounding lands 24, 190–1, 208, **208**
　landscape park 21, 63, 65, 188, **188**, **189**, 190–1, **190**
　location **224–5**, **226–7**, **238–9**, **242–3**
　moorlands 78, **142**, 194
　prehistoric sites 162, **162**, **172**
　routeways, roads and drives 136, 138–9, **138**
　Salisbury Lawn **185**
　sheepwalk 63
　water supply and fountains 152
　; *see also* Edensor (Derbys)
Chee Tor (Derbys) 178, **178**, 179, **179**, **236–7**
Chelmorton (Derbys) 15, 42, **43**, 62, 72, **224–5**, **226–7**, **242–3**
chert **85**, 121–2, **122**, 158, **228–9**
Chester, Earls of 187
Chester Road Mill (Cheshire) 150
Chunal (Derbys) 43, **224–5**
Churchdale Hall (Derbys) 193, **238–9**
churches
　Anglo-Saxon 19, 21, 47, 55–6, 184, 209
　medieval 19, 27, **34**, 36, 56, 183, **183**, **236–7**
citizen-archaeology/history 221

Clarence Mill (Cheshire) 150
Clayton Mine (Staffs) **96**, 100, 108, **108**, **109**
Clemonseats (Derbys) 18, **18**
climate 5, 11
Cluther Rocks (Derbys) 123, **228–9**
coal mines
  eastern moors 113–14, **113**, **114**
  locations **228–9**
  overview 94–5, 110
  Ringinglow Seam 110, 111, 112, 113
  steam engines/engine houses **110**, 112
  tramways 112, 134, 144, 146, 148, **148**
  western moors 110–12, **110**, **111**, 148, **148**, 217, **218**, **219**
  Yard Seam 110, 111, 112
Coalpit Rake (Derbys) **95**, 96, **228–9**
coffin roads 220
Cold Eaton (Derbys) 35, **35**, **224–5**
Combermere Abbey (Cheshire) 18, 20, 35
Combs Moss (Derbys) 30, **31**, 32, 110, 112, 123, **224–5**, **228–9**
Combs Reservoir (Derbys) **154**
commons
  Carsington Pasture 75, **75**
  disputes over 211–12
  monastic granges 18, **18**, 70
  routeways 131, 132, **132**, 136, 138–9, **138**
  Thorpe Pasture 75, **75**
commons, enclosure of
  Bakewell 64, **64**, **65**
  Castleton **72**, 73–4
  dew ponds 86, **87**
  grouse moors 186
  new farmsteads on 13, 54, 216, **217**
  Parliamentary and private 70–2, **72**
  rectangular fields 13, 14, 15, 58, **59**, **62**, 63, **71**
  routeways 136
  community knowledge 221
Conksbury (Derbys) 50, **224–5**
Coplow Dale (Derbys) **40**, **224–5**
copper mines 5, **91**, 93, 104, 115, 214, **228–9**; see also Ecton Hill mines (Staffs)
Cork Stone (Derbys) 168, **234–5**
Cotesfield Grange (Derbys) 18, **18**, 53
county boundaries **2**, 11
Cow Low (Derbys) 179, **236–7**
Cracken Edge (Derbys) 125, 128, **128**, 146, **146**, **228–9**, **230–1**

Cracknowl Pasture (Derbys) 63, **226–7**
Cratcliffe Rocks hillfort (Derbys) 164, 176
Cressbrook Dale (Derbys) **3**, **222–3**
Cressbrook Mill (Derbys) **150**, 151, **232–3**
Cresswell Crags (Derbys/Notts) 172
Crich (Derbys) 115, 119, 134, 144, **228–9**
Cromford and High Peak Railway 112, 120, 129, 134, **135**, 144–5, **145**, **200**, **230–1**
Cromford Canal 119, 134, 144, **145**, 152, **230–1**
Cromford (Derbys) 21, 134, 149, 152, **224–5**, **228–9**, **242–3**
Cromford Mill (Derbys) 150, 152, **232–3**
Cromford Sough (Derbys) 92, **97**, 152, **228–9**
Cronkston Grange (Derbys) 18, **18**, 53, 70, **226–7**
Cronkston Lodge (Derbys) 54, **54**, **224–5**
Crookhill Grange (Derbys) 27, **28**, 53
crosses, Anglo-Saxon 19, 21, 47, 50, 177, 184, **184**, 209
Crow Chin barrows (Yorks) 171, **234–5**
cupola furnaces 93, 115, **115**
Curbar (Derbys) 47, **205**, 208, **224–5**, **242–3**
Curbar Edge (Derbys) 124, **205**, **228–9**
Curbar Gap (Derbys) **205**

D

Dale Dike Reservoir (Yorks) 154
Dam Cliff (Derbys) 179, **236–7**
Damflask Reservoir (Yorks) 154
Dane, River/Valley 10, 20, 30, 213, 214, **214**, 223; see also specific locations
Danebower Colliery (Derbys) 110, **110**, **228–9**
Dark Peak **7**, 9, 26–7, 62; see also remote places cultural landscape zone; Valley Heartlands cultural landscape zone; specific locations
Darley Bridge (Derbys) 93, 97, 100, 139
Darley Churchtown (Derbys) 21, 40, 42, 50, **224–5**
Darley Dale (Derbys) 56, **224–5**
Darley (Derbys) 27, 184, 204, **236–7**, **242–3**

De Ferrers family 16, 126, 187, 216–17
Deep Dale (Derbys) 180, **236–7**
deer parks 25, **25**, 63, **69**, 187, 188–9, **188**, **189**, 208, **208**, **238–9**
Defoe, Daniel 124, 194
Dene Quarry (Derbys) 129, **228–9**
Derby, Earls of 16, 126, 187, 216–17
Derbyshire Bridge (Derbys) 156, **156**
Derwent Moors **78**
Derwent Reservoir (Derbys) 146, 147, 154, 155, **155**, **224–5**
Derwent, River/Valley
  agriculture 63
  charcoal production 117, **117**
  Dark Peak 9, 26, 27–8, **28**
  location **223**
  mills 150, 151, 152
  mines and quarries 93, 95, **95**, 97, **97**, **124**
  parks 189; see also Chatsworth Estate (Derbys)
  prehistoric sites 158–9, **164**
  railways and tramways 134, 146, 147, **230–1**
  reservoirs 146, **149**, 154, 155, **155**, **224–5**
  Romano-British sites 177–8
  settlement 39, 42, 53, 187, 204, **205**, 208–9, **208**, **209**, 219
  shale valley 9, 21
  smelting industries 114, 115, **228–9**
  Upper Derwent 27–8, **28**
  walls and hedges 65
  white coal kilns 116, **116**
  World Heritage Site 1
  ; see also Hope Valley (Derbys); specific locations
Devonshire, Earls/Dukes of
  Bubnell 24
  grouse moors 71, 77, 159
  Hartington 16–17
  lime kilns 88, 120, 121
  mines and quarries 93, 111, 113, 115, 126, 148
  Peak tourism 194
  Wetton 45
  woodland plantations 186
  ; see also Chatsworth Estate (Derbys); Edensor (Derbys)
dew ponds 13, 86–7, **87**, **226–7**
Dieulacres Abbey (Staffs) 51, 187
Dirtlow Rake (Derbys) 103, **103**, **206**, **228–9**
Dobb Edge (Derbys) **172**
Doctor's Gate road 136, **230–1**
Domesday Book 15, 16, 20, 35, 40, 150, 211, 216
Dove Dale 180, 186, 194, **195**, **238–9**

Dove Holes (Derbys) 112, 118, 119, 129, **129**, 144, 163, **224–5**, **228–9**
Dove Holes Tunnel 134, **230–1**
Dove, River/Valley
  caves 172
  settlement 204, 210, 213, 214–15, 216–17, **216**, **217**
  South-West Peak 10, 30, 32, **32**
  walls and hedges 65
  White Peak 6, 13, 17
Dowlow (Derbys) 129, **228–9**
dual economies 82, 93, 217
Duffield Frith (Derbys) 34, 186, 187, 188
Dunnington Mines (Staffs) 104, **228–9**

E

Earl Rake (Derbys) **206**
Earl Sterndale (Derbys) 17, **242–3**
Ecclesbourne, River 34, **223**
Ecton Hill mines (Staffs)
  cupola furnaces 115
  deep workings **99**
  gunpowder work 92
  importance 93, 214
  location **228–9**, **242–3**
  pipe workings **96**
  prehistoric workings 93, 104
  steam engines 98–100, **99**, 108, **108**, **109**
  wealth 93
Ecton Hill Park (Staffs) 189, **238–9**
Edale (Derbys)
  Booths 23, 220, **220**
  historic landscape character assessment **249**
  Hope manor 207
  location **222–3**, **226–7**, **232–3**
  peat cutting 220, **220**
  searchlight battery earthworks 199, **199**, **240–1**
  settlement 21, **23**, 23, 187, 219
  shale valley 9, 21
  walls and hedges 65, **67**
Edensor (Derbys) 21
  church 183
  field barns 83
  before landscape park 69, **69**
  after landscape park 190–1, **191**
  location **224–5**, **226–7**, **232–3**, **242–3**
  mill 150
  rabbit warren 63
  settlement 42
  vernacular buildings 37
  ; see also Chatsworth Estate (Derbys)

Elderbush Cave (Derbys) 172
Eldon Hill (Derbys) 129, **129**,
  228–9
Elkstone, Upper and Lower
  (Staffs) 32, 33, **33**, **62**, 63,
  88, **224–5**, **226–7**
Elton (Derbys) 43, 62, 104, **224–
  5**, **226–7**, **242–3**
enclosure *see* commons, enclosure
  of
Errwood Hall (Derbys) 156, **156**
Errwood Reservoir (Derbys) 155,
  156, **156**
Etherow, River 9, 154, 186, 219,
  223; *see also* Longdendale
Ewden Height (Yorks) 197,
  240–1
Eyam (Derbys) 40, 45, 184,
  224–5, **226–7**, **242–3**
Eyam Hall (Derbys) 193, **238–9**
Eyam Moor (Derbys) 9, 27, 125,
  222–3, **224–5**, **228–9**

F

Fairbairn, John 101
Fairfield (Derbys) 14, 42, 211,
  224–5, **242–3**
Fallinge Edge (Derbys) 123, 208,
  228–9
Farey, John 87, 88, 90, 117
Fawfieldhead (Staffs) 63, 186,
  214, **226–7**
Fenny Bentley (Derbys) 34, 36,
  192, **224–5**, **238–9**, **242–3**
Fernilee Gunpowder Works
  (Derbys) 156, **156**
Fernilee Reservoir (Derbys) 155,
  156, **156**
field barns 17, 64, 81–3, **81**, **82**,
  87, 99, **226–7**
field walls 65, 67–8, **67**, 72, 79,
  226–7
Fiennes, Celia 132, 194
Fin Cop hillfort (Derbys) **14**, 173,
  176
fireclay 95
Five Wells Neolithic tomb and
  barrows (Derbys) 165, **166**,
  234–5
Fivewells Farms (Derbys) 54,
  224–5
Flagg (Derbys) **5**, 15, 45, **58**, 62,
  222–3, **224–5**, **226–7**,
  242–3
Flash (Staffs) 217, **218**
flats, mining 92, 95, 96
Flockton tunnel (Yorks) 144
fluorspar mines 5, 93, 95, 103,
  105, **105**
Foolow (Derbys) **8**, 40, 47, **222–
  3**, **224–5**, **226–7**, **242–3**
forests, hunting 185, 186–7, **187**,
  213

Fox Hole Cave (Derbys) 172,
  234–5
Frank i' th' Rocks Cave
  (Derbys) 172, **173**, **234–5**
Friden (Derbys) 145, **230–1**
fringes of the Peak 10
Froggatt (Derbys) 208, 209,
  224–5, **242–3**
Froggatt Wood (Derbys) 115,
  116, **116**, **228–9**
Froghall (Staffs) 115, 119, **228–
  9**, **230–1**

G

ganister 91, 95
gardens 185, 193
Gardom's Edge (Derbys)
  20th-century wartime use 197
  location **224–5**, **226–7**, **228–
    9**, **234–5**, **240–1**
  millstone production 124, **124**
  prehistoric period 158, 159,
    160, **160**, 171, 176
  Romano-British period 79
  use through time 29–30, **29**,
    30
Gateham Grange (Derbys) 20, **81**,
  226–7
gateposts and gateways 80, **80**,
  81
geology and topography
  Dark Peak 9, **9**, **10**
  fringes 10
  impact on people 3, **3**, **4**, 5
  Shale Valleys 9
  South-West Peak 10
  Southern Valleys 10
  variety 3
  White Peak 6, **8**
Gib Hill barrow (Derbys) 165,
  170
Gibbet Moor (Derbys) 159, 162,
  162, 197, **240–1**
global warming 5, 11
Glossop (Derbys)
  Ardotalia Roman fort 136, 177
  exclusion from National
    Park 195
  farmsteads 187
  location 224–5, 232–3, 242–3
  manorial centre and market 42
  mill 151
  urbanisation 27, 56, 219
  water supply 149, 155
Golden Carr Road **131**, **230–1**
Goldsitch Moss Colliery
  (Staffs) 110, 217, 219,
  228–9
Goyt, River/Valley 10, 17, 30, 39,
  144, 155, **156**, **223**, **226–7**
Goyt's Moss (Derbys) 30, 32, 110,
  111–12, **111**, 148, 156, **218**,
  224–5, **228–9**

Goytsbridge (Derbys) 156, **156**
Gradbach (Staffs) 95, 117,
  228–9
Grange Mill (Derbys) 129,
  228–9
granges, monastic 18, **18**, 27, 50,
  51–3, **51**, **52**, **53**, 70
grazing 11–12, **12**, 73, 74
Great Hucklow (Derbys) **224–5**,
  242–3
Great Longstone (Derbys) 37,
  193, **224–5**, **238–9**, **242–3**
Green Low barrow (Derbys) 165,
  234–5
Greens Mill (Derbys) 151, **232–3**
Grey Ditch, Hope Valley
  (Derbys) **206**, 207
Grey Marble 121, **228–9**
Grimshawe, Samuel 156
Grin Hill (Derbys) 88, 112, 118,
  119, 120, **120**, 129, 194,
  226–7, **228–9**
Grindleford (Derbys) 56, **224–5**
Grindlow (Derbys) 52, **224–5**,
  242–3
Grindon (Staffs) 30, 32, 47, **224–
  5**, **242–3**
guide stoups/posts 130, 132,
  133, 138, 142, **142**, **230–1**

H

Haddon Hall (Derbys) 25, **25**, 36,
  191, 192, **224–5**, **238–9**
Haddon Park (Derbys) 25, **25**, 63,
  189, **226–7**, **238–9**
Hall Dale Quarry (Derbys) 129,
  228–9
halls/houses 25, **25**, 36, 64, 185,
  192–3, **192**, **193**, **194**, **238–
  9**; *see also* Chatsworth Estate
  (Derbys)
Hamps, River/Valley 10, 30, **39**,
  65, 213, **223**
Handley Bottom (Derbys) **205**,
  242–3
Hanson Grange (Staffs) 35, **35**,
  50, 51, **224–5**
Harewood Grange (Derbys) 51,
  53, 208, **208**
Harland Edge (Derbys) **142**,
  230–1
Harpur Hill (Derbys)
  Hoffmann Kiln 120, 145
  location **228–9**, **230–1**,
    240–1
  munitions storage 196, **196**,
    199, 200–1, **200**, **201**
  quarries 119, 129
  railways 144, 145
Harthill deer park (Derbys) 50,
  63, 189, **226–7**, **238–9**
Harthill Moor (Derbys) 9, 164,
  176, **222–3**, **224–5**

Hartington (Derbys)
  location **224–5**, **226–7**,
    236–7, **242–3**
  market centre 14, 16, 42, 45,
    211, 213, 216
  monastic granges 70
  urbanisation 54
Hartington Frith (Derbys) 186,
  187, 216, **216**
Hartington Hall (Derbys) 193,
  238–9
Hartington parish
  (Derbys) 16–17, **16**, **17**, 183,
    216–17, **216**, **217**
Hassop (Derbys) 24, **24**, 63, 208,
  224–5, **238–9**, **242–3**
Hassop Hall (Derbys) 191, 193,
  208
Hathersage (Derbys) 21, 22, 23,
  42, 47, 124, 125, 204, **224–5**,
  242–3
Hayfield (Derbys) 187, 189, 219,
  220, **238–9**, **242–3**
Haylee Farm (Derbys) **61**, **226–7**
Hazard Mine (Derbys) 103, **103**,
  228–9
Hazlebadge (Derbys) 49, **224–5**
Hazlebadge Hall (Derbys) 192,
  238–9
Hazleford Hall (Derbys) 193,
  193, **238–9**
Heathcote (Derbys) 17, 86, **224–
  5**, **226–7**, **242–3**
Heathy Lea Brook (Derbys) 113,
  141, **141**
hedges 65–8, **66**, **67**, 190, 208
Heights of Abraham, Matlock Bath
  (Derbys) 96, 105, **105**
Hen Cloud (Staffs) 168, **168**,
  169, **234–5**
henges *see* stone circles and
  henges
High Mere (Derbys) 86
High Peak Trail (Derbys) 144,
  145
High Rake Mine (Derbys) 100,
  100, 101, 103, **228–9**
Highlow Bank (Derbys) **132**,
  230–1
Highlow Hall (Derbys) **36**, 193,
  224–5, **238–9**
Hillcar Sough (Derbys) 97, **97**,
  228–9
hillforts **14**, 173, **174**, **175**, 176,
  176, **206–7**
Hillhead (Derbys) 129, **228–9**
Hindlow (Derbys) 129, **228–9**
historic landscape character
  assessment 1–3, 5–6, **5**, 244,
    245, **246**, **247**, **248**, **249**,
    250–1, **251**
Hob Hurst House (Derbys) 163,
  234–5
Hognaston (Derbys) 34, **224–5**,
  242–3

Hollandtwine Mine (Derbys) 103, **103**
hollow-ways 130, 132–3, **132**, 136, **137**, 138–9, **138**, **141**, 220, **220**
Holme and Holme Hall (Derbys) 50, **55**, 56, 64, **64**, 193, **224–5**, **238–9**
Holme Bank Chert Mine (Derbys) 122, **122**
Holme Hall Mine (Derbys) 122, **122**
Holt House (Derbys) 193, **238–9**
Hope (Derbys)
 castle 22, 182, 206, **206**, 207
 church 184
 forest 187
 location **224–5**, **226–7**, **232–3**, **236–7**, **242–3**
 manorial centre and market 41, 45, 187, 204, 206–7, **206**, 213
 mill 150
Hope quarry and cement works 118, 129, **228–9**
Hope Valley (Derbys) **22**
 agriculture 62, 73
 Brough Cupola **115**
 community landscape zone **203**, 204, **204**, 206–7, **206**, **207**
 development 56
 hedges 65
 historic landscape character assessment **249**
 location **222–3**
 Romano-British sites 136, **137**, 177
 settlement 22–3, 23, 206–7, **206**, **207**, 219
 shale valley 9, **9**, 21
 urbanisation 56
 ; see also Castleton (Derbys); Mam Tor hillfort (Derbys)
Hope Woodlands (Derbys) 27–8, 207
Hopton (Derbys) 34, **224–5**, **242–3**
Hopton Hall (Derbys) 34
Hoptonwood (Derbys) 144
Horse Lane, Monyash **137**, **230–1**
Houndkirk Moor (Yorks) 196, **240–1**
How Grove (Derbys) 103, **228–9**
Howardtown Mill (Derbys) 151
Howden Reservoir (Derbys) 27, 125, 146, 154, 155, **224–5**
Hulme End (Staffs) 20, 134, 230–1
human – environment interaction 3, 5, 10–11
Hurdlow (Derbys) 17, 18, **18**, 43, 144, **230–1**
Hurst Reservoir (Derbys) 155

I

Ible (Derbys) 62, **224–5**, **226–7**, **242–3**
Ilam (Staffs) 34, 34, 224–5, 242–3
Industrial Revolution 56, 118, 133, 150, 152
Iron Age sites 22, 159, 160, **160**, 164, 172, 173, **173**, 176, **176**, 178; see also Romano-British sites
Ivonbrook Grange (Derbys) 51

J

Jessop, William 152

K

Kent, William **185**, 190
Kinder Reservoir (Derbys) 155
Kinder, River 219, **223**
Kinder Scout (Derbys) 9, 26, 155, **164**, 176, 186, 195, **222–3**, **224–5**
King Edward of Wessex 182
King Sterndale (Derbys) 48, **49**, **224–5**
Kirk Ireton (Derbys) 34, **224–5**, **242–3**
Knar (Cheshire) **214**
Kniveton (Derbys) 34, **224–5**, **242–3**

L

Ladybower Reservoir (Derbys) 27, **149**, 155
Lamaload Reservoir (Cheshire) 155
landscape parks 21, 63, 188, **189**, 190–1, **190**, **191**, **238–9**
landscapes, Peak
 Dark Peak 26–30, **26**, **28**, **29**, **30**
 Shale Valleys 21–5, **21**, **22**, **23**, **24**, **25**
 South-West Peak 30, **31**, 32–3, **32**, **33**
 Southern Valleys 34–5, **34**, **35**
 White Peak 13–20, **14**, **15**, **16**, **17**, **18**, **19**, **20**
Langsett Reservoir (Yorks) 154, 196, **240–1**
Lathkill Dale (Derbys) 76, **76**, 100, 170, **212**, **226–7**
Lathkill Head Cave (Derbys) 212
Lathkill, River 6, 13, 21, 76, 86, 189, 210, **223**
Lawrence Field (Derbys) 40, **224–5**

lead mines
 archaeological interest 96
 distribution 5, **91**
 locations **228–9**
 loss of 103–4, **103**
 orefield **94**
 overview 92–3
 Romano-British 177, **180**
 small mines 82
 Southern Valleys 34
 terminology 95
 White Peak 6, **8**
 ; see also mines; specific Mine
Leawood pumping engine (Cromford Canal) 144, **145**, **230–1**
Leek Frith (Staffs) 186, **187**, 187, 213
Leoni, Giacomo **192**
Liffs, The (Derbys) 181, **181**, **236–7**
limekilns
 commercial kilns 118–21, **119**, **120**, **121**, 194
 field kilns 88–90, **89**, **90**
 locations **226–7**, **228–9**
limestone quarries 76, 118–21, **120**, **121**, 129, **129**, 145, 146, 195, **228–9**; see also limekilns
Linch Clough (Derbys) 114, **228–9**
Little Hucklow (Derbys) **40**, 48, **224–5**, **242–3**
Little Longstone (Derbys) 42, **224–5**, **242–3**
Little Park (Derbys) 25, **25**, 189
Litton (Derbys) 48, **49**, 57, 62, 70, 213, 213, **224–5**, **226–7**, **232–3**, **242–3**
Litton Edge (Derbys) **90**, **226–7**
Litton Mill (Derbys) 151
Lodge Moor (Yorks) 115
Long Hill road **140**
Long Low barrow (Staffs) 165, **234–5**
Longdendale 9, 26, 39, 125, 152, 187, 219, **224–5**
Longnor (Staffs) 32, **32**, 42, **62**, 125, 213, 214–15, **215**, **224–5**, **242–3**
Longshaw Estate (Derbys) 78, 186, **226–7**
Longstone Edge (Derbys) **12**, 73, 129, **222–3**
Longstone Hall (Derbys) 37, **238–9**
Lower Green Farm (Staffs) **39**, **224–5**
Loxley, River 154
Ludwell (Derbys) 216, **242–3**
Lutodarum Roman centre (Derbys) 177, **236–7**
Lyme Hall and Park (Cheshire) 32, 63, 189, 191, 192, **192**, **224–5**, **226–7**, **238–9**

M

Macclesfield (Cheshire) 30, 56, 149, 150, 155, **232–3**
Macclesfield Forest (Cheshire) 186, 187, **187**, 213
Magpie Mine (Derbys) 100, 101–2, **101**, **102**, **228–9**
Magpie Sough (Derbys) 97, **228–9**
Mam Tor hillfort (Derbys) 22, 173, **175**, 176, 206–7, **206**
Mandale Mine (Derbys) 100, **228–9**
Manifold, River/Valley
 caves 172
 location **223**
 railway 134
 South-West Peak 10, 30, 33, 65, **99**, 213, 214
 Southern Valleys 34
 White Peak 6, 13, 210
'manor,' defining 6
manorial centres and markets 21, 34, 41–2, **41**; see also specific town/village
map of Peak District **2**
Mappleton (Derbys) 34, **224–5**, **242–3**
Marple (Greater Manchester) 56, 118, 119, **228–9**
Masson Mill (Derbys) 150, 152, **232–3**
Matlock Bank (Derbys) 54, 55, **224–5**
Matlock Bath (Derbys)
 location **224–5**, **238–9**
 mines **95**, 96, 104, 105, **105**
 railway 134, 194–5
 spa town 54, 55, 186
Matlock Churchtown (Derbys) 21, 41, **224–5**
Matlock (Derbys)
 Bailey's Tump 198, **198**
 limestone gorge 21
 location **230–1**, **238–9**, **242–3**
 manorial centre and market 204
 quarries 129
 tors 194
 urbanisation 56
Meadow Place Grange (Derbys) 53
meadows, hay 73, **74**
Meerbrook Sough (Derbys) 97, **228–9**
meres 13, **49**, **74**, 86, 211, **226–7**
Merevale Abbey (Warks) 18
Metcalf, John 140
Middle Hills (Derbys) 30, **224–5**
Middleton by Wirksworth (Derbys) 129, 210, **211**, **224–5**, **228–9**, **242–3**

Middleton by Youlgreave
(Derbys) 166, **224–5**,
242–3
Midhope Armoured Vehicle Firing
Range (Yorks) 197
Midhope Reservoir (Yorks) 196,
240–1
milestones/mileposts 130, 142–3,
143
Millclose Mine (Derbys) 93,
228–9
Millers Dale (Derbys) 129,
228–9
mills **55**, 56, 76, 149, 150–2,
150, **151**, 219, **232–3**
Millstone Edge (Derbys) 124,
125, **228–9**
Millstone Grit sandstone 9, 10,
123–5, **123**
millstone production 123–5, **123**,
124, **228–9**
mines
archaeological remains 95
Ashford Black Marble 118, 121
barytes 5, 95, 103, 151
calcite 5, 95
canals, underground 107, **107**,
112
chert 121–2, **122**
coal see coal mines
compressed-air drilling
engines 93, 108, **108**, **109**
conservation concerns 103–4,
103, **104**
copper see copper mines
distribution **91**
drainage soughs 76, 86, 92, **97**,
97, 102, 112, 113, 152
fireclay 95
firesetting 92, 106
flats 92, 95, 96
fluorspar 5, 93, 95, 103, 105,
105
ganister 91, 95
gin circles **100**, 101–2, 103,
103
Grey Marble 121
gunpowder work 92–3
lead see lead mines
locations **228–9**
miner-farmers 82, 93
orefield **94**
overview 91
pipe workings 93, 95, 96, **96**,
104, **212**
prehistoric 104–6, **105**
pumping engines see pumping
engines
rakes **8**, **92**, 95, **95**, 96, 100,
100, 103, **103**, **206**
scrins 95
terminology 95
winding engines 93, **93**, 98–9,
99, 100, 101, 102, 108, **108**,
110, **111**, 148

woodpecker work 105, **105**
zinc 93, 214
; see also smelting industries;
specific mines
Minninglow (Derbys) 136, 144,
145, 165, **186**, 221, **230–1**,
234–5, **238–9**
Mixon (Staffs) 88, 214, **226–7**,
242–3
Monsal Viaduct (Derbys) 134
Monyash (Derbys) **212**
commons 212
field systems 62
historic landscape character
assessment **5**
Horse Road **137**
location **224–5**, **226–7**,
242–3
market town 40, 45, 210, 211
meres 86, 211
topographical zone, relationship
to 42
village green 48, **49**, 211
moorlands
Dark Peak 9, **9**, **10**, 26–7, **26**
enclosure 62, 70–1, 77, **77**
grouse moors 58, 70, 71, 78,
78, 159, 186, **226–7**
peat cutting 217, 220, **220**
rambling 195
South-West Peak 30, **31**
travel networks see travel
networks
; see also specific Moor
Moritz, Carl Philipp 64
Morridge (Staffs) 30, **224–5**
Moscar (Derbys) 117, **228–9**
Moss Rake (Derbys) 103, **103**,
206, **228–9**
Mossy Lea Reservoir
(Derbys) 155
Mottram Tunnel 152
Mouldridge Grange (Derbys) 53,
70, **226–7**
Musden Grange (Derbys) 50, 51,
224–5

N

narrow-rig ploughing 83, 85
Narrowdale Hill (Staffs) **19**, 20
national park boundaries 195
natural places, revered 168, **168**,
169, **234–5**
Navio Roman fort and vicus
(Derbys) 136, 177, 206–7,
206, **236–7**
Needham Grange 17, 18, **18**,
52–3, 70, **226–7**
Neolithic sites
barrows and chambered
tombs **20**, 165–6, **166**, 167,
168, **186**
cairns 159

caves 172
rock art 171
stone circles and henges 163–4,
163, 170, **170**
Nestus Pipes (Derbys) 96, 105,
105, **228–9**
Nether Haddon (Derbys) 25, **25**,
47, 49–50, 63, 189, **226–7**
New Mills (Derbys) 30, 56, 149,
151, **151**, 152, 195, 219,
224–5, **232–3**, **242–3**
Newcomen, Thomas 98
Newton, George W 152
Newton Grange (Derbys) 35, **35**,
50, 51, **224–5**
Nine Ladies stone circle
(Derbys) 164, 165, **234–5**
Nine Stone Close stone circle
(Derbys) 164, 168, **234–5**
Noe, River/Valley 21, 23, 45, 151,
206, 219, **223**
North Lees (Derbys) 116, **116**,
177, 178, 192, **228–9**,
238–9

O

Oaking Clough coal mines
(Yorks) **113**, **228–9**
Odin Mine (Derbys) 96, **206**,
228–9
Offerton (Derbys) 23, 49, 50,
224–5, **242–3**
Offerton Hall (Derbys) 23, 50,
193, **204**, **238–9**
Offerton Moor (Derbys) 9, 27,
222–3, **224–5**
Old Ash Mine (Derbys) 96, 106,
106, **228–9**
Old Grove Mine (Derbys) **60**
Old Millclose Mine (Derbys) 96,
100, **228–9**
Old Woman's Stone (Derbys) 164,
234–5
Ollersett Moor coal mines
(Derbys) 110, 112, **228–9**
Ollersett Moor Reservoir
(Derbys) 152
One Ash (Derbys) 50, **51**, 52,
184, 211–12, **224–5**, **236–7**
Onecote Grange (Staffs) 52
Onecote (Staffs) 63, **226–7**
Orchard Common Colliery
(Staffs) 110, 111, **228–9**
ore hearths 114, 115, 116, **116**
Organ Ground Farm (Derbys) 54,
224–5
Outram, Benjamin 144, 152
Over Haddon (Derbys) 76, **224–5**, **242–3**
Owler Bar coal mines
(Derbys) 113, **228–9**
Oxlow Rake (Derbys) 103,
228–9

P

packhorse routes 117, 130, 136,
137
Padfield (Derbys) 43, **224–5**
Padley and Venables 125
Padley Wood (Derbys) 116,
228–9
Paine, James 150, 190, **194**
Palaeolithic sites 172
Paradise Mill (Cheshire) 150
'parish,' defining 6
parks see deer parks; landscape
parks
Parliamentary Enclosure
Awards 58, **59**, 60, 62–3, **62**,
64, **64**, 68, 70–1; see also
commons, enclosure of
Parsley Hay (Derbys) 18, 134,
230–1
Parsons House (Yorks) **4**, **222–3**
Parwich (Derbys)
church 183
field systems 34, 85
Hall 193
irregular settlement 41, 47
location **224–5**, **226–7**, **236–7**, **238–9**, **242–3**
manorial centre and market 34,
35, **35**
paths 47, 130–1, **131**; see also
hollow-ways
Paxton, Joseph **56**, 191, **191**, 193
Pea Low (Staffs) 20, 20, 165,
234–5
Peak Cavern (Derbys) 45, 172,
234–5
Peak Dale (Derbys) 118, 119,
129, **224–5**, **228–9**
Peak District Mines Historical
Society 103
Peak Forest Canal 119, **134**, 144,
152, **154**, **230–1**
Peak Forest (Derbys)
atypical settlement 40, 48, **48**,
210, **210**
field barn 82
field systems 63
heart of Royal Forest 187, **187**
limekilns 118, 119, 121, **121**
location **224–5**, **228–9**,
242–3
Peak Forest Tramway 119, 134,
144, **230–1**
Peak Tor (Derbys) 189, **238–9**
perspectives 10–12
picturesque, the 186, 194–5, **195**,
238–9
Pilsbury (Derbys)
castle **18**, 182, 217
dew pond **87**
field systems 17, **18**
location **226–7**, **236–7**,
242–3

settlement 216, 217
Pilsbury Grange (Derbys) 17, 18, **18**, 52, 70, **226–7**
Pilsley (Derbys) 24, **24**, 48, 208, **224–5**, **242–3**
Pin Dale (Derbys) **93**, 129, **228–9**
pipes (mine workings) 93, 95, 96, **96**, 104, **212**
Porter, River 154
prehistoric sites
  barrows and chambered tombs 20, **20**, 160, **161**, 165–7, **166**, 167–8, 170, 171, **196**, **234–5**
  cairns 30, **30**, **78**, 157, 158–9, 160, **160**, 162, **162**
  caves 172, **173**, **234–5**
  dating 159, 160
  distribution 167–8
  field systems 29, **29**
  hillforts **14**, 173, **174**, **175**, 176
  locations **234–5**
  meaning to prehistoric people 167–8
  mines 104–6, **105**
  modern reuse of **196**, 201
  modern tree plantations at 186, **186**
  natural places, revered 168, **168**, **169**, **234–5**
  place, assessment of 169
  pollen analysis 159
  preservation on grouse moors 78, **78**
  rock art 168, 171, **172**, **234–5**
  settlements and farmsteads 30, 158–9, **158**, 160, **160**, **161**
  standing stones 164, **234–5**
  stone circles and henges **10**, 158, 162, **162**, 163–5, **163**, **164**, 170, **170**, 171, **234–5**
  stone tools 158
  survival of 157–8, **157**, 159
  timber buildings 157–8
  understanding/ interpreting 160, 165, 169, 171
  walls 79
  ; see also specific site
Priestcliffe (Derbys) 15, 40, 73, **74**, **84**, 85, 212, **224–5**, **226–7**, **242–3**
Pugin, Augustus **56**
pumping engines 93, **93**, 97, 98, **98**, 99, **99**, 100, **100**, 101, 102, **102**, 108, **108**

Q

Quarnford (Staffs) 186, 189, 217
quarries
  Black Marble 118, 121
  chert **85**, 121–2, **122**, 158
  Grey Marble 121
  limestone see limestone quarries
  locations **228–9**, **238–9**
  modern 22, **23**, 129, **129**, 195
  overview 118
  railways and tramways 119–20, 128, **128**, 134, 144–7, **145**, **146**, **147**
  sandstone see sandstone quarries
  slate 37
  tufa 76
quicklime 88

R

rabbit warrens 25, 50, 63, **69**, **226–7**
railways and tramways
  coal mines 112, 134, 144, 146, 148, **148**
  development of 134, **135**
  locations **228–9**
  quarries 119–20, 128, **128**, 134, 144–7, **145**, **146**, **147**
  tourism, impact on 194–5
  trans-Peak 133–4
  ; see also specific railway/ tramway
Rainster Rocks (Derbys) **157**, 179, **236–7**
rakes **8**, **92**, 95, **95**, 96, 100, **100**, 103, **103**, **206**
Ramshaw Rocks (Staffs) **80**, **226–7**
Ramsley Reservoir (Derbys) 155
Redmires military training area (Yorks) 196
Redmires Reservoir (Yorks) 152, **240–1**
Redsoil Mine (Derbys) 101, **101**, 102
Reeve Edge (Derbys) 126–7, **126**, **127**, **228–9**
remote places cultural landscape zone 219–20, **220**
reservoirs 17, 27, 146, **149**, 152, **153**, 154–6, **154**, **155**, **156**
Revidge 30, **224–5**
Rhodeswood Reservoir (Derbys) 154
Ricklow Dale (Derbys) 121, **228–9**
ridge and furrow field systems 83, **84**, 85, **85**, **86**, **226–7**
Rivelin Reservoir (Yorks) 152
Roaches, The (Staffs) 30, 95, 110, 117, 168, **168**, **169**, **224–5**, **234–5**
road furniture 130, 142–3, **142**, **143**
roads
  coffin roads 220

linking settlements 131
locations **230–1**
modern 134, 139
passable roads 140–1, **140**, **141**
Romano-British 18, 130–1, 136, 177
straight roads 136, **137**
turnpike roads 139–43, **140**, **141**, **142**, **143**, **230–1**
Robertson, John **56**, **191**, 193
Robin Hood (Derbys) 29, 113, 141, **141**, **230–1**
Robin Hood's Stride (Derbys) 164, 168, **234–5**
Roche Abbey (Yorks) 212
rock art, prehistoric 168, 171, **172**, **234–5**
Rodknoll (Derbys) 63, **226–7**
Romano-British sites
  administrative centres **174**, 177
  caves 172, **173**
  dating 179
  farmsteads and hamlets 79, **84**, 85, **157**, 177–81, **178**, **179**, **180**, **181**
  field systems 179, **179**, **180**, **181**
  forts 22, **174**, 177, 206–7, **206**
  locations **230–1**, **236–7**
  mines 104
  overview 177
  roads 18, 130–1, 136, 177
  ; see also specific site
routeways see travel networks
Rowland (Derbys) **242–3**
Rowsley (Derbys) 25, 129, 134, 139, 150, 189, 195, **224–5**, **238–9**, **242–3**
Rowter Rocks (Derbys) 168, 171, **234–5**
Royal Forest of the Peak 14, 21, 27, 39, 40, 71, 74, 186–7, **187**
Roystone Grange (Derbys) 53, 70, 79, 178, 181, **226–7**, **236–7**
Rushup Edge (Derbys) **71**
Rutland, Dukes of 25, **25**, 76, 78, 155, 159, 186, 191, 192

S

sandstone quarries
  building stone 125–8, **127**, **128**
  locations **228–9**
  millstone production 123–5, **123**, **124**, 126
  railways and tramways 146–7, **146**, **147**
Scott, Giles Gilbert 183
scrins 95
Senior, William 27, **28**, **46**, 63, **69**, **188**

settlement
  18th- and 19th-century farmsteads 54, **54**
  changes in pattern 202
  Dark Peak 27
  deserted 49–50, **50**
  industrial sprawl 56
  irregular villages 47–8, **47**, **48**
  local identity 202
  locations **224–5**, **242–3**
  manorial centres and markets 41–2, **41**
  monastic granges 50, 51–3, **51**, **52**, **53**, 70
  nucleated and dispersed 37–40, **38**, **39**, **40**
  overview 5, 36–7
  planned villages 42–6, **43**, **44**, **46**
  prehistoric 30, 158–9, **158**, 160, **160**, **161**
  remote places 219
  reservoir-building, impact of 155
  Romano-British 177–81, **178**, **179**, **180**, **181**
  in Royal Forest of the Peak 187
  Shale Valleys 21, 204
  South-West Peak 30, 32, 213–14
  Southern Valleys 34
  towns 54–6, **55**, **56**
  vernacular buildings 37
  village greens 48–9, **49**
  White Peak 13–14, 210–11
Seven Stones of Hordron (Derbys) 164, **164**, **234–5**
Shacklow Wood (Derbys) 116, 151, **228–9**, **232–3**
Shale Valleys 7, 9, 21, 204; see also specific locations
Shatton (Derbys) 49, **224–5**
sheep-throughs 80
sheepwalks 25, **25**, 63, **64**, 75, **75**, **188**, 189, **226–7**
Sheffield Clarion Ramblers 195
Sheffield Plantation (Derbys) 40, **224–5**
Sheldon (Derbys) 100, 101, **224–5**, **242–3**
Shilito Wood (Derbys) 53, **53**
Shutlingsloe (Cheshire) 30, **224–5**
Sims, James 100
Sir William Hill prehistoric site (Derbys) 159, 160
slaked lime 88
Slaley Corner (Derbys) 103–4, **104**
Slaley (Derbys) 40, **224–5**
smelting industries 93, 95, 114–17, **115**, **116**, **117**, **228–9**
Smerrill (Derbys) 50, **50**, **224–5**
Smith, Thomas **185**
smoots 80

Smythson, Robert 192
Snitterton (Derbys) 96, 106, 189, **224–5**, **226–7**, **238–9**
Snitterton Hall (Derbys) 193
Soham (Derbys) 216, **242–3**
soughs, drainage 76, 86, 92, **97**, 97, 102, 112, 113, 152, **228–9**
South Carolina Farm (Derbys) 54, **224–5**
South-West Peak **7**, 10, 30, **31**, 32, 65, 88, 213–14, *see also specific locations*
Southern Valleys **7**, 10, 34; *see also specific locations*
Speedwell Mine (Derbys) 107, **107**, **228–9**
Staden (Derbys) 40, 178, **224–5**, **236–7**
Staffordshire moorlands 39, **39**
Stanage Collieries (Derbys/ Yorks) 114, **114**, **228–9**
Stanage Edge (Derbys/ Yorks) 115, **123**, **131**, 136, **137**, 154, 164, 171, **222–3**, **224–5**, **228–9**, **230–1**
Stancliffe Hall (Derbys) 193, **238–9**
standing stones 164, **234–5**
Stanley Moor (Staffs) **119**, **120**, **228–9**
Stanshope (Staffs) 20, 40, **224–5**
Stanton (Derbys) 42, 125, 159, **224–5**, **228–9**, **242–3**
Stanton Moor (Derbys) 9, 97, **97**, 164, 168, **168**, **222–3**
Stanton quarry 125, **228–9**
stiles 80, 81
Stodhart tunnel (Derbys) 144
Stoke Flat (Derbys) 159
Stoke Hall (Derbys) 97, 193, **194**, **238–9**
Stoke Sough (Derbys) 97, **228–9**
stone circles and henges **10**, 158, 162, **162**, 163–5, **163**, **164**, 170, **170**, 171, **234–5**
Stone Edge (Derbys) 115, 139, **228–9**
Stoney Middleton Dale (Derbys) 119, 129
Stoney Middleton (Derbys) 13, 129, **224–5**, **228–9**, **242–3**
Strawberry Lee Grange (Yorks) 53
Street Roman road, The 136, **230–1**
Strines Reservoir (Yorks) 154
strip lynchet field systems 83, **84**, 85, **85**
Swine Sty prehistoric site (Derbys) 159, 160, **161**
Swineshaw Reservoir (Derbys) 155
Swythamley Hall and Park (Staffs) 32, 63, 191, **224–5**, **238–9**

T

Taddington (Derbys) **5**, 15, **15**, 43, 62, 73, **74**, 210, 212, **224–5**, **226–7**, **242–3**
Taddington Moor (Derbys) 15, **15**, 43, 54, **166**
Taylor, John 101
Thatch Marsh Colliery (Staffs) 110, 111–12, **111**, 148, **148**, **228–9**
Thirklow (Derbys) 118, 119, **228–9**
Thornbridge Hall (Derbys) 193, **238–9**
Thornhill (Derbys) 22, 62, **224–5**, **226–7**, **242–3**
Thorpe Cloud (Derbys) 75, **75**, 195
Thorpe (Derbys) 34, 44, **224–5**, **242–3**
Thorpe Pasture (Derbys) 63, 75, **75**, 180, **180**, **226–7**, **236–7**
Thor's Cave (Staffs) 172, **234–5**
Three Shires Head 20, **224–5**
Throwley Hall and Park (Derbys) 36, 50, 189, **189**, 192, **224–5**, **238–9**
Tideslow Rake (Derbys) **8**, 103, **222–3**, **228–9**
Tideswell (Derbys)
  church 183, **183**
  location **224–5**, **226–7**, **236–7**, **242–3**
  manorial centre and market 42, 45, 187, 207, 210, 211, 213, **213**
  Parliamentary Enclosure 58, **59**, 62
time-slice mapping 5–6, **5**, **244**, **245**, **246**, **247**, **248**, **249**, 250–1, **251**
Tissington (Derbys) 34, 85, 183, 189, 193, **224–5**, **226–7**, **236–7**, **238–9**, **242–3**
Tissington Trail (Derbys) 145
Toddbrook Reservoir (Derbys) 152
tombs, prehistoric *see* barrows and chambered tombs
topography *see* geology and topography
Torr Vale Mill (Derbys) 151, **151**
Torside Reservoir (Derbys) 154
tourism 107, 155, 194–5
'township,' defining 6
tramways *see* railways and tramways
travel networks
  braids 132
  canals 118, 119, 134, **134**, 144, **145**, 152, **154**, **230–1**
  changes over time 132–3

coffin roads 220
guide stoups/posts 130, 132, **133**, 138, 142, **142**, **230–1**
hollow-ways 130, 132–3, **132**, 136, **137**, 138–9, **138**, **141**, 220, **220**
Long Hill road 140, **140**
milestones and mileposts 142–3, **143**
packhorse routes 117, 130, 136, **137**
paths **47**, 130–1, **131**; *see also* hollow-ways
railways and tramways *see* railways and tramways
road furniture 142–3, **142**, **143**
roads *see* roads
turnpike roads 139–43, **140**, **141**, **142**, **143**, **230–1**
Trentabank Reservoir (Cheshire) 155
Tunstead Quarry (Derbys) 129, **129**, 166, 195, **224–5**, **228–9**, **238–9**
turnpike roads 139–43, **140**, **141**, **142**, **143**, **230–1**
twentieth-century conflict landscapes
  anti-aircraft searchlight batteries 198, **198**, 199
  First World War 196, 197, **197**
  military training areas 196–7, **197**, 199
  munitions storage 196, 199–201, **200**, **201**
  overview 196
  prisoner of war camps 199
  Second World War 196, **196**, 197, 198, **198**, 199–201, **199**, **200**, **201**

U

Underbank Reservoir (Yorks) 196, **240–1**
Upper Padley (Derbys) 36, 189, 192, **224–5**, **238–9**
urbanisation 54–6, **55**, **56**

V

Valehouse Reservoir (Derbys) 154
Valley Heartlands cultural landscape zone **203**, 204, **204**, **205**, 206–9, **206**, **207**, **208**, **209**
vernacular buildings 37
Via Gellia (Derbys) 13, 210, **211**, **224–5**
village greens 48–9, **49**

W

walkers and ramblers 195
wall furniture 80–1, **80**, **226–7**
Wardlow (Derbys) 42, **43**, **224–5**, **242–3**
Wardlow Hay Cop (Derbys) **8**
Warren, The (Derbys) 178, **236–7**
Warslow (Staffs) 30, **33**, 33, **47**, **47**, **224–5**, **242–3**
wartime landscapes *see* twentieth-century conflict landscapes
water supplies
  dew ponds and meres 86–7, **87**, 211
  Lathkill Head Cave 212
  reservoirs 149, **149**, 152, **153**, 154–6, **155**, **156**
  rivers and streams 76, 149
  springs 43
Waterfall (Staffs) 30, **224–5**, **242–3**
Watergrove Mine (Derbys) **4**, 98, **98**, **222–3**, **228–9**
Waterhouses (Staffs) 30, **224–5**, **242–3**
Waterlees (Derbys) 179, **236–7**
Watt, James 98
Welbeck Abbey (Notts) 27, 53
Wellfield Rake (Derbys) **92**, **228–9**
Wensley (Derbys) **84**, 85, **224–5**, **226–7**, **242–3**
Wetton Hill (Staffs) 45, **224–5**
Wetton (Staffs) 44, 45, **46**, **82**, 211, **224–5**, **226–7**, **242–3**
Whaley Bridge (Derbys)
  canal 134, 144
  coal mines 151
  exclusion from National Park 195
  fire house 112
  location **224–5**, **230–1**, **232–3**, **242–3**
  railways and tramways 134, 144
  settlement 27
  turnpike road 140
  urbanisation 56, 219
Whatstandwell (Derbys) 97, 116, **228–9**
Wheston (Derbys) 40, 58, **59**, 62, 213, **213**, **226–7**, **242–3**
Whiston (Staffs) 115, **228–9**
white coal and kilns 95, 116, **116**
White Edge road **133**, **230–1**
White Peak 6, **7**, 13–14, 62–3, 210–11; *see also specific locations*
Whitworth, Joseph 193
Willersley Castle (Derbys) 152
Wincle (Cheshire) 32, **224–5**
windfarms 75, **75**
winding engines 93, **93**, 98–9, **99**, 100, 101, 102, 108, **108**, **110**, **111**, 148
Windy Knoll (Derbys) 196, **240–1**

Winnats Pass, Hope Valley
(Derbys) **22, 207**
Winster (Derbys) 42, 62, 70, 82,
193, 204, **224–5, 226–7,
238–9, 242–3**
Wirksworth (Derbys)
Anglo-Saxon origins **47**, 184
Barmote Courts 204
church 47, 183
exclusion from National
Park 195
location **224–5, 228–9, 234–5,
236–7, 238–9, 242–3**
manorial centre and market 34,
41, 54, 204
mines and quarries 129
modern housing 56
Parliamentary Enclosure
Awards 34
settlement 47

standing stone 164
topographical zone, relationship
to 42
Woodhead Pass turnpike 139,
219, **230–1**
Woodhead Reservoir
(Derbys) 154
Woodhead Tunnel 134, **230–1**
woodlands 11–12, **12**, 186, **186**
Wormhill (Derbys) 42, **44**, 48,
224–5, 242–3
Wren Nest Mill (Derbys) 151
Wyatt, William 101, 102
Wye, River/Valley
location **223, 230–1**
mills 150, **150**, 151
prehistoric sites **166**
railways 134
Romano-British sites 178, **178**,
179, **179**

settlement 204, **205**, 210, 211,
213
shale valley 9, 21, 24, **25**
White Peak 6, 13, 14, 15

Y

Yorkshire Bridge (Derbys) 155
Youlgreave (Derbys) 42, 85, 183,
204, **224–5, 226–7, 236–7,
242–3**

Z

zinc mines 91, 93, 214
zones, cultural landscape 203
Limestone Core 210–13, **210,
211, 212, 213**

locations **203, 242–3**
remote places 219–20, **220**
South-West Peak 213–17, **214,
215, 216, 217, 218, 219**
Valley Heartlands **203**, 204,
204, 205, 206–9, **206, 207,
208, 209**
zones, topographic character 6
Dark Peak 9, **9, 10**
fringes 10
maps 7, **222–3**
Shale Valleys 9
South-West Peak 10
Southern Valleys 10
White Peak 6, **8**